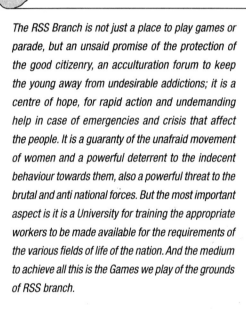

The RSS Branch is not just a place to play games or parade, but an unsaid promise of the protection of the good citizenry, an acculturation forum to keep the young away from undesirable addictions; it is a centre of hope, for rapid action and undemanding help in case of emergencies and crisis that affect the people. It is a guaranty of the unafraid movement of women and a powerful deterrent to the indecent behaviour towards them, also a powerful threat to the brutal and anti national forces. But the most important aspect is it is a University for training the appropriate workers to be made available for the requirements of the various fields of life of the nation. And the medium to achieve all this is the Games we play of the grounds of RSS branch.

— Shri Balasaheb Deoras

Lost Years of the RSS

Lost Years of the RSS

Sanjeev Kelkar

SSAGE   www.sagepublications.com
Los Angeles • London • New Delhi • Singapore • Washington DC

First published in 2011 by

SAGE Publications India Pvt Ltd
B1/I-1 Mohan Cooperative Industrial Area
Mathura Road, New Delhi 110 044, India
www.sagepub.in

SAGE Publications Inc
2455 Teller Road
Thousand Oaks, California 91320, USA

SAGE Publications Ltd
1 Oliver's Yard
55 City Road
London EC1Y 1SP, United Kingdom

SAGE Publications Asia-Pacific Pte Ltd
33 Pekin Street
#02-01 Far East Square
Singapore 048763

Published by Vivek Mehra for SAGE Publications India Pvt Ltd, typeset in 11/13 pt Book Antiqua by Innovative Processors, New Delhi and printed at Chaman Enterprises, New Delhi.

Library of Congress Cataloging-in-Publication Data
Kelkar, Sanjeev.
    Lost years of the RSS/Sanjeev Kelkar.
        p. c.m.
    Includes bibliographical references and index.
    1. Rashtriya Swayam Sevak Sangh — History. 2. India — Politics and government — 1947-. 3. Hinduism — Relations — Islam. 4. Hinduism and politics — India. 5. Hindutva. 6. Hedgewar, Keshav Baliram, 1889-1940 — Political and social views. I. Title.

DS480.84.K43   320.540954 — dc22   2011   2011003282
ISBN: 978-81-321-0590-9 (PB)

The SAGE Team: Elina Majumdar, Aniruddha De and Deepti Saxena

To Shri Balasaheb Deoras,
Chief of RSS, 1973–1994,
The misunderstood giant,
The balance wheel of RSS and Parivar.

To the followers of the RSS, in the hope that they regain,
through his thinking, the need to rediscover and represent
the RSS of the original,
and destroy the unacceptable rabidness, inconsistencies,
imbalances and distortions it has become a victim of.

To all my friends adhering to other ideologies
to introspect, to reach the truths about themselves
and to shed the obsolescence pervading therein.

Thank you for choosing a SAGE product! If you have any comment, observation or feedback, I would like to personally hear from you. Please write to me at <u>contactceo@sagepub.in</u>

—Vivek Mehra, Managing Director and CEO,
SAGE Publications India Pvt Ltd, New Delhi

Bulk Sales

SAGE India offers special discounts for purchase of books in bulk. We also make available special imprints and excerpts from our books on demand.

For orders and enquiries, write to us at

Marketing Department
SAGE Publications India Pvt Ltd
B1/I-1, Mohan Cooperative Industrial Area
Mathura Road, Post Bag 7
New Delhi 110044, India
E-mail us at <u>marketing@sagepub.in</u>

Get to know more about SAGE, be invited to SAGE events, get on our mailing list. Write today to <u>marketing@sagepub.in</u>

This book is also available as an e-book.

Contents

———•✦•———

List of Abbreviations		ix
Foreword by Kumar Ketkar		xi
Acknowledgements		xxv
Introduction		xxxi
1.	Original Design of the RSS: An Analysis	1
2.	Political Ethnography of the RSS	34
3.	Dominant Tendencies of the Golwalkar Era	63
4.	Withdrawal, Return and Ascent of Deoras	98
5.	The Emergency and Post-Emergency	131
6.	The BJP, the Parivar and Deoras: 1980–85	163
7.	Catapulting the Hindu to the Centre Stage	190
8.	Road to Political Power and Its Aftermath	205
9.	The Unipolar World and the RSS' Response	229
10.	The Future, If Any	247
11.	The New Hindutva (Violent) Forces	280
	Epilogue: The Problem of Ideologies	303

Postscript: *Ayodhya Judgement and*
Bihar Assembly Elections   310
Appendix 1: The 'Dashera' of Dalits and
the Dashera of RSS   314
Appendix 2: The RSS Constitution   324
Glossary   333
References   335
Index   341
About the Author   353

List of Abbreviations

————•✦•————

ABPS	Akhil Bharatiya Pratinidhi Sabha or All India Representatives' Council, the highest decision making and ratifying body of RSS
ABVKA	Akhil Bharatiya Vanavasi Kalyan Ashram or All India Tribal Welfare Organisation
ABVP	Akhil Bharatiya Vidyarthi Parishad or All India (College) Students Organisation
BJP	Bharatiya Janata Party
BJS	Bharatiya Jan Sangh
BMS	Bharatiya Mazdoor Sangh or Indian Labour Organisation
CWC	Congress Working Committee
KKM	Kendriya Karyakari Mandal or Central Executive Committee of RSS
OTC	Officers Training Camp, held every year since 1929 or so during summer in about 50 places in the country to train *swayamsevaks* in leadership qualities. A few years after Golwalkar took over as the chief of the RSS, the same was called Sangh Shiksha Varga or camp for teaching the RSS way of thinking

| RSS | Rashtriya Swayamsevak Sangh or National Volunteer Corps |
| VHP | Vishwa Hindu Parishad |

Foreword

————— • ✦ • —————

This is not just a book. It is a 'treatise' with a difference. It is not a doctoral dissertation, yet it has all the elements of objective analysis and interpretation. It is research based and substantially documented. Though it has an autobiographical dimension, it has no personal bias, no predilection, nor rancour! Indeed, it has a strong purpose to make us introspect and examine all the premises which we hold closely, even passionately, often prejudicially and sometimes possessively!!

We frequently encounter people, particularly in this country, who refuse to inquire. They feel it is a betrayal to the 'cause' they held so dearly. They think it is immoral. Even blasphemous! The result is—we do not grow, neither individually nor collectively. This intellectual and emotional stagnation results in inertia. Finally, this inertia destroys our life at personal, social as well as national level.

The title of the book, *The Lost Years of RSS*, may sound to some as provocative. Actually, it is inquisitive, but our intelligentsia regards being inquisitive as provocative. Also it must be stated that the title is also slightly, but inevitably, misleading. The book is about the RSS, from its concept and foundation to its today's predicament. A similar exercise could be undertaken by any Communist, Socialist or a Gandhian. In fact, by anyone who regards his conviction is superior to the 'reality' he is in.

The author of this book is not just a medical consultant. He is a highly experienced Management Expert and Strategic Consultant, a grassroots worker and also an institution builder. A social activist and a nationalist, without any chauvinism, religious or cultural! Compassion and commitment have been his driving forces. That is why he chose to work in totally poor and backward rural area for long years. He could have given up and settled in a cosy metro city or settled abroad. Yet, he chose to change the world around him.

Born in Nagpur and educated in Mumbai, he has lectured and taught in many places world over. He has travelled all over the world and interacted with a vast range of people. His career spans from his rural stint to highly complex medicine to multinational pharma industry to professional education for doctors. He has seen medicine from a 360-degree perspective. It is necessary to know these aspects of Dr Kelkar's personality.

Though well known in his field, he is not known as an author in the area of Humanities. He has written professional papers and monographs, but not anything like this treatise. I must add that this book is truly profound and written in an extremely elegant language. Without pretensions of erudition, the book delves into philosophy and science. The author knows that any discourse or debate is not possible without that perspective. One cannot, similarly, discuss the RSS without the current global scene. And the global scene cannot be understood without the process of globalisation. In turn, economics, technology, sociology and psychology become relevant.

Dr Kelkar is very well read and has a sound understanding of the fundamentals. He does not get bogged down by these dimensions. He refers and elaborates on them only when necessary and strictly in context. Sure, his personal as well as political association has been with the RSS and the BJP. But it is obvious that he did not get trapped psychologically, ideologically or politically. Without an open mind and global perspective such a book could not have been written.

For whom is it written? What was the motivation? The title might wrongly suggest that it is addressed to the rank and file of the RSS, its sympathisers, supporters or those curious, but neutral about the RSS. Well, it is addressed for them. But actually its audience is much larger. Indeed, this thesis would be relevant to all schools of thought—Left, Right and Centre. The sweep of his argument can be seen right in the table of contents itself.

The Epilogue is titled 'The Problem of Ideologies'. He begins by raising a very fundamental question—of 'ideology'. How do people get into ideological traps? And what keeps them happy there? If ideology is an abstraction of reality, then why are there so many of them, when the reality around is the same? Of course, the reality is not absolutely same to Indians and Africans, Americans and Arabs. But that is more because of geography and history. Fundamentally, all are human beings, with almost entirely similar characteristics. Colour of the skin or hair may differ; external body features too could be different. But the processes and functions within the body and even mind are not.

Why do people need an ideology? Why do they prefer some and hate other ideologies? He goes deep into genetics, neurology, biology and psychology to understand this. He discusses the ideas of religion and faith, and their socio-psychological function, the notion of God and the practice of worship. Then he tackles the complex question of ideology and human behaviour. The author clearly feels that to comprehend RSS, one must know the mindsets. Not only of the Sangh Parivar, but of all those who embrace ideologies—anyone!

It is only after that he comes to the idea of Hindu. I do not
want to argue with the author about the very term 'Hindu'
and its origin, or the misnomer 'Hindu religion'. There are
some 'accepted' but ahistorical ideas about Hindu religion,
and also about 'Hindu civilisation' as separate from Indian
civilization. Even the idea of Hindu nation or Hindu Rashtra
is not shared by various followers. Most RSS followers,
activists and sympathisers too are confused about the idea.
Hindu Mahasabha, Arya Samaj, Ram Rajya Parishad, Jan
Sangh, BJP, etc. add to the confusion. The author discusses
the idea of Hindu Rashtra and its origin. Naturally he also
deals with the most divisive idea of Hindu and Muslim
nationalism. He traces the history of founding of the RSS and
the canvas in the early 20th century, the legacy of Lokamanya
Tilak and the arrival of Gandhiji on the national scene. Then
he tackles the Marxist ideology and the idea of revolution
that came to India from Europe.

It is obvious that the author has taken a lot of trouble in
collecting rare references that are highly relevant to the theme.
Many important instances in the history of the RSS that he
quotes are not known to most. Even the observations of Dr
Keshavrao Hedgewar and his real 'line' are thickly shrouded.
Dr Hedgewar founded the RSS in 1925, but continued to work
for Congress till 1937. He believed that the 'Hindu' society
was divided, weak and totally disorganised. Hindus are
individualistic, not 'nationalistic' in their temperament. The
early 20th century in India was a melting pot of ideologies. It
is in that period that Lokamanya Tilak and social reformers
like Gopal Ganesh Agarkar clashed. Gopal Krishna Gokhale
appealed Gandhiji to come to India and lead people.

There was already a conflict between Gokhale and Tilak on
the way in which to approach Indian independence. Gandhiji
arrived on the scene even as Lokamanya was released from
Mandalay. Slowly the baton was handed over to Gandhiji.
In the same decade, Russian Revolution took place. Tilak
was inspired by that revolution. Veer Savarkar as well as
Comrade S.A. Dange both regarded Tilak as their source

of inspiration. Vinoba Bhave, N.C. Kelkar as well as Dr Hedgewar trace their legacy to Tilak. Communist nucleus was formed in 1921, and Communist Party in 1926. Gandhiji was in full command by 1920–21. It is just around that time that Dr Babasaheb Ambedkar emerged as the voice of the Dalits. The movement for Chavdar Tale, the symbol of Dalit emancipation, commenced in 1927, that is just two years after the RSS was founded. Briefly, this was the politico-ideological backdrop, each ideology influencing the other.

The RSS acquired 'Brahminical' character and seemed to defend *Chaturvarna*. But in its foundational theory, Hedgewar was opposed to the discriminatory caste system. So was Savarkar. Both worked hard to erase the caste inequality from the Hindu society. So did Gandhiji, who was the Congress leader, for the party Hedgewar worked. The Communists, of course, regarded caste as an evil and class war as real agenda. The Indian people were thus brought under multiple ideological streams. Often they overlapped and equally frequently they clashed.

The defining differences emerged on the so-called Muslim question. Though Hedgewar believed in the Indian plurality, his goal was Hindu consolidation. He never advocated hatred of Muslims and urged inclusive approach. But he clearly distinguished between 'appeasement' and 'inclusive approach'. Slowly the streams began to flow separately. When Pandit Nehru became a second line of command, another dimension evolved — that of modern (European) secularism. But Indian philosophical and intellectual tradition also had great secular ethos, from Ashoka to Akbar. The Congress managed to bring together, even integrate all streams, and with it all kinds of people from all castes, classes, creeds and religions. That was a challenge before the RSS. And it continues to be. Coincidentally, the militant movement for Pakistan started taking shape from 1940.

The Second World War had started just a year before, in 1939. In the same year, Subhash Chandra Bose broke away from the Congress. Despite Gandhiji's appeal across the country, Bose emerged as an icon. In the initial years, Adolf Hitler was on a winning spree in Europe. The struggle against British imperialism was partly inspired by the Nazi victories. But liberal, secular and socialistic in outlook, Pandit Nehru chose even to confront Bose. The Congress was divided internally, with a section sympathising even with the RSS. But as the war progressed and the Red Army began to fight back, the mood changed.

The 'Quit India' movement was launched in 1942. The timing for this movement was important. Congress under Gandhiji and Nehru consolidated the freedom movement. The other political forces, from the Hindu mobilisers right down to the Communists, got marginalised. Almost all the paradigms of politics underwent change by the '1942' movement. It is since then that the RSS is accused of keeping away from the freedom struggle. So are the Communists, who are accused of being 'traitors' to the cause. Really speaking, the 'Quit India' movement evaporated rather soon. But it had captured the imagination of people. The countdown for Independence, and also Partition, began with that movement.

The author has concentrated on the period after Dr Hedgewar's death in 1940. He only traces the ideological debates of the 1920s, but does not elaborate. That is because he perhaps believes that with Hedgewar's death, the RSS changed course. The Golwalkar era begins in those turbulent times, precisely, from 1940. The RSS from 1940 to 1948 is one phase. The RSS after Gandhiji's assassination in 1948 is a different entity, particularly after the ban. The author has drawn a vivid picture of these most difficult years. There was no pragmatism in it. There was no enthusiasm in those years. The Jan Sangh was launched in 1951 with the full blessings and support systems of the RSS. The RSS–Jan Sangh relationship was evolving. The RSS was a backseat driver and the Jan Sangh with a 'learner's' license. But the new recruits to the Jan Sangh, with no background of the RSS, were different. Yet the authority of the RSS continued to exert its influence through Jan Sangh.

Golwalkar kept the RSS insulated from the reality. He allowed it to function in its own imagination, taking itself too seriously. The uncanny thing was to keep the RSS out of any activity that had day-to-day relevance and importance to the life of people. More and more 'front' organisations came into existence. The 'Parivar' began to expand. But they were the stepchildren of the RSS work, neither of importance nor sanctity. As a result, throughout the Golwalkar era nothing nationally significant happened at the hands of the RSS. Barring the slow numerical progress of the RSS and the Parivar, nothing much changed. The RSS became increasingly distant to people. Inertia of this nature saps the strength. Creativity dies. It does not release energy for big projects. That is what happened. The RSS inertly aged by 23 years after the ban was lifted.

The original idea of the RSS was to have just a small band of activists/leaders—about 3 per cent urban and 1 per cent rural. The idea was to control, coordinate and guide the Hindu society by this dedicated band. But India was too plural—culturally, linguistically and religiously—to be 'guided'. The RSS could neither understand this plurality nor its Indian secular ethos. Also, it could not comprehend the growing influence of the West on the new middle class.

The political incarnations of the RSS, namely Jan Sangh and the BJP, are still struggling. It was inevitable that there would be internal ideological turmoil within the RSS. Those outside the RSS regard it as a monolithic and mono-ideological organisation. The critics treat all the Sarsanghachalaks in the same manner. Many commentators even consider all Hindu politics as one entity. They cannot and do not distinguish between Hindu Mahasabha and the RSS and even the BJP. There is indeed a symbiotic relationship among them, but also sharp contradictions. This monograph will clear some of the bitter truths about this complexity.

Guru Golwalkar died in 1973. Deoras succeeded him. Deoras and Golwalkar had two different approaches, especially after the 1948 ban. Their differences reached such a level that Deoras virtually left RSS for 10 years of *sanyasa*. He came on the scene fully in charge only after Guru Golwalkar died. Deoras crafted a different strategy. The year 1973 was when Indira Gandhi had emerged as the supreme leader. Under her leadership, Pakistan had partitioned and Bangladesh was born. The 'Two-Nation Theory', based on religion-based nationalism, was exposed as hollow. It was a Bengali language- and culture-based national identity that split Pakistan. With that one stroke, the Islamic as well as Hindu Rashtra concepts were proved bankrupt. Again, India was at a turning point. On the one hand, there was towering leadership of Indira Gandhi, while on the other was a challenge posed by Jay Prakash Narayan. With the glory of new powerful India, a parallel tendency of decay had also set in.

The international economic crisis, fueled by oil price rise, had brought India to its knees. The global drought, known as the 'Drought of the Century', further intensified the crisis. Scarcity, price rise, corruption, bureaucratic indifference added to the discontent. Jay Prakash Narayan, with the halo of great freedom struggle, consolidated that mood. The entire opposition, which was wary and defeated since 1971, smelled an opportunity. In the year 1973, Balasaheb Deoras succeeded as Sarsanghachalak. Deoras decided to take a plunge.

And with that plunge, he changed the class character of the RSS to a mass character. Purely from the 'nationalist' point of view, Deoras could have joined forces with Indira. But he chose JP, to fill the rapidly expanding opposition space. The Jan Sangh and the socialists, the CPM and the Swatantraites joined the JP movement. Indira was cornered, but perceived her continuation as an absolute essential born out of the egomaniacal impression of herself that no one else is suited to rule the country. She was forced to declare emergency to prevent what she believed would be political chaos. The entire top leadership of the opposition was arrested. It is at that point that Deoras also established contact with Indira

Gandhi. There is surely a contradiction in this strategy. Yet there is a sort of commonality in approach. Balasaheb Deoras was trying to reach out to masses. His effort was to bring the RSS in the national mainstream. If not JP, it would be Indira Gandhi. From 1973, the RSS was at the crossroads.

The crisis of 1973 was followed by anarchy brought about by the railway strike in 1974. The emergency brought order, but the discontent went underground. When Indira Gandhi called for election, the discontent surfaced. That was how the Janata Party came into existence. But for Deoras, the Jan Sangh would never have merged in the Janata Party. For the first time Jan Sangh dissolved its identity. But the RSS chains remained. Some may call it as the RSS bond. Depends on perspective and perception. The socialists and liberals in the Janata Party questioned the 'dual membership'. It was not membership that was questioned. It was the 'loyalty'. The schizophrenia was too much for the RSS to bear. The Janata Party went into oblivion, never to emerge, except in splintered forms. Under the RSS guidance, that is, under the leadership of Deoras, the JS became the BJP. One wonders why like others they did not go back to their original form. Would it have made a difference? Would it have retained its original character of a cadre-based party? Was that essential? But the principle of remaining in the national mainstream remained. It took almost two decades for the BJP to form and lead NDA to come to power. The author has extensively analysed the travel of BJP in a hard-hitting manner. BJP may learn from it even now. Indira's second coming, and her assassination four years later, reduced the BJP to just two seats in 1985, as Rajiv wave swept the country. But the Deoras strategy remained on course.

Yet again, the RSS was faced with the dilemma. Now it surfaced in the form of Ayodhya Movement, which brought in the idea of militant Hinduism. The BJP-led NDA would not have come to power without the Ayodhya–Babri Syndrome. Nor would it have been able to spread the net of political allies without the Deoras strategy. But in the 50 years since the founding of the Jan Sangh, the RSS had travelled a lot. Not in linear manner, but searching, exploring and experimenting. It was during this phase, after 1991,that the world changed and with it India.

It was a great coincidence and also a consequence that the socialist world collapsed. Along with that came globalisation, liberalisation and privatisation. The Jan Sangh and the BJP were initially the champions of free market, and opposed to the idea of socialism and state control. And yet they got totally confused by the pace of global events! RSS and Parivar minus BJP opposed the new world. The RSS could not decide whether it stood for *swadeshi* or globalisation; Whether it wanted control or liberal economy? It could not decide whether the new economy and new technology should be welcome. The RSS had not just missed the bus. It had missed the flight.

One of the significant contributions the author has made comes here. He has drawn a precise picture of the processes of globalisation—of what it did to India. He has squarely placed the RSS or the overall right wing in this context. He has exposed the stereotype and bankrupt thinking of them. This has never been done before.

Today, the RSS and its Parivar does not know how to deal with the new world. The setbacks the BJP is suffering are actually hard blows in the face of the RSS. That some members should ask the RSS to take over the BJP and run is anachronism. Any organisation can grow only by adapting to the environment. Organisations are like organisms. Organisations are socio-political corporate organisms. The RSS must leave the political entity, the BJP, to evolve and adapt to the new world. By keeping the BJP on a leash, even the RSS is losing credibility and relevance. After the death of Deoras, the RSS is yet again in a sort of identity crisis. BJP's identity crisis is merely a shadow of that. The intellectual bankruptcy, egoism, and morbid attraction to power politics has come to the fore. One question will always be asked by the political pundits and historians. And also by the old RSS leaders, activists and sympathisers: Why, after achieving power, the BJP could not grow? Why could the power that the BJP had acquired not help the RSS spread its tentacles? Just as the CPM failed to expand, the BJP and the RSS too failed. Are there similar reasons? Perhaps yes, though both will resent the comparison. The similarity is that both the groups/organisations/parties failed to see the changes. Both the organisations were out to change the world, as per their vision. Both did not understand that the world was changing already. In fact, the world was changing much more rapidly than they could cope with. Or even imagine. The forces of technology, the decline of ideology or more precisely the decline of demagogy were the features of the new world. There is nothing wrong in having an ideological base. Surely it helps to comprehend the world. But ideology is not a prison. It is a construct. It is a structure. It must be flexible, open and ready to absorb the new ideas. Just as openness does not mean wilderness, having a structure does not mean closing windows. Indeed, to have windows, you must have structure. But with open windows!

Jaswant Singh was expelled in the most undemocratic manner. Missile hurling from Yashwant Sinha and Arun Shourie left a bad taste. For the first time the coterie of big D 4 emerged. No one in the BJP felt ashamed of it.

Everyone else other than the BJP is pained to see the debacle of the main opposition party. It is not the ideology of which all other political parties are in opposition. Yet they recognise the necessity of a strong opposition, especially the right of centre. Of a strong and vibrant, alert opposition for the sake of democracy. And BJP is completely unaware of this sentiment and the duty it has to do. Could there be a greater state of degeneracy? The loser in the process is India, the magnificent Indian society, with all its glory and great civilisation.

It is no small wonder. The author has used such a long and eventful canvass of the country and the world so well. And against that he has put forward his thesis in just one monograph. He has discussed his ideas about a large number of issues quite commendably. The main theorems he has argued can be summarised as follows: Under the name of 'cultural orientation' Golwalkar made the RSS a sect. This was never intended in the original design. That also made RSS irrelevant to the time and to the masses. This alienation began with 1942. It continued till Golwalkar passed away. These are the 'Lost Years of the RSS' in failing to make its full impact. Deoras attempted to reverse it; he succeeded till he was in charge.

All the dominant tendencies of the Golwalkar era returned with Deoras passing away. The tendencies of militant Hinduism, rabid chauvinism and publicity craze got added. The new, hitherto unknown tendencies to create controversies went fundamentally against one prime Hedgewar principle. It was — 'by opposition from none' style of working — '*Sarvesham Avirodhena*'!

RSS must redefine its role, its idea of India, its understanding of being Hindu! A question can be legitimately asked: What is the future of the RSS? Or more precisely, is there future for the RSS? But then 'future' is 'when'? In politics, 'future' is often till the next election. The really patient and long-distance runners look for a decade. So, let us say, the future of the RSS in 2020. The year 2020 has acquired an aura of sorts. The former President of India, APJ Kalam, expects India to be a superpower in that year. That was also the RSS dream. Indeed, most of its followers dreamt of that status, even at an earlier date. They blamed Gandhiji and Pandit Nehru for keeping India behind in the race.

Privately they eulogised Adolph Hitler for building a 'superpowerful nation'. They forgot that the Nazi icon had to shoot himself in head. And he also brought Germany on its knees! They also did not realise that Hitler stands condemned in Germany itself. Except of course among some lunatic neo-Nazi groups; or among some scattered nostalgic groups. But, by and large, Germany wants to rise beyond the Hitler era. Even beyond the militaristic ambitions. Can we imagine what would have been Germany without Hitler?

Which means, can we imagine recent history without the Second World War?

These questions in history, with their 'ifs' and 'buts', could appear frivolous. But they are not. In algebra or even geometry, we play on imaginary numbers and lines. That is useful to underscore and establish a formula, a point or a statement. We can do that even in sociology or politics, of course, with caution and moderation. So to repeat the question: What does future hold for the RSS?

The author has raised many fundamental questions in this regard. All the RSS tenets have to be defined. The context is that of the constitution, state and the modern times. A positive resynthesis and expansion should be thought of. Or slowly it would lose its relevance. Like the hardcore comrades, the swayamsevaks would look like ghosts from the past. I do not know how the readers would react to *Lost Years of the RSS*. If, however, the activists and supporters take a hard look, it could make a difference. I think that is the purpose of this book. The author wants *Perestroika* in the RSS. He is all praise for Mikhail Gorbachev, for he changed the world. RSS too can. But will it?

Kumar Ketkar
Chief Editor, Loksatta, Mumbai,
ketkarkumar@hotmail.com
4 March 2010

Acknowledgements

——— • ✦ • ———

My good fortune is to have as friends many free-thinking men, who were willing to give me information, an inside as well as ringside view of the organisations concerned, joining me in arguments to lead to the correct interpretations of events. Each represented a special shade of thought, of character, but the same loyalty and readiness for sacrifice. Late Bhaskar Kalambi, Late Damodar Date, Late Prof. G.B. Kanitkar, Late Shivray Telang, Late Prof. Yeshwantrao Kelkar, Late Gajananrao Gokhale, Wamanrao Parab, Madhu Chavan, Madhu Deolekar, Balasaheb Dixit, Ram Kulkarni, Aravind Sakhalkar, Anandrao Bhagavat, Rajabhau and Sadanand Damle, Ramesh Patange, Bal and Mohan Apte, Vikas Mahashabde, Vinaya Khadpekar, Sulabbha Kanitkar, Neena Patel, Vijay, Sudha and Kamal Patwardhan, Yashwant Thorat and Patwardhan, Mrudula Lad, Madan Das Devi, Sudhir Joglekar, Ganesh Joshi, Satish Marathe, Nana Junagade, Late Sadanand and Arun Vaidya, Bal Chitale, Rambhau Naik, Bimal Kedia, Suren Thatte, Madhukar Moghe, Manohar Mujumdar, Dada Naik, Ved Prakash Goyal, the Kocharekar brothers, Ajit Pandit, Shekhar, Kishore Oak family, Aravind Navare, Gokhales Subhash and others, Chandu Mendhe, Suresh Babar, Vidyadhar Tamhankar, Mahendra Mhatre, Aravind Joshi, Satish Risbud, Aravind Bhave, Dr V.K., P.K. and Manohar Kunte, all from the Mumbai unit of the RSS, were people I grew up with in the RSS.

Late Babarao Bhide, long-time chief of Maharashtra; Sureshrao Ketkar, Late Rambhau Mhalgi, Dr B.G. Muley, Late C.P. Bhishikar, Late Nana Dhobale, Late N.H. Palkar and Dr Swarnalata Bhishikar, from Pune, have left lasting impressions. Late Dr Ram Aloorkar and Dr Ashok Kukade from Vivekananda Hospital, Latur; Dr R.S. and Vibhavari Dandavate; Pramod Kulkarni from Udgir; Sukhdeo alias Nana Navale and Dr Satish Kulkarni and the doctors from the Dr Hedgewar Hospital from Aurangabad have been of great help to understand the society and RSS, and have had positive influences on me.

My friends and co-workers from Karnataka, in a manner my second home state, H.V. Seshadri, N. Krishnappa, S. Ramanna, Sitaram Kedlay, Rajgopal, Dr V.V. and Veena Bapat, all from the RSS, were witness to many matters of great revelations and enormous educational value. Chandrashekhar Bhandari and Late Ajitkumar, both full-timers from RSS Karnataka; B.S. Seshadri, retired Income Tax Commissioner, Bangalore, whose ideas matched mine; B.G. Vasant, T.K. Muthanna, N.S. Ponnappa, Shivkumar, M.C. Gokhale, K. Thimmappa, K.G. Uthappa, A.P. Suresh from Coorg with whom I worked for long years under the umbrella of the organisation; Raghavendra Rao, B.N. Murthy, M.N. Nagaraj, Sadanand Kakade, Baburao Desai, all from Vishwa Hindu Parishad, Bangalore, Karnataka unit, the shared experience of working with whom led me to my thesis.

Late Dr Sujit Dhar from Kolkata, with his subtleties of expression, indicated to me many a truths. Dr Dhanakar Thakur from Ranchi, whose fast-paced activism gave me a balance of action. Ashok Singhal, of VHP, during our travels together in 1989, occasioned lot of discussion. I received help from Mr Arun Shourie; Retd Prof. Imtiaz Ahmad of JNU; Dr Rajput, Retd Chief of NCERT; Raja Javalikar, a retired Air Force Officer; Anil Bal of Flywell Industries; Jay Nair from Dr Reddy's; Abhijit Sane, my nephew; Arnab Sadhu; all from New Delhi.

Among my socialist friends, it was with Prakash Bal that the idea of this book arose first and was vindicated by many others in all the different circles I move. Kumar alias Prof. J.K. Joshi from Ahmedabad, the lifelong friends and ideological adversaries from the Lohia socialist group, mainly from Goregaon, Mumbai, composed of Mrinal Gore, P.B. Samant, Damodar Samant, D.G. Prabhu, my teacher, Vasudha Patil, Kamal Desai and many others, were a constant counterpoise who made me think that their ideas as well should be mentioned. My other close friends who hold positively different views were Nanda and Vidyagouri Khare, strongly opposed to the RSS ideas; Sudhir and Aparna Deo, having different views of the matter have discussed with me. Profs Usha Gadkari, Vivek Gokhale, Suresh Despande, Leela Deshpande, Vijay Bhagadikar, P.G. Borawar, Dr Vijay Chouthaiwale and Ajay Dhakras have been my discussants and listeners, genuinely interested in the outcome of this book.

Among my lifelong and close Muslim friends, Dr Qais and Dr Mrs Tasneem Contractor and Asgar Ali Contractor gave me a good idea of how the Muslim mind thinks generally and about the RSS, which was of value in order to balance things. Dr Shaukat Sadikot and Dr Nadeem Rais, the quintessential modern, liberal Muslims, close friends, have made my life richer. Mr and Mrs Mohammad, Mrs Afzal, Tanweer Ahmad, Shakil Ahmad, Latif Magdum, Prof. Nafeesa, Khadim Chhote Miyan and many others from Rashtriya Muslim Manch have been friends who do not leave any doubt in my mind that Muslims will welcome Hindus to come close to each other.

It is the Nagpur circle that finally shaped and firmed up the ideas, and a coherent structure emerged. Many who helped me have seen the RSS for more than 70 years. Dr M.K. Salpekar, a veteran who grew up with Deoras, as did Late Krishnarao Bapat, Late Dattopant Thengadi and Late Moropant Pingale, M.G. alias Baburao Vaidya, Digambar B alias Mama Ghumare, both former editors of *Tarun Bharat*, have shared important viewpoints. Late Prof. Krishnarao Bhagadikar, Late Adv. P.S. Badhiye and Prof. Rambhau Tupkary had a lot to say for the RSS and Deoras. Rambhau Bondale was helpful in providing quite a lot of original material from the RSS archives; a couple of dialogues with Mohanrao Bhagwat helped. Prof. Bachhuji Yvavahare, Sudhir Pathak of *Tarun Bharat*, Nagpur, Dr Jayant Deopujari and Jagadish Sukalikar have helped me with materials and ideas. Shripad and Sanjay Dani, Manohar Deshkar, Baba Gulkari were deep and early influences.

The seeds of my rebellion found an ally in Virag Pachpore as early as 1997. The most frequent interaction was with Dilip Deodhar, the outspoken futurologist and extremely well-informed writer on the RSS deserves special mention. Virag Pachpore read through the chapters several times, giving his critique. Much that has been possible and achieved in these pages is because of these two.

I grew up in a diehard RSS but radical and freethinking family. The paramount influence was my father, Late Kesheo Kelkar. My uncles, Raghunath, Madhav and Late Anil, influenced me deeply and early, largely shaping my character, along with my mother, Pramila, and my aunts, Mangala, Meena and Sudha. My wife, Dr Sanjeevanee, and my children, Nachiket and Tejaswinee, never subscribed to my ideological moorings but were a constant support.

Many may feel surprised about the Foreword by Mr Kumar Ketkar, who describes himself as from 'Comrade School', a strong critic of the RSS, for agreeing to write it, or my choice to ask him to do it. Mr Ketkar is a veteran journalist of over 35 years' experience, presently the Chief Editor of the prestigious Marathi daily *Dainik Lokasatta*. He did not even know me. From the word go, we hit it off well, underlining the power of transparent and non-motivated dialogue. I am immensely grateful to him for the good words he has for me and also for the Introduction that explains some of the key issues of the monograph even more forcefully.

Finally, I must thank wholeheartedly and gratefully Ms Elina Majumdar, the Commissioning Editor from SAGE Publications, for taking this first-time author through all the stages of publishing a book with patience, empathy, encouragement and support, and Aniruddha De.

I also thank SAGE Publications for accepting this work for publication.

Introduction

———— • ✦ • ————

The only prophet not let down by his disciples would be the *Paigambar*. Across a millennium, his disciples have continued without dilution all the acts the Prophet Mohammad had asked them to do, without doubt and without rebellion. The founder prophet of the Rashtriya Swayamsevak Sangh (RSS) is no *Paigambar*, but it is the same story—the Apostle Paul and Jesus Christ, a Prophet let down by his own chosen immediate successor. The pilot only brought about a small change in direction, but his ship went astray from the original path. Then there was a brief period of reverting to the original, only to give way to a return of the lost years, this time losing the original to a shameful decadence. This book is an attempt to prove this thesis.

Thematically, this monograph is constructed around the analysis of the important overarching issues which have never left the RSS and its critiques. It is not a coherent, chronologically written history—rather, it discusses the major turning points in the 82-year-old history of the RSS, from the point of view of the believer as well as the opponent. I begin this monograph with the original ideological conception of the RSS, its political ethnography and the growth of the organisation with it. The monograph then goes on to discuss the Partition era: the first ban imposed upon the RSS, the subsequent demoralisation and the turn the RSS took under Golwalkar for the next 20 years. The Deoras era, beginning in 1973, ends with the demolition of the Babri Masjid. This era, I argue, saw partial, and at times considerable, negation of traits from the Golwalkar era, leading to an RSS that had to be counted in every aspect of the nation's life. The monograph then points out where the original lessons have been forgotten and the decadence rising out of it. Having dissected the problem, finally, the monograph offers concrete solutions for the same and for the future of the RSS.

The monograph has as its backdrop the socio-political situations of India from the early years of the 20th century, beginning with the end of the Tilak era, with its belief in the great tradition of the country. It takes a detailed note of the rise of a parallel and somewhat alien Communist ideology at that time, posing an intellectual challenge by interpreting history in terms of dialectical materialism and the economic root of all problems. It discusses the rise of – and fascination with – socialism, the influence of M.N. Roy and his radical Humanism, as well as the rise of the Scheduled Castes Federation of Dr Ambedkar and its concern with the downtrodden populace of free India. Furthermore, it takes into consideration the beginning of the Gandhi era. The conception and creation of the RSS cannot be understood without taking into account these developments, which will make their appearance, time and again, in various places in this monograph.

I have attempted to place the beginnings of the RSS in its context, amidst the constant flux and upheavals that the nation was undergoing at that time. To this end, I have had to narrate, in considerable detail, the early development of the RSS. I have dealt with the economic, political and cultural thought of the RSS, as well as its views on minorities and the influences it bore in the first 15 years of its existence. It was necessary, as I have already mentioned, to take into account issues which were integrally related to the shaping of the RSS. Dr Hedgewar, the founder of the RSS, passed away in 1940. A most turbulent epoch, beginning with the 'Chale Jao' (Quit India) movement in August 1942, followed, ultimately leading to the vivisection of the Motherland. This was a trying period for the RSS. I have used the considerable material available in the RSS archives on this period to show how the RSS' behaviour started changing. Tendencies alien to the Hedgewar era started creeping in, becoming subtly — at times, strongly — manifest. This, I believe, is the most important achievement of this monograph, offering a highly original and radically different interpretation of the era: no one inside or outside of the RSS has sought to do the same. This radically different interpretation is supplemented by an attempt to view it in today's context, which is sufficiently distant from the time of the events under consideration. This distance provides us with a better opportunity to view the topic at hand with greater impartiality.

My quest to reinterpret this era led me to that period between 1952 and 1962, 10 odd years in the course of which a person as significant as Deoras stayed away from the RSS. It is a period most tenaciously guarded by the RSS hierarchy, and it has taken considerable time and effort on my part to unearth the details concerning the era. As I learned more about it, I was further convinced that my thesis on the Lost Years has its roots in the Deoras' thinking at that time.

Golwalkar's thought, meanwhile, offered me an opportunity to compare Hindu thought and Communist thought, and to show how close some of their basic tenets were. Indeed, the parallels continue till this date. It is one of the major discoveries of this work. In large tracts of discussion in this monograph, several different ideological/fundamental tenets — from that of the left and the extreme left to the right and ultra right, as well as the centrists, leaning either way — come together in seamless juxtaposition. I would consider myself rewarded if the provincial and national leadership following ideologies other than that of the RSS also peruse this treatise.

The Golwalkar era and his persona have overshadowed the Hedgewar and the Deoras eras. Deoras and Hedgewar, in contrast with Golwalkar, were built differently, thought and acted differently. For a more holistic and balanced perspective on the RSS, more information on the former two should be available, which is what I have sought to do here. This is an open-minded interpretation of the ways of Hedgewar, Deoras and Golwalkar, a critical analysis of their contributions to the RSS as well as the effect they left upon the organisation and polity. This, in my opinion, is one of the major strengths of this book. Once these varied elements and nuances become clearer, the RSS and its history can be seen in a different light in the present day context. I, therefore, beseech the reader to peruse this account with *tabula rasa*, a clean slate.

The last, and a rather considerable, segment of this book contains accounts of events from 1998. This section, as far as I am concerned, consists of the crux of the narrative, as it depicts the difficulties faced by the RSS to understand and interpret the unipolar world that came about after the collapse of Communism in 1989, and every other development that followed. I am pleased to be able to draw a good picture of the tremendous social, political, and particularly, economic impact of globalisation on the Indian society, as well as ways of handing these changes, which is in sharp contrast to the way the RSS thinks.

I was raised in, and worked for, RSS for 25 years. I have worked in and travelled all over the modern corporate world. Having had this rare opportunity, I could address the issues plaguing the RSS about understanding the present and the immediate future, as well as the issues about the organisational structure of the RSS, its function and future impact. I am happy that I am able to talk of the many possible solutions while delineating the difficulties plaguing the RSS and its future existence and growth.

In the Postscript, 'The New (Violent) Hindutva Forces', I had a further opportunity to reiterate and clarify many issues which may not have had adequate space in the flow of narrative earlier. I have included as Appendix 1 an article I wrote on Dr Ambedkar's birthday in 1997, 'The Dashera of Dalits and The Dashera of RSS'. This will help the reader to know where I come from. The second appendix is the latest and revised version of the constitution of the RSS. This will help the reader understand how the RSS is organised and how it functions.

The originality of the monograph, if any, may lie in three elements. Firstly, as I have already mentioned, it is a completely different interpretation of the RSS and its Parivar, especially in comparison to the received and accepted conventional wisdom, both from within and outside the RSS. It puts forward an alternative thesis in the name of truth and justice. The second is that it takes into consideration the many broad as well as subtle similarities between the political ideologies of the left, the right and the centre. It may help stop the unjustifiable sniping across fences and help people to understand their own internal milieu. This could help them to come together for a larger cause more openly. The third and final element is the biological basis I have given to human behaviour in matter related to ideology. A long career in medicine helped me find explanations for hitherto unexplained aspects of human behaviour, which has been the cause of considerable discord.

The accretions over the RSS stone are a mile deep. Myriad beliefs and counter beliefs, accusations and counter accusations, assumptions made from a distance and inferences drawn from close quarters prevail in the observation of behaviour of the RSS and its members. The print and electronic media, with their constitutionally embedded biases and prejudices, have persistently and relentlessly reinforced a particular image of the organisation. It has resulted in the distortion of the original beyond recognition. Not all of these processes have been rooted in truth and honesty, or attempted to do justice to the RSS. There are surprising levels of naivety, myopia and unwillingness to accept the truth when confronted with one. This is an attempt to clear the accretions thus accumulated, to go back to the roots, the essence of the RSS, for the reader to get a clearer picture of the RSS. It is an attempt similar to the one Martin Luther undertook to go back to the fundamentals of Christianity. Having brought the essence in clear view, I will discuss the lost years of the RSS and the corrupted version that came into being. This will form the backdrop of my reinterpretation of everything that happened from the year of the death of Dr Hedgewar, the founder, in 1940, till date.

Wishing to peel off all accretions in a small monograph is an arrogant claim, and I wish to make this claim with as much arrogance as I can summon, because I believe that we, as a nation, stand to gain by it. Those who have an in-depth understanding of the RSS do not wish to be vocal—there is a certain amount of terror associated with it. Therefore, I consider it an ordained duty on my part to record that which I believe is the essence of the RSS, that which has been corrupted. I have to risk the possibilities of being labelled a renegade or a believer, with both camps rejecting the contents of my monograph as untrustworthy. All I can say in support of this work is that it is a product of 20 years of study, and of a lifetime as an insider activist, with first-hand information and experience of the RSS.

Sanjeev Kelkar

1

Original Design of the RSS: An Analysis

——— • ✦ • ———

Dr Hedgewar, the Founder of the RSS

A born burning patriot, Dr K.B. Hedgewar was a medical doctor by profession. He was a member of the anti-British revolutionary group, the Anusheelan Samiti, in Calcutta, where he received his degree. Over years he realised that it was beyond the common man to undertake revolutionary acts consistent enough to overthrow the British. Such acts would necessarily remain infrequent, so some other instrument would have to be developed to drive the British colonisers away from India. Despite this realisation, however, he helped revolutionaries across the country from his base in Nagpur for many years to come (Sinha 2003: 20–23). Furthermore, after returning to Nagpur, he involved himself in many social and political activities. His contacts were numerous and his role always that of a helping hand. He maintained a catholic attitude towards all tasks, however big or small, provided the task in question was inspired by patriotic fervour.

In the freedom movement of 1921, Dr Hedgewar was arrested and charged with 'seditious activities'. He then made his own defence in the court, which the judge labelled as 'more seditious than his actions' (Palkar 1967). He founded the Rashtriya Swayamsevak Sangh (RSS) in 1925 on Dashera day in Nagpur. Dr Hedgewar was a Tilakite Congressman, and he continued to work for the Congress till 1937, holding many important posts—a period of 12 years after the formation of the RSS. The Congress, for him, was the political arm which would help him achieve his goal of an independent India. He was not particular about the means used, provided the circumstances were suitable to achieve independence. However, Dr Hedgewar was disturbed by the fact that only a handful of British had managed to rule over a country as vast and ancient as India. He concluded that it was the failings of the 'the disorganized and weak Hindu Society with innumerable other vices that had crept in its life blood' that led to such a situation—the Rashtriya Swayamsevak Sangh (National Volunteer Corps), popularly known as the RSS, was his answer to this problem (Palkar 1967).

The Fault Lies with the Hindus

Dr Hedgewar was convinced that the Hindus, as a community, were divided on numerous counts. They had turned upon themselves and lost their lives' goal. They were not an organised force; as a result, they could not work together. They did not have a temperament for *parakram*, that is, valour; as a result, even if they were beaten, or if their symbols of honour were violated, they did not react. They were weak and hence ruled by others. Unless the Hindu society was made strong and organised towards the fulfilment of a common goal, they would be able to do precious little to emancipate the nation. The Hindus are the majority community with whom the welfare of this country is irrevocably tied, but

2

the community at that time existed at its weakest. Hence, as *ab initio* or the first principle, the community needed to be strengthened.

Dr Hedgewar was further of the opinion that the Hindus did not possess a nationalist, common civic character. They were individualistic in nature. The Hindus had to first mend 'their own house', which had rotted from within. A united, organised leadership with character, a body of people who will work hard and throughout their lives for the society, keeping their personal lives minimal and behind the welfare of the society, submerging their self for the larger aim, was all too necessary.[1]

Golwalkar speaking in the years 1940–46, says,

> Hindus are naïve and simpletons, who deal with their (undeserving) enemies also with respect. There are innumerable divisions within, they are disorganized; they themselves are responsible for all the injustice meted out to them. Parochialism, linguistic, religious and sectarian differences, individualism above the national interests are their glaring faults. They have neither self respect nor self pride; nor do they have any pride in their glorious past; they have forgotten self reliance to solve their problems. They take pride in emulating the others. They have become the haters of themselves. Such a race cannot survive. (Golwalkar 1981)

The Historical Background of 1920s (Thengadi 1989)

India, in the 1920s, was in a state of tremendous upheaval, inundated with social, political and religious activity. Every act was united by a common thread: the dream of achieving independence, lit by the fire which Tilak had set in all hearts. By 1920, various schools of political thought had emerged on the national horizon, from Communism to the Hindu Mahasabha and the Muslim League. Their members could be found working in and under the umbrella called the Indian National Congress. The Congress in the Tilak era was

3

widely inclusive in nature, despite the fact that a majority of the leaders then were believers in the Hindutva, be it Bal Gangadhar Tilak, Bipin Chandra Pal, Lala Lajpat Rai, Annie Besant or Aurobindo Ghosh, to name a few.[2] In Tilak's time, Jinnah was a different man. He had taken it upon himself to defend Tilak against the British judiciary. As early as 1910, Jinnah had moved the condemnation resolution against independent constituencies for Muslims at the 25th Congress in Allahabad. There are several instances within the Congress and the Muslim League in the early years of the 20th century where they had worked together. Tilak was in favour of pushing forward Jinnah and others like him for talks, since they represented the nationalist Muslims of the times. It was considered in the interest of the nation. Even then, Tilak was sceptical; he felt that while it was important to foreground the nationalist Muslim leaders, it should not lead to unnecessary appeasement of the Muslim community. Tilak, who treated all religions as equal and believed that everyone should be free to practice their faith, did not support the appeasement of any one religious community. He was not sympathetic to the Khilafat movement, but he did not oppose it either. L.K. Advani, in his book on Jinnah, is also of the opinion that Jinnah wanted to go back to India after the Partition and assume the old familiar role of the ambassador of Hindu–Muslim unity, among other things (Advani 2008: 50).

The Changing Face of the Congress under Gandhi (Thengadi 1989)

There is no denying that the demise of Tilak and the emergence of Gandhi marked the addition of two new weapons and one new idea in the arsenal of the Congress. The first new weapon was the unprecedented idea of unarmed Satyagraha—the insistence on truth sans arms. It was a weapon that revolutionised all political struggles of the downtrodden in India as well as the rest of the world and continues to be effective till date. Even the most meagre and powerless individual could take up Satyagraha and fight against injustice. Gandhi had sensed the potential strength in Satyagraha as a weapon, thereby cementing his place as one of the greatest epoch-makers of his times.[3]

The second weapon Gandhi introduced was that of non-violence, as a part of Satyagraha. Those demonstrating against an outrage must do so in a non-violent way, Gandhi believed, clearly recognising the limitation of the common man in his capacity to resort to violence. He converted this limitation into a principle with great effect. His disciples, however, took it to an extreme, opposing the volunteer corps in a conference of the Congress, claiming that it looked militaristic. They made Gandhi's very effective weapon ridiculous. Critics have observed that non-violence looks good only in the hands of those who have power, not in the hands of those who are without any. Furthermore, Gandhi's insistence on non-violence took away the moral sanction of all actions of the revolutionary groups, including that of Subhash Chandra Bose, to which young men continued to feel attracted at that time. The Congress has, thereafter, wiped out any credit whatsoever due to these revolutionaries in achieving India's independence in an act that can be only termed ostracism.

The one new idea proposed by Gandhi was his firm belief that unless all Muslims joined the struggle for independence with the Congress, independence could not be achieved. The way he went about achieving this alliance, however, is not acceptable. Within a few more years, Gandhi managed to sideline Jinnah as a representative in any talks with the British, choosing instead those who were often perceived as anti-national and fundamentalist Muslim leaders.[4] In November 1919, Gandhi delivered his presidential speech in the All India Khilafat Parishad, offering it a blank cheque of support. Khilafat Committees were formed all over. Minor to major skirmishes started by Muslims took place all over the country. Kemal Pasha was busy dismantling a historical relic in Turkey; Gandhi, on the other hand, was busy doing something that was irrelevant to any Indian Muslim.

Shortly after this, Gandhi refused to pass the resolution against slaughtering of cows in order to avoid hurting the sentiments of Muslims. The Mopla revolt in Kerala was, beyond doubt, an instance of eruption of Muslim communalism, killing at least 1,500 Hindus and converting 20,000 (Malkani 1980: 13). Gandhi's remark on the event was, '[The] God fearing brave Moplas have fought for what they think is their religious duty in a manner they think is religious' (Malkani 1980). He praised the killer of Swami Shraddhananda. Even his *ahimsa* did not come in the way of the slaughter of cows, Hindus or the Swami. He declared the slogan of 'Alla hu Akbar' nobler than 'Vande Mataram' (Malkani 1980), and further wrote that he would surrender Hindustan to the Amir of Afghanistan if he attacked India. In the name of taking Muslims with him, Gandhi had alienated a number of groups within the Congress. More and more people found it difficult to continue in the Congress, especially if they had a difference of opinion with Gandhi, not just on the Muslim question but also on other issues.

Dr Hedgewar was clear about his stand on Muslims. He was of the firm belief that the nation is a single indivisible entity. He was clear that the language of minorities and majority would build separatism into the fabric of the nation, leading to dire consequences, and should therefore have no place at all in the national struggle. He was of the opinion that such actions would only help the growth of communalism. The Muslims would start feeling that remaining separate from Hindus and bargaining with them all the time would be in their interest. This would forever end the hope of Hindu–Muslim unity. It would hurt the nationalist Muslims whom Gandhi sidelined — the next day, the same nationalists might also adopt separatism to be counted, respected and to be able to bargain. Dr Hedgewar, like many others, has proved prophetic in his predictions about the future of Gandhi's policies. He was in favour of Hindu–Muslim unity, but disagreed with the way Gandhi went about it. The principle that the Congress enshrined as 'territorial Nationalism' has therefore been called 'unrealistic Muslim appeasement' by the RSS (Thengadi 1989).

Dr Hedgewar believed that the biggest obstacle in the achievement of Hindu–Muslim unity was the weak, disunited and disorganised state of the Hindus. An unequal friendship between the strong and the weak cannot last. Dr Hedgewar was not a Muslim-hater. Even the state gazetteer, which had all the details of his pro-revolutionary activities, wrote, 'He was a strongly Hindu minded man, who believed in the principles and ideals of Hindutva. But he cannot be said to be against the other religions and faiths. He founded and is the chief of an organization called RSS' (Thengadi 1989). While Hedgewar contributed to the work of the Hindu Sabha, there was no confusion in his mind about nationalist Muslims and other anti-national elements. In Hedgewar's early days in Kolkata, he had a number of prominent Muslim friends, some of whom he was close to.

The Gandhi Experiment of Muslim Appeasement

A nation can carry on with experiments over long years to know what turns out to be right and not so right. We will call Gandhi's 'unrealistic Muslim appeasement' (Thengadi 1989) as an experiment of taking the Muslim along with the Hindu majority 'at all costs'. That was one of the most important paradigms of his political agenda. There is nothing wrong with such an experiment. However, by belittling the Hindu sentiment, he hurt many people like Dr Hedgewar or Savarkar.

The Reaction

A large number of Hindus were unable to forget the Muslim history of various outrages, loot and atrocities committed on women. There were others who did not think of Muslim history either as atrocious or particularly unjust. People who thought that Muslim appeasement comes at the cost of loss of honour of Hindus or trampling upon their sentiments were shouted against and made to feel guilty as if a crime was being committed. There was a long period during which people were ashamed to call themselves Hindus.[5] Anyone who said anything good related to the word 'Hindu' were brow-beaten. They were asked to forget the killings, loot, plunder and the abduction of Hindu women or the desecration of the Hindu places of faith and honour. Those who disagreed with this kind of falsification were not allowed to hold an opinion.

The much-maligned Hindu groups prophesied that such appeasement would not bring the Muslims in the mainstream, but would in fact foster a sense of separateness or a tendency to make arrogant demands and get whatever they wanted. This ultimately proved right. The democratic privilege to think and express such prophecies was denied by Gandhi. Talking about power or strength went against the ubiquitous *ahimsa* or non-violence. This has continued even till today. It has been successfully hammered into the brains of people that accumulating strength or power is a heinous crime, which is a tragedy of our nation.

Evolution of the Political Philosophy of Dr Hedgewar—The Short-term Goal

At this juncture, Dr Hedgewar made a distinction in his mind about short-term goals and long-term vision. The short-term goal was the ouster of the British, necessary to protect the

Hindu society, Hindu Dharma and Hindu culture. This was the vow that the RSS volunteers used to take in the pre-independence period (Malkani 1980: 200). Hedgewar never really gave up the idea of an organised movement, even an upsurge, till as late as 1939. He wanted to see the country freed in his lifetime (Palkar 1967). In his last illness — which was possibly an instance of abnormal brain function due to severely raised blood pressure — even in his semi-conscious and delirious state, he used to say, 'Come on, the World War has started and we are so much behind times' (Palkar 1967). He considered the Second World War an excellent opportunity to drive the British out of India, but it was not meant to happen.

Those who think that killing Muslims was the prime passion with which Dr Hedgewar started the RSS may note this dominant trait of his thought. He did not think that an alternative to the Congress was necessary. However, at that time he had also reached the position that unless the society as a whole did not unite, matters could not be helped. He pondered deeply upon the possibility of bringing the Hindus of India together, inculcating a feeling of honour among them, unite them under the banner of something that was common to all of them, lofty enough to live and sacrifice for, till the end. Hedgewar asked, wherein lay the soul of the Hindu society? What were its principal traits, its reasons behind surviving for so long? What were the reasons for the downfall of this society that had a glorious past and had produced a string of national heroes, philosophers and saints? Its soul, he realised, lay in Hindutva, and the answer to the problems posed by him lay in welding the Hindus together in the bond of Hindu Nationalism. This was the identity of this nation. To restore it, Hedgewar decided, would be the basis of his efforts. To achieve this, he would have to create an organisation of people with a nationalistic, sacrificing outlook, who would dedicate themselves to the organisation of the whole of the Hindu society. I shall elaborate more on this later.

What Does the RSS Stand For?

The ideas with which the RSS began are simple and few. The RSS volunteers have been reciting a prayer every day for over six decades — it is the elementary declaration of the RSS (Malkani 1980: 198). The prayer, composed in 1939, does not talk about freeing the country from the British or the enemies of the nation, or killing them. The prayer says,

> We the children, the integral parts of the Hindu Nation, have girded our loins to do your work, O almighty God. Grant us such might as no power on earth can ever challenge, such purity of character as would command the respect of the whole world, and such knowledge that will make easy the thorny path we have voluntarily chosen. May we be inspired with the spirit of stern heroism which is the soul and ultimate means of attaining the greatest temporal prosperity and spiritual bliss.... May our victorious organized power of action...fully protect our Dharma and lead this nation to the highest pinnacle of glory!!

To achieve this he wanted men to be welded together in the shape of an organised force, along with other characteristics. Dr Hedgewar was equally clear on the fact that he looked at the RSS not as one more organised force within the Hindu society, but visualised the whole society as a united and organised one — the RSS was merely a tool to achieve this end. This was an ingenious contribution on his part. In Dr Hedgewar's vision, the RSS would ultimately wither away once the organisation of the society was achieved. Indeed, he repeatedly stated that the RSS was not interested in celebrating its jubilees.

Need for Organised Behaviour and Strength

The RSS was also founded to inculcate a 'Common Civic Nationalist Character' in the Hindus, using techniques of the

British military (conversations with Late Prof. Bhagadikar 2007; Tupkary 2008). There was no doubt that Dr Hedgewar was impressed by the British army and its discipline, courage and splendour (conversations with Late Prof. Bhagadikar 2007; Tupkary 2008). Deoras, his heir apparent, was fond of a number of English military marches like 'Marne', 'Be Prepared', 'Sturdy', 'Scout' and 'Falkland', all which were played by the RSS. Militarism was synonymous with discipline, splendour and power, not fascism. Dr Hedgewar believed that these attributes of the British character made it possible for them to win over India and other nations. He considered contact with Britain a boon for India and said so often, and as late as 1935. Along with the disciplined civic–nationalistic British character, Dr Hedgewar was equally impressed by their achievement of modernity (D. Deodhar 2004). When Balaji Huddar went to Spain to take part in the Franco-German war, Dr Hedgewar had instructed him to learn not only about military methods but also about what was the latest in the army (conversations with Shrikant Joshi, a long-time personal secretary to Deoras).

In an RSS branch, their programmes and drills in the open grounds do not have an 'Indian' equivalent as a model for moulding the character of a man. Dr Hedgewar believed that daily contact, working together, walking together and having a bond of camaraderie alone would lead to the development of a united force with a united mind, leading to the unity of the Hindu society as a whole. Dr Hedgewar's genius also lay in the fact that he introduced purely Hindu elements in the British model, like *guru dakshina*, offering monetary contribution to the sacred flag for the upkeep of the organisation, or the Hindu Samrajya Dinotsav, the day of Shivaji's coronation. The choice of Dashera as the foundation day of the RSS was also an instance of this. The RSS model was thus devised to make the Hindus as a whole strong and united. It was not for aggression as a habit or article of faith. It was a form and a tool chosen at that time to develop a positive outlook towards matters in the country's history worth being proud of.

Need for Nationalistic Mind and Civic Discipline

The most dominant influence the RSS technique sought to force upon its volunteers was socially appropriate 'civic behaviour' — to place others first, to place the nation first in one's thoughts and actions. The RSS upheld this mode of acculturation as its principal *sanskar*. Attention was paid to the growth of managerial and leadership capability of members. A neat working method with an aesthetic quality was implicitly integrated in all the workings of the RSS. Numerous small matters were insisted upon. These were as much a part of the making of the organisation as they were of the making of a man. That there cannot be a dichotomy in one's public and private character, both of which should be unimpeachable, was an 'a priori' condition. That alone could give one's social life a pure, lustrous credibility. It was a must. Above all, Dr Hedgewar wanted people who would live all their lives sacrificing their energy for the welfare of society, who would merge their individual egos in the large consciousness of the society with Mother Bharat as its symbol.

An Organisation for the Post-British Independent India— The Long-term Goal

Dr Hedgewar had sensed that, sooner or later, the English would leave the country. He had also sensed that, as an independent nation, India would need the right kind of people — political freedom was just one stop on the way. Harold Laski has said, 'The problem of democracy is the problem of right men' (quoted by Thengadi [1986]). Dr Hedgewar, in his farsightedness, wanted to produce honest men of credibility and character, who would make every effort to undertake right actions in the various spheres of national life post-independence. His basic diagnosis of the problems faced by Indian society was that India did not have the right kind of people, with impeccable integrity, who could come up with the solutions to those problems. This diagnosis is as valid today as it was 84 years ago, when the RSS first started. The need for such men of integrity is universally applicable now, as it was then.

'RSS is a power house from where energy in the form of well moulded, nationalist men with unblemished character will go out in to the various spheres of National life, influence and set it right' (Palkar 1967). This is a position numerously stated in the annals of the RSS. Throughout his life, Dr Hedgewar emphasised that he wanted 3 per cent of *swayamsevaks* in the urban centres and 1 per cent in the rural areas who could provide the masses with necessary leadership. He considered these percentages sufficient to change the picture and show a direction to the society. Arnold Toynbee, who recognised the need for such people in a culture, has put the necessary number of people who can and will lead at 10 per cent — this 10 per cent can offer leadership to the remaining 90 per cent in the society (Tupkary 2010).

Dr Hedgewar laid down the practices of equality, homogeneity and brotherhood before the members of the RSS. He did not allow notions of caste, high or low, and especially that of untouchability, to enter the RSS ethos. His acts of stopping marriages between young girls and old men, of encouraging and supporting inter-caste marriages even at that time, stopping exploitation of the devotees in Ramtek at the hands of both Hindu priests and Muslim fakirs, and so on, clearly speak of his social ideas.

Dr Hedgewar's aim was to establish, politically, a 'republic in India and socially Congress should strive to stop exploitation of the masses under the capitalist system, world over' (Thengadi 1989: 86). He sent in a resolution to that effect at the 1920 Nagpur Congress (Malkani 1980: 8). This skeleton framework of a future world was enough for him to start the RSS.

The modus operandi of the RSS, as evolved by Dr Hedgewar, was unlike any other sect or religion within the Hindu Dharma (I shall elaborate upon this later). This eliminated the long-term possibility of the RSS becoming another sect and made it capable of absorbing people of every sect within it. This characteristic of the RSS was strikingly different from that of any other sect that arose in the broad Hindu fold. Whereas sects always caused some kind of a separation, the RSS stood for their unification, not under the name of Dharma, but that of an unusual social/quasi-political organisation. This stands testimony to Dr Hedgewar's multi-faceted genius.[6]

The RSS as a Reaction to the Muslim Arrogance

There is also no denying that the anger towards the growing Muslim atrocities and arrogance in the early 1920s, coupled with the Gandhi way of dealing with them, contributed to the formation of the RSS in 1925. The propaganda, or the position taken by a large number of people in this country, about the RSS is: 'Muslim hatred on one side and a military fascist mechanism to kill Muslims was the only basis of formation of the RSS.'[7]

There are two matters that we, as a nation, must rethink. Both matters relate to the Muslim issue in this country, in the light of the history of the past 90 years. One position to rethink is that Muslim appeasement — or drawing Muslims to the mainstream 'at all costs', however one may put it — has done enormous harm to the nation. The second position to rethink is that the policy of Muslim appeasement has done no great harm to the nation. If someone upholds the latter position, then I have nothing to offer except point out the price we paid for independence, the price we are still paying, in some form or the other, in the shape of Pakistan, which has recently been internationally called the epicentre of Muslim terrorism.

One could even take a third position: that it was the rise of Hindu fundamentalism in India that has led to the Muslim reaction and not what the Hindu fundamentalists call Muslim appeasement. Going back, it was the formation of the RSS that created the insecurity in the minds of Muslims. This historically anachronistic proposition can be quickly answered. The RSS, born in 1925, had not become a force to reckon with till 1942. The efforts to draw Muslims into the mainstream were fully on since 1919 by Gandhi. The violence during the Khilafat Movement in Malabar was perpetrated by Muslims in and around 1922. The RSS did not even exist then.

The Violent Anti-Muslim RSS Psyche

Taking a completely contrary view, let us accept that the RSS does have such violent tendencies. There were scores of those pre- or post-Independence riots, so rampant in the 1960s in Bhivandi, Malegaon, Nasik, and a thousand other places in India. Let us assume that they were instigated and conducted by the RSS and that they massacred Muslims. What is the situation on ground? What does the Government of India have to say on it? The Home Ministry's report on 'Bhagalpur Riots', for example, does not uphold this premise. Quoting this report, the Home Ministry stated in Parliament in 1974 that all the 22 main riots were started by the Muslims throughout the country, against Hindus (conversations with Shrikant Joshi, long-time personal secretary to Deoras). Not one court had ever indicted either the RSS or a single RSS volunteer at that time. The RSS was not in power. The Jan Sangh was a minor political party. And yet we are to assume that they were so clever that nowhere could the police get hold of a single RSS volunteer, nor find any damning evidence against them. Surely this skill of theirs should inspire the Naxalites and the Anandamargis to ask them for advice! Is the RSS so powerful or influential or fearsome that all the judges of the judiciary gave them a clean chit? Or were all people manning these judicial and police machineries secret admirers of the RSS that they just let go, happy in their own minds that 'well, it is good that Muslims got killed'? If the RSS has indeed always been in possession of a killer's mentality, how can we explain the killings and other atrocities suffered by the RSS in Kerala at the hand of the Communists, as well as during the Emergency? And why were the *swayamsevaks* asked to keep calm at all costs at the time of Gandhi's murder when the Congress gangsters killed many RSS workers? Such questions remain unanswered.

Hindu, Hindutva, Hindu Dharma and the RSS

The inability to fully and convincingly define who a Hindu is has been held against the validity or legitimacy of the concept of 'Hindu' as applicable to the people of India. The idea has been consistently negated.[8] Life and consciousness are universal, and defy definition even today, when so much is known about the body and the brain and their functioning. No one, however, denies their existence. Then why object to the concept of a 'Hindu', and by the same token, 'Hindu Dharma'? Taking a more mundane view, the Hindu Code Bill is applicable to all who call themselves Hindu, as well as Sikhs, Jains, Buddhists and any other person who has otherwise not been characterised by other religious connotations. That Hindus exist is a reality. Savarkar went to the length of writing dozens of pages on the matter, citing evidence after evidence to show that there existed people called the 'Hindus' and that they had a well-demarcated land of their own ever since the time humans gained consciousness of themselves (Savarkar 1979). It is a living reality of thousands of years. What did Mr M.C. Chhagala, the former Chief

Justice of India, mean or understand instinctively when he said, 'I am a Muslim by religion but Hindu by race?' (quoted by Deoras in his speech in Alandi, near Pune, in 1987). What about the common identification of Haj-going Muslims of the yesteryears as one from 'Hind'?

There are a few strong issues that do really go against the authenticity of the name 'Hindu'. One is the failure of Hindus of various creeds, from Cho Ramaswamy to Satyajit Ray, to call themselves one.[9] Everything that Ray and Ramaswamy are, do, and believe in comes from the folds of Hindu practices, culture and tradition, but they deny that larger inclusive term 'Hindu'. The second thing that goes against the term 'Hindu' is the divisions of people of every conceivable kind. The long list leading to smaller and smaller fragments is unending. They are conscious of only that small fragment as their identity, even when the larger entity that comprises all these fragments is their final identification. Mechanisms from earlier times, aimed to achieve cohesion within the Hindu society, had become ineffective. Furthermore, the mechanisms active in the later part of Hindu history were never directed towards a larger goal of uniting the Hindu society as a corporate whole to which every individual and community belonged. Their concern was limited to a sub-caste at best. Those were the forces which created the high and low in the Hindu society. They were the ones who tore the fabric of unity into shreds. They were the ultra-orthodox bourgeoisie who were more concerned with their own purity as a caste, who failed to recognise this overarching Hindu consciousness. All these elements seem to negate the very validity of the concept of a 'Hindu' as a well-defined ancient inhabitant of this land. The first principle of the RSS, as devised by Hedgewar, was to create and regain the same, to call upon all to merge their small consciousness and ego into this larger ego-consciousness and stand united.

A Small Step but a Huge Leap

How tremendously difficult has undertaking this simple step proved to be? Spreaking of the Hindus, how many of them have actually been able to sublimate their narrow caste consciousness into something much larger and higher? It did not work. What happened to all the divisive tendencies within the Hindu fold, despite a larger platform being made available? Did it improve? No. Did anything that the reformists wanted actually happen in the Hindu society at large? Far too slowly, far less universally, far less as a habit of the polity, not till it was pushed down their throat by law. The RSS, much more than any other agency, has met with fair success in the elevation and broadening of this consciousness.

The RSS accepted this degenerated Hindu society as theirs, like a tender notice, on an 'as is and where is' basis, to take and improve (Palkar 1967). Is there anything fundamentally wrong in offering this ideal to people? If this ideal is indeed wrong, then what other larger ideal can we place in front of the people for them to become a nation, a united and strong society? If we replace the Hindu nation with the Indian or Bharatiya nation, does it really change anything except that it dilutes the focus slightly on the Hindu? Do we thereby mean that the Muslim and the British rule are as glorious a part of Hindu history as any other? Then why did Hindus fight against both for hundreds of years, identifying them as the enemies? Or are we of the opinion that neither do we need to be united as Hindus nor be strong, and therefore do not need a larger ideal? If that is the opinion, then we will have to answer a lot of questions.

Why did we fight the Chinese or even Pakistan four times? Why do we shout against American imperialism? Is not it because somewhere it pinches us as a society? Is the degenerated state of our Dharma the cause or reason for us to abandon our Hindu identity? If so, then why do we routinely praise all the reformers born in the Hindu fold? For whose betterment did they work? And why do we fondly refer to the RSS an orthodox organisation, truly or falsely, that wants to keep all the ills of Hinduism going? Is it not because we want the society better in a different way? Whose or which society is this? When Assam was divided into the Seven Sisters, not one name, with the exception of Nagaland, came from any other tradition but from the traditions of the Hindu culture. All the names of our naval fleet, our Light Combat Aircraft and our tanks are Hindu names. The RSS does not decide these at least. When the RSS says 'Hindu', it is this entire tradition they identify with.

The Question of Substitutes

The radicals, the atheists, the anti-religionists, the moderns, the anti-ritualists, and so on, have constantly attacked and criticised the rigid, ritualistic, fossilised Hindu religion. They have tried to erode the structure and create a vacuum. Unfortunately, they have succeeded in doing neither. The fact remains that they have not been able to replace the older degenerate values with the new and modern ones, fill the empty space with their own values and make those values acceptable to society. The society should have embraced those values in place of the old ones, but it did not. The radicals were of the belief that they had succeeded in removing the legitimacy of Hindu practices and motifs, be it good or bad. None of them realised their failure to substitute them with newer ones. They could not make the society 'modern'. Meanwhile, the people were denied the succour they were receiving from that obscure religion. Aggressive radicalism produced, for a while, a sheepish attitude among the Hindus who observed the age-old practices. Even then the situation did not improve, though it should have. What the radicals blithely want to ignore is that this blessed society remains as orthodox today as it was in the past.

Hindutva

'Hindutva', incidentally, should not mean 'Hinduism', since there is no -ism, that is to say, dogma called 'Hindutva'. A proper understanding of the word 'Hindutva' would be 'Hindu-ness', and where that 'Hindu-ness' lies. There are innumerable elements in the present and the past of this culture. No one Hindu can be seen as subscribing to all of it. The contradictory opinions on what is right and wrong in this 'holdall' of Hindutva are so numerous that it is difficult to decide what causes one to possess this Hindutva (Savarkar 1979).

On a personal level, one may be said to have inherited Hindutva by being born to Hindu parents. Such a person would inherit the whole of the experiences, the accumulated psyche, what Carl Jung would call the archetype of that culture. Like genes, which transfer physical characteristics in humans, 'the memes' are the memory genes that are transmitted. These endow a person with some innate understanding of Hindutva.

Savarkar has simplified the issue of Hindutva by saying that everything that the Hindu race has done, thought of, expressed, accumulated or dispersed for so long is all that comes under the umbrella of Hindutva. This goes on to form the archetypal of this race and will be handed down over generations. It identifies our race, our geographical unity and our cultural psyche. Mr Naikar[10] may denounce his heritage, but he remains a Ramaswamy, which comes from the culture he has inherited—he has not changed his name to, say, Fazal Mahmood. Hindutva, as I have already said, is a holdall. However, that does not mean that the RSS proudly accepts all the degeneracy therein. Had they done so, they would have had no a priori cause to exist at all.

Savarkar has further spoken of the bonds of blood of common traditions, common culture and common sense of 'ours' and 'not ours', of friends and foes, of those who consider Hindustan as their Fatherland and Motherland. We have a history, we have the same ideals and the common process of acculturation. These are his next characteristics of Hindutva. The most contentious of his claims here is the concept of *punyabhoomi*, the place of salvation an individual looks for through worship. The RSS has effectively negated and resolved this issue by saying that 'the Muslims of this country as of now have not come from outside. They have changed their religion but not their forefathers' (Bondale Unpublished). Therefore, they have a place in this country.

Responsibility of Defining Modern Hindutva

The question often raised to RSS volunteers by their baiters is: of this mass and mess of Hindutva, which elements do you subscribe to? The RSS must list them in detail. There are certain assumptions in this demand. It strongly presupposes bourgeoisie tendencies, a non-acquaintance with or denial of modern science, denial of modern ways of thinking. It is assumed that the RSS, marooned in the degenerate past, possesses an obscurantist mindset. The articles of blind faith in astrology, rituals, superstitions, theism, ritualistic religion, Tantra, the *mantras*, *upasana*s and innumerable such other come up for denouncement, depending upon the questioner's preference. In short, what these questioners want to know is whether the RSS also denounces and praises what they do. If the RSS was to produce a list of what they did or did not believe in, a hundred different intellectual questioners would still criticise it since one or more of the elements they wanted would not have been mentioned.

Does this confused situation absolve the RSS from the task defining it? Far from it. Popular conception may believe otherwise, but despite its reluctance, the RSS has managed a fair blueprint over the years. Dr Hedgewar had read the Savarkar thesis of Hindutva. Replete with inspiring tales of the past and its glorious traditions, the thesis served Dr Hedgewar in his purpose to an extent. Golwalkar is credited to have given greater details and content to the notion of Hindutva, but the concept, as it exists today, is mostly the elaboration of the principles laid down by Dr Hedgewar in the early days. The details, then, developed over years.

Golwalkar, in his further elaboration of the notion of Hindutva, emphasised upon the concept of other religions as well as that of respect, something only Hindus are capable of. He propounded that there are many paths to attain godhead, none of which are to be spurned. He put forward an ideal: 'Let all the living beings, not just humans be happy, healthy, without disease, let every one see Bhadra, or the godliness, emancipated consciousness, sacred feelings of brotherhood' (Golwalkar 1966: 2). It is not possible to translate into English the concept of Bhadra in its full and totality. He contrasted the Western idea of 'greatest good of the greatest number' with this Hindu ideal.

Golwalkar also underlined the thesis of the unity of the universe. Everything, from inert material to the highest evolved humans, is one with the ultimate reality, Golwalkar proclaimed. The same principle permeates in all. Golwalkar further emphasised that this oneness with the ultimate reality need not eliminate all the characteristics of different communities, since by developing their uniqueness, they grow to their full stature and happiness. Beyond that, however, Hindus have enunciated the principle of recognising all diversity as essentially moving towards or being a part of the ultimate reality, leading to a harmonious synthesis. Such a principle seeks to eliminate the sordid spectacle of man setting himself against man. The idea of a world-state that erases and levels every nation of its genius is foreign to Hindus. Their innate catholicity is unique to this world. The Hindu society has a mission in this world to be the torchbearer of harmony and to elevate the rest to a superior state. The Krinvanto Vishwam Aryam was an effort on the part of the Hindus to spread this message all over the world, without resorting to violence (Golwalkar 1966: 1–11).

Along with Gandhi (and Lohia, whom Golwalkar knew well), Golwalkar was the only one to propose trusteeship to the affairs of the world. He decried accumulation of wealth for the sake of self-aggrandisement and upheld the principle of *aparigraha* of the Bhagvat Gita, as Gandhi did, denouncing those who only sought to accumulate wealth as thieves. Both Golwalkar and Gandhi negated the possibility of forever satisfying one's needs and emphasised upon limiting them as a tenet of Hindu philosophy. They negated the theory of Social Contract and visualised society as an organic corporate whole, where there could not be any conflict between the individual and the society. Both decried competition as unhealthy. The source of happiness, according to both, was inside oneself, through the means of looking for salvation and union with the Godhead.

Both Gandhi and Golwalkar emphasised upon the principles of ethics and morality as the foundation for wielding power. They saw political power, including that of kings, as subordinate to the power of ethics, which was upheld by the sages in society. We will return to this point in greater detail at a later occasion in the book.

Golwalkar had recognised the power of the sectarian chiefs — the Mathadheeshas. He levelled down their egos and their ideas of self-prestige, and yoked them to social causes, especially the removal of untouchability, something they had not contributed towards for over a millennium. He, furthermore, continued, for 33 long years, to inspire the *swayamsevak*s in the service of Bharat Mata, evoking the glorious past of the nation.

Political and Economic Content of RSS-inspired Hindutva

There is a general belief that the RSS or any of its affiliates do not have any economic or political aspects to their programme. This is far from being true, but there are reasons and circumstances that did not foster an environment suitable for the surfacing of these aspects of the RSS' programme in the decades of post-Independence India. I will treat this all-important aspect at two different places in this monograph, once in Chapter 4, which examines the dominant tendencies of the Golwalkar era, and the second time in connection with the Jan Sangh, the BJP and other affiliates later.

Hindu Dharma

The Hindu Dharma is not a religion like the Semitic religions with one prophet, one book and one God, a rigid discipline and a strong force of social cohesion. It is a federation of religions and sects of all conceivable modes of worship. Each of the sects or religions that were born in India, thus contributing to its large catholic view, did so out of some need to improve upon the existing ways. To Hindu Dharma, the formation of newer and newer sects is merely a matter of liking or finding resonance with certain concepts or religious practices. It not only tolerates all, but also welcomes them in its fold. Proselytisation, a strong element of at least two out of the three Semitic religions, therefore has no place in Hinduism. Yet Dharma is a much larger concept, something which Golwalkar brought to the forefront in his thoughts.

He characterised this Dharma as the one which 'sustains' society, allowing social beings to live a fulfilling life. To do that, it lays down certain laws and principles which must form a part of the human endeavour. These principles generally have nothing to do with religious practices but of the behaviour of people in conducting mundane actions. It directs the actions for the greatest good of all. Gandhi identified Dharma as Truth. Golwalkar pointed out that by enforcing this Dharma, one attains both material wealth as well as spiritual development. Dharma thus sustains and nourishes society.

Hindu Rashtra

We will now discuss the all-encompassing idea of the Hindu Rashtra, the concept for which the RSS is hated most. This is the most controversial concept in the whole of the RSS' configuration. Those who instinctively feel it to be a real, tangible concept that has been in operation for thousands of years, who see it beyond the sectarian, divided society as an overarching concept, do not go into the exercise of proving it to themselves. Many of them are in the RSS. The objectors on the other hand put out a number of theories to disagree with these three ideas put forth by the RSS: Hindu, Hindutva and Hindu Rashtra. Hindu Rashtra is the largest inclusive concept, incorporating Hindu, Hindutva and Hindu Dharma, as well as much more. In discussing these three, the overlaps are difficult to separate and may perhaps be understood in the following light. The charges levelled by the critics are:

1. The idea of a Hindu Rashtra is false and historically invalid. There is little similarity among the so-called Hindu communities of different denominations. They are not one commonality.
2. There never existed a political state that can be identified with the Hindu Rashtra. It was a mere matter of hundreds of kingly principalities which fought among themselves.

The RSS typically counters the first criticism by saying that, superficial differences notwithstanding, the traditions in the Hindu Rashtra are common. Their objects of reverence are common. The Hindu gods have common origins though diverse forms and names, and the religious practices differ but the philosophical moorings do not. To draw a cohesive picture of this country's common history, one can consider the testimony of the historical accounts. Why should the Ramayana have a Kambh and a Tulsidas version? We can draw up a long list of such things, but it would be tedious for readers. Enough material is available for anyone who wishes to verify that the nation is at least culturally united. No proof would be worth anything to those who do not wish to accept this. However, I will seek to approach the problem from another angle for their sake.

Let us start by agreeing that the Hindu Rashtra never existed, that it was always just a mass of people staying on a vast land, where every kind of difference existed. No harmony was ever possible, the sects looked down on each other, the castes lived with their endogamy and immiscibility. It was never a homogeneous or one society. It was a society built upon the enshrined doctrine that men are unequal, that they must exist in a hierarchy. It was a society that gave rise to untouchability. Tolerant by appearance, this society was intolerant within, creating divisions between sects and between classes. Let us accept that this is the truth and that Golwalkar and Hedgewar had made a fundamental scholastic mistake in taking up the position that the Hindu Rashtra had existed for many thousand years. Many more glaring examples and scholastic objections or examples of deterioration can be added, though they are not necessary to make the point any stronger.

Is there any sense in accepting and believing a completely false idea like the Hindu Rashtra as the truth? Is there any advantage to be gained here? Could we rectify the situation we have criticised here by holding on to a concept which engenders such glaring instances of degeneration and intolerance while being fully aware that the concept is completely false? To give an example: to an atheist, God is a worthless and false concept; the world has accepted a false notion. This concept, however, gives the world and its many believers, the Muslims, the Christians, the Jews, and so on, succour, support, tranquillity, a place to seek strength, and a thousand other things. The concept, thus, has its advantages. What advantages would we gain if we embrace the false idea of the Hindu Rashtra?

The advantage is this: since we have decided to accept this non-entity as an entity, we now have a directly defined area which we can attack and improve upon. We can now take a stand on what we should preserve and what we should discard. Whatever we do will improve this fictional Hindu Rashtra. Since we accept Hindu-ness as its basis, we are accepting reforms within it. Many of those reformist values are modern values. They cleanse and clear. If reforms occur, it may start looking more like the kind of religion the modern mind would like to see. A thousand ills will go away, such as the practise of immolating a wife on her dead husband's pyre. If she does not immolate herself, then her head will not be shorn, widows will marry again, the seven prohibitions of travelling, eating, and so on, will go away. Women will learn and progress, and they will compete with men. They will be equal. The extortion called dowry will go away. Untouchability should and probably will go away from the very heart of the people. The myriad classes and castes will hopefully also disappear along with their notions of high and low. Superstitions will lessen. All of this might happen because there is a larger whole, a corporate whole, however false, to which it will all be directed. The differences that arise and the biases that play havoc with the lives of people will go away. There will arise some common codes and principles which will be acceptable to all.

The second critique of the Hindu Rashtra is a real, formidable objection, and it needs to be understood against the backdrop of the very real problem of communication in the vast landmass that was Bharat. It extended from Kandahar to Thailand. It had huge geographical variations, countless mountain ranges, jungles and deserts. It should be obvious how difficult it must have been to establish a single empire from one end to the other of this landmass. As late as the time of Shivaji and Aurangzeb, five different Muslim principalities ruled the country. Even if only one empire had existed, it would have been impossible to govern the land in any other way than merely through the extraction of taxes. This is historical truth notwithstanding the belief—or perhaps fact—that this country ruled by many was culturally one.

History will show that time and time again, empires built by the *chakravartins* and the *samrats* have come into existence in India, and lasted at least a couple of hundred years. The concept of the *Ashwamedha Yagnya* indicated that the necessity or desire to have a single ruling authority was well perceived and recognised. The story of Sri Ram shows us, even accepting—for the sake of argument—that it is a fabrication, that the land he ruled over conceptually attained the status of an empire, stretching from the north to Ceylon. Ram bestowed their states back to Bibhishana and Sugreev, as well as all others. To whom did they owe their loyalty? Even in the time of the Mahabharata, all the kings who gathered in Kurukshetra had to decide who was the owner of the kingdom of Bharatavarsha. The empires of Chandragupta Maurya and the Gupta dynasty extended well beyond the present limits of India, even if it did not cover all of present-day South India. Ashoka, after converting to Buddhism, extended his reach through the spread of Buddhism to distances and territories unimaginable at that time.

The Gupta dynasties, Harshavardhana, Kanishka, Vikramaditya, Shalivahana, the Pulakesin, and the kingdom of Vijayanagara are similar examples. Shivaji made an attempt to fuse the power of Jaysingh with his own to liberate the whole country. Guru Govindsinghji wanted to fuse his might with Shivaji's kingdom to establish one *raj*. The way the Peshvas liberated the country from Attock to Cuttack need not be lost sight of. Political unity was not unheard of in India. It must be admitted that, despite this, the country had been re-divided. It must also be admitted that political unity was not a defining characteristic of early India. This is because political unity, ultimately, is established by the state—impossible till modern times, mainly because the country was too large. Both the state and the nation are Western concepts, arising only about a few hundred years ago. What grants political unity in the Western countries is a nation state of relatively small size, generally with one language and one dominant race, which makes it governable. Yet, even within a nation state, there could exist several nations as shown by the USSR, not all of which were Russian, but of diverse origins and faiths. In India, similarly, several states existed that belonged to one common lineage, unlike Russia. It is cliché to keep repeating that all their diversity had a common cultural foundation, but the truth remains that culturally, they were one nation.

How did this cultural commonality, this common foundation develop? Were there visionaries who without the use of force brought about this assimilation? The answer to both questions is a resounding yes. The more important issue is the superhuman feat the sages of this country achieved against the odds of distances. It was through the cultural unity of this country — by spreading common messages, common cultural practices, common ideas, principles, philosophy — that these sages tried to keep this land as one country, despite the variations that occurred. Shankara was the greatest living example of that tradition as late as 800 AD. The claim of the RSS, therefore, is that India is culturally one nation, even if the name 'Hindu' is recent.

Golwalkar brought in some truly unusual insights regarding the apolitical, self-sufficient and interdependent nature of Hindu social structure and governance in order to fortify his argument. The king, represented by the state in modern times, was but one part of the national life. For the people belonging to the four classes and numerous castes, living their life as ordained by the priests was more important. It was to this aspect that the sages had paid attention. The king was neither the centre of power nor were the kingdoms the be all and end all of the people. When these kingly principalities started failing to rise as one without an emperor, Hindustan was defeated at the hands of invaders. Long ago it had succeeded in assimilating the Shakas, the Kushanas, and the Huns, in the times of Vikramaditya and Shalivahana. This was because the cultures of those temporary victors proved inferior to that of the Hindus. The Hindus were defeated by the Muslims because they failed to understand the mindset of these invaders and did not come together to defeat them; in fact, many joined hands with them against the native kingdoms.

Territorial Nationalism versus Cultural Nationalism

The real issue at stake in the fight against the Hindu Rashtra is the question of territorial nationalism versus cultural nationalism. Nehru, a believer in territorial nationalism, propounded that all those who reside on a piece of land constitute the nation. This was in consonance with the Gandhi experiment of taking Muslims along with the majority. India was a geographical entity that would, after independence, transform into a political one. The propounders of non-territorial, historical or cultural nationalism, meanwhile argued that the Muslims came to India as invaders, first, to loot, and then to rule and convert. They still retain this mindset of the victor. They have neither respected this country's traditions nor this land as the sustaining principle of their life. Their loyalty does not lie here. Therefore, they cannot be included in the concept of the nation. The next and the immediate question that arose here is: then where did these cultural nationalists want the Muslim population of India to be? Such a strong position was enough to lead Nehru to fanatical opposition of these people.

These ideas demand the definition of a nation and a state, and brings us to some of the fundamentals of Golwalkar's thought, its contradictions as well as some of the serious charges of fascism within the RSS, and to the Golwalkar school of thought in particular. We will take these matters up in the next chapter.

Notes

1. These are the consolidated, oft-repeated ideas most basic to the thought of Dr Hedgewar. They will be found in dozens of places in RSS literature from his times to the same till date. The volumes *Shri Guruji Samagra Darshan* (Golwalkar 1974a, 1974b, 1975, 1978, 1979, 1981), included in the list of references, is also a collection of his statements variously expressed in that volume.

2. The historical background of the 1920s and the changing face of the Congress under Gandhi, as documented in this monograph, are sourced from an extraordinary volume edited by Bhanu Pratap Shukla, based on the writings, speeches and conversations of D.B. Thengadi. Mr Shukla, in an amazingly seamless manner, brings together in his volume a fine picture of the currents prevailing at the time of the rise of the RSS, in a manner that only a Nagpurian who had witnessed the era can draw. The picture is similar to that portrayed by Durga Das in *India from Curzon to Nehru and After* (1969), and numerous others who have written of the era, but no one could have sketched a better narrative from the RSS point of view.

3. Ironically, it is the RSS which has made use of Satyagraha in its best and true spirit, while fighting the illegal ban of the organisation in 1949 and 1975. The non-violent Satyagraha it employed at those times are but two examples of the RSS making use of this weapon. It is necessary to understand at this stage that there are far too many aspects of similarity between Gandhi and the RSS, as we have already seen and will again see later. The recent aggressive behaviour of the Parivar for the last dozen years or so is so out of character that the author was forced to present his interpretation of the matter in this monograph.

4. Hindsight allows us to consider the possibility that anyone who presented a challenge to Jawaharlal Nehru's leadership was systematically sidelined by Gandhi. Jinnah and Subash Chandra Bose are two glaring examples of it. In the massive three-volume work of Mr Govind Talwalkar, former editor, *Maharashtra Times*, on the transfer of power (Talwalkar 1980, 1982, 1984), he has brought out the stand taken by Mr Jinnah in all the negotiations aimed at getting Pakistan. The only way it can be explained (as suggested by Talwalkar in the first volume) is that Jinnah wanted to settle the score with Gandhi for the spurning he received during the freedom struggle.

5. An industrialist once said in a discussion on a national TV channel, 'Today's growth rate is surging forward from what was historically

"the Hindu growth rate"'. Mr P. Chidambaram felt obliged to mention that it was politically correct to say 'Indian Growth Rate'.

6. In passing, I would like to address those who have demanded for long that the RSS take Muslims along with them. This background should perhaps help them understand how practically impossible such a proposition would be. Let alone the long-standing hatred and the lack of trust between the two communities, when the RSS has not even been able to unite all Hindus under its banner, there is little doubt that it would have only been utterly unsuccessful if it had also attempted to bring Muslims and Christians under the RSS umbrella in their formative phase of strengthening themselves and consolidating their belief systems!

7. For long, the RSS has been accused of being a fascist organisation in the mould of the Aryan German Hitler. I have contemplated upon this a great deal. At that time, there was undoubtedly a fascination towards Adolf Hitler, not just in the RSS but also in general, since he brought about a total transformation of a beleaguered, indebted and inflation-ridden nation into a proud nation in a short period of time, from 1933 to 1939, when the war began. The achievement of nationhood, coupled with the imperial challenge he threw at England, and his declaration of Germans as an Aryan race, led to this fascination and admiration — this is understandable as well as justifiable.

In those times of limited transmissible information, it was not possible to know first-hand the havoc that Hitler played upon the lives of the people — Jewish, as well as others — with the aid of the SS, the Brown Shirts and the Gestapo. It must also be remembered that the massacre of the Jews came to be known to the Allied Forces much later, only when defeat started looming large on Hitler's Germany. By then, all of the sensible world — the RSS included — had ceased to have any good words for this monster.

Looking back at the dozen formative years I spent in the RSS, I do not recollect a single story about Hitler, or a story that glorified him, being told in the RSS programmes. On the contrary, the British evacuation of Dunkirk was a favourite, illustrating to us the bravery, nationalism, planning, organisation and steadfast nature of the British in the face of adversity.

8. The three reasons I worked for the RSS for many years were: first, the RSS' man-making mission made immense sense to me. I felt that it was a fundamental need of the nation that was being addressed by the RSS; the second reason was that the leadership of the organisation would never allow it to become another Hindu sect; and the third was my belief that they would not compromise on ethics and principles

under any situation. When I saw that none of the three were operative any longer, I left the RSS.

9. In 1970, the now-defunct *Illustrated Weekly* from Mumbai asked many prominent people what they thought about being a Hindu. The reply of the great Satyajit Ray was, 'I am not a Hindu, I am a Bengali.'

10. Mr Ramaswamy Naikar was a social political thinker of Tamil Nadu in the middle decades of the 20th century. He was opposed to Brahmins, apart from being an atheist, and, in general, a denouncer of everything that went as a common tradition of this land.

2

Political Ethnography of the RSS

———— • ✦ • ————

As I mentioned at the end of the previous chapter, I will now discuss the very serious objection of the Hindu Rashtra being a vindictive concept, excluding the Muslims and threatening to exterminate them.

Delineating the Thesis for Nationhood

Towards the close of 1938, Hedgewar wanted to delineate the concept of the 'nation' in greater detail. This job was given to Golwalkar, who derived his thesis substantially from a book written by Babarao Savarkar, the elder brother of the revolutionary V.D. Savarkar, titled *We or Our Nationhood Defined* (henceforth referred to as *We*). The original 1939 publication *We* was later altered. Four different versions of the text exist. Golwalkar ultimately disowned the ownership of the whole endeavour saying that it was a mere translation of an original essay called *Rashtra Meemamsa* (Critique of the

Nation Concept) by Babarao Savarkar (D. Deodhar 2006). This is the book which has been quoted for so long as the indicator of the fascist tendencies of Golwalkar and the RSS, as the evidence of the venom they have for Muslims in particular. The matter is further complicated by the fact that *We* was used by the RSS workers till 1960, when Golwalkar's *Bunch of Thoughts* became available as a text (D. Deodhar 2006). Looking at the way it is written, it is difficult to accept that Dr Hedgewar consented to the free use of this book, but in less than a year and a quarter after the book was published, Hedgewar passed away as a result of the chronic debilitating disorders he had been suffering from. *We* also highlights some of the strong and aggressive beliefs of Golwalkar as a person. Some of them continued to be important in his later life, while some of them were completely abandoned by him in the course of time. These are issues I will return to in Chapter 3, titled 'Dominant Tendencies of the Golwalkar Era'.

Meanwhile, focusing on the matter at hand, the charge against the Hindu Rashtra can be framed thus: 'Hindu Rashtra' is a vindictive concept, spewing hatred towards people of all non-Hindu religions who have been residents of India for so long. It is a vengeful concept. It excludes non-Hindus from any rights and declares that they do not even deserve a place in India.

The Clamour and Controversies of *We*

Strictly following the pre- and post-war political thinkers of the West, Golwalkar in *We* discusses the concept of the nation and whether it is applicable to the idea of the Hindu Nation (Golwalkar 1939). To put forth a brief summary: a nation is said to come into existence when there is a common piece of land for a people who belong to a common race, tradition, culture, religion and, preferably, language, who have common aspirations and a shared sense of who their friends and foes are. Lokanayak Aney has corroborated this idea in much detail by an erudite discussion in his foreword to *We*. As per the corroborations and Golwalkar's own thesis, the most salient point of Golwalkar's discussion is this: since Hindus alone answer to this description of 'nation' in India, they are therefore the only ones who constitute the nation in this land (Golwalkar 1939: 2).

Paraphrasing Golwalkar, his thoughts on the Muslim community of India seem to be thus: though the land is common, yet the Muslims do not share any of the traditions of Hindustan — their religious loyalty lies outside the country, their religious tradition accepts a genealogy of prophets who do not belong to this land. While not naming them directly, Golwalkar calls Muslims traitors in *We*. They, he argues, consider themselves to be the conquering invaders of India and seek to win back the power they have now lost. Quoting the 'Minority Treaty of League of Nations', Golwalkar then points out that in a nation state, a national race and a foreign race cannot coexist. Citing the instance of Czechoslovakia, he further presses forth his contention that forcibly bringing together two or more nationalities will not result in territorial loyalty to the nation. We have very recently seen these very nations, the Czechs and the Slovaks, as well as the Yugoslavian conglomerate, breaking into pieces. As far as logic and the then prevailing situation goes, Golwalkar has every reason to claim that there exists a national race and a foreign race. Aney, in his foreword, honestly supports the main thesis of the book, the pure concept of what 'nationhood' is:

> There is much in this small book with which I am in agreement with the author....The author's book is in my opinion a natural and perhaps an inevitable and much needed reply to the theory of blank cheque which is generally attributed to Mahatma Gandhi and those who think like him. (Golwalkar 1939: xx)

This was the face within the Congress that Nehru was allergic to. This was the Hindu group within the Congress which Gandhi was aware of but managed to keep in check for long.

Reading *We*, the reader, however reluctantly, realizes and regrets the strong overtones in the text that serious writing disallows. What follows in the form of expectations from the other communities, to say the least, is difficult to accept. Aney reacts to it by adding,

> The strong and impassioned language used by the author towards those who do not subscribe towards his theory of Nationalism is also not in keeping with the dignity with which the scientific study of a complex problem like the nationalism deserves to be pursued... (Golwalkar 1939: xviii)

The balanced attitude of Dr Hedgewar towards the Congress and his continuing to work with it as late as 1937 is in sharp contrast with that of Golwalkar, who, too blunt for etiquette, said, 'In these strange times — traitors are enthroned as national heroes and patriots are heaped with ignominy' (Golwalkar 1939: 2). The 'traitors' being referred to are obviously the Muslims who shared honours on the Congress platform, and whom he believed to be fundamentalists and anti-national.

To facilitate our understanding, it is necessary to point out that Golwalkar has specifically avoided the question of the relationship of the nation and its state with these 'foreign races' in *We*. Aney observes, 'Hindu Nation as a Sovereign State is entirely a different entity from the Hindu Nation as a cultural nationality.... The author in dealing with problem of Mohammedans' place has not always borne the difference between these two' (Golwalkar 1939). By doing so, Golwalkar harms his own thesis, as well as that of the RSS, as we will see later. *We* creates an impression that the Muslims are not in the mainstream and goes on to deny them any political rights whatsoever. *We* has also left the question of the place of Muslims in an independent state of India unanswered. Even if he had discussed the issue as a matter of statecraft and said what he wanted to (which we will come to), it would have softened the critique somewhat. Obviously he was not willing to be conciliatory on that issue.

This is serious consideration, since Golwalkar was referring to millions of people living in this land. They could not be merely thrown into the Arabian Sea, after all. Whatever the community in question may say today, their genes have been mixed with that of the Hindu populace, even if it has been by marriage, abductions and conversions. As a race they are now closest to the race residing in this land before they came here. For someone who was to later position himself as a far-seeing statesman, it should have been apparent to Golwalkar that attitudes of exclusion—a strong trait in Golwalkar—do not solve a problem. A solution which looks at the inclusion and acceptance of divergence, disparities and antagonism alone solves the problem.

The remedies Golwalkar suggested overall are: those who fall outside the fivefold limits of nationalism can have no place in the national life unless they abandon their differences; adopt the religion, culture and language of the nation; and completely merge themselves in the national race. Until then they could only be foreigners, be it friendly or inimical. Ironically, the same Golwalkar was fond of saying that 'Nature Abhors Uniformity' (Golwalkar 1966).

'Having no place in national life' is not the same as 'we appeal them to join the National life', or that 'in the State they have their place, provided they are not a public nuisance'. On one hand, Golwalkar speaks of Hinduism as the most catholic of all religions, one which tolerates, nay, respects all the different modes of worship; on the other hand, he demands the abandonment of all differences. Which differences? Certainly not religious, since he respects them! It is such a demand that cannot be complied with by anyone living in any part of the world other than his native land, and is quite difficult to be followed even by those who do reside in their native land. What was the need for this monochromatic view?

The second demand, of adopting the religion, culture and language of the nation, is even more absurd. What is adopting a culture? Performing *pujas* and making pilgrimages to holy Hindu sites? It is indeed perplexing as to why Golwalkar could not conceive of respecting the culture of the nation's forefathers instead of adopting the same. That would be a reasonable request. Deoras spoke in this tenor. On the question of language, we must point out that Muslims of the various different provinces speak the native language of the province they reside — this was as true at Golwalkar's time as it is now. There is no tact in demanding complete merger at a time when separatism is afoot, appeasement is giving wind to it, and as the RSS or Golwalkar, one is completely powerless in reigning in the situation. This holds true even today. The entire text of *We* runs counter to the main thesis of the RSS, that is to say, 'All the problems of this country lie in the fact that the Hindu society today is weak, disunited, disorganised. Unless that is made strong nothing is possible.'

Golwalkar continues, 'The foreign races in Hindustan must learn to respect and hold in reverence Hindu religion... must entertain no idea except the glorification of the Hindu race and culture' (1939). I would like to ask any sane man if the way the Hindu religion and culture is today, or was in 1939, can be held in reverence even by a Hindu and entertain no idea except the 'glorification' of the same? How can one demand such respect? We will have a detailed look at this unqualified, unconvincing eulogy of Hinduism as one of the main traits in Golwalkar's thought in the later chapters.

His last and perhaps the best is, '[The foreign races must] either lose their separate existence or merge... or stay in the country wholly subordinated to the Hindu Nation, deserving no privileges...not even the citizen's rights' (Golwalkar 1939). This demand should be beyond tolerance even to an RSS man. Such a demand is the demand of Savarkar, not the RSS.

Belief System in the RSS Then

We know as a fact that from the time of Dr Hedgewar, the RSS did not subscribe to the religiously preconditioned brand of Hindutva propounded by Savarkar, which did not leave any place for the Muslims in this country. Whatever Golwalkar may have written in *We*, his public and private conversations and speeches since 1940 have never reflected these hard, extremist thoughts.[1] Referring to *Bunch of Thoughts*, and the chapter on the nation's enemies in particular, one finds that Golwalkar has pointed out the anti-national, pro-Pakistani, quarrel-mongering attitude of his contemporary Indian Muslims, as well as their hatred of Hindus. The hardest he has been on this group is in his assertion that such people are not the sons of the soil. Clearly accepting the status of citizens given to them by the constitution, his point is restricted to the question of loyalty to this land. This position of Golwalkar has remained throughout, which, of course, stands to reason, since the sustenance of such Muslims has also come from this very land.

As late as 1939, Dr Hedgewar had taken Savarkar around the RSS *shakha*s and made the *swayamsevak*s to listen to his thoughts. Golwalkar gave a vote of thanks in one instance. In those 15 minutes, Golwalkar, while thanking Savarkar, made amply clear the differences between his brand of Hindutva and the RSS brand. He also conveyed the unwillingness of the RSS to work as the political or youth wing of a political party. It was a scholarly speech, spoken with polite audacity (conversations with D.B. Ghumare, senior journalist, June 2007).

We may further quote L.K. Advani on Golwalkar in August 1942 in Karachi in order to obtain a clearer view, 'Muslims should know that they belong to the same race as Hindus. Their forefathers were Hindus. Their culture and civilization is Indian and not Arabic' (Advani 2008).

The Politics of the Early Years to Establish Golwalkar

Though Deoras was much younger than one of the most trusted lieutenants of Dr Hedgewar, Appaji Joshi, there is no doubt that he was the heir apparent. Yet Hedgewar ultimately chose Golwalkar over Deoras. Golwalkar's tremendous command over several languages, especially English, was considered a great asset to spread the work of the RSS in south India. His knowledge of many subjects was another asset. Hedgewar's choice of Golwalkar supposedly had the consent of people like Appaji Joshi (Palkar 1967). However, when the announcement took place, Appaji was surprised because he did not think Golwalkar had the requisite political sophistication to lead the RSS, since he was new to the Sangh and not experienced enough (Anderson and Damle 1987: 63, note 85). The first cry of dissent was raised in Pune, asking, 'Who is this *dadhiwala* (bearded man) being thrust upon us?' The well-wishers outside were also apprehensive about the RSS after Dr Hedgewar, something which Deoras has said on more than one occasion (Anderson and Damle 1987: 40).

The magnanimity of Deoras lies in the fact that he did everything to establish the leadership of Golwalkar in the RSS. From 1940 onwards, Deoras used to accompany him to many places for a few years as Hedgewar's emissary to suppress notions of dissent.[2] Deoras was aware of the general perception that the new leader is a 'peculiar' person. However, for this disciplined soldier, however differently Golwalkar may have been built, however new to the RSS, it was enough that his mentor Dr Hedgewar had named Golwalkar the chief. Therefore, he did everything in his power to establish Golwalkar's leadership, since he knew that his word still counted above all in the RSS at that time.

Anderson and Damle note 'that Ghatate might well have fabricated Hedgewar's choice or planted the idea in the dying man's mind (to make Golwalkar the chief of RSS after him)' (1987), but there is no way this rumour can be verified.

Other people close to the dying Dr Hedgewar have denied it (Anderson and Damle 1987: 68). There has also been a speculation that Golwalkar had mesmerised the dying man, again without any evidence to support such a claim. All this is not common knowledge within the RSS. The establishment of Golwalkar's dominance over the years has effectively led to the suppression of such rumours, as well as the fact that leadership did not come easily to Golwalkar.

Soon enough, Golwalkar defied the early opposition he faced. According to my father, Golwalkar once said,

> Dr. Hedgewar has appointed me in the position of [the] Sarsanghchalak. If anyone sitting here has any objection to it, tell me now. If someone does it tomorrow, I will throw him out of [the] RSS like a stone in the rice, just as Mahatma Gandhi did to Dr N B Khare.

Golwalkar's uncertainty, however, remained for a long time. He was very much his own man. He had his own design about where he wanted to take the RSS. If C.P. Bhishikar (1982) is to be believed, then Golwalkar wanted to continue the unfinished work of Hindu Sanghatan of Swami Vivekananda through the RSS. Golwalkar strongly believed that he was Vivekananda reincarnate, to the point of losing himself in the intoxication of such a belief at least on one instance (conversations with Dilip Deodhar, 2007–08; conversations with D.B. Ghumare, senior journalist, June 2007; conversations with Late Prof. Bhagadikar Krishnarao in 2007). He wanted the RSS to have a cultural thrust, espousing the ideal of cultural nationalism.

The Golwalkar Aversion to Political Power

Golwalkar wanted to keep the RSS undefiled and pure, of a lofty and unimpeachable character, which alone would allow it to remain in a position to dictate terms. This fear of slipping from the pedestal led him to programme the cadre in a particular fashion, especially in the domain of political power. The world renowned ballerina Isadora Duncan said, 'The man who has had no opportunity to sin is not a sinless man. Those who remain sinless even when confronting an opportunity are' (Duncan 1927). Golwalkar and his men did not want to face temptation and remain pure, like stainless steel.

The dominant tendency in Golwalkar was the abhorrence of (political) power and, therefore, of attaining the same. His psyche was suspicious and contemptuous of power. He sincerely believed that political power was not all that necessary for the work of national reconstruction that he had undertaken through the RSS. 'Power corrupts and absolute power corrupts absolutely': Golwalkar first said this with reference to the Communist regime in Russia, but soon it became a general statement of the RSS creed of staying away from political power (Golwalkar 1960). The mindset of Golwalkar and others around him was to shun political power but control the same. The Indian psyche respects sacrifice more than any other people and adores those who sacrifice. The most potent effect is achieved when a person shuns something what other people like most: power. Such people typically project themselves as akin to the sacrificing Hindu *rishi*s who controlled the unruly kings by the power of Dharma. The king merely receives a salute, but the *rishi*, who makes the king, desires prostration (conversations with Dilip Deodhar 2007–08). Real-life instances of sacrifice by people such as M.K. Gandhi, Bal Thackarey, Sonia Gandhi and many others make this point clear.

Golwalkar did not want to deal with political work and power because he did not want the responsibility of delivering the goods that was demanded of a politician. Golwalkar thus called politics too small a part of the human life, too unimportant. He rationalised his stance by saying that politics is not central to the life of a nation. He thus made it an indifferent object of no significance. He added a dirty connotation to the term by calling politics a *varangana* or a prostitute. What he garnered for the RSS were the assets from the political work done by the RSS men he provided for the Jan Sangh, without wanting the liabilities of the hard work to deliver the goods (conversations with Dilip Deodhar 2007–08). On the converse, he and his disciples like Thengadi wanted the smug satisfaction of being the critics and the watchdogs who do not achieve anything themselves but are always there to point out the failures and inadequacies of those who commit themselves to some action and may fail.

Golwalkar constructed another argument, that the RSS would create a force outside politics that will influence, control and even cleanse politics from the outside (conversations with D.B. Ghumare, Senior Journalist, June 2007). This was the power wielded by the ancient saints and sages of the Vasishtha and Vishvamitra tradition, who sought only the society's welfare. It was a grand vision that moved everybody; it boosted the self-esteem of the majority and of the Brahmins in Maharashtra in particular. However, it was too idealistic a vision—the history of RSS itself has shown it to be impractical and impossible. Even when staying out of power, the RSS men turned out to be easily fallible. In fact, the RSS' score on that count is quite bad. Some solace the RSS men may derive is through the satisfaction that none of the political party workers of any other creed are any different.

Golwalkar further theorised that all cultures and societies sustained by political power perished with the same. Scholars may either prove or negate this theory—I admit it is beyond the limits of my competence to do the same. The converse of this argument, that the strength of a society should reside with the people (which is true but not enough, nor easily realisable), however, drove the RSS men away from acquiring that power. The proof of so serious a charge is the persistent tendency of Golwalkar and his likes to shirk away from creating details and conveniently avoiding any work that will be required for such a task, outside that ordained for the man making the plan. Within the narrow confines of the organisation, Golwalkar did not legitimise the need for power.

Politics of the Congress and the RSS during the First Ban

Following the (re)translated letter from Sardar Patel to Golwalkar after the first ban on the RSS was lifted, it is possible to understand what these men thought of each other and their respective organisations.

> Brother Golwalkarji...the situation of the country is such, the events are taking place with such speed that we have to fix our vision on the present and future, taking it away from the past. I hope you will think of RSS, Congress and the Government in this manner....Only those who are close to me could tell how greatly happy I was in lifting the ban on RSS. (Sardar Vallabhbhai Patel, in a letter to Golwalkar DO No. 512–DPM/49 dated 21–23 July 49, New Delhi)

Patel, in his letter dated 19 August 1949, had accepted that

> there is no doubt that RSS has served the Hindu Society. Where people were helpless, the young men of RSS went there, protected the women and children and did a lot of work for them [that is, the refugees from Pakistan]. I believe that the RSS men can fulfil and fructify their emotions of patriotism by entering Congress. (Golwalkar 1979)

From 17 to 23 October 1948, Patel met Golwalkar several times about lifting the ban, but Patel instead insisted on the RSS becoming a part of the Congress. Patel was delaying the removal of the ban to see if the RSS merged with the Congress — he was a politician who would look for any source to fortify his organisation. Golwalkar was no less shrewd, and while he sought to cooperate with the Congress, he had no intention of merging the RSS with the Congress or joining the Congress. The language of cooperation used by

Golwalkar was not that of a beggar but of an equal who has full knowledge of the strengths of both the organisations in their own spheres. It is also clear that Golwalkar felt his and the RSS' cooperation with the government to be a natural sentiment (Golwalkar 1979).

As long as the possibility to work with the Congress remained, Golwalkar evaded Shyama Prasad Mukherjee, who wanted the RSS' collaboration to start his own political party. Mukherjee had serious differences on the issue of admitting Muslims in the Hindu Mahasabha. The Hindu Mahasabha rejected this admittance outright, which led to Mukherjee leaving the Hindu Mahasabha.

The antagonism between the Congress and the RSS that the polity today is accustomed to is a much later phenomenon. Suffice it to say that from 1942 to 1947, during the Partition and its aftermath, there was alignment between the two, tacit or otherwise. To indicate the level of understanding, it will suffice to point out that Patel had asked Golwalkar to meet Raja Hari Singh of Kashmir in 1947 to make him agree to join the Indian State, which Golwalkar complied with (Golwalkar 1981).

The Need for Political Power Arises

Gandhi's murder led to the ban on the RSS. No one had the time, nor any desire, to stop and think if those very people who had saved Delhi and the people in it, who had served the refugees and who had lost 5,000 of their comrades in protecting the same, who had saved Srinagar Airport and had fought the Muslim onslaught could want to murder Gandhi. No one was ready to speak on behalf of the RSS even after the ban was lifted and the RSS was given a clean chit in the murder of Gandhi. This was far more disturbing to many, because it was not a matter of isolation — it was ostracism by the very society for whom these men had recently shed their blood. The former nationalists were now traitors. There had been little effort from within the Congress, Patel included, to remove the ban on the RSS. Patel had clearly told Nehru that the plot of Gandhi's murder was hatched by the Hindu Mahasabha, and the RSS was not involved. The RSS was framed by various forces, including Nehru. The correspondence during the period of ban does not reflect favourably on the democratically elected new government of the sovereign, democratic Indian Republic, where the primary and fundamental basis of democracy and jurisprudence, dialogue, was not practised in dealing with this ban.

When the deadlock continued despite a massive Satyagraha, Dani and Deoras sent a message through the emissary to Patel saying, 'If you are not going to remove the ban we have other ways [meaning entering politics], to carry on the work (Chouthaiwale n.d.: 19). Patel could not have missed the threat and was shrewd enough not to allow such a force to go into direct antagonism with the Congress in politics. Finally, on 12 July 1949, the ban was withdrawn unconditionally without any apparent reason or without any justification as to why it had been operative for so long.

The Demoralisation Sets In

The first general elections ensued in 1952. The nascent Jan Sangh fielded candidates wherever possible. The rudest shock they received was in the Punjab elections, where the work done by the RSS men for the protection of the Hindus and the refugees was fresh in the minds of the people. All the Jan Sangh candidates in Punjab were defeated. One fails to understand why people still voted for the Congress, especially in Punjab, and did not seem to buy into the new nationalistic party even after the holocaust of Partition. In face of the spectre of electoral debacle and the failure to achieve recognition for the work done in Punjab, demoralisation set in. It started off a process of rethinking, of inspecting what their past actions were, and what had happened to them. The backlash of the Partition, the fact that the vivisection of the nation did take place in spite of the RSS being there, was not easy to accept or tolerate.

Even after the ban was lifted, the unsympathetic attitude of the government and its repressive and oppressive measures continued. Job opportunities, which at that time were mostly government jobs and small to begin with, were denied to the members of the RSS. There was a glaring need to rehabilitate those who had offered Satyagraha, family-wise as well as financially. The organisational spirit itself had broken. There were huge debts. The growth curve of the organisation had severely regressed and reversed. The spate of young full-time workers who had left their homes for many years in 1940 and 1942 started returning home, broken. The situation as a whole put a question mark on how they were going to continue the organisation in the future.

The strongest effect was that of disillusionment, which slowly set in — disillusionment with the pure ethos of worship of the Motherland, with the concentration of man-making in the *shakha*s. After 22 years of so much sacrifice, if this was the fate of the organisation, then it was not wrong for many to challenge the very basis of the work. The rising tide of opinions was expressed mainly in two ways. One relatively small group wanted the RSS to abandon its work altogether and transform itself into a political party, support another party, or form a new party with some existing party, since all that mattered was really the political power to propagate the RSS' ideas and ideology (Anderson and Damle 1987). The second group, however, was larger and believed that the Sangh and its *shakha* work alone were not sufficient — they had to get into the various areas of national life, including politics, and make an impression of their thoughts. Strong opinions over adopting different methodologies to achieve the aim were expressed by many diehard workers, mostly from Maharashtra, with a significant chunk of full-timers from Delhi as well as Bihar, who later left the RSS (Pimpalkar 2002a: 08).

Politics of Handling Dissidence

The most notable among the dissenters was Dr V.V. Pendsey, who finally decided to develop models of schools which would impart the same ethos and acculturate students for the role and responsibilities of leadership — the now famous Dnyan Prabodhini of Pune. He was later disallowed to attend the RSS branches. Madhukar Deval argued similarly and was openly and bitterly critical, although Pendsey did not do that (conversations with Vasant Tamhankar 2008). Deval went away to start the Sri Vitthal Sahakari Seva Sanstha, a cooperative society for the most downtrodden untouchables in Miraj, in the then Bombay Presidency. At home, the Deoras brothers wanted to enter politics as the most immediate priority. Deoras wanted the Sangh to get into a variety of work while the work of the RSS continued. Golwalkar found it difficult to cope with this situation. He used to get upset and angry over it (Pimpalkar 2002b: 08).

Golwalkar handled these myriad dissenting opinions and the entire situation rather badly. The Pune group consisted of brilliant devoted *swayamsevak*s with sacrifice on their nameplate. Their understanding of the RSS ethos was no less than any other. But they were freethinking men. While these men argued, they did not do so with an idea of starting an organisation parallel to the RSS. They wanted to get into other areas with the blessings and the concurrence of the RSS, and its moral support for their ideas. Golwalkar's refusal to accept their viewpoint hurt them. The prevailing attitude in the RSS about Dnyan Prabodhini, for instance, was 'as impossible, incompatible and unacceptable as onions and garlic on Ekadashi [on a day of fasting in Maharashtra]'. Golwalkar took their desire for a new way of doing things as a

49

personal affront, a failure on his part. 'Egos clashed', was one of the simplest explanations given to me by Shri D.M. Date, a level-headed, highly placed full-timer of RSS (conversations with Damodar Madhav Date 1975–80). One may not credit the dissidents with the best of behaviour, given their youth, brilliance and freethinking. But one may not be able to exempt Golwalkar from some responsibility either.

That there were elements inherently correct in the demands of these heretics must be appreciated. The reaction of the common RSS *swayamsevak*, 'if Guruji does not agree with it there must be something inherently wrong in it', is not acceptable. The fact that Golwalkar did, or 'allowed to happen', exactly what these heretics wanted, in the next year or two to come, supports their position.[3] But it happened at the cost of, and after the exclusion of, the dissidents from mainstream RSS work. Not even a year lapsed before the Akhil Bharatiya Vidyarthi Parishad (ABVP) was formed to become active in the university and college arena and politics. One after another the Jan Sangh and the Bharatiya Mazdoor Sangh followed; in addition the work in *vanvasi* (tribal) areas began in right earnest in 1952.

Golwalkar separated the works of these organisations once he sent some of his core workers to man the new fields. He virtually disowned these fields, which later came to be known as the Parivar organisations of the RSS, in public as well as in private, by reiterating his position that he found it *'vichitra'* (peculiar) and that he did not have much hope from it. His reaction to the work of these organisations, particularly politics, was bitter. He considered it as a contraption. He was of the opinion that if it worked, he would accept it, but if it did not, it should be dismantled (V.D. Deoras 2000). The most painful aspect of this dismissal was his attitude that every other type of work, politics included, was potentially useless. He started the work, but took away their sanction. And on top of that, he expected an unflinching allegiance to him and, more specifically, to his persona.

The Politics of Non-inclusive Culture Begins

With this began the politics of non-inclusive behaviour and the functioning of non-inclusive practices. All the other types of work and the people doing them were tacitly or overtly given the status of second-class citizens, RSS work being the main and the only true work. This bred two more tendencies. The first was to not 'recognise' any good work done by the *swayamsevaks* outside the RSS. The second one was to not own the work done by these organisations. A sense of contempt towards those who worked in these other organisations set in. The major attribute of the Golwalkar era is this disdain and indifference. The RSS hierarchy became supreme. A post in the party endowed the members with every attainable virtue, however mediocre the people holding these various posts might have been. There was, furthermore, an honour attached with these positions. A desire to be a part of it and enjoy the status never really left many of them.

The organisation no longer remained a tool for achieving social unity but became a reason in itself to survive. It became a career, an occupation in the manner of some sects. The rituals became more important, even more sacrosanct as days went by. There were cycles of the daily, weekly, monthly and yearly meetings and programmes. The tenacity of the full-time workers and the diehard *swayamsevaks* is a wonder in itself. In those bleakest days, many of them worked hundreds of miles away from their homes, often hungry, sustaining on *chana* and *murmura*, often sleeping on pavements and open verandas because they had nowhere else to go. They were prepared for the possibility of their lives ending in struggle, like that of a dog by the roadside. They were the heroes of the struggle to keep the RSS intact organisationally and to retain as many of the members from drifting away. These countless heart-rending episodes are at par with the sacrifices the RSS men made during the days of Partition. The Partition days ended in a few months, but the sacrifices of these men continued for over 15 years before the RSS started finding some general credibility within society again. Golwalkar rebuilt the organisation through this painful process.[4] But it also became unchangeable and mechanical. As early as 1950–55, the RSS had lost the charm of its early years and had become tedious and unappetising.

The meticulous Eknath Ranade, who gave managerial inputs, drew the lines of reporting, function and other processes and, to a large measure, structured the organisational hierarchy, could have inadvertently caused this change towards rigidity (conversations with Virag Pachpore 2007). A hierarchy is functional and relates to capacities in a live and adaptive business model. It is important but not sacrosanct. In the RSS at that time, however, it became so. Mediocrity was enshrined in the hierarchy. Scholarship was of little consequence and was unwelcome. Anyone thinking outside the box was a natural outcaste.[5]

The Politics of Consolidation

Golwalkar was intolerant to shortcomings and had a very sharp tongue. He was intolerant of fools and wished to keep the sycophants away. He could, therefore, often be insulting, hurtful, contemptuous, especially with those who did not agree with him (conversations with D.B. Ghumare, senior journalist, June 2007). His humour was cutting, full of barbs; it often made one feel sheepish or humiliated. He could not suppress his desire to show his erudition everywhere. His affection was for those who conformed to his ways of thinking or those who believed in many of the religious rituals of the day. Golwalkar was ruthless and pretty much heartless over these matters.

The RSS as a Sect

The following discussion owes a serious debt to my senior friend Dr R.H. Tupkary (*Sanghatana Ani Sanghatitata*, 2008). We did not realise it at that time, but the RSS had increasingly started assuming the characteristics of a sect. The RSS had by then taken a position of not being affected by the social, political and economic turmoil that was occurring in the country. Like the tradition of the saints in medieval India who helped the Hindus to retain their belief system but neglected the far more important matters like invasions of aliens, the threat to existence itself under it, national security and the unity or the organisation of the society, the RSS began to act in a similar manner. People went around with a laughable seriousness, exactly as they do in a religious sect, as if they had found the ultimate truth and were the chosen people to spread it around. There was a spiritual man at the top, a realised soul, as in a sect. Demand for an unquestioning surrender to his persona was in obvious evidence. Unless there was an order from the top, nothing would move. Like a sect, there was no challenging this hierarchy. Those who remained within the hierarchy exhibited the tendency to have faith in the one and only brand of the RSS, as one would have faith on one's own church. If we follow the one prophet, one book logic, the RSS had as its holy book *Bunch of Thoughts* and Golwalkar was its prophet. Like in a sect, there was a popular acceptance that the man at the top understood everything and that all knowledge had been revealed to him.

Why do we need to question these developments? Let us be very clear here: this is how a sect is born or gets founded. Slowly, the Sangh began to centre around the chant of 'Guruji' alone. To keep the record straight, we must acknowledge that there were a few people who produced considerable written material that was made available and circulated within the RSS. But the fountainhead of logic and content in the organisation, its main ideas, came from what Golwalkar thought.

A sect typically does not allow any leeway to the taste, intellect or self-awareness of an individual (it is not the same as ego or fascism). The RSS became a closed system, proving this thesis. There was no scope for change. To all problems there was only one answer. The people had an unshakable belief. They had even evolved a language and the rituals of a sect: if the head was meeting with the *swayamsevaks*, everyone must go in with a *tilak* on his forehead. The cadre bore external emblems and styled themselves like their head. They were not much concerned about whether this was fruitful or where it all was leading to. A volunteer had to face apparent condescension if he wished to discuss something with the hierarchy. After all, where was the need to discuss anything? The RSS was a sect; the answers to all questions had already been laid out.

In majority of the sects formed, the appeal essentially is that of the emotional solace one gains by joining it. Rational, radical, intellectual understanding or scientific proof is not something that appeals to most people. The vast majority in the RSS wanted that emotional succour, the sense of belonging, and a sense of security. That was available to them as long as they did not start questioning and remained implicitly faithful. In fact, there were very few who said that their understanding and approach was based on the intellectual appraisal of the RSS' thesis and no other element.

Is a sectarian arrangement of implicit faith, command, and obedience, an intellectually closed system, the same as fascism? T.V.R. Sastri, attempting to remove the ban on the RSS, wondered how an organisation where people were not compelled to join could be fascist. The examples of fascism as we know and have seen have something inherently based on either hunger for power, usually political, or/and a tendency to conquer and destroy. Both these desires are usually rooted in the hatred of a people, or an idea of an enemy, or an ideology. With fascism comes violence, both in deed as well as emotions. The RSS, however, was a sect that had explicitly stated that power was not their goal. If it bore any hatred, it did not act on the same. Whatever fascism there might have been in the RSS, in the sense that its leader had absolute command and had the capacity to evict members if they were not obedient, it remained within the organisation as an instance of internal dictatorship. We should also note that actual eviction of members was extremely rare in the RSS. The RSS in the Golwalkar era was simply converted into a sect by Golwalkar and his faithful, who were happy to remain there.

Young men like me did not find an appeal in the *'arsha'* or the scriptural language to which the RSS and Golwalkar continued to resort to. The RSS under Golwalkar claimed that evil would be defeated by the spread of brotherly love and the methods of the Sangh, but the organisation suffered from a lack of focus on details and any guidance about managing glaring practical problems. Meanwhile, vested interests continued to evolve with time.

The RSS was never meant to be a sect. That was one of the two reasons I was a part of the organisation, the second reason being the 'no compromise' attitude I believed existed in the organisation when faced with the right cause. It was to be an eternally growing, moulding body, one which evolves, one which changes in response to the time and tide to achieve what is good for the society, one which is capable of embracing and incorporating one and all faiths or sectarian beliefs. This is what the RSS ceased to be. This was the beginning of the 'lost years' of the RSS.

The Dilution of the Achiever's Psyche

The founder of the RSS, Dr Hedgewar, had repeatedly said that the RSS was not interested in celebrating its jubilees and centenaries. It merely wanted to achieve the aim of consolidation of the Hindu society, '*Yachi Dehi, Yachi Dola*' (while this body is alive and these eyes can see). This was an achiever's psyche, not ready to wait but to force itself on the sands of time and bring about change in the situation one had inherited simply through one's effort. Deoras, the direct disciple of Dr Hedgewar, thought exactly the same way. He was a man of action, ready to bite more than he could chew. This is an attitude typical of those who want to achieve something. Golwalkar gave the RSS its most decisive turn in the backdrop of massive setbacks, the rise of dissidence, dilapidation of the strength of the organisation, and societal aversion and loss of sympathy towards the organisation.

Golwalkar abandoned the achiever's psyche and declared RSS work as an all-time necessity. A job of nation building cannot be a one-time job. He explained his thesis with many examples and made a philosophy out of it. In an attempt to do justice to Golwalkar, we must concede that any other idea, possibly stricter than this, might very well have broken the terribly beleaguered organisation at that time. We may even concede that he administered the second dose of modest heroism through the 1940s to the 1970s, to which people could relate. It offered them a target larger than their life but demanded only moderate sacrifice and moderate courage. It gave them a sense of power, of being together and being a part of an organisation. It gave them confidence to face the disadvantages in life at a time when India was poor, starved and had locked itself into a state of stasis. This brand of patriotism and heroism did not demand the courage of revolutionaries. The sense that the RSS and Golwalkar gave them was that they were preparing for a war, gathering strength to address certain issues. The feeling was that they were the ones who would finally have to do what was good for the country. The most damning effect of this newly developed psyche was that it paved slowly the way for the RSS to become a sect among other things.

These were sensations heady enough to intoxicate, but not enough for one to lose balance altogether. They served to sustain faith across the vast organisation. The tendency to avoid conflict was also what finally gave the illusion away — the RSS was ready to boot and had nowhere to go. This is the paradox. Because of his implicit faith in his working method, Golwalkar developed considerable strength, but he did not put it to the grind during the post-ban period for a long time. By adopting this attitude after the near lethal blow of the first ban, it was possible to bear with the ostracism. With that the RSS went into a shell and avoided exposure to society and to the media. They did not pursue a case, following the old logic of avoiding publicity, since it is potentially harmful, forgetting that it could not be relevant anymore in independent India.

This eternal walker's psyche was also an antidote to those who demanded diversification and called for achievement in other areas as well. In a subtle way, it was a message that the true work lay in the RSS. Any other form of work was of a reactionary nature, embroiled in the rough and tumble of daily business and likely to pollute one. While refusing to do anything else, the RSS also adopted a saintly posture, looking down their nose at every other work. In the process, it started forgetting that it was supposed to achieve, along with the rest of the Hindu society, something on a much bigger scale — fulfil a grand vision and attain synthesis. That made the RSS a stagnant organisation, one that did not appear up to date. The RSS chose to work quietly to build the nation, whatever that might have meant.

The most diabolical effect this direction taken by the organisation was to remove the edge not only of urgency but of a temperament that was restless, reactive and proactive (refer note 4). It put an end to the RSS' characteristic intolerance and refusal to accept the situation as it existed and a strong desire to change it. This took away any appeal the challenges had to *Parakram* and *Purushartha*, the virility and the manhood of the RSS, two elements Golwalkar talked of all the time.

There was great responsibility, but no time-bound agenda for achievement. The RSS thus became insipid. It started attracting only a rather restricted type of men who were happy to be associated with the mundane, repetitive work and restfully end the day with a mildly intoxicating sense of having done the work of the nation. With this came complacency. The organisation was identified by and with the full-timer workers, who had been battered in the recent traumatic events. They had nothing to go back to in the outside world. They had lost their capacity to earn their own keep. Still, things were being looked after. Who then had the need for an achiever's psyche and take so much pain? All that was needed was to declare oneself eternally dedicated to the work of the RSS and abandon the necessity of upholding time-bound achievements as a creed. In this change of attitudes also lie some of the answers as to why the Deoras era did not last after him and why the organisation was not very responsive to Deoras even during his time, to which I will return duly.

This was the beginning of the lost years, when the RSS aged inertly. It lost the strength of its youth.

The Political Thrust and Political Sensitivity of the RSS

Of the first three phases of the RSS, the Hedgewar era was clearly endowed with a political thrust, given that we were not a free nation at that time. Dr Hedgewar's burning desire to free the country from the British rule could not have given it anything but a political thrust. When a nation talks of independence, it is talking of political power. Dr Hedgewar had chosen the Congress as his political organisation to work for independence. The longing for freedom was one of the greatest factors pulling the youth to the RSS. Independence was a tangible goal. The best part of it was that they never hid their political intentions, but took care that they did not give the British any handle to wipe them out.

The Political Situation and the RSS

There is a panoramic view of the RSS across the years available now. For all their avowed disinterest in politics, at least twice a year the RSS would pass resolutions, once in front of the all-India representative body and once in front of its highest governing body. All the resolutions from 1950 to 2007 have been compiled in an English and a Hindi version (The RSS 2008). It is claimed in the introduction that before Independence this practice did not exist, since the single-point political agenda of the organisation was independence. A cursory look at the index will reveal that a large number of these resolutions are political in nature, with many pointing to the situation in the subcontinent, while others involving issues of international politics where situations that did not augur well for India have been mentioned, worried over and/or criticised. Such issues include Pakistan–America relations, the increasing influence of Russia in and around the world, the possibilities of aggression from Pakistan and China, solutions to the Kashmir problem, and so on, most of them guided by the perceived danger to the integrity of the nation and the welfare of the people of India.

A review of the resolutions shows the RSS coming out openly in opposition to the reorganisation of states on linguistic basis in 1955. It had strongly criticised Nehru for the accusations he had made against the RSS regarding the riots and unrest. In 1959, they had demanded the return of the Kashi Vishvanath Mandir to the Uttar Pradesh (UP) government and to the people since the Supreme Court had decided in favour of it. Such acts have also been linked with 'emotional integration with Muslims', which otherwise would be difficult. The RSS further demanded that the Government should function in a native language (read Hindi) and not English, because otherwise the nation would not be free from the mental slavery of England. It was vocal about the increasing control of the Government and the reduction of individual freedom. During situations of national crisis, however, the RSS has repeatedly sought to work closely with the Government and appealed to its cadre to do so. In the 1960s, sensitive to the scarcity of food due to undependable and meagre rainfall and imports, the RSS had chalked out work plans to tackle famine and carried out those plans well.

By 1971, persecution of Hindus in Bangladesh started featuring in these resolutions. In 1974, the RSS aggressively attacked the Communists for their violent philosophy and means which were destabilising the country, while defending the non-violent stand of the RSS. It accused the Centre of corruption and of being responsible for inflation in the country. The RSS also accused the Centre that it wanted to lay all blame for its failure to control the widespread unrest in Bihar and Gujarat that had erupted at that time on a scapegoat. It is important to note that the communal riots, repeatedly blamed on the RSS, repeatedly find strongly worded denials and demands for judicial enquiries in these resolutions.

In 1977 (the Deoras era at its peak), the resolutions mentioned the formation of an apolitical platform to bring the Muslims, Christians, Parsis and other religious communities together and reviewed its working. They further expressed appreciation towards the Janata government for inviting the RSS' cooperation in the 'Adult Literacy' campaign, which it had given wholeheartedly. The RSS' awareness of the international superpowers and their capacity to undermine the sovereignty of India, to bring India under economic and other forms of imperialism, is evident in these resolutions, as is its determination to resist the same. It also supported Om Prakash Tyagi's anti-conversion bill and blamed the Christian missionaries' opposition of the bill as evidence of coercion, bribery, and so on, which the RSS believed was symptomatic of the way in which they carried out conversions in India. This too is a recurrent theme in the RSS' resolutions. The most recurrent themes revolved around movements seeking to secede from the country, most frequently in the North-East and Punjab in corresponding years. It may, however, be added that these resolutions were more an appeal to the government to look into these destabilising situations than anything else.

This sketch of the RSS' stance on various political issues, I hope, will lay down the basis of understanding the RSS in its later years. With this, let us now turn to some of the most vexing issues about Deoras and his distancing of himself from the RSS' daily work.

Notes

1. One would find it difficult to believe that the assertions of *We* never found repetitions after 1940. Dr Hedgewar had clearly advised Golwalkar to modulate the strong language he was used to in his early years in the RSS. Dr Hedgewar insisted that one who wishes to unite and organise people cannot speak harshly. Golwalkar took the advice to heart. It took him a few years to tone himself down, but he achieved it in immense measure.

2. Strongly disciplined as Deoras was, he helped established the leadership of Golwalkar in the RSS in the early years. In 1942 and 1952, he obeyed Golwalkar out of that same sense of discipline. Over years, Golwalkar strengthened his leadership by elevating men who thought like him to key positions. When Deoras became the chief of the RSS, he had to deal with men who did not always accept him and his thoughts the way they did Golwalkar.

3. There are differences of opinion as to whether it was Golwalkar or Deoras who was behind the idea of creating a Parivar, a network of organisations in many fields of national life. Shrikant Joshi clearly states that it was the doing of Deoras. Golwalkar did not like such things. Deodhar, however, gives all credit to Golwalkar. Many disliked the Deoras viewpoint of the RSS actively supporting such initiatives, becoming responsible for their work, achievement and owning them up as RSS work.

4. Most RSS *swayamsevaks* (volunteer cadre) know about the subtle change from the 'achievement in this lifetime' to the eternal walker's psyche, but have remained unaware of its effects, extending into the Deoras years. This created serious resistance to the ideas of Deoras, especially in the front of political power.

5. Eknath Ranade, after building the Vivekananda monument, started the Vivekananda Kendra (Centre) and developed a system of choosing young men and women with a temperament for social service even under difficult circumstances. They were then rigorously trained and sent as full-time workers to such difficult areas as Arunachal Pradesh. Since 1942, the RSS had developed its own system of full-time workers which, like the Vivekananda Kendra, had no assurance of future, no pay nor any other form of security. Baba Bhide, the then deputy chief of RSS in Maharashtra, questioned Ranade on his scheme of creating lifelong selfless workers, asking him whether he thought the RSS system of full-timers as inadequate. He also asked Ranade whether he considered the RSS as so insufficiently able to deal with the national situation that Ranade felt the need for an alternate organisation. The major attribute of the Golwalkar era was the disdain and indifference the men in the organisation received.

3

Dominant Tendencies of the Golwalkar Era

——— • ✦ • ———

The principal issue that I wish to address in this chapter is whether the dominant tendencies of the RSS in the Golwalkar era are, in any fundamental way, different from the tendencies of the organisation under Dr Hedgewar. The monumental book written by Mr V.R. Karandikar, *Teen Sarsanghachalak* (1999), strenuously makes a tenuous argument that they were not very different at all. It is an intricate and also a dangerous question to raise, since it threatens to challenge this most fond and deeply entrenched belief within the RSS.

The thesis of man-making as one of the most essential requirements of the nation, along with the conviction that this is a Hindu Rashtra with a past one can be proud of and the tremendous belief in the RSS methodology of working and man-making, is common to Hedgewar, Golwalkar and Deoras. The tendencies of the Golwalkar era, the ways of thinking, the modes of behaviour, the various externalities and the projection or aversion towards work, however, are in stark contrast with the Hedgewar and Deoras eras. These differences have cost the nation dear, and any and every political ideology in this country will benefit from the lessons of these differences and should learn not to suppress them.

The Aversion to Publicity

Golwalkar was a highly spiritual man with a pure and idealistic, and hence, perhaps, unworkable vision of the work of the RSS. To him publicity was poison to the character, harming the ethos of the organisation. His creed was the submersion of the ego in the collective consciousness of the society, which was the surrogate for Mother Bharat herself. 'Do we publicise what we do as service to our own mother?' was his insistent refusal for publicity. Equally importantly, he had held the media in contempt. He did not trust them. He believed that publicity gives a false sense of power, to others as well as to the RSS. It put the *swayamsevaks* in danger of becoming publicity hounds. He did not like *swayamsevaks* indulging in acrimonious public squabbles and hit out hard against mischievous propaganda. Paraphrasing him: The silent work speaks for itself. Pure love and affection alone win hearts, arguments but increase acrimony. By sharing joy and sorrows, by being with people in their need, one can win them over and bring them to the RSS and its *shakha*. In short, there was 'an extreme excess' of no publicity — in the words of Bhishikar — in the Golwalkar era.

Everyone was aware of the wisdom of staying away from publicity in the pre-Independence Hedgewar era, when India was under an alien ruler. It was earthly wisdom to avoid the ire of the foreign rulers, arising out of 'their' perception of the RSS' power. The RSS too was a small organisation at that time and had to be protected at all costs. The application of the same logic to 1942 or 1946, when the situation was very different from 1930 and the independence of the country was in sight, was nothing but ridiculous. This continued even in the post-ban years for a long time. That certainly was following an obsolete and anachronistic principle to a nauseating extent. It was done with great fervour.

Deoras initially changed this by issuing press releases. The releases would at least give them an official material to write from. Whether they do it or not is a different issue. But then there is something to argue from in case of controversies (notes made by Bapurao Varhadpande on the 1939 Sind meeting). Golwalkar had little interest in all these. Countering the propaganda clearly was one of the aims of Deoras. He was not averse to publicity, although he had a very balanced view of the effects it might cause on the young RSS. The clear differences in the attitudes of a pragmatist and a purist, that is to say, Deoras and Golwalkar, were visible as early as 1939 (photocopied resources obtained from the RSS Headquarters, Dr Hedgewar Bhavan Mahal, at Nagpur, including recordings of various speeches, question–answer sessions, press interviews, jottings by personal secretaries or attendees from the Headquarters; hitherto referred to as HQX Resources).[1]

The Costs the RSS Paid

This aversion to publicity shrouded the work of the RSS in secrecy, leading to the perception that the organisation was uncommunicative and dangerous. After all, unwillingness or failure to communicate always creates suspicion and misunderstandings. The people who tried to figure things out, especially from a distance, to understand the happenings in the RSS did not form a favourable idea of the outfit. Ambivalence, doubts and confusion over what the RSS was remained. A few, no doubt, undertook a daily journey to the RSS grounds to understand the organisation closely, but it was necessary nonetheless that there exist a generally favourable atmosphere about the movement. This did not happen. Politically motivated opponents positively harmed the image of the RSS, and there was no counteracting mechanism from within the organisation. More importantly, in their self-righteous and haughty attitude, they did not even think that something was seriously going wrong for them, for their organisation and their ideals. The RSS remained a vague entity to the people, and its men remained faceless (Nene 1986: 40).

The Left-wing politicians, along with the Congress, managed to slander against Hindu ideas by developing an effective stranglehold on the mass media for a very long time. The Left-wing politicians and Socialists in India, more than anyone else, have been more successful in establishing an aura of intelligent, radical, liberal and egalitarian modernism around themselves, projecting themselves as so to the media. They created an inferiority complex in others. Furthermore, they were extremely successful in legitimising themselves and what they supported while destroying others' legitimacy by attacking them. The Left-wing politicians have an excellent network, which works most effectively in helping create hugely lustrous images of themselves and tarnish that of others whom they want to destroy. They do not like anything in India that goes by the name of 'Hindu'—they are the most ferociously united group seeking to execute its destruction. Unfortunately, the RSS, till date, does not recognise how much it has cost them in their failure to counteract this vicious propaganda.

The Anti-intellectual RSS Psyche

The idea and the pride of having 'no need for anything above the shoulders, their best attribute being collective behaviour', prevalent in the RSS cadre at that time was nauseating. There was no discussion, no spark of scholarship on any problem that beset the nation at the ground level. They refused to admit any other matter as necessary for betterment or development. Scholarship may not create a good worker, but that a good worker must develop some scholarship was never taken on board. This was in contrast with Dr Hedgewar's insistence that his workers, particularly those who went out as full-time workers (*pracharaks*), complete graduation. There was a tradition of scholarship among the Socialists, but they were derided by the RSS hierarchy as *vachiveer*, that is to say, those who gab, do not work and cannot raise and maintain an organisation. There was a failure to appreciate the need of the ordinary *swayamsevak* to be prepared to argue others out.

Golwalkar was a well-informed man, but his popular outward image was that he did not even read newspapers. The cadre therefore followed suit, believing that the job of reading and thinking was something 'given' to the likes of a Thengadi or a Deendayal. The sacrosanct declaration of the ideologues, Golwalkar and Thengadi, was: 'We are here to give the light of eternal principles, you work out the details.' It was elitist, egoistic and irresponsible towards the worker, who was beset with the task of sorting the problems of the society through his work. Golwalkar fashionably asked the then Bharatiya Jan Sangh (BJS), the original avatar of today's Bharatiya Janata Party (BJP), if they had a shadow cabinet of experts if or when they came to power. The answer was 'no'. This limitation was set partly by the absence of praise of scholarship outside the limits set by Golwalkar, Deendayal and Thengadi. Later, with the death of Deendayal and the absence of foresight in the leadership, there was no one who saw the need for this for a long time.

Enshrining Mediocrity

What the RSS enshrined was the converse of scholarship—it upheld and praised mediocrity. With the lines of organisation becoming harder, the injunction from the top was to not concern oneself with anything other than the work one is responsible for. Any inquiry or interest was admonished. There were many fields in which the RSS was trying to put up alternative models. The discouragement from knowing everything resulted in not a having a wide range of ideas to think about, the absence of a grand vision of themselves. This is one of the reasons why even today the RSS cadre does not have an intuitive experience of their already huge collective power. This derision of scholarship has cost the RSS dear in terms of its own needs as it grew and faced challenges, especially when it came to power or when it initiated social work within their fold. The work became narrow, repetitious and monochromatic. This ploy of compartmentalising, straight-jacketing a worker, was used by many at different levels of organisation: The officers know everything, and once you go higher, Guruji Golwalkar knows best what is expected from each one. Hence do what has been asked of you.

Free flow of information has long been considered the prerequisite of a live, intelligent and learning organisation in business. By the use of controlled information, the RSS controlled people, but along with it took away their energy, imagination, creativity and originality. It was not the right thing to do, even from the point of view of daily rote. As a result, the RSS did not attract people of diverse talents, nor could it retain them. All they could retain were those who were intellectually better equipped to accept the rigidity of thought and act, and preferred to remain faceless.

The Incompatibility of Constructive and Agitational Work

Golwalkar strongly believed that constructive work (which the RSS believed was their brand) and the confrontational and agitational work, as was believed to be the Lohia Socialist brand, do not go together. My friend Prakash Bal put it beautifully as 'the prison, the spade and the ballot box'. Golwalkar denounced it as a reactionary mode of work: 'Once the cause for reaction is removed the work collapses' (Golwalkar 1974a: 44–54).[2] The agitational work was labelled as *rajasik*, that is, 'valorous', and it held a strong attraction for many, but by adopting such work the RSS would deviate from the *satvik*, that is, the 'saintly' path it had chosen for itself. The lure of one would destroy the other. The work that needed to be done constantly was the work of man-making and the achievement of the goal of Hindu Rashtra that required no external stimuli. All of us believed in what we thought was the implicit wisdom of this thesis. Later, Deoras proved this to be inappropriate.

The Tendency to Avoid Conflict, the Falsettos of Logic

The serious errors arising from the above tendency more or less decided the part not played by the RSS in three major events in the life of the nation: 1942, 1946, and the prevention of the vivisection of the nation. It was justified by using every trick of Freudian rationalisation — transference, projection, and so on — which later was to become the *sine qua non* of the Golwalkar era.

The RSS' analysis and prediction of what could happen to the 1942 movement turned out to be fully correct. Golwalkar predicted that 1942 was not planned well and that it was doomed to fail. According to Mr K.P.S. Sudarshan (statements I will analyse after I cite them below), Golwalkar said,

> ...the leaders of the agitation have not consulted any of the other organizations who strive for the nation's freedom. There is no effort to distribute work and responsibility to each according to their capacity and liking. We do not (however) make it a point of prestige that we were not asked. (Sudarshan 2006)

Golwalkar further said, as Mr Sudarshan observed,

> Our work anyhow was limited to Maharashtra and MP. Both
> states are at the centre of the country and if there could be
> an attack the people will feel frustrated. Hence Sangh will
> not participate, but on an individual level *swayamsevak*s can
> participate in it. (Sudarshan 2006)

One might ask: where would the attack come from? This was clearly fence-sitting on the part of the RSS. Was the 1942 movement not a movement for freedom? The RSS called itself a nationalist organisation. Its vow required each *swayamsevak* in the pre-Independence era to declare that he would work for the freedom of this nation. Freedom was a strong thread in the thinking of Dr Hedgewar. Does such an organisation need an invitation to come and join a movement? What was at work was the conflict-avoiding psyche of Golwalkar. While accepting the fact that all his predictions turned out to be correct, was it proper for the uninvolved RSS and Golwalkar to sit back in their office, criticising the same? Would it not have been more correct for the RSS to get involved in the movement, supply the necessary manpower, the strength and the initiatives to fill the gap of leadership? At times, leadership needs to be wrested from the hands of those unworthy of being leaders. For that is required a sense of timing, courage, foresight and fortitude (the very virtues Golwalkar expounded as desirable in the cadre) to use the opportunity to rise with the people and be remembered. The people in turn would identify themselves with the leader. Every action and move need not be predetermined.

The records in the RSS archives indicate that the importance of 1942 was not lost sight of. It led the RSS to debate, for three full days, whether to participate in it as the RSS or not. That indicates severe differences over the final stand. Deoras wanted a substantial section of the RSS to jump into the 1942 movement and, later, to lead a political party himself, while another section continued to do the routine RSS work (conversations with Dilip Deodhar 2007–08).

When Deoras made this proposal, Golwalkar was worried. For many, Deoras was the RSS, and the RSS cadre would have therefore undoubtedly followed Deoras. The RSS that Dr Hedgewar had asked him to look after, then, would be finished—what would Golwalkar lead? The final decision therefore was not to participate in it as the RSS, although the individual *swayamsevak* remained free to participate in it by himself. Golwalkar thus failed to grab the opportunity that 1942 presented.

The romance of the Quit India Movement in 1942 (which Golwalkar failed to predict, even though he successfully predicted its failure), along with the effect of the memory it left on generations to come, is one of the reasons why the non-participation of the RSS in 1942 is discussed so frequently.

Many believe that the RSS would have been wiped out if it had participated in the 1942 movement.[3] I do not, however, believe the same. Deoras must have sensed the magic and the romance of the movement as well as the opportunity to expand base and assume leadership, which is why he argued in favour of the RSS' participation in the movement. He had seen Dr Hedgewar safely leaving the RSS in the hands of Dr L.B. Paranjape in 1930 to go and demonstrate against the oppressive Forest Act, prepared to be jailed for at least one year. The idea behind this move was to draw in some new like-minded daredevils towards the organisation, recruiting them for RSS work; Deoras' logic in 1942 was probably the same. Whatever might be the reasons, the fact remains that the political activism of Hedgewar's RSS went out of the window as early as 1942.

There is also another possibility that may justify Golwalkar's actions in 1942. Having taken the responsibility of the RSS from Dr Hedgewar, he could have considered it his sacred duty to preserve the RSS as was handed over to him and not allow it to be destroyed by throwing it into such actions. There is some credence to this mode of thought, considering the way he fought with Patel and Nehru during the first ban of 1948 to bring the RSS out intact and continue with the organisation. For him, preservation of the RSS was everything. It is possible that Deoras and others had greater understanding of the flexibility of the RSS and its capacity to assume myriad forms. This could be the reason that led later to the bitter debates after the first ban, which we have already discussed. Looking at the way Deoras balanced agitational and constructive work after 1973, when he himself became the Sarsanghachalak, there is little doubt in my mind that he would have reinvigorated the RSS, even if the excursion of 1942 had wiped it out. Golwalkar, however, may not have been able to do the same. Golwalkar's years in the RSS began in 1935–36. They were too few compared to that of Deoras, who evolved with the RSS from 1926 onwards.

When disallowed participation in the 1942 movement, Deoras, the disciplined soldier of the Hedgewar mould, obliged without question. Characteristically, he went back to the same cadre he wanted to join the Quit India Movement with and appealed to thousands to come out of their houses and work full-time for the RSS in his famous utterance of 'Now or Never', which paid huge dividends.

Looking back, even after giving benefit of doubt to Golwalkar and the RSS leadership, assuming that these men knew the situation well enough not to participate in 1942, there is something inherently absurd in this logic. Avoiding doing something that everyone should be doing raises the phantoms of attacks and frustrations of people. It is but an act of shying away from the responsibility of plunging in and giving strength to a movement which had caught the imagination of the nation and caused trepidation to the British rulers.

The movement of 1942 was not a short-lived movement. According to Nehru, there were at least 538 places where firing took place, without including the numerous stray incidents. The reported number of killings, at 1,028, is a gross underestimate (Shourie 1998). The year 1942 inspired novels. People remained in that agitated state for a while. The stigma on the RSS, meanwhile, also remained, and no amount of clever arguing on the part of the RSS could convince those who wanted the organisation to be present and active in the movement.

There was one illogical step in the Golwalkar argument which was cleverly glossed over. In 1974, Deoras used the following argument to support the Jay Prakash Narayan-led agitation: there will always be circumstances in society that are unjust and will need action to destroy them (conversations with Mr D.B. Ghumare, senior journalist, in June 2007). Had Deoras applied the Golwalkar logic of 1942? Walter Anderson has accused Golwalkar of showing no public interest in 1942 (Anderson and Damle 1987). Lately, people have even been bold enough to doubt as to whether Dr Hedgewar, if he had been alive, would himself have taken the same stance, or if his response might have been different. A different response might not have brought India's independence nearer, but even the Congress would have had to think about the RSS anew and the fact that they could wrest control of a movement that had been orchestrated by the Congress. The Congress then would have had to reconsider the RSS' spirit, and pay greater attention to the organisation to work together in the future. The RSS lost an opportunity to increase its mass base across all strata, which they claimed to have been their principal organisational goal.

The RSS' failure to appreciate charisma in national life was obvious. No intelligent human being will believe that walking with a few scores of people to Dandi and lifting a fistful of salt in defiance of the British Raj in 1930 drove the foreign rulers away from this country. But the Dandi March is nonetheless a matter of terrific pride to all Indians (the RSS included, I hope). The power of Gandhi's charisma, the romanticism that he evoked in the entire country, is what shook the British. The RSS, however, remained confined within its elitist ways of thinking and showed an unwillingness to identify with the people in what were their highest sentiments. Had the RSS participated in the movement of 1942 openly, even symbolically, the Congress would not have dared to ban the organisation on the false allegation of Gandhi's murder. This would have helped the RSS to become stronger with public support. Who knows if it could even have led to the avoidance of the vivisection of this country?

There are, however, some other aspects to this story, certain contradictions and injustices that cannot be ignored and must be brought out into the open. The Communists, especially the radical humanist M.N. Roy, who were receiving substantial money from the British directly, are never singled out for their failure to participate in the movement of 1942. Dr Ambedkar was nowhere in the struggle, and his party received part of the same money through Roy, as Shourie (1998) has pointed out. But one is not supposed to talk about it, let alone characterise Dr Ambedkar or anyone else on the sole strength of this one failure. For the benefit of my Dalit friends, let me be clear at this point that I understand Dr Ambedkar's argument when he claimed that an upper caste Hindu-dominated Congress government in independent India would not do anything for the downtrodden Dalit masses, and therefore preferred the security offered by the British government and avoided action against it. I am sympathetic to this refrain because it is true that for a very long time, upper caste Hindus had done nothing for the so-called lower castes and the untouchables — neither had they intervened to prevent the mass conversion to Buddhism later in 1956.

The point, however, is that none of these gentlemen or their parties are ever attacked about their non-participation in 1942, whereas the RSS is singled out for the same. It must also be forcefully stated that the RSS *swayamsevaks* played a significant role in the movement in their individual capacity as thousands of them had joined in. The society at large, the Congress in particular, as well as the persistent Socialists, have accused and defined the RSS' character in terms of this non-participation, but they have completely and unjustifiably suppressed the work the RSS *swayamsevaks* did during 1942. Detailed accounts are available, but I have not seen the media allocating a pittance of praise to the RSS.

The RSS and the Partition of India

The RSS had grown leaps and bounds from 1942 to 1946, under the threats of the Muslim League, the conflagrated situation of the country, the demand of a partition to create a Muslim nation and the aftermath of the 'Direct Action' sanctioned by Jinnah against the Hindus. Hindus had started looking at the RSS as their saviour. Wherever Golwalkar went, hundreds of thousands gathered to listen to him. The organisation had acquired a mass base, of which moving descriptions have been given by many who have written about it. The Partition had become a distinct possibility — freedom, it seemed, would come only to a truncated India.

Prof. Mushirul Hassan (1997) of Jamia Millia Islamia has drawn an extremely vivid picture of how the madness of wanting a partition developed and swept across the country in so short a time. He has lambasted the Congress in unequivocal terms and singled them out for their failure to control and not yield to the madness that shook the nation, and later blaming the Muslims for all that happened. Still, one of the first arguments from the RSS was: 'No one thought Gandhiji will allow partition and we believed in him' (Golwalkar 1978, 1979). This is too simplistic to believe in, given the way the conflagration had spread. The second was far more shallow and ridiculous, as detailed by Mr H.V. Seshadri, the former Sarkaryavaha of the RSS, in his *The Tragic Story of Partition*. He quotes Nehru, 'If Gandhiji had insisted on not accepting partition we were prepared to go to jail once more' (1998). I have seldom come across a more classic instance of naivety; it is insulting, to say the least.

The third argument placed forth by the RSS was: 'Where was the strength to raise the flag of opposition to the partition?' All the documents I have studied, however, speak proudly and admiringly, in almost superlative terms, of the huge rallies that Golwalkar held in the sensitive areas of India, all the way down to Maharashtra in 1946, till the ban. In the eyes of the people, he was the great hope and the RSS the only saviour for those likely to be affected by the Partition. They were flocking under the RSS flag (Golwalkar 1978, 1979, 1981; Datye July 1981; Swaroop 2004: 86–94). What did not exist was a front that clearly stood up and opposed the 'partition'. The RSS cadre may have been small, but was this not the same organisation that claimed the 3 and 1 per cent well-trained *swayamsevaks* in towns and villages respectively would be enough to lead the Indian society? The huge numbers attending the RSS rallies were not considered a force sufficient enough for the RSS to have given a direction to rise against the Partition. If one reads the speeches of Golwalkar from that period, one finds him appealing all the time for valour, courage and sacrifice, recalling Shivaji's victory even with such few foot-soldiers. Many senior *pracharaks* and important people were asked to draw detailed reports of where the attacks from the Muslim might come from, how they could be countered, what kind of preparations were needed, and so on. Raghu Ranade, one such *pracharak* close to Golwalkar, was among those who were charged to the core like thousands of others, ready for the kill and action (conversations with RSS insiders Dr L.S. Joshi and Sudhir Pathak). And yet, the RSS withdrew at the very last moment. It led itself to constructing other equally clever arguments and rationalisations about accepting the Partition.

Could the RSS have opened up such a front? For the sake of argument, let us say that opening such a front by the RSS was possible. Who in the country, except some frenzied Muslims in Uttar Pradesh and Bihar, wanted the Partition? No one, including the Baluchs, Pakhtoons or Sindhis, who now are a part of today's Pakistan, wanted it. The people would have stood behind the RSS. For all we know, Gandhi would have found his movement suddenly fortified. True leadership is that which rides on the wave of adversity and/or opportunity.

With the Partition, Gandhi saw his lifetime dream of Hindu–Muslim unity shattered, however illogical and unhistorical it might have been, and he broke down. At the fag end of his life, 'Direct Action' also broke the spirit of Gandhi as he had to witness what bitter fruits his lifelong effort to bring the Muslims to the mainstream had borne. Direct Action was the most glaring evidence of the Muslim temperament, and the effect of the utter nonsense of Muslim appeasement for decades. Many had warned against it, but they were spurned by the Congress. Many accepted the Partition, but considered it a Himalayan blunder. Even the spirit of Nehru broke under it. However, no one was ready to believe they had acted wrongly about Muslims.

The RSS has not given any account of Golwalkar meeting Nehru several times in those days (Golwalkar 1979). Why was the rebellion not raised? Why were the preparations suddenly withdrawn? Why did all the build-up come to nothing? People like Raghu Ranade were so disgusted that they became haters of the RSS and of Golwalkar. Ranade later became a Communist.

The next argument put forth by the RSS in defence of their inaction is that they were concerned about a civil war breaking out and feared that the Hindu brethren in the frontier regions would be massacred and devastated. If the RSS had started a full-fledged agitation, riots would have spread all over the country, causing far too many losses. The bloodshed would have increased manifold. One must therefore ask, did or could they prevent either the civil war or the massacre by not opposing the Partition? The answer, as we know from history, is no, they did/could not. For as great a cause as the abolition of slavery, Lincoln waged a civil war and won. He was not a charismatic leader; it was the cause he espoused that had the popular sentiment of northern America pitted against that of the south. If the vivisection of the country was not as big a cause as abolition of slavery was, then what else does the RSS as a nationalistic body stand for? Is one's own survival of a ban more important than sacrificing oneself against the cutting up of the nation? Furthermore, has allowing the Partition not caused even a greater problem for India and for the world for the past 63 years? Is that consequence lesser than raising a rebellion? The RSS as it existed would have been finished in the bargain — that was the stock argument, the consequence the leadership was afraid of (conversations with RSS insiders Dr L.S. Joshi and Sudhir Pathak). Again and again, whatever may be the situation, however grave, preservation of the RSS seems to be the ultimate aim. It is ironic that these are the same people who praise Tilak for his '*Punashcha Harihi Om*', that is, 'I will start again', after he came out of six years of horrible imprisonment in Mandalay.

Paradoxically and ironically, it was finally the RSS volunteers who fought for the Hindus, retaliated for the sake of the Hindus and stopped the madness of genocide from spreading across the border. After the Partition, no one in this country should have had a bad word against the RSS. The RSS jumped into the fight to fortify those bases of the Hindus under threat from the Muslims. Five thousand *swayamsevak*s died for the cause. The Srinagar airport, and hence, by implication, Kashmir itself, was saved by the RSS men. Delhi was under protection of the RSS men, including all the top Congress leaders. Glorious accounts of what the RSS did during the days of the Partition are available (which we will discuss in greater detail in the course of this book). The point is, if they were capable of this sort of a heroism, why did they not try and prevent the root cause of the trouble? When the RSS was saving their own brethren, Gandhi was virtually accusing Golwalkar and the RSS of perpetrating violence. It is ironic that the RSS spoke of their revered Mother Bharat day in and day out, and yet did nothing save merely contain the aftermath of the vivisection. Once again, the RSS lost out on what would have given them an eternal place in the hearts of the citizens of this nation.

To quote K.P.S. Sudarshan again, '...if RSS and Congress had come together, it might have been possible to avoid partition. But the way the propaganda was going it would have appeared that RSS was against freedom and its acquisition...and not against partition' (Sudarshan 2006). Since when did the RSS start caring so much about public opinion? For those who were, and even today are, ready to work to rebuild society and the nation till 'eternity', since when has freedom getting postponed for a few more years become a reason not to come together with the Congress, with whom there was more alignment at that time than historians have cared to show? To show Golwalkar in the right light is presently, and for a very long time, the favourite pastime of the RSS hierarchy. They are therefore resorting to unconvincing and hollow arguments and stretching them beyond all reason.

It is unsurprising, therefore, that only Sudarshan could have come up with the next argument: 'Britons knew the presence of Hindu sentiments even in Congress and they wanted the RSS and Congress to clash which would have resulted in Britishers to retain a grasp on India, hence Golwalkar avoided taking an open stand against the partition' (Sudarshan 2006). This statement presupposes that the Congress would have come in conflict with the RSS over this issue. It does not state if a dialogue was initiated and if the Congress, and more pertinently, people like Patel, had repulsed any such joint action.

The contradictions of the first ban of 1948 vis-à-vis the Partition needs further analysis. In order to get the ban (imposed on 4 February 1948) lifted, when all democratic ways of dialogue, argument and judicial approaches, efforts of the well-meaning intermediaries failed, the RSS put up a historically unmatched Satyagraha, an agitation that has been a matter of wonderment even today. Eighty thousand *swayamsevaks* went to jail in protest, and stayed there for long months. The newly elected Nehru government had a massive majority at the centre. Even with this RSS-hating government at the helm of affairs, a drastically diminished public sympathy and vicious propaganda from opponents, Golwalkar showed the courage and produced the strength to get the ban removed. How is it that the same individual argued that he did not have enough strength and power to raise the banner against Partition when as big a cause as the division of his beloved motherland was at stake? By avoiding conflict except when it came to saving one's own skin, Golwalkar and his RSS thus became culprits in the eyes of history.

Obsession with Symbolism

In 1952, the RSS formed the backbone of the movement of collecting signatures for the demand of 'Gohatya Bandi', the famous anti-cow slaughter movement. This remained a significant consideration till at least 1969 in the RSS lectures. These lectures emphasised on how the village economy is centred around the cow and cattle, and how useful the cow (as well as oxen) is throughout her life and after. In the agricultural situation then and even now, there was nothing wrong about the construction of that logic of cow preservation. This thrust of the movement would be in line with other economic thoughts of the RSS or Deendayal. But the thrust was of a symbolic nature, around which Hindu sentiments could be rallied. Unlike Gandhi, the RSS was neither here nor there. Gandhi was fearless in making such statements. These people talked about it in a similar language, but without Gandhi's audacity, force and emphasis. This, I think, was the biggest problem of the RSS in those years.

This obsession with symbolism in the Golwalkar era has lately taken a diabolical form in recent years in the shape of politicisation of symbols. The Sethu Samudram is supposed to be the construction Lord Ram made to reach Sri Lanka and rescue Sita. What does the Sethu Samudram controversy over whether it should be tunnelled to shorten shipping routes, which took place as recently as 2007, led by none other than the RSS, suggest? I have read the RSS' resolution on the matter. Nowhere does the resolution mention the ecologically damaging dimensions of the proposed project, which, I am told, exist and are worthy of concern. The resolution as it exists appears highly irrelevant in the present state of the nation, when more fundamental thinking is expected from the RSS. The RSS, it seems, is content to indulge itself in these frivolous activities of extremely high degree of irrelevance, as if nothing else matters at present.

Building the Vivekananda Rock Memorial as a place of pilgrimage, as a symbol of national pride and common belief, was again an exercise in symbolism. It was the second movement in the course of a dozen years that the RSS became famous for. I have no problem with the idea itself as well as the wonderful monument Eknath Ranade has created. As a Hindu and as an Indian, I am proud of it. But as a radical, I am bound to ask, if this surplus energy was available, why was a lot of it not being spent in more concrete tasks and areas of direct benefit to people in terms of their earthly life?

Forming a Vishwa Hindu Parishad (VHP) in 1964 was considered more important than a body for farmers' interests. That body was finally formed as the Bharatiya Kisan Sangh in 1983. The VHP is hailed as a landmark creation of Golwalkar. Within three years, that is, in 1966, all the *Dharmacharya*s of the Hindus came together on a level platform. It indicated that all of them had given up (at least outwardly, or on such occasions) their egoistical insistence of their hierarchical privileges, their own sense of high and low among themselves. In one voice they declared that there is no sanction to untouchability in the Hindu religion. On this instance, Golwalkar has been described to have been virtually dancing with joy, forgetting the normal restraint and decorum so characteristic of him (conversation with Sadanad Damale, an office-bearer of the RSS, Mumbai, 2007–08). As a young boy, I was also stunned and elated by the fact that Golwalkar had actually thought of a way of getting these bourgeois, ultra-orthodox and, to my young mind, not-so-respectable creatures together and had managed in doing the same and getting them to declare that untouchability was wrong.

The Golwalkar logic that we did not realise fully at that time but accepted wholeheartedly was: 'Those who believe in untouchability and consider it sanctioned by Dharma will not listen to Golwalkar or to any political leaders. They will listen to their own *Peethadheeshas* and/or *Mathadheeshas* (the sectarian chiefs). To have them reject untouchability as unsanctioned by Dharma will be useful.' However momentous that event of getting the *Dharmacharyas* together on the same platform might have been, it remained a symbolic effort, an elitist logic and appeal. Since 1966, the VHP has not been particularly successful in attracting the downtrodden and the neo-Buddhists to the VHP–RSS fold. How much of the dirt in the religion, how many of the taboos and the archaic or redundant beliefs has the Parishad attacked and managed to remove? Have religious practices improved? Have they managed to reduce superstition and help develop a healthy faith? This is a VHP typically lost in symbolism, then and now. No wonder the VHP was also the result of a stereotype psyche.[4]

What little the VHP could achieve from 1966 to 1974 for the removal of untouchability, one Deoras lecture did much more than that and much more effectively in 1974. Mayawati, on the other hand, quite recently, showed surprising imagination and boldness—she took the challenge of making a U-turn head on. Putting behind the ignominies she had heaped on Brahmins, Khsatriyas and Vaishyas, she went back to them and made a grand alliance of them with the Dalits and the downtrodden. This was a great piece of social engineering that swept her to power in Uttar Pradesh. The RSS in the Golwalkar years was always lost in its own spectacular shows in such movements.

The question, however, does not end here. If Golwalkar could think of this in the 1960s and achieve it in 1966, what was he and the RSS doing when millions were preparing to cross over to Buddhism for 20 years, and did so in 1956? Dr Ambedkar waited for a long time, perhaps for someone to come and stop him with a convincing appeal, an evidence of amended behaviour for him to remain in the Hindu fold, but nothing happened. Neither Golwalkar nor the RSS, not even Gandhi did anything to prevent that. It was unrealistic to expect that the upper caste Hindu society would do something about it.

An Unconvincing View of the Past

The litany of India's past glory prevalent in the RSS had its reasons, which the critics must understand. A principal theory behind the formation of the RSS was to give back the Hindu society a sense of pride in themselves, of their past, of their traditions, a sense that they are not a condemned and useless race one should be ashamed of, but in fact are a part of a race that has had a glorious life of thousands of years. The young generation today might find it difficult to believe that a time existed around the 1920s when people were ashamed of calling themselves Hindu. The eulogy of past glory was to give them a quiet and just, self-assured and decent pride that could give tremendous meaning to the inner minds of the Hindus in the 1930s.

The eulogy and litany of past glory, carried out in inspiring poetic imagery, pleased the upper-caste elite who dominated and supported the RSS. Golwalkar claimed that the Hindu society, in the beginning, was a homogeneous society with equality and of a single class. But this society was short-lived. The increasing complexity of the society led to the development of the original fourfold caste system, which has managed to last all these years. In practical terms, it is this system — that of the fourfold distinction of castes — of which they spoke so highly (Yerkuntwar 1960; Golwalkar 1974a, 1974b, 1975, 1978, 1979, 1981).[5] It led to a stated/unstated position that whatever else may happen, the world cannot move away from the fourfold system.[6]

The downside of this elitist logic of deliberate positivism led to a strong unwillingness to point out and condemn the evils of the past in unequivocal terms. It also led to a dangerous tendency not to align the organisation with any burning issues or social needs, or to stand up and speak out against what was downright bad. It left the RSS in a situation where people started wondering if the RSS was even aware of these problems. The counter-argument was typically Golwalkarian, and is scattered throughout his lectures, writings, collections, and so on. He insisted,

> By focussing on the mistakes of the past and by talking about it all the time, say the worst evil of untouchability, are we helping it to be ousted or entrenched? By focussing on the shortcomings you are further demoralizing the already beleaguered society. This will not awaken their Purushartha, the manhood. (V.D. Deoras 1974: 17–21, Golwalkar 1966: 461–68)

The argument has sense, but the effects are diabolical. You are speaking of a wonderful past life, but never mentioning the evils of the present. How is everyone else to understand that you detest from the core of your heart a practice like *sati* or untouchability? The nation has, after all, witnessed what the Hindu orthodox mind is during the Roop Kanwar episode. The series of incidents featuring the *Khap panchayat*s has left the nation shocked — that such horrible relics from an earlier set of religio-social injunctions are still so strongly operative in society, and that the orthodox are so completely immune to thinking is beyond belief. Where is the proof of your intentions? You look like a *sanyasi*; the exterior, the language and the behaviour of your office-bearers, the important people of your organisation, are clearly upper-caste (read Brahminical), and yet you expect the masses to believe that you love them and that they are as much a part of the larger Hindu entity, of which the RSS is the modern visible form?

Many within the RSS were instinctively aware that it glorified the figure of the selfless Brahmin of the *Chaturvarnya* system, who acted as the controller of the affairs of the king and the society, without having any personal stake in the same. We were aware of this being perceived as an open defence of *Chaturvarnya*, in direct opposition to what is modern. Govind Talwalkar openly blamed the RSS and Golwalkar for it years later, by pointing out that such orthodoxy lends legitimacy to others' (read Muslims') orthodoxy as well. Surprisingly, these RSS men were smug and disdainful towards such arguments, either unable to recognise or unwilling to understand and accept that the non-Brahmin society could feel alienated.

That derecognising the wrong and allowing it to have no place in our heart and behaviour is the only way to convince the people wronged was something that the RSS failed to recognise themselves and was one more instance of its elitism which has not helped its cause in the least. The RSS functions in a world that relishes action and criticism as the testimony of one's intentions and true beliefs. Speaking out against evils is considered a matter of courage and is praiseworthy since it indicates one's commitment to the cause. The puritanical stance of Golwalkar, however, led to a refusal for open, visible action towards the removal of social evils (till 1966). The RSS thus was perceived as being supportive of social evils instead of being against it. The behavioural evidences of the obsession with ritualistic religion and Hindu social systems gave the RSS a sectarian look. It did not produce a modern, forward-looking image, but led to a popular perception that the RSS has at its root ideas of revivalism, status quo-ism and obscurantism. I will take up this issue again when I discuss the sociopolitical and economic ideas of Deendayal Upadhyay.

Golwalkar had an undying fascination for the past, which led him to discuss *Chaturvarnya* with the editor of *Nava Kal* in 1968. The emotional attraction of the past made him overlook the fact that any defence of the system was uncalled for, that it had tremendous potential to be misquoted and misrepresented, and that extremely strong protests would be raised against it, pushing the RSS back by several years. This is precisely what happened. The defence of the 'uncorrupted' original was uncalled for at that time. At that juncture, the credibility of the RSS was once again being established in society. The RSS was coming out of its self-imposed as well as society-imposed isolation. It was finally being accepted by the society again. However, the RSS and Golwalkar were both attacked for their backward stance, which set the clock back for the organisation by several years. This is a fact the hardcore supporters of the RSS will never admit. For them, Golwalkar cannot err on any count, even though history tells us otherwise. It is unfortunate that the cadre were angry not because their credentials as a socially just organisation were being attacked, but because their 'Guruji' was attacked.

The painful contradiction we experienced in the shape of these tags of Brahmanism, revivalism, even obscurantism and orthodoxy, inequity and social injustice made our life in the RSS uncomfortable.[7] We found ourselves fretting over the unwanted labels that had stuck to the RSS. I was uncomfortable about the Brahminical face it bore which served as an alienating influence on the majority, but it remained there nonetheless as it was. On the other hand, we truly enjoyed the classless atmosphere of harmony, love, affection and equality within the organisation, where the mass of volunteers came from all strata of society. There was a sense that we were contributing to the development of a homogeneous society which had no place for high and low, backwards and forwards, economically or socially – a society to build a powerful nation upon. This belief and faith in the changing national situation, which we ourselves were bringing about by organising the Hindus, found itself mixed with the stigma of an organisation of this brand – that is to say, orthodox and Brahminical – without having to resort to gaining political power.

The Political–Economic–Social Philosophy

In the interest of scholarship, it must be reiterated that Golwalkar had a dream of a non-confrontational, non-competitive, cooperative and interdependent classless society. The Communists in their own model of the ideal society also wanted to eliminate competition as well as conflicts arising in the society from and between classes. The Communists wished to achieve this classless society by removing these competitions and conflicts through systematic central planning. The RSS' construction of the ideal society, meanwhile, was based on the concept of a decentralised state, with small units using intermediate and appropriate technology while remaining interdependent and cooperative. Deoras, in 1965, knew of these similarities and clearly stated that even those who believed they were ideologically very different from the RSS realised, in the course of discussion, that there were in fact many similarities between the two dissimilar schools of thought. If the alien words of the Communists could ever be put aside, it would be evident that their biases about the RSS did not stand to reason (B. Deoras 1965).

Is there anything fundamentally wrong with this Hindu model of an ideal society? If we look at the world in the Tofflerian manner, following the theory of the waves of civilisation, the longest was the first wave, which lasted for 10,000 years (Toffler 1985). Cooperation, interdependence and lack of conflict on a day-to-day basis within a community were much in evidence through these years, within each society, if not between them. Stephen Covey (n.d.) has spoken of interdependence as a major idea in modern business models. There is often talk of cooperation and partnerships at the business-to-business level. Even Jet Airways and Kingfisher could negotiate for the benefit of both companies. The idea of partnership has also taken root in present day literature on patient care. Ecologists and environmentalists call this kind of system 'sustainable', which has now become a buzzword.

In its daily practices, this Hindu model was based on the cyclical use of renewable resources only, or mainly. The use of non-renewable resources was sparing. The stark reality of the fast depletion of non-renewable energy resources, of the need for recycling and conservation, which is now a part of scholarly discourse all over the world, was understood by Golwalkar and Deendayal about 30 or 40 years ago. The case against big dams made by the intelligentsia of today was made by these two gentlemen in the 1960s, who were then accused of being anti-development.

With the gradual imposition of industrialisation in what was otherwise an agricultural society, both the Communists and the RSS found two different ways to put an end to the inevitable conflicts that arose in order to develop a homogeneous society. At the heart of both their dreams was the central idea of 'subordinating the individual interest to the larger interest of the society', that is, sacrificing the individual. The RSS tried to develop this emotion from within an individual so that he surrenders his self and interest for the interest of society by his own will, fostered by the acculturation process within the RSS. The Communists forced it on the individual from without, through communes, through cooperative farming. These measures, incidentally, led to widespread pain and agony, killing 20 million people to enforce their creed. This did not happen in the RSS, as it recognised at the same time the personal needs of the individual, the need for his freedom and to some extent his creativity to survive within any system of organisation or governance. However, the RSS was accused of being a fascist organisation while the Communists were not blamed!

Paradoxically enough, the Communist structure gave rise to different classes again (typically, four classes), depicted in 1957 by Djilas in his famous book, *The New Class*. And it was the middle intellectual class — the equivalent of the Brahmin — that seemed to dominate the scene. Golwalkar and his colleagues, like Thengadi and others, were always firm on the notion that *Chaturvarnya* is 'the' model. Djilas merely proved this yet again on the backdrop of a vicious temptation of creating a classless society. Yet, the problem that I as a youngster then faced was: 'Is there or is there not a solution for ending the inevitability of various social classes, and the possibility of organising things in a way that is different and better?' A corollary of this question was, how could class and caste consciousness in India be eliminated or reduced to miniscule levels? I got that answer to this question in 1974, from Deoras.

Further interpretation of the RSS thinking leads us to their insistence on a decentralised mode of production and services. Sustaining society through an empowered agriculture, as well as small- and middle-level technology appropriate for machine-manufactured goods was the central argument of Deendayal's *Bharatiya Artha Neeti*. It draws a neat picture of production which was famously called by Deendayal 'not mass production but production by masses!' (Upadhyay 1971). The Bolshevik Revolution on the other hand took Russia in the direction of a large infrastructure based on centrally controlled economy, leaving no initiative with the individual. The Israeli Kibbutz was a hybrid of both streams, but required unlimited voluntary human sacrifice for society. After 50 years' existence, the Kibbutz has now outlived its mission and is breaking up (S.H. Deshpande 1983).

The RSS ideologues found that the nearest equivalent of such a model existed in the *Chaturvarnya* system and was sustained by the four *Varna*s and the four stages or the *Ashram* system. The hierarchy of classes was in the following order: intellectual, politico-administrative, trading and labour. Each of the four stages sequentially occupy roughly a quarter of a person's lifetime. Celibacy, the first stage, is the stage of learning, followed by that of the householder whose activities sustain society. In the next stage, that of retirement, the householder willingly steps out of his home and serves society without self-interest. In the final stage, he renounces the world in order to do penance for attaining *moksha*. The third stage of the system, that of retirement and selfless social service, has now become the talk of the modern world. Thity-three years ago, Nanaji Deshmukh and P. Parameshwaran embraced the same; just a few years ago, N.R. Narayana Murthy of Infosys was seen following that same path. The ancient Indian thinkers have given their second tenet of *Ashram Dharma*, that of conjunction with the *Varna Dharma*, laced with sacrifice, that too of power. Gandhiji, incidentally, was a firm, declared and avowedly strong follower and believer of the *Varna–Ashram Dharma*. The dishonesty of Indian politics lies in singling out the RSS as *Manuvadi*s while leaving Gandhi out of the equation. Except for Ambedkar, no one has criticised Gandhi on this point (conversations with Dr L.S. Joshi 2007–08).

There was also a third principle propounded by Deendayal and Golwalkar which no one had effectively utilised till then. It was the principle of *Purusharthas*—what a man is expected to achieve in life and how he does it. Those were the *Purushartha*s of *artha*, that is, earning money, *kama* to satisfy one's bodily desires, to follow *dharma* or the rightful path, and attain *moksha* or salvation. What the genius of Golwalkar and Deendayal did was to place *artha* and *kama* bracketed between *dharma* on the left and *moksha* on the right side of the axis. That raised the thesis that the limits of creating and enjoying *artha* and *kama* should be governed by *dharma* and aimed at *moksha*. Deendayal always said that the paucity or excess of *artha* or money is detrimental to the individual (which we now witness in the new generation of software technology professionals).

In a competitive and ruthless society, there will be destruction, which both the Communist and the RSS systems understand and detest intensely. Deendayal and Golwalkar were extremely sensitive to the carnage that happened in Russia, the power of an absolute Communist regime that could force a model of administration down the throats of people. It led to human suffering, as was evident in the massive exterminations in Communist Russia, following its dogma. Deendayal and Golwalkar wanted the Indian masses spared of this suffering. Hence, their model was directed towards the upliftment of large masses of India as the first essential. Therefore, they were in intellectual opposition to the Nehruvian model of development. Like the Russians, Nehru went for a large infrastructure, heavy-industry-based model, which did not yield immediate results but guzzled a lot of money. Not mass production, but production by the masses — this symbolises everything about the RSS' model of economics. This economic model, propounded by Deendayal in 1965 and infused by his integral humanism, however, still had some static and restrictive features. Since this model was so focused on fulfilling the necessities of a community, it would have certain curtailment of individual creativity and might at times have killed the tendency altogether. It would also not liberate the energy of the people to undertake more and newer initiatives, as happens in a capitalistic society.

This line of thinking has also led to a protectionist, inward-looking economic practice, coupled by a tendency to avoid conflict. Thengadi, for instance, consistently harped upon India being a universe in itself which has no need to relate to the external world. Nothing could be more unacceptable and ridiculous than such a statement. The RSS model might have, concessionally speaking, started as a model repurposed for India, but could not be forcefully advocated for various reasons.

Fritjof Capra and others have talked about it as the Yin and the Yang, the female and the male principle respectively.[8] Human nature seems to oscillate between the two tendencies, depending upon the situation. The cooperative ideas represent the Yin and the aggressive, conflicting one the Yang, the Oriental and the Occidental attitudes. The 'cooperative' societies are like extremely large water bodies, which do not begin to emit a stench instantly. But once they do, it becomes very difficult to clean them — this is the problem we are facing today.

The Teutons, the Bourbons, the Nordics and the Slavs in the Dark Ages, typically, were static societies. Once the masculine principle began to dominate, they rode out into the seas, became imperialists, fought wars, created injustice, but also created vibrant societies that caused new developments (whether for good or bad is a separate issue). They turned this world into a new world. If their aggression and spirit created problems, it also made the individual free and developed a system that he could afford to be fearless in, as in the American democracy (what happened to whistleblowers like S. Manjunath of Indian Oil Corporation in November 2005 is the contrast between the two democracies, American and Indian). Darwin sanctified the Yang principle by declaring the basis of life as a 'struggle for existence' and the 'natural selection of the fittest' (1998).

To return to my larger point in this entire discussion: the so-called bourgeois, revivalist, obscure, anti-modern, anti-development economic model of the RSS, in effect, had elements that needed better understanding, indeed, *deserved* better understanding than what it had received.

Golwalkar and Democracy

More surprisingly, to Golwalkar — and hence to all others in the RSS — democracy was the only system that was acceptable because it is the 'least evil system' of governance. Deoras on the other hand was staunchly in favour of it. Golwalkar, in his derision towards the Indian Constitution, called it a patchwork quilt of American, British, Irish and Canadian democratic models, which does not reflect the Indian psyche, its cultural peculiarities and needs. Whatever may be the veracity of these accusations, the Indian polity had started to consider the Constitution as the base of modern India. It had started having faith in the Constitution as the fundamental basis of the organisation of this country.[9] People had a feeling that the RSS leadership had some uncomfortable ideas about the Constitution and the democratic construction of the nation. It did not earn any goodwill for the organisation. If Golwalkar, Deendayal and Thengadi did not like the Constitution, did they produce a charter of what they would have liked to see in the Constitution? Did they submit it to the Constituent Assembly? Unfortunately, they did not! They opposed the federal nature of the constitution but knowingly ignored Ambedkar's wisdom of making it unitary in spirit with a strong centre and making the states dependent on it. Dr Ambedkar was equally or even more concerned about the fragmentation of this country, and hence provided the scope for a strong central government in the Constitution. The latest sortie of Mr Sudarshan on Constitutional review, in the presence of Air Marshal Tipnis for the 2006 Dashera function of the RSS in Nagpur, was uncalled for. This position has been attacked by people like Jyotirmay Sharma as an indication of Golwalkar's fascist tendencies – or more directly, as a proof of the same (J. Sharma 2007).

With the tenets just described, the RSS, the BJS and the Parivar could not force themselves upon the Indian society when they were young and energetic, thereby unfortunately losing their years. With all its erudition and philosophy, which action of the Sangh in the Golwalkar era led to any widespread and welcome or a healthy change in the national life? The frank answer would be: none!

The Exact Contribution of Golwalkar

The sacrifice made by Golwalkar for the RSS can be rarely matched by an example of an individual anywhere in this world. He saw the organisation through all kinds of odds. Our issue with him here is not regarding what he did for the RSS – that is beyond any question and doubt. The issue is what he did do 'with it'. By his incessant efforts post-ban as well, when the sympathy had died down, Golwalkar still created a huge and an intensive network for the RSS, right down to the village level. He taught people to think in unitary manner, trained them in the discipline and the lore of Bharat Mata and established a whole set of values. They spoke in one language, with one mind.

Golwalkar did the job of knitting the organisation together while also expanding it. That needed a defence of the faith in an atmosphere where the majority was unwilling to listen or agree, or had well-articulated, diehard opposition to the same. Sustaining such a colossus of belief across a vast organisation across a vast country would have been possible only by an unshakable, open-eyed but unending faith in the eternity and immortality of Hindu society and its ability to see a nation through the rough and tumble of times. Golwalkar had that faith, and it served as the bedrock to the floundering RSS. He was fearless to stand in opposition and stuck to his position on many issues. For example, he had warned of the aggressive tendencies of China seven years before the Chinese invasion. Nehru called him a warmonger.[10] His best and the biggest contribution to the RSS is that he sustained this belief in Hindu Rashtra and of organising Hindus to keep them united and strong. The reader need not agree with the principle, but he cannot but agree with the contribution, the sacrifice and the enormous effort Golwalkar had undertaken for that task. One need only imagine, in a conscious effort at soul-searching, what would have happened to the Hindus and Hindu society if the RSS or Golwalkar had not been around in this country at all.

It was at around the Deepvali of 1969, the festival of lights, that one problem was, in some ways, strongly exposed by S.H. Deshpande (1969). His question was blunt: had the RSS decided to allow the strength of its youth to be put to no other use except the RSS *shakhas*? Were they going to pickle it so that no one could use it until it matured? It was a long essay; the impression was logically correct but factually wrong. The RSS, as the article declared, had nothing to do with anything other than the daily *shakha* work and gathering strength. The fact is, despite such accusations, Golwalkar had managed to develop a huge Parivar organisation network in a dozen different fields, many of which had done extraordinary work through the ordinary-looking RSS men. This well-meaning article had little idea about this achievement. But such articles can scarcely manage to belittle the multifaceted genius of Golwalkar.

Notes

1. The 'HQX resources', as I will be referring to them, include motley paper recordings of various speeches, question answers, press interviews, jottings of personal secretaries or attendees from the RSS headquarters. Of note is the fact that it contains documentation of the all-important Sind Meeting of 1939, a year before Dr Hedgewar died, the meeting that gave the RSS the shape it has to date.

2. Throughout the literature on the speeches, meetings, discussions and talks with the workers, Golwalkar from 1940 onwards, has expressed this thought directly and indirectly, and in a somewhat positive manner. Golwalkar maintains all along that the only work that needs to be done is to unite and organise the fragmented Hindu society into a large corporate entity through the daily work of the RSS. He had no interest in any other type of work, except for that of the Vishva Hindu Parishad.

3. We had a direct test of the tremendous potential of the RSS to assume myriad forms to carry out its work, to keep its organisation intact and to even carry out underground work during the Emergency in 1975–77. If it could be done at the frontline workers' level so easily, it would be unjust to say that Deoras could not have reinvented the RSS with ease, even if it had wiped itself out in 1942, or in 1946 while opposing the Partition.

4. *Peethadheesha*s or *Mathadheesha*s are the sectarian chiefs of the monasteries each sect builds for itself. The followers of that sect revolve around the monasteries, which act as sites for religious congregations. By definition, they are not people who would look beyond their sectarian sentiments. These sects have never been in the habit of acknowledging that they are part of the larger whole of the Hindu federation of religions, the Hindu Dharma. The sectarian chiefs

are highly egoistic, practising exclusivity against all others. No one but Golwalkar could have achieved the momentous feat of making these chiefs and their followers aware of the fact that they are part of this larger entity. No one could have managed to make them see that there are evils in the Hindu religious and social culture that are incompatible with today's world and got them to come together for such a declaration. Golwalkar alone could have convinced the chiefs to use their powers over their followers to help discard old ideas and think differently, which he successfully did, at least to a certain extent.

I do not wish to belittle this achievement at all. It is one of the most significant achievements of Golwalkar, a task that was carried forward by the Vishwa Hindu Parishad (VHP). My issue lies with the symbolism, which, to my knowledge, has neither led to a drastic change in the psyche of the orthodox nor has in any way appealed to the modern Hindu mind.

5. The oft-quoted *Samagra Darshan* (Full View of Philosophy) volumes appear to repeatedly sing the song of Bharat Mata and the glorious past of the Hindu society with an unmistakable underlying sense of belief in the mainstream fourfold *Chaturvarnya* system of the Hindus, without directly speaking of it. The bourgeois upholders of the *Chaturvarnya* system like B.S. Yerkuntwar, drenched deep in the ritualistic side of this system, have never tired of espousing it for over 48 long years. The utter incompatibility of Deoras with this thinking earned him laurels of hatred from only one man in his life, Mr Yerkuntwar.

6. All the volumes of Golwalkar's *Shri Guruji Samagra Darshan* (Full View of Philosophy) repeatedly speak of the past glory of the Hindu civilisation and at dozens of places refer to the fourfold system of caste, more often indirectly, which is why I have cited the specific instances in the text.

7. I have lived under this persecution mania for years. One of my closest friends in medical college, towards whom I had extended a helping hand when he needed it, abused me at the end of a dozen years of friendship as the sort of hateful Brahmin Maratha people like him detest. The trigger for this outburst was my involvement with the RSS. Unlike many others, I do not possess a thick skin – it hurt.

8. I owe these ideas to Prof. G.B. Kanitkar, during our discussions in 1989.

9. The power of having a democracy structured in its detail by the Constitution entered the Indian consciousness with what they achieved during the 1977 elections. When T.N. Seshan started implementing the constitutionally provided restraints on the conduction of elections, there were strong checks, leading to a better execution

of this romance of democracy that we call election. During that time, P.V. Narasimha Rao was in office, and everyone, high or low, was and could be called to court as accused. It was at this time that the faith in the constitution really solidified. The process has taken almost 40 years.

10. At once paradoxical and magnanimous, the same Nehru who had called Golwalkar a warmonger invited the RSS to participate in the Republic Day Parade in 1962, in the full splendour of its outfit. It was a tribute that Nehru paid to the tremendous role the RSS volunteers played during the Chinese aggression in helping the army. It is also well known that Lal Bahadur Shastri had called upon Golwalkar, along with the leaders of all other political parties, to help coordinate the war effort in 1965.

4

Withdrawal, Return and Ascent of Deoras

————— • ✦ • —————

The Golwalkar Model Wrenched Free

The establishment of Golwalkar's leadership, the differences over 1942, the failure to raise a united front against the Partition, the Partition itself and its terrible aftermath, Gandhi's murder and the first ban on the organisation, the demoralisation and the dissidence — it was a tumultuous era for the RSS; in one particular way, a defining moment. And it is also a period marked by the strong differences between the two most important people in the RSS: Golwalkar and Deoras. This is a period that is most guarded in RSS history, the one with the least information available. It is a period that the first- and second-generation RSS members in Nagpur speak of all the time, but without having much information at hand.

Deoras Withdraws from the Day-to-day RSS Work

Deoras' withdrawal from day-to-day RSS work happened sometime between 1952 and 1955 and lasted nearly for a decade. One version of the narrative says that there was only on one occasion a strongly worded disagreement between Golwalkar and Deoras on the issue of using funds of the RSS for the political work that Deoras undertook (conversations with D.B. Ghumare 2006–07). The counter-narrative claims that Deoras borrowed money to finance the survival of the RSS during the ban and after. When it came to repayments, Golwalkar and all others treated these debts as the personal loans of Deoras. Deoras was an extremely capable achiever, very self-respecting and an illustrious man. He did not tolerate this attitude – he could not have, because it was not for himself but for the RSS that he had borrowed money. By common consent, he was the manager and the owner of the RSS. He *was* the RSS (conversations with Dilip Deodhar 2007–08). The insult went deep, and he distanced himself from the RSS. The debts were paid off in 1956 by collecting the Golwalkar Honour Fund for the occasion of his 51st birthday. There is another version of this narrative, which claimed that Deoras took it upon himself to liquidate the debt since much of it had been incurred on his word. People who had paid the money upon his word were now coming to Deoras for the repayment of the loans. Deoras attempted to do this by developing his agricultural lands in Amgaon Karanja and by running one of the Bharat stores. Both these notions have little support or credence (V.D. Deoras 2000: 25).

Another equally important issue was the struggle between the activist orientation of the RSS and the *shakha*-only orientation, which reached its peak and had its principal casualties from 1942 to 1952. The RSS had gone into a shell, insulated itself and slowed greatly as an organisation. Its appeal was slowly being lost. The *shakha*s were moribund.

Diversification had, to some extent, diffused the tensions. It was obvious that the original process would require years to rebuild the organisation. The Deoras brothers were uncomfortable with the likely speed of rebuilding and wanted to get over the process as quickly as possible. It was here that the real disagreements between Deoras and Golwalkar on the means for the end might have begun.

Deoras wanted to spread the RSS in whatever possible way, in areas other than the RSS *shakha*. There were possibly *swayamsevaks* who may have thought of breaking up the *shakha* model itself and trying other things, although Deoras was not among them. Given the undying, implicit and never-diluted belief of Deoras in the working methodology of the RSS,[1] and the way he held the men and the huge organisation together, he could never have given up the *shakha* altogether (conversations with Advocate P.S. alias Bhausaheb Badhiye, Nagpur 1997). Viewed this way, the conflict looks benign; it is even possible to believe that Golwalkar and Deoras could have continued together. Where then did the true intensity of the debate lie? For that we need to know some background, as well as some more information on these two differently built individuals.

Golwalkar caused the final break on the issue of the Bharatiya Jan Sangh (BJS) and the malfunctions it was suffering from. Dr Mukherjee had unfortunately died in 1953, and an egoist like Moulichandra Sharma was in command. The political ambitions of the BJS were severely curtailed by the huge defeats in the first general elections, particularly in Punjab. Dilip Deodhar claims that Deoras proposed to Golwalkar that he himself would go forth to head the BJS, all attempts hitherto to make it a strong political party having failed, while Golwalkar continued to look after the RSS (conversations with Dilip Deodhar 2007–08). Deoras was fully a goal-oriented man, who said, 'Wherever I go I will be the number one, and that would include being a General or a Prime Minister depending on where I go.' He would have succeeded in developing the Jan Sangh better than anyone else. He once told his friend Narayan Baitule, after the ban was lifted, 'RSS has more power than one may imagine. Do not get disheartened. One day I will become the prime minister of this country' (conversations with Dilip Deodhar 2007–08).

Golwalkar refused to allow Deoras to go into politics. If Deoras left, most of the RSS would leave with him, and where would that leave Golwalkar's leadership? Invoking the promise they both had made to Dr Hedgewar, that they would look after the RSS together, he virtually emotionally blackmailed Deoras from doing what Deoras thought was the immediate need of the hour — to take the mission forward among other matters (conversations with Dilip Deodhar 2007–08). Deoras was now caught in the same situation as 1942 — discipline against his better judgment. Golwalkar won the crafty game, since he knew that Deoras would not breach discipline. This time it was a little too much to take and Deoras had no recourse but to move away from the RSS.

The most sensible and necessary course of action, as dictated by practical reasoning and analysis, was being spurned, that too by none other than the head of the organisation whose leadership Deoras had struggled to establish. Deoras' point of view was unacceptable to Golwalkar. It was, no doubt, a suffocating experience. What would a man in possession of considerable judgment do under the circumstances? He could either leave and sit quietly or rebel. He would, in all possibility, do what he thought should be done while outside the fold of the organisation. The agony that Deoras must have felt over it, the tremendous patience he showed while biding time, without any mutinies or public voicing of differences, any attempts at a split or division, was extraordinary. He put the organisation and the ideal above his ego for a long time. The thought of it alone sears the mind, even after so many years. It is not the feat of an ordinary man. The superhuman control he had shown has no parallel in history. Any issue that was outside the RSS' perimeter was still being referred to Deoras. He was the central contact with the 'other works' and guiding them. I feel certain that in the interest of the organisation, the nation lost an idea and an action it needed badly. To quote Alexander Pope,

Born for the Universe, narrowed his mind
And to party gave up what was meant for mankind.
(Thengadi 1986: 13)

The full-time workers who came back first went to Deoras. He took care of their pain, their wounds and their demoralised spirit. He rehabilitated them in civil life. He was not bitter, agitated and angry over it as Golwalkar was, but quietly digested the situation. Deoras never lost a man. He was still the motivator par excellence of the RSS, not Golwalkar (conversations with the Late Prof. Krishnarao Bhagadikar 2007).

One of the coups Deoras managed to pull during this isolation was to take over the Narkesari Prakashan and its newspaper that was to become the mouthpiece of the RSS. It underlined the need for internal communication and external retaliation. Aggressive, unafraid and all-inclusive journalism seems to be his idea of defending his thesis at that time (Pimpalkar 2005). Deoras became its chief, trying to make it a complete, competent and professionally run paper. If there was anything in the starkest contrast with Golwalkar's aversion to publicity or public retaliation, it was a newspaper of their own — and yet it started, under Deoras' patronage.

There is no doubt that Deoras' exit left the entire RSS with enormous worries. His friend and close colleague, Mr Madhavrao Muley, could not understand if Deoras had left the RSS altogether or was still a part of the organisation, as was Mr Chaman Lal in Delhi (conversations with Late Prof. Krishnarao Bhagadikar 2007). The place that Deoras occupied in the hearts of people was deeply entrenched. The enormous affection and reverence they had for him were unmatched. People went to Deoras to ask what the matter was. To them he replied, 'Do not be after me and bother me. It is a matter between me and Guruji.' On being pressured further he would say, 'Whatever may be, but I will not allow Sangh to split in a Guruji Golwalkar Sangh and a Deoras Sangh; this is not what Dr Hedgewar has taught me' (V.D. Deoras 2000: 7). Deoras has been called, even in this period, the 'owner' of the RSS, or its leader, by none other than Golwalkar in an entirely unsarcastic manner (conversations with D.B. Ghumare 2006–07). He was, however, prepared to wait, and did what he wanted after 1973.[2]

Setting and Achieving Goals

As long ago as 1945–46, Deoras had given a message to the college-going volunteers:

> Organisation, Mobilisation and Action! [These were the original words Deoras used in that lecture in Marathi.] Organisation phase does not continue *ad infinitum*. Once it assumes certain strength or mass, the man power put to action in the various fields of the national life and creates the desirable change. In this phase of mobilisation RSS will create a flexible and loose network of all these forces. After that we act in a time-relevant manner to achieve our aim. Unless we do this, RSS will become a sect and loose all its relevance to the upliftment and building of society. It will become a ritual. (Joshi 1996: 12, 13)

No one could have missed the point. Be it in 1942, starting work in other fields of national life, or the action of 1954 about the BJS, Deoras' mantra, no matter how appropriate, had no takers.

D.B. Ghumare, who was a college student at that time, says, 'In the speech "the most appealing and inviting" was the language [read the English words used by Deoras], which illuminated the path with such consummate ease.' The three words — 'organisation', 'mobilisation', 'action' — could be sequential or simultaneous and might feed into each other.

The quote was never repeated that forcefully later. Ghumare said, 'What could not be achieved by thousands of books and lectures could be achieved by the blunt, frank or candid utterances of Deoras, with innate characteristics of brevity, simplicity, and straightforward content' (conversations with D.B. Ghumare 2006–07). That is the central paradigm of an achiever and the call for the achiever.

Golwalkar and Deoras expressed themselves differently, processed things differently and prioritised differently. The article we are referring to also comments upon what Golwalkar continued to say — repetitively, untiringly (to the point of boredom, in this author's humble opinion) — over the years: 'Devotion to the motherland, sacrifice and high illustrious character.' But this statement by Golwalkar did not answer the question, what next, what do we want to achieve? 'Sequential' was the sanctioned principle in the Golwalkar era. It was never accepted that the mass is sufficient to mobilise for any action whatsoever. He stretched the phase of gathering strength so far that expecting him to put this force to mobilise for taking up action, or to receive his sanction for the same, was a frustrating undertaking.

Sense of Time and Timing

Deoras had a much keener sense of time and timing compared to Golwalkar. His 'now or never' in 1942 is a testimony of that. According to him, the years after the ban were the most crucial years lying ahead, a time for the RSS to free itself from all that it had come to be identified with, including Gandhi's murder. The RSS needed people who would talk in favour of the organisation in various fields of national life. One could not take a defensive posture and withdraw in a shell, in a self- and society-imposed isolation. This was the time to become aggressive and make an impact. Political power is one of the most important strengths, and the RSS, as far as Deoras was concerned, needed to try everything to attain it.

Sangh *shakha* alone would not achieve what they wanted to achieve—this was a time the RSS would not get back if they did not encash it at that very moment, and by not doing so, they were losing time and getting pushed backwards. People with a sense of timing are restless and eager to strike at any possible opportunity, which they are always on the lookout for. For Deoras, the time was running out; for Golwalkar, it was an eternally ongoing work. Deoras was not going to take the insults on the Sangh lying down; Golwalkar, the tranquil *sanyasi*, wanted to continue unaffected.

Golwalkar Gets a Stronghold on the RSS

In this Deoras-free period, the RSS received the imprint of Golwalkar in full measure. He saw to the fact that his imprint on the organisation becomes deep and indelible. Given the traditional, or, more appropriately, the orthodox minds accumulated in the RSS, the ascetic, bearded exterior of Golwalkar, the stories of his penances, of his Ramakrishna Mission background and his authority over them and in the spiritual field, formed deep impressions upon the cadre. There could not have been anything more pleasing than his belief in a hundred matters in the tradition, ranging from Ayurveda to *Chaturvarnya*, to the strongly orthodox orientation of the Nagpur and/or Indian Brahmins. His other-worldly orientation, which magnified over the years, added to his charisma. His undoubted and tremendous sacrifice for the RSS topped it all. Indians like to become devotees, perhaps even more than they like the deeds performed by their ideal—Golwalkar offered the RSS cadre that very opportunity, to become his devotees.

Golwalkar concentrated upon establishing his unquestionable authority in the RSS hierarchy by creating a provincial *pracharak* post that reported to him directly, and not to the provincial head. According to Anderson and

Damle (1987), by this key manoeuvre, he managed to have the authority directed to him. It is said that the men he handpicked and raised through the structure of organisation became his protégés (conversations with Dilip Deodhar 2007–08). Golwalkar appointed Deoras as his successor, but did not leave him with many who would follow his line. I have been often perplexed by this aspect of the RSS: why were majority of the initiatives of Deoras either spurned or not able to last beyond his regime? One reason, as I have already discussed, lies in Deoras' lack of involvement in the daily affairs of the RSS in one of the most trying periods of the organisation. There is another explanation, which I believe answers most of the questions—I will discuss the details of the same in the course of the next two chapters. It is not an explanation I enjoy offering the reader.

The RSS Centrality Paradigm of Deoras

In the following section, I will further highlight some of the crucial differences between Golwalkar and Deoras. This is where he wrenched the Golwalkar model further free after he became the chief of the RSS.

These words and the paradigm of thinking indicated are not there in the voluminous literature of the RSS. These words—the paradigm of RSS centrality—convey that the RSS is finally responsible for anything that should happen, happens otherwise, or does not happen in the country. Whether they make it happen through the Parivar organisations or do it on their own, it ultimately arises from the RSS and returns to the same. My own conviction, having known Deoras personally and well, is that while he believed in the paradigm of centrality of the RSS, not many in the RSS did the same.

Once an individual becomes a *swayamsevak*, whatever he does, from lending a helping hand in an Andhra disaster to running a school in Arunachal, is the work of the RSS, irrespective of the label stuck on it as a Parivar organisation. Therefore, no work done by a *swayamsevak* should be looked down upon. No task arising out of an express desire of the RSS or any *swayamsevak* is something other than or outside the work of the RSS. On this point, most of the cadre and many office-bearers have had great confusion in their day-to-day interactions with society. Outsiders have never understood this complex relationship and have long deluded themselves that they have an insider's knowledge of things. The naivety and foolishness of the ridiculous 'facts' or 'information' such people have bandied around very often has no bounds. Logistics, economics, other reasons have caused differentiation and classification of the various works undertaken by the RSS, which entails systematisation. It was expected that these projects would ultimately achieve independence, especially financial, and self-determination. The loose network was to lead to interdependence, finally connecting them to the overall RSS value system. This goal was to be achieved by all these projects. That is what adhering to the centrality paradigm really means.

Deoras' RSS centrality is a vision of its work and a way of behaviour. It is based on character, intensity of involvement, credibility, visionary understanding, love, the largeness of mind, clarity of understanding of ground realities and an unshakable faith in the RSS of Dr Hedgewar at all costs (and not what has become of it). This RSS centrality is well expressed in one favourite saying of the 'old timers' of the RSS: 'You may earn your blood and flesh anywhere, but remember and never forget that your bones are made of Bhosalas [the then kings of Nagpur].' It is an extremely strong, unbreakable attachment to the root of the RSS of Dr Hedgewar.

The Misunderstood Deoras

One might ask, since Deoras was away for so many years, why did he at all come back? All accounts of his return try to politely point out that Sri Guruji's stand was vindicated and accepted by Deoras as correct. Deoras realised the futility of the various works that many wanted to start, and that would not be the best thing to do. These accounts are at best naive and at worst instances of a deadly tendency that had started taking root in the Sangh at that time, which was to uphold Golwalkar's image at all costs, against all odds. We have good measures to reliably indicate such a claim. This tendency was operative then and is continuing even now.

In 1962, the *samadhisthal* (the shrine) of Dr Hedgewar was completed and inaugurated. This was when Deoras returned to the RSS fold. In 1965, after the death of his dear friend Bhayyaji Dani, he became the Sarkaryavah, the CEO in modern terms, of the RSS. His thoughts and inclinations at that time can be easily guessed if we consider a small incident, which was never (allowed) to be repeated. As the RSS General Secretary, he addressed the entire important cadre of the BJS in 1974. From 1965, he had undertaken some structural reorientation of the RSS. I have attended one such occasion and still remember the simple structure he had put forward, which looked entirely feasible. The most important message in his project of reorganisation was that the *shakha* unit should be a socially alert unit. There were ideas about adopting a low income settlement, adding at least one social work outside the *shakha* work to one's repertoire and extend the contacts to people other than RSS. Each branch had to do it. If the reader looks at the first page of the book, he or she will find a description of what an RSS branch is expected to do. There is no parallel to it in the huge ocean of RSS literature.

Successors who are the carbon copies of their predecessors can have no positive impact upon an organisation. It is therefore not sacrilege to believe that the first three supremos of the RSS were different in many ways. Artificially compressing them in one mould or striving to believe they were complimentary and relevant to every age can be a psychological need, but it cannot be an act of scholarship for truth. While the ideological premises of the three RSS leaders were never different, their thoughts on the ways to achieve their goals were at times radically different. Deoras could take much more liberty with activism than even Dr Hedgewar, since in the latter's time, India was a slave nation. The marked difference between the styles of Golwalkar and Deoras is the only way to understand many paradoxes in the journey of the RSS.

Balasaheb Deoras, to me, was the most misunderstood Sarsanghachalak of the RSS. It is paradoxical that outsiders understood him well and clearly, but the RSS cadre by and large did not understand him, or did not want to do the same. Prof. Ram Shewalkar, a learned man, not necessarily an RSS admirer, from Nagpur, put it well: 'The leadership of Deoras was inclusive, drawing people within it and affectionate. It was rooted in realistic understanding of the situation. Still it was strongly mission oriented and belonged to the present. The leadership of Golwalkar was spiritual, saintly and ritualistically oriented' (1996: 34).

Deoras was not well understood within the RSS since the perceivers were already steeped in a lore he did not sing. He did not offer them spirituality—instead, he criticised traditions and unscientific accumulations in the culture, and so on. He was neither orthodox nor traditional. He was modern. The biases, hardened beliefs, if not outright bigotry, present within the cadre made them unable to accept for consideration his new ideas, new ways of thinking and practice. Their own belief system and their limited ability— the biggest obstacle of the cadre and officials in the process of understanding him—did not allow them to prepare for change. Deoras did not stand on esoteric stations, but he certainly was on a higher plain, on a wavelength others found difficult to understand. It should not have been far beyond general level of perception, but in spite of that, all these factors operated in mixed proportion at various and crucial times against his cadres' familiarity with him. One of the most appropriate and pithy appraisals of who this man was came after he became the chief: 'From the skies of spirituality to the earth of reality' (S.H. Deshpande 1996). Purists reacted to this differentiation strongly.

That Deoras was a man of forthrightness and downright practical thinking, the very image of the founder, was known. He was an interested, knowledgeable and experimenting farmer, who had the wisdom of those who have lived and toiled with the soil. He was an avid defender of modern science, medicine and democracy; he detested matters religious and persistence on singing the glories of the past. It is highly debatable if he believed in God, or if in any way needed Him. For him, the thread ceremony was outdated and he disliked attending them. He had even threatened to walk out if he was made to attend one without his knowledge (conversations with Damodar Madhav Date 1975–80).

On the other hand, he would make it a point to attend an inter-caste marriage, as did Golwalkar and Dr Hedgewar. He was known for his pistol-shot responses, sharp, quick and short. Above all, Deoras was a modern man. He once said, 'People who wear modern clothes do not always have modern minds' (Deoras, in conversation with RSS volunteers in May 1980, in Pune, during the Officers Training Camp). That he could suggest—in 1950—that his niece go out with her ' "would be" and get to know each other' was perfectly normal for him (Joshi 1992: 21). The year 1973 was in. The accession of Mr Deoras was to mean a complete change in the style, functioning and thinking of Golwalkar's RSS, deeply entrenched in the former Sarsanghachalak's thought for over three decades. The cadre was not aware of what was to come. Every one of these aspects about Deoras and his regime could make the people surrounding him unable to fathom him, and make them uncomfortable.

One of my problems between the years 1967 — when I first understood what the idea of the RSS meant — and 1973 was my inability to find some 'resonance' within the RSS, its official language and ways of functioning and thinking. When Deoras became the Sarsanghachalak, I found this resonance with him, suddenly and completely. Equally strong was my impression that only a few within the RSS were aware that some 'new phenomenon' has occurred at the top, and that they would have to take notice of a somewhat different chord resonating and understand the same. It meant little to others.

Golwalkar had, from 1944 onwards, called Deoras the '*asali*' or true chief, and himself the '*nakali*' or the false chief of the RSS. But in 1973, Deoras was being viewed against the decades of Golwalkar's reign, and the cadre wanted him to be like Golwalkar and not regain Dr Hedgewar through him. Such was 'the programming' Golwalkar had achieved. By then, the sectarian character of the RSS had set in. The cadre, instead of remembering him as the protégé of the founder, instead of recognising that his ways of thinking were different and were more like the founder than the recently deceased Golwalkar, expected him to continue with the Golwalkar ways of thought, action and externalities. Golwalkar had, by then, mesmerised them.[3,4]

Deoras as the New Chief of the RSS, June–July 1973

In the first top-level meeting one month after the death of Golwalkar, what was repeatedly said by individuals placed at highest positions in the RSS hierarchy on the occasion was, at its least, uncomfortable. They 'expressed' that Deoras would get their 'full cooperation'.

To those who had learnt what the RSS stood for under Dr Hedgewar, this expression is something that stood at odds with the culture of the RSS. Some said that since Deoras had also received guidance and enlightenment from Golwalkar, they expected he would continue to work in the same way as Golwalkar. No one mentioned the singular fact that if anyone wanted to see an image of the founder—the way he thought, the way he talked—they only had to look at Deoras. In 33 years, the founder had become irrelevant for the hierarchy at the top. The document (published later) that provides us with the details of this occasion produces a sense of acute discomfort, as though 'cooperation' was being forced out of those who were speaking in the function, as though there was little they could do about this man replacing Golwalkar, however they might feel. They expected that 'he will advance RSS in the way Golwalkar has shown them'. Only two persons spoke not about cooperation, but 'uncompromising allegiance' or *sampoorna nistha*. The radical difference between the attitudes and inclinations of the cadre and the officers with Deoras is thus seen from day one (RSS 1973: 9–14).

In the same meeting, Deoras gave a moving account of the numerous qualities of Golwalkar, but also pointed out that Golwalkar had been a late entrant at the RSS and that initially, he was perceived as a strange man. He also drew a distinction between the people Dr Hedgewar had developed and those who had developed under the leadership of Golwalkar (RSS 1973: 13). It is a subtle but important distinction on his part. In this first top-level meeting, Deoras declared that 'the power RSS had accumulated will increase the more we spend it on appropriate, well planned deployment'. This was the most important declaration of the occasion. He had planned to put forward some radical ways of looking at the Hindu social systems and the way the RSS should think about them. The grain and the content of it could have been understood to be in contrast with the way Golwalkar expressed himself, and was disallowed by the administrative chief as 'anything belittling Golwalkar will not be allowed'. Deoras thus omitted it (conversations with an insider who does not want to be named August 2007).

The First Few Indications

The first indications of a change in direction under Deoras came quickly. In December 1973, six months after Deoras took over from Golwalkar, he opened his heart to the volunteers of Nagpur with a belief that they would understand him:

> There is crisis of character and credibility...the responsibility of what needs to be done will come over to us and we will have to accept that. We have avoided many of them. We have put in an effort to stay away from them. This will not do...What has to happen and what should not happen, must happen out of the efforts of RSS...What RSS today is and as it should be in the context of the situation have a wide gap. I am not in a position to boldly say that our worker will not fall to temptations...There are serious problems like social inequality, economic exploitation, caste related problems, the failure of new systems to take root and form when the older ones are breaking down, with the perversions that has caused. We have to think beyond the usual solutions of law and agitations or constitutional rights. We have the responsibility of finding answers. (Balasaheb Deoras, speech at the Winter Camp of the RSS, Dr Hedgewar Bhavan, Nagpur, December 1973)

Was there so drastic a change in the national situation that barely six months after the demise of Golwalkar, Deoras had to say, 'We cannot avoid our responsibility any more'? The message is clear and vibrant. There could be little doubt as to what he had in mind, even in 1950. That had been stifled at that time. Pent up for decades, he was finally free to express himself in front of his most trusted Nagpur volunteers.

This was where the RSS was wrenched free of the Golwalkar model. Within a few years of his return to the organisation after nearly eight years' break, Deoras sought to convert the 'eternal walker psyche', which he detested and denied in 1965, to the 'achiever's creed'. About politics, the second most contentious and detested issue in the Golwalkar era, Deoras famously quipped, 'It is like a bath room in the house. Because the danger of slipping is greatest there, do we build houses without it?' (Lokhiteishi 1994, as reported by Atal Behari Vajpayee). To Deoras, it counted as a denial of the RSS' myriad responsibilities. They were, after all, an organisation founded to build the life of this nation.

Inclusivity Begins

One of the very first things that Deoras did after becoming the Sarsanghachalak was to visit Mr Madhukar Deval, the rebel of 1950. He ran one of the landmark projects by an RSS man, a hallmark of excellence and the stamp-bearer of the RSS culture, as was Dr V.V. Pendsey's Dnyan Prabodhini. They remained pariahs, without any recognition from the RSS as long as Golwalkar was around. He never forgave them for their rebellion. In the Golwalkar era, people obtained some kind of a vicious or perverted pleasure in denying this recognition to the best and most loyal members of the RSS. This tendency was far more pervasive than even an insider might suspect. To go to such a person in the capacity of the new Sarsanghachalak signified hundred different things: 'I, as Deoras, could not have done anything to bridge the rift then; it was beyond my power. But as the chief I visit you to say that you were always "our own" and we belonged to you; we recognise your work as our work, let bygones be bygones.' Later, he told a gathering that Dr Pendsey continued to be a *pracharak* till that date. Pendsey, who had been disowned by Golwalkar and stripped of his title as a full-time *pracharak*, happily agreed to that.

Those who have never been in the RSS will never understand how much such 'recognition' means to the *swayamsevaks*, especially coming from its chief or the organisation as a whole. I will leave it to the reader to decide if this is another evidence of fascism, in the form of allegiance to the leader. To return to our point, Deoras' visit to Deval was one of most ego-less acts I have ever seen. It asked for forgiveness and achieved deliverance. Later, he made several public mentions of Deval's work as work done by a *swayamsevak*.

Deoras' Tête-à-tête with Press Begins

In one of the very early press conferences in Bangalore, Deoras pointed to the work being done by the Saraswati Shishoo Mandirs (kindergarten schools), a thousand strong. He made it clear that he considered it RSS work, truly praiseworthy since it sought to inculcate the right attitudes among small children (*Onward March* 1974). On the link and line between the Jan Sangh and the RSS, he was quite forthcoming in his long and open answer,

> We did not want to be isolated either from society or politically. So we strengthened Mukherjee's Jana Sangh. Patel wanted RSS cadre to join Congress, but Nehruji did not allow that; hence we are not there in Congress. But that I would like our *swayamsevaks* to join different political parties so that the political untouchability will end; these *swayamsevaks* can still come together on the *shakha* grounds and think about what is common to all of them than what differences they have among them. (*Onward March* 1974)

As early as October 1973, Deoras spoke of a federation of nations with India that went as far as Iran, Malaysia and Singapore. It was on the lines of European Economic Community, which he sensed to be a strong political deterrent to both Russia and America at that time, and was aware of the details of its formation and functioning. He blamed the mainland Hindus not discharging their responsibility towards the North-East for the huge conversions taking place there. He spoke about the work done by the Vivekananda Kendra and others in stalling proselytisation, countering the secessionist tendencies in those areas as the work of the RSS. When questioned on the dominance of the English language, he shot back saying that all the major languages of the world should be taught in the universities to deal with the world better. He did not, characteristically, talk of Sanskrit (*Onward March* 1974: 22–45).

When questioned on the then current topic of a committed judiciary, he replied, 'Why judiciary? No one should be committed in life so that one remains open to new ideas' (*Onward March* 1974). On the military, he said, 'Military is a sensitive area and criteria of admission should be in the national interests and not political expediency' (*Onward March* 1974). For him, 'Socialism meant better deal for weaker sections, and not state capitalism or nationalization' (*Onward March* 1974). He mentioned that with this interpretation, the RSS was also a Socialist organisation. While pointing out the huge differences among people in defining either Socialism or Communism, he also had a good word for the Communists. He said, 'They gave us strong ideas on the weaker sections, in economics, but they misinterpret everything one says which we do not like' (*Onward March* 1974). He did not think there was anything wrong in the Russia–India Pact of 1973. He considered it 'as a national necessity since we were a weaker country and need support in oil, arms etc' (*Onward March* 1974). One of his best statements came when some journalist whimsically asked him if the RSS would cooperate with the government for the ill-functioning Public Distribution System of essential commodities. He promptly responded by saying that the RSS had its branches everywhere – if the government wanted their help, they would cooperate with the government.

Activism and Agitation Gets Green Signal

In 1974, the student's agitation of Nava Nirman against the corrupt Chimanbhai Patel ministry was a high laudable peak of our national life. When accused of fuelling this agitation in a press conference, Deoras shot back, 'If our RSS had such strength to control and fuel such an agitation I would be a happy man indeed!' (*Saptahik Vivek 1974*). It is an open secret that he encouraged the *swayamsevaks* and the Vidyarthi Parishad to be a part of the movement. In all movements where the *swayamsevaks* participated, the typical Deoras argument was, 'Are the RSS volunteers not the citizens of this country? Don't they have their problems and difficulties as citizens in biding their life? If they feel that they can get a redress this way why should they not be a part of such movements?' (discussion between Deoras and D.B. Ghumare reported to author). It meant a lot to people like us. There was no Golwalkar there to call these movements as 'reactionary' and 'short lived', or to accuse the participants of being 'destructive elements'. There was no scholarly lecture on the fundamentals of RSS work, or that the RSS should not have to do anything with 'political movements'. Gone were the clichés about 'non-involvement' and 'long-range goal'. Deoras 'openly approved fight against corruption' — period.

The national situation in 1974 was terrible. The nation was besieged with poverty, corruption, nepotism and lack of credibility. The suffering populace had to cope with the horrible spectre of nothing to look forward to, of food shortages, of high prices, of being plagued and plundered by the licence–quota–permit sharks. The opposition was demoralised. The 'drought of the century' had just occurred in 1972. The Vidyarthi Parishad, with Sushil Modi, the deputy chief minister of Nitish Kumar in Bihar from 2006 onwards, started an agitation against corruption as the main plank. The movement caught on. RSS *swayamsevaks* got involved in it and the RSS offices across the states were used for this purpose. There was actually a considerable neglect of the RSS work then, which 'worried the purists' (conversations with D.B. Ghumare 2006–07). The certainty of brutal and oppressive measures taken by the Government was more than obvious. The need for a leader with credentials was felt.

Jay Prakash Narayan (JP) was therefore approached. He had his misgivings about the RSS, but he agreed to their proposal nonetheless. JP is later said to have given resounding tributes to the RSS to his close contacts. Once JP got involved, people like Thakurdas Bang and others went, and in the typical style of the Socialists, they sat on the 'jaggery heap' the RSS cadre had created and carried the banner as theirs.

Deoras knew this in detail and also the neglect of RSS work. His question to those purists was,

> The situation there is grave. We stay at home but venture out to work, to see a picture or visit others, or to agitate. But we do return home. If our volunteers show an unwillingness to come back to RSS work after tasting the field then we should feel concerned. Presently there is no need. This work is more important. (Discussion between Deoras and D.B. Ghumare reported to author)

It was pure pragmatism. It was the first demonstration of the idea that there would be matters the RSS would take in their hands and be responsible for. It was the first demonstration that the RSS as an organisation is not averse to conflict, agitation and confrontation. The 'constructive work' meanwhile continued. Deoras demolished a huge myth and lived up to his own theme of 'organisation, mobilisation and action'.

He deputed Nanaji Deshmukh to be close to JP. The movement met with unprecedented success. It was the first act of the RSS to give a decisive turn to the country's future course. It set the political stage afire, virtually setting the stage for the Allahabad High Court aftermath and the Emergency. And the rest is history. JP's movement was not mired in symbolism. It was a concrete, down-to-earth act, a measure that immediately gave the RSS an immense credibility of being relevant to the present context, of being sensitive to the common man's day-to-day issues, from which it had once eschewed responsibility. The RSS was now lending its force to bolster the same. Would Golwalkar have allowed this participation if he were still around? This is not a moot question, but a real concern. For the first time, Deoras had a free hand to do what he thought was proper. This was the first of Deoras' acts that changed the course of the destiny of the nation.

Changing the Exterior of the RSS

Deoras wanted or, at least thought of attempting, a change in the exterior of the RSS *shakhas*. On an occasion in 1973, my uncle, a close friend of Deoras, had gone to see him. I was with him at that time. Deoras said, 'I feel that change of content of sports in RSS is worth trying…It is desirable that some experiments may be carried out even with non Indian sports' (Kane 1996).[5] This topic must have been alive in the inner and higher circles for long. I heard about it years after that, in Karnataka, where I worked for the organisation. Both Deoras and Golwalkar attended Dilip Deodhar's 'full pant' RSS branch. He had an encouraging attitude towards those who wanted to do something like these experiments (Lokhiteishi 1994: 41). The higher-ups did not like the idea. They were not ready for it, and opposed it as the sacrosanct being defiled. They stuck to the archaic model that continues even today. For Deoras, the physical form of what happens in the *shakha* was changeable. In 1946, he said, 'To consolidate the society, from starting a fire to extinguishing it, anything and everything is a program' (Lokhiteishi 1994: 42). Deoras had to wait for long before he could inject some different dimensions to the rituals of the *shakhas*.

Thinking Paradigms and the Masterstrokes of Deoras

The occasion was the famous Vasant Vyakhyanmala, a century-long institution of scholarship in Pune, the cultural bastion of Brahminical Maharashtra. Once a year, prominent people deliver a series of lectures on different subjects during spring. As the chief of RSS, Deoras spoke there on 'Hindu Unity and Equality' in 1974. The damage caused by the controversial 1968 interview of Golwalkar in *Nava Kal*, on the *Chaturvarnya* system, was ultimately undone by Deoras in this speech. It hit the followers harder than it did the outsiders. It silenced the Left-wing criticism completely on this issue for long years in Maharashtra, where the critics were most vocal.[6]

Deoras talked of some 'emotional basis of being the children of the motherland having a past which we have spoiled as well as did well with, is necessary. Emotions are necessary but they are not sufficient' (speech at the Vasant Vyakhyanmala, Pune 1974). He emphasised that:

> Practical experience of this unity, homogeneity, love and equality especially to those deprived of it, is necessary. The divisions of the *varna*s, casts and untouchability were the causes of division and fragmentation that led to the foreign domination. The contradiction of having a culture which has many good things that even the world has acknowledged, but has also developed many deficiencies which cannot be denied but have to be addressed. (Speech at the Vasant Vyakhyanmala, Pune 1974)

He then attacked the mentality of 'making a virtue and a science of the inherited differences and inequities man is born with and declared that there is no manhood in it' (speech at the Vasant Vyakhyanmala, Pune 1974).

> Inheritance is a limited matter. The attempt should be to minimise its effects by allowing the environment to be shared equally by every body, by special efforts, help, or by some particular ways of education, or some other arrangements. The system of caste or *varna* has no relevance to holding together and building the society up (towards equality). The caste or the *varna* system is getting dismantled. All well meaning people should see how effectively it disappears and it is desirable

to see that all of us think that way. (Speech at the Vasant Vyakhyanmala, Pune 1974)

He went on to defend the free mixing of castes and *varnas*, including eating together, working together and sharing common spaces. 'It has reduced the intensity of the caste based behaviour' (speech at the Vasant Vyakhyanmala, Pune 1974). He insisted,

> The limited happenstance of marriages outside the castes must become the norm, the usual, and the universal. For that the educational level, economic level and living standards should become equal, irrespective of castes. Then the castes will disappear as they should. The more the communities and the localities become mixed, that they are not caste based, education becomes universal as do the opportunities, easier it will be to intermarry. It cannot be forced and we have to be patient and encouraging.

Deoras did not hesitate to meet the issue of untouchability head on. The RSS had talked of homogeneity earlier as well, but had not 'battled' for 'social justice'. He called it an 'extremely painful and unfortunate occurrence of hundreds of years, a mistake'. He characteristically declared that it should 'go and go lock stock and barrel'. He quoted Lincoln who said 'if slavery is not wrong, then nothing is wrong in this world. Similarly if untouchability is not wrong nothing in the world is wrong' (speech at the Vasant Vyakhyanmala, Pune 1974).

Deoras did not spare the 'glory of the past' psyche either. As early as 1965, he had said that 'the only driving idea that one needs to have is to bring glory to the society in which one is born. If you have a glorious past it is better. A glorious past, however, does not mean that the future will be glorious.' He clearly said, in a tone not many would like,

> Just because a matter is old, or of long standing, it cannot be good! If it is irrelevant today it has to go away. Why

should anyone feel bad about it? The limits of the pride in the past should be laid by what is scientific and proved by modern knowledge. One must adopt this kind of approach if one is serious about organizing the society in an equal and homogeneous one. (Speech at the Vasant Vyakhyanmala, Pune 1974)

His direct pointer was to 'all' Hindus, asking them, 'Do you think and behave in this modern way? One should' (speech at the Vasant Vyakhyanmala, Pune 1974). Then he went on to attack the 'tendency to avoid contact with the world and blame others like Britishers for the deteriorations or perversions like untouchability or casteism'. 'Those who build walls around themselves are declaring of their deficiencies and are unsure of themselves' (speech at the Vasant Vyakhyanmala, Pune 1974).

An important term that he used twice was *parivartan*, that is, 'change'. It is impossible that he was unaware of the tenuous argument emphasised in the RSS, that is, 'progressive unfoldment', which emphatically denied 'change'. Deoras' proclamation was an unexpected matter and it did emphasise that 'change' was not some kind of an anathema for the RSS and its thinking, as it was being made out at that time. People like me have suffered from the untenable exercise of defending 'progressive unfoldment', which in itself is fine, but becomes irrational if it starts denying change as a necessary mechanism. These were the things young boys like me had unconsciously waited for the RSS to express, knowing well that the general RSS psyche was unfortunately at variance with it. The kind of difference of expression that we saw with Deoras was very enchanting. I cannot imagine a more egalitarian approach. At the same time, the fact that the 'Hindu bulk mind' was too primitive to understand this man caused us great pain.

The next in the line of his attack was the prevailing, dominant psyche of the Savarna Hindus, ubiquitous in the society and also within the RSS. He challenged the notion of 'created by god, the *apourusheya* principle'. He insisted that what exists in 'matters religious' can be changed.

> We must be able to think in consonance with the new times. New discoveries have been made. New science has come. Can we write that the solar eclipse occurs because Rahu and Ketu are swallowing the sun in the school text books? The environment has changed. Environment has become as important as heredity. It can mean in that context only one thing—that it should be shared. (Speech at the Vasant Vyakhyanmala, Pune 1974)

Deoras clearly asked 'if it is okay or workable or acceptable for anyone who intends to consolidate the Hindu Society to keep dwelling on even the wrong of the past or rationally examine and reject without feeling bad about it' (speech at the Vasant Vyakhyanmala, Pune 1974). This was sacrilege in the tradition of the RSS.

In that lecture, Deoras described the traditional view of the *Chaturvarnya* with 'checks and balances'. His way of expression not only had 'acceptability outside Sangh', but also the 'power' to silence the motivated, orchestrated criticism from various quarters. It was not a matter of changed times, but of a changed and logical way of expression. For example, the traditional Hindu mind and the bulk of the RSS cadre has never taken into account the central fact that no defence of the *Chaturvarnya* system is possible today because, as Deoras put it simply,

> Education today is imparted in Educational institutes and not in the home environment any more. Printing technology was then not there, now it is. The age of industrialization had set in to create a necessity that education should go out of the house. When that happened the four fold system became obsolete. (Speech at the Vasant Vyakhyanmala, Pune 1974)

He clearly disowned the perversions in tradition and indicated the fallacious acceptance of observance of rituals as a sign of either purity or good character. It was in his emphasis on a more desirable 'social awareness in people' that his modernism came to fore with force. He wanted the *swayamsevaks* to talk about material prosperity and social problems, be acquainted with the powers of the new age and era, and the effects that it had on society and have a good knowledge of its solutions (B. Deoras 1965). This was said a few years after he came back to the RSS. In 1974, his opinion had not changed at all on this matter. Every point that he touched upon appeared as a new language and paradigm which he opened for the traditional Hindu mind. It was pleasing when Deoras said, 'There is a large group of people, even within Sangh, who thinks this way. I pray that Dalits identify and stand with them. It will ease the matters. That will bring in an atmosphere of equality' (speech at the Vasant Vyakhyanmala, Pune 1974).

> Our Dalit brethren have suffered a great deal for millennia. All of us have pain in our mind about it...Our behaviour should be conducive for ending the inequality...Criticism over such issues arising out of pain and agony, out of affection towards the section of people...who suffered, is the right kind of criticism. Otherwise it is motivated. We will then drag the battles of past in the present and spoil the future for everybody.
>
> I assume that Dalits do not want compassion or a paternalistic attitude, but a place of equality that they will wrest by their own effort. It is necessary that they are given every kind of help. They must take all of it. It is their right to demand the help. It is up to them to decide how long they should use it. Ultimately the equality that has to come in will be without these struts, but of their own abilities...To develop this nation, Hindu consolidation is essential. For Hindu consolidation social equality is essential. (Speech at the Vasant Vyakhyanmala, Pune 1974)

Within the RSS, there are two or three distinct streams. There are people at various levels who not only think but have actualised and internalised what Deoras said above. To do more justice to them, their natural egalitarian mind was already deeply disturbed that the problem of untouchability existed, which found resonance in Deoras' proclamations. My own uncomfortable feeling about the covert *Chaturvarnya* system continuing to exist stemmed from a sense of apprehension. There is little doubt that if this covert system is allowed to operate within Hindu society, it will not allow untouchability to get eliminated. In fact, it will positively strive not to eliminate the existence of Antyajas (the lowest and the last born of the caste categories), and not desire to maintain equality and free mixing across the classes. I do not think that those who speak in that language understand the fact that it will not end untouchability and inequality as their strongest primary concern. Consequently, these promoters do not think of checks and balances about how to prevent it from developing the same.[7]

The second stream consists of people who have accepted these lines of thinking, but find more pleasure in talking about the great past attributes of Hindu society. This group also has, deep inside, a certainty that the fourfold system will return. This group is large in number. The third stream of the ordinary bulk cadre is the one worried over the loss of jobs and opportunities due to reservations for the Dalits and other backward groups. They are mostly undisturbed by the existence of caste, inequality, untouchability; at their worst, they are in favour of many of these things. This large group has, rightfully, raised the following question in the minds of the Dalits, 'How can we believe your organisation? We do not see those few who do not believe in untouchability and behave differently.'

Deoras issued a clear warning: the way we behaved ourselves, the way we spoke, thought, expressed ourselves and retaliated gave out wrong signals. In fact, behaviour and expression on a man-to-man basis is something the Sangh behaviour has always lagged behind in and lacked in substance, be it with Muslims or Dalits.

Throughout Deoras' speech, the address is to the Savarnas,

> It is their doing. The onus to change and to convince the untouchables is on them. They have to take the beating, to genuinely feel the pain over what they did. It is for them to understand that the big problem has to be solved. It is necessary to understand that hard words are bound to be used; it is the expression of the agony of centuries by Dalits and the Savarnas cannot complain. (Speech at the Vasant Vyakhyanmala, Pune 1974)

Today the castes have no problem eating with other castes and sharing their meal. Similarly, intercaste marriages also have become a norm. This is likely to happen between people of different castes who have equal or similar backgrounds of economy, education and a commonly shared atmosphere of mixed societies.[8]

This is coming a long way for the RSS, given the way the RSS' thinking apparatus operates. When the highest body of the RSS representatives nationwide met over the issue of reservations, there was a heated discussion, and an impasse developed. Deoras (and Rajendra Singhji) intervened, saying, 'Imagine for a moment you were born in such a situation and then think about whether reservations should continue or not' (Seshadri 1996a: 7). The message went home.

The Deep Divide Becomes Apparent

A peculiar aspect had developed in the dominant and majority psyche of the Sangh which was at variance with the way Deoras thought. When Deoras emphasised upon equality as necessary for Hindu unity, he laid down a clear principle which could, to an extent, contain the interest groups. Till 1983, the organisation neither responded to the letter nor the spirit of this lecture of 1974. At that time, the word 'equality' was replaced by someone with 'homogeneity', which was supposed to take the concept to a higher level. When 'equality' is converted to 'homogeneity', the true meaning behind the concept is shrouded, even as it becomes elitist, more symbolic and befuddled. That leads to a possibility of accepting inequality as long as there is homogeneity. Then some could be more equal than others, a strong trait in Golwalkar's leadership, at least as far as the hierarchy went. Equality is more direct, more appealing because it is simple and understood by everyone. Equality is the modern word. Deoras did not voice his displeasure over this elitism. Sources say that he did not have a high opinion of the one who changed it.

It is noteworthy that every word that was said about him on his death had a connection with this message of social equality as essential to Hindu unity. People have been unkind to him to say that all efforts to homogeneity and equality started after Meenakshipuram in 1982. Even Golwalkar, equally unjustifiably, has wrongly been assumed to support untouchability till the 1966 declaration of all the saints of India. We have seen the contradiction in that. However, there was no such contradiction in Deoras' efforts to establish equality. It helped demolish the isolation of the RSS. It helped, to a considerable extent, to destroy the sectarian character it had assumed.

Everywhere he went, Deoras started the question-and-answer sessions more emphatically. He encouraged the practice of free thinking 'expressed'. No less a person than the then organisational chief Mr H.V. Seshadri (1996: 2) has spoken of this with tremendous appreciation.

There are people close to Deoras who have said that they could not understand why he was doing all that. They give credit to Deoras as the man mostly responsible for shaping all the work in the 'other fields'. Even then they thought it unnecessarily brought the burden of Parivar work onto the RSS. There was a certain amount of accountability expected, which these people thought was unwanted. But the larger issue, which I think these people ignored, was the message that all work is in its final essence the work of the RSS and it is the RSS' responsibility to set things right in the long and the final run.

It is now generally agreed that Deoras introduced rapid and sweeping changes in the general approach and expression in the Sangh. The 'Hindu' was catapulted on the centre stage by 1985–88, to change all the paradigms of Indian life. Which aspect of this drastic change, which took place from June 1973 to, say, 1985, could not have been attempted before 1973? The answer to this question is simple: the real change that had happened was at the top. We will discuss this matter some more in the later chapters.

Notes

1. Advocate P.S. Badhiye has told the following story to the author, corroborated by the personal secretary of Deoras, Shrikant Joshi, about the undying faith of Deoras in RSS work. In the Gadarwada conclave of the RSS workers circa 1952–53, when Deoras' strong opinions about diversification were well known, a lecture on the primacy of the work of the RSS was scheduled. To everyone's utter surprise, Golwalkar told them to ask Deoras to deliver it. Deoras unfolded the pure vision of RSS work for two and a half hours in the most stunning manner, without a single reference to his own well-held opinions, to the utter amazement of all. F. Scott Fitzgerald has commented on a first-rate intelligence saying that it can hold two completely different viewpoints at a time in excellent balance. No further comment is necessary.

2. This essentially is my interpretation of what must have been going on in the mind of Deoras during those years he was sitting out. It has been endorsed as correct by seniors who had not articulated it themselves over so many years.

3. The external as well as internal Golwalkarisation of Deoras was systematically attempted. One may even accuse the RSS heads of making Deoras' originality unrecognisable, as seen in the various pages of Chouthaiwale's booklet (n.d.). When the demand for the externalities is so strong, it is not difficult to understand how completely ineffective the intellectual, logical appeal of this modern mind would be. Deoras may have traded this off in order to avoid hurting sentiments, but he did not receive either a rational and radical response or a change in attitude towards the shedding of obsolescence

and turning to modern scientific ways from the followers. They remained the bourgeoisie they always were.

4. The monograph written by M.K. Chouthaiwale (n.d.) gives a detailed account of how Deoras was persuaded to adapt to the religious rituals, the *pujas* and the *yagnyas* people did for him, how he disliked being called the *Param Poojaniya*, as well as at least a dozen more instances of things Deoras detested. Deoras gave up his preference for meat so as to not hurt the sentiments of the members of the RSS. This merely confirms our charge that Golwalkar made him the chief of the RSS, but did not leave him with followers of a nature akin to him.

5. Deoras, in his youth, was fond of hockey and cricket. Of test cricket, he said, 'It requires concentration, tenacity, strength and the need to play as a team.' It is needless to say what the remarks of the orthodox would be on this issue.

6. On the first death anniversary of Mr Deoras in 1997, I published a series of articles on him. Much of the second article has been included above. Within an hour of the morning papers reaching home, I got a phone call from Prof. Bhau Lokhande, a scholar from among the Ambedkar circles in Nagpur. We did not know each other. Prof. Lakhande said, 'If this is the true picture of RSS then we, the hitherto untouchables, now the Neo-Buddhists, are with you.' We have been great friends since then.

7. To clarify further what I mean by these words, I must refer here to an 18-hour long discussion I had with one of my mentors, Prof. G.B. Kanitkar. We were talking about his proposed treatise on explaining and expanding in greater details the thesis of Deen Dayal Upadhyay's integral humanism. My constant refrain to the Professor was, how do we provide a guarantee to prevent the development of untouchability, the narrow, limiting caste-consciousness, as well as the strong feelings of high and low that come with it, in the model presented by integral humanism? Undoubtedly, the model of integral humanism speaks the language of the interdependent, non-conflicting, cooperative society. It immediately has the overtones of the hitherto prevalent *Chaturvarnya* system, to which Deoras had already raised strong objections.

The result of this long argument was that the candid professor agreed to rethink the entire structure of the book, keeping these points as the primary considerations, while expanding the thesis of integral humanism. He agreed that this was the number one question that all the proponents of the model of integral humanism had not even considered. This restructuring effort proved to be too onerous for my ageing professor, who died at its altar without being able to put together the framework in detail.

8. I have often wondered about both Dr Ambedkar and Mr M.K. Gandhi, as to why their efforts could not succeed to the extent they should have. Gandhiji went and stayed in the Bhangi Colony in Delhi and Dr Ambedkar in Rajgriha in Bombay. The untouchable communities, nonetheless, remained where they were. It was in 1974 for the first time that anybody emphasised upon free mixing of castes within the society in such clear and practical terms as Deoras did.

5

The Emergency and Post-Emergency

————•✦•————

The Emergency as a Boon

The Emergency was one of the few good events in the 60-year-old life of independent India, comparable only to the processes of liberalisation in 1992, whatever the antecedents of both. Europe faced two holocausts, the USSR and China inflicted great misery upon its people — India, in comparison, did not suffer anything worse than unending, uninterrupted poverty and unemployment, lowly levels at which life was somehow led and completed. The infamous Emergency was independent India's first experience of suppression of freedom, of fear of the state apparatus and a sense of impotence against the ruler and the oppression being meted out, involving the entire nation across all the layers. People required such an insult to be inflicted upon them to realise what parliamentary democracy could mean, its value to individual life and the contrast it presented to the experience of the Soviet and Chinese brand of totalitarian regimes, and be wiser with it. Even the *panwallahs*, from the lowest rungs of society, and the vast, illiterate masses responded to this challenge and opportunity gallantly and wisely, establishing democracy more firmly than all the previous years could. The Emergency galvanised the nation.

The years preceding the Emergency were of great upheavals. There was serious drought for three years running, in 1969, 1971 and 1972. It undermined the food grain situation, leading to high prices and increasing suffering for the people. Meanwhile, internationally, the Watergate scandal took place in 1972; it was one great test of the American democracy. Two reporters followed all the leads at great peril to themselves and unearthed the black deeds of Mr Nixon. American democracy impeached Nixon. The whole episode stood in sharp contrast with the undemocratic Indian Emergency that soon followed, with the R Document being proscribed in India. The Nixon episode underlined the fundamental fact that he was an American citizen first, also incidentally the president of America, and hence liable for judicial action, not above it.

The Iraq War started in 1973 with effects rippling all over the world. All things put together, the suffering of the common man in India had reached unbearable proportions. Mrs Gandhi even sanctified corruption as a way of life. Jay Prakash's movement started, leading to the Emergency being clamped upon the nation.

The Oppression

Mrs Gandhi had already become paranoid over the Jay Prakash–RSS alliance, and the enormous and extensive support that the Lok Sangharsh Samiti and the Chhatra Yuva Sangharsh Vahini were receiving. Months before, it was becoming apparent that, among other things, these two would be the targets soon. With the landmark judgement of the Allahabad High Court, everything changed.

Twenty-seven organisations, including the RSS and the Jamat-e-Islami, were banned. Deoras identified the opportunity presented by the ban as a leap forward, correctly predicting the likely timeframe of the crisis, almost as soon as he was arrested at the Nagpur railway station. The message that reached us was, 'What could not have been achieved in twenty years will be possible in two years' (conversations with Damodar Madhav Date 1975–80). No one thought it would come true. Deoras identified the crisis as the 'war of nerves' — whoever remains without blinking will win. On both counts, he was prophetic.

There were large-scale arrests. All the political bosses and leaders of the 27 banned organisations were jailed. The Jamat-e-Islami and everyone else were jailed together, many of them with Deoras in the famous Yerawada Jail in Pune. Newspapers remained quiet, fearing the administration's wrath. There were numerous places where they, or the bureaucrats, were out to show that they were more loyal to Mrs Gandhi than even King Sanjay. Atrocities followed and spread all over. There were reports from Kerala that RSS volunteers were subjected to such torture as running heavy printing roles over their thighs, crushing their muscles. Not one hand lifted in retaliation. Months went by. Authorities from all over cautioned the government against such treatment and asked the administration not to play with fire.

Studying the period and the major role the RSS and Deoras played in lifting the Emergency will be beneficial. Today, if our life is better, a considerable credit will go to these two. On the occasion of 20 years of the Emergency being lifted, *The Times of India*, Bangalore published at least 11 articles titled 'Emergency Remembered' (Baru 1997, Bidwai 1997, Karlekar 1997, Kothari 1997, Lazman 1997, Malhotra 1997, Palkhiwal 1997, Sen 1997, Shastri 1997, Subrahmanyam 1997, Subramanyam 1997). Only two articles mention in some non-significant way the role of the RSS. On the 30th anniversary of the Emergency, Dr Usha Mehta (2007) published a book on the fight that was put up by people in 1977. Barring Socialists' accounts, I believe there is no mention of the RSS at all. Be sure this is not the historical truth. 'One man Churchill and twenty miles of English channel stood between Hitler and victory', Deoras had thundered in the post-Emergency era. 'In the same manner I will say one man Jay Prakash and RSS stood between totalitarianism and democracy' (unpublished recordings of speeches, discussions, interviews, jottings by personal secretaries and attendees — RSS Headquarters, Dr Hedgewar Bhavan Mahal, Nagpur). If there are any literal truths in the era of the Emergency (or in any other era), this is one of them. Characteristically, Deoras did not take credit for himself.

The Peace and the Protest Offers

Deoras wrote to Mrs Gandhi twice, asking her to lift the unnecessary Emergency and remove the ban on the RSS, seek redressal for her problem in the law courts and restore democracy to utilise the strength of people for the all-round development of the nation. He assured her that the RSS would cooperate with the Government (Chouthaiwale n.d.).[1] It went unheeded. When the elections were declared, the organisation to fight the elections was put quickly in place, even in the remote areas of the country, only by the RSS. Mrs Gandhi knew the meaning of it. The PMO sent a confidential emissary, a skilled negotiator, to meet the underground RSS leaders. He placed an offer in front of Lala Hansraj Gupta, Bapurao Moghe and Brahmadeo. Paraphrasing the lengthy offer, which was more a threat:

> The RSS volunteers in jail will languish there.... Their families will be in dire straits. They and their families both have lost the nerve. People are opposed to the RSS. Congress will win. All the underground leaders will be arrested and dumped in the jail. The only way out is to severe your relationship with the Janata Party and remove yourself from the election

process. If the RSS leaders promise this all the leaders and the volunteers will be released from jail and after the election it might be possible to remove the ban on the RSS.

This was a diabolical threat that could have scared anyone. The leaders sent back the following reply with the emissary, 'Immediately after the Emergency Deoras had extended a hand of co-operation to which you did not pay attention. Now the time has slipped past. Now everything will be decided upon the war of election' (Chouthaiwale n.d.).

When all doors to break the impasse appeared closed and the future bleak, action was necessary. Deoras spoke of his wish to go on a fast unto death to break the stalemate. The reply came back post-haste, 'The communication is blocked out completely. The news and the effect from such an undertaking will not have any effect as it will neither reach the masses nor the deadened conscience of Mrs Indira Gandhi. Hence it is not acceptable'[2] (Chari Unpublished). The tone is clear. If the circumstances were favourable, it could have been considered. Deoras, had he undertaken the fast, would be a dead man in a matter of few days. The accusations of the RSS and Deoras' shameful surrender to Mrs Gandhi could be looked at afresh in the light of this.

There was demoralisation everywhere. Mr Achyutrao Patwardhan, the senior Socialist leader, called upon the Socialist rank and file to say, 'The grassroot level organisation of the RSS alone is intact. Go to them. They will help you' (conversations with Damodar Madhav Date 1975–80). When the impasse reached a peak and culminated into a deadlock, Deoras decided to protest. So did the Socialists. Of all, 80 per cent of all the protestors were RSS men, while all others put together made 20 per cent.

On 4 December 1976, *The Economist* of London spelled out the position of the RSS clearly:

> The underground campaign against Mrs Gandhi claims to be the only non left wing revolutionary force in the world, disavowing both bloodshed and class struggle. Indeed it might

even be called right wing since it is dominated by the Hindu communalist party, Jan Sangh and its 'cultural' (some say paramilitary) affiliate the RSS. But its platform at the moment has only one non ideological plank; to bring democracy back to India.

The Economist went on to delineate the roles various political social forces were playing at that point of time, echoing Achyutrao Patwardhan:

> The ground troops of this operation (the underground movement), consists of tens of thousands of cadres who are organized to the village level into four man cells. Most of them are RSS regulars, though more and more new young recruits are coming in. The other opposition parties which started out as partners in the underground have effectively abandoned the field to Jan Sangh and RSS. (Sehgal 15 May 1979)

The RSS was at the vanguard of the mass movement of peaceful Satyagraha, the famous Gandhian instrument, best used by the RSS in both the bans it had to endure. Nearly 80,000 volunteers went to jail. Thousands remained incarcerated for months on end, 19 months at its maximum. The RSS supported their families by providing money, clothes and food. The organisation remained intact. There were secret meetings everywhere. We moved around with the Criminal Investigation Department (CID) on our track. Two of the five cousins that we were went to jail under DRI (Defense of India Rules). A hundred friends of mine were under MISA (Maintenance of Internal Security Act) for long months. On one occasion, we were asked to actually create a mess of our footwear in contrast to the orderly way in which we were used to keeping them wherever we gathered, lest we were detected by that sign. The underground press churned out pamphlets, small and big, everywhere in the country to keep people informed. Young girls often distributed these pamphlets.

The RSS volunteers asked their bosses inside and outside the jails, 'What will happen?' The quiet and the confident reply of people like Moropant Pingale or Thengadi or Date was: 'This is an unnatural situation which cannot go on. No dictator from Mr Ravan to Mr Hitler has survived the holocaust they created. This will also end.' Deoras also empowered those outside by another of his by now famous quotes, 'I may be the one Sarsanghachalak inside the jail but there are six other Sarsanghachalaks roaming outside free. They have a better idea of the situation outside. Whatever they decide to do will have my support and sanction' (published verbatim by *Vivek* in 1976). That infused new vigour in the fight against the Emergency. It was around this time when Deoras ended one strong tradition in the RSS, at least within his own mind, that of *Ekachalakanuvartitva* — the notion that the order of that one leader is to be followed implicitly without doubt, question and challenge. This was, however, also the tenet that had created, fostered and perpetuated the image of the RSS as a fascist organisation. Deoras replaced it by *Sahachalakanuvartitva*, that is, by the consensus of the leaders.

Finally, the elections were declared with as little time for preparation as could be legally allowed. According to a recorded account, Deoras insisted with Madhu Limaye and George Fernandez that they fight the elections (Bondale, unpublished). Limaye and Fernandez thought there would be large-scale irregularities, capturing of booths and other such things that would lead to their defeat — therefore they sought to boycott the elections. Deoras persuaded them to reject this mode of thought, by pointing out that 'if the elections were not fought Mrs Indira Gandhi will be in a position to claim that the people are behind her and she will get support abroad as well' (Chouthaiwale n.d.). He appealed to all those who were being released from the jail to consider that they were not free and to therefore whole-heartedly participate in election work instead of going home. The RSS was officially ushered into the election arena by Deoras.

An unsteady alliance of the Congress (O), the Bharatiya Kranti Dal of Mr Charan Singh, the Socialists and the

Bharatiya Jan Sangh emerged. Babu Jagjivan Ram's Congress for Democracy (CFD) went with them. There is a shroud of mystery around the merger of the BJS into the Janata Party. Some sources from Mumbai office of the RSS told me at the time of the 1980 debacle that Deoras had advised against this merger, since he was well aware of both its pitfalls — the loss of identity for the BJS and the intolerant attitude of all other political parties towards the RSS (conversations with Dada Naik, Incharge, RSS office, Navyug, Mumbai).

There has not been any corroboration from other people asked in Mumbai, like Damodar Datey, Abaji Thatte or Madhukar Moghe. Deoras has also been reported as saying, 'Could the merger have been avoided?' The emotional, poetic (and some say, the power-hungry) Vajpayee was supposedly insistent and was fairly carried away by the idea of the merger, as was Advani (Swaroop 2007).

The RSS workers witnessed the bickering and the personality clashes between Morarji Desai and Charan Singh, Jagjeevan Ram, Ramakrishna Hegde and Chandrashekhar early, even before they had won. It was seen again during the farcical oath-taking at Rajghat. The complete disregard for any consideration of the national good, and of the opportunity and the responsibility that was thrust upon them by destiny, were on display. Advani put it thus in a nutshell, 'Charan Singh could never reconcile himself to number 2 to Morarji, however, he detested much more being under Jagjeevan Ram for obvious reasons' (2008). The RSS men may not be greatly learned scholars, but the most ordinary *swayamsevak*, in comparison to these great men, was aware of where the national interest lay. The victory was a golden opportunity, when for the first time a clear and massive mandate for a non-Congress government was given by the electorate. Many seem to think that the Janata experiment broke down — and was destined to do so — because of the ideological extremism and disparity of viewpoints within the parties that came together more as a reaction to the Emergency than anything else. The primary responsibility of the debacle goes to the

Socialists. They derived a certain kind of pleasure from destroying, dividing and running through something that was doing well, which prevailed even in this instance. The second reason behind the debacle was their adherence to the obsolescent in their ideology. They knew that they had changed. They knew the RSS had changed, and that they were now in a position to understand it better. But they could not break out of their old mould.[3] The third reason behind the debacle was the typical mentality of being critical without taking on any responsibility, even when an opportunity was provided. That finally ended the experiment. A close parallel to this was witnessed in the actions of the Left parties with respect to the UPA government in 2007, as Advani has observed (2008).

A New Deal by the Free RSS

Deoras was released from prison and the ban on the RSS was lifted on 21st March 1977. The charter of demands that was placed by the mixed conglomerate of the Janata Party was mainly worded to ensure the restoration of democracy in the country. It may appear surprising or even suspicious to the readers that the charter of demands made no mention of the RSS' ban, or demand the removal of the same. Deoras lifted the charter above the partisan politics and showed great maturity to restore a much higher value, that of democracy, which would automatically lead to the restoration of many other precious norms. Deoras was one of the few who understood what exactly this victory meant for the nation and for the RSS. The RSS had emerged victorious and riding on the wave of immense and limitless credibility. They were looked upon with awe and respect, as the saviours who had brought freedom to the nation.

As was done by Golwalkar after the first ban was lifted in 1949, Deoras started on his historical march of victory after the Janata Party was established at the centre. He had several messages to deliver, but the situation at this time was very different from that in 1949. In 1949, the RSS had managed to be rid of the false accusation of being accomplices in Gandhi's murder, but the political situation was adverse, tyrannical and oppressive. The RSS' popularity had surged, but the costs had been tremendous in terms of manpower and loss of credibility, the prevalence of hatred and disaffection, and so on. The nation was paying the human and other costs of the Partition, including the murder of Mahatma Gandhi. In 1977, it was a purer achievement; the costs were high, but were more than doubly paid off by the victory. The crest of the credibility that the RSS was riding at that time was the single most important difference—their political colleagues were now in power with absolute majority.

The first message of Deoras was to 'forgive and forget' Mrs Indira Gandhi, the very woman who had put him and thousands of others in jail for 19 months, not to mention her other misdeeds. Golwalkar showed tremendous maturity with his proclamation that 'those who rose against us are our own brothers and we will not start the cycle of revenge....It is our very own government of the independent India and we are not going to fight it' (Golwalkar 1979). There was great political wisdom in such a stance under the circumstances.

The RSS Opens Doors for Muslims

Deoras was utterly conscious of the ties he had developed with the Socialist and the Jamat-e-Islami brethren. People like Madhu Limaye were ready to put on the *khaki* half knickers and line up at the RSS branches. The more urbane Madhu Dandavate expressed his embarrassment when Deoras asked him for his time for a meeting. Dandavate replied saying that he would come to Deoras when he commanded, in the garb of a *swayamsevak*. The period of honeymoon was intoxicating and short. More than anyone else, Deoras had sensed the historic moment and had made a decision, which he then acted upon. On his release from prison, Deoras declared that the RSS was considering opening its doors to the Muslims. Both the RSS and the Jamat-e-Islami members were in jail together, a place where nothing much could be hidden from each other. They had come closer, become friends and had covered considerable distance in understanding each other. The time had come to make that epoch-making declaration, that the RSS was actively considering opening their doors to them.

In 1977, it was only logical that this 'liberal and liberated' image be reiterated and expanded so that the persecution of the RSS over the Muslim problem ended. Deoras did it effectively, and it went well with his stance. He openly announced that if Muslims believed that India was their country, that their past was in this land and that they were ready to comply with the minimum demands of the rituals of the *shakha*, the 'doors are open' (Bondale, unpublished). With this move, Deoras also attempted to address the realistic need to demolish the isolation of the RSS, in the interest of the society at large as well as the RSS itself. He made recurrent attempts, directed outside the organisation as well as inwards, to put an end to this isolation. The outward-directed effort was clearly to obtain that implicit as well as overt sanction that people give to an organisation or a concept, which becomes one of its greatest strengths.

In his tour, Deoras made it a point to meet Muslim leaders wherever he went, chatted with them and invited them to participate in his informal meetings. Muslim leaders in their turn made it a point to go and see him. During one such meeting in the RSS headquarters in Nagpur, the Muslims who had come to see the RSS leaders became restless. On being asked what the matter was, they responded saying that it was time for their *Namaz*. They were asked if they would have any problem if an arrangement was made in the RSS headquarters itself for offering *Namaz*. They agreed to the proposition. And so they offered their prayers facing the west and Mecca in the RSS headquarters, and then rejoined the talks with Deoras.

Whoever he met, Deoras was always found leaning lower than the person he met in greeting, including Muslims. The responsive body language of all of them is apparent in photographs. In the meetings with the elders, leaders and other dignitaries which Deoras held wherever he went, he was asked about the entrance of Muslims in the RSS. He would respond openly to these questions. The gist of all such recorded minutes of dozens of his meetings would be: We have to increase the frequency of meeting together. We are thinking of about six to seven occasions in a year where these meetings will take place, exchange of ideas will take place. The goodwill will continue to develop and increase. We can think more about this initiative. There is no need to hurry over it. Expediting it will create unnecessary difficulties and hurdles in the process. But let us go on (Bondale, unpublished).

How was this received? Variously! People like me instantly grasped the significance of this initiative. The atmosphere was ripe and the time most opportune. It had the potential to once and for all rid the RSS of the various labels it had acquired, like that of being Muslim haters, the vitriolic effects of which had scourged and burnt the RSS for nearly 30 years before and after Independence. Deoras had the instinctive understanding that the RSS was strong and could hold the Muslims to their heart and help them adjust in this new stream. This was the time the thesis of Hindu Rashtra could have been expanded, added upon and made more inclusive. This declaration actually reflected the confidence of Deoras in his RSS.

There were people like the firebrand orator Jagannathrao Joshi, the only man who could pale Atal Behari Vajpayee in the art of oratory, the then Jan Sangh leader, who was among those who delighted over it. In a meeting, he called upon the women sitting apart in his booming voice to come to the centre of the hall, saying, 'Arey, when even the Mussalman has come in to the RSS why are you sitting away?' (at a ceremony organised on the 61st birthday of Dr Abaji Thatte, which was attended by the author). The message was unmistakable. Was it surprising? Not really. Not for people like me. It is and was natural. It was what needed to happen, and it had happened under Deoras.

The Civic Receptions

Nani Palkhiwala and Mohammad Karim Chhagala presided over the civic reception that the city of Mumbai hosted to felicitate Deoras over the victory. Chhagala had already declared then, 'I am a Muslim by religion but a Hindu by race' (quoted by Deoras in his speech at Alandi, near Pune, 1987). Chhagala had come under severe and impolite criticism for this declaration, from the orthodox as well as highly educated Muslims, some of whom were my friends. Deoras reiterated his persistent appeal to 'forget and forgive Mrs Gandhi'. He then addressed the issue of the Brahmin dominance of the RSS. Characteristically, he narrated a long list of all the top RSS leaders at that time and mentioned after each name the caste that person belonged to—it had only a few Brahmins. The Kerala RSS had a huge following of Pullayas and Ezhavas, the most downtrodden and backward communities in the state. In Uttar Pradesh, the Kurmis and Lodhs were in the RSS and the Brahmins were in the Congress. The Socialists were headed by S.M. Joshi and N.G. Gore, two archetypal Chitpawan Brahmins, even though they were not supposed to be Brahmin-dominated parties. After addressing this issue, he dwelt upon the subject of admitting Muslims into the RSS and opening the organisation's doors to them. This was by and large the pattern of the initiative undertaken by Deoras in the immediate post-Emergency days.

Reaction of the Muslims

What was the Muslim mind then? Whether the Jamat-e-Islami was the most representative body of Muslims or not at that time is rather unimportant. During the Janata regime, a situation developed when the Janata rule appeared to be very likely to crumble. Disaster loomed large in the horizon. At this time, Muslim leaders approached Deoras with a request to make every effort to save the regime. What was the connection? Belief in the man and his integrity alone can explain this step taken by the Muslim leaders, not to mention the transparency that marked all his actions. In one of the interim periods in February 1978, even the Shahi Imam Abdullah Bukhari visited an RSS branch in Punjab, and came out singing praises of the RSS, 'Both of us do the same thing. We free people from oppression' (Ketkar 1985: 5, 10, 13, 14, 22).

Devendra Swaroop wrote an article in *Panchajanya* on 9th April 1978 titled, 'The Auspicious Beginning of National Unity'. He has given several instances where responsible, educated community leaders of Muslims attended the RSS-organised functions in Meerut, Kolkata, Akola and Imphal (Swaroop 2004). Each and every Muslim leader reiterated that they had been misled about the RSS. They said that walls of distrust had been erected between the two communities, but they had now come to know each other well. They would, now and hereafter, jointly solve the problems they faced. In Kolkata, the editor of *Tariqu e Millat* quoted the Quran to say that all religions aim at the same goal. In Akola, the Jamat leader said, 'So far we have been enemies in the name of religion. We will not repeat the mistakes now' (Swaroop 2004: 86–94). In Manipur, a Jawaharlal Nehru University (JNU) professor presiding over the valedictory of an RSS camp said, 'The Hindu Rashtra as envisaged by RSS is not a religious but a nationalist connotation' (Swaroop 86–94). He exhorted the

144

minorities to understand 'Bharat as their motherland, where a hoary tradition of culture has been flowing. We have to become members of a family. Constitutional guarantees will not help the welfare of Muslims.'

Father Monis in Mangalore, Karnataka; a Dalit in Meerut; a Sikh saint in Patiala—all sang praises of the RSS. In the Urdu *Dawat* it was said that this hand of friendship and exchange of thoughts should be continued with fortitude, and the venomous propaganda should be made ineffective. Nani Palkhiwala called the RSS men as willing to sacrifice to the utmost for the sake of the nation. A little ahead in time, in April 1979, Mr Shamsul Haq Khan, an MLA in the Maharashtra Assembly, speaking on a resolution to ban the RSS drill said,

> I have known RSS since 1957. Out of my own experience I say that RSS is not communal. Many Muslims, Christians and Parsis I know, for many years, have been visiting RSS. If RSS wants to unite Hindus what is wrong with it? This nation is called Hindustan. Whatever the religion, finally everybody is a Hindu or a Hindustani here. An organisation like RSS that inculcates discipline and character is essential for this country. (Ketkar 1985: 5)

In 1979, Mr Sayyad Bhai spoke on the concept of the secular state in a symposium on the occasion of the Ganapati Utsav in Revenue Colony, Pune. Responding to the questions from the audience, he said, 'To say that RSS is against Muslims is false. RSS stands against those who create the feelings of dissidence and secession, be it Muslims, Hindus or anyone else. RSS is most certainly not against the nationalist and the true Muslims' (Ketkar 1985: 10).

The *Organiser*'s editor, V.P. Bhatia, wrote a series of articles about the Pakistani Punjabi poets writing about Lord Krishna and their affection for him. No one made a hue and cry over it. The Muslims were delighted to have Atal Behari Vajpayee attending the *mushayara* on the sands of a Mumbai *chowpatti* and reciting his poetry. He was the star attraction. In an

inter-community dinner in Mumbai, Maulana Nadvi, the
Imam of Mumbai said, 'All Indians must live like brothers'
(Ketkar 1985: 5, 10, 13, 14, 22). Deoras met Sheikh Abdulla
of Jammu and Kashmir in 1979. The National Conference
backed the BJP for the election of the mayoralty of Jammu.
On being questioned about the alliance, Sheikh Abdulla shot
back, asking, 'Are the Jan Sanghis not Indians? Are they not
men?' (Ketkar 1985: 5, 10, 13, 14, 22). A little later in time, in
1980, Mr C. Mohammad Koya, the then Chief Minister of
Kerala, said, 'The RSS bogey cannot be used any longer to
frighten us' (Malkani 1980: 107). As late as 1 August 1980, a
ceremony of releasing a long-playing record with two songs,
one dedicated to Dr Hedgewar and the other to Golwalkar,
was held. The songs were sung by no less a person than
Sudhir Phadke. The function was presided over by Deoras.
The meeting opened with all those present standing up to
pay homage to Mohammad Rafi, who had died the previous
day.

The Reactions within the RSS

The RSS cadre was told that in the expanded perimeter of
Hindutva, non-Hindus could also come in and be accommodated—they could be even allowed to come into the
shakhas. The reactions were instantaneous and many. Even
at the level of the national representative body of the RSS,
the Akhil Bharatiya Pratinidhi Sabha, Deoras was lambasted
by none other than the then provincial deputy chief of
Maharashtra, the famous criminal lawyer of Pune, Baba
Bhide. Deoras heard him through patiently. Baba Bhide's
accusations made it appear as though the RSS of Hedgewar
was on sale. It was being broken down in pieces and hacked
to death. How does anyone expect the RSS to forget the
atrocities Muslims have committed upon the Hindus, Hindu
women and Hindu religious places, Deoras was asked. Why

was he speaking of letting the same Muslims into the fold now, out of the blue?

Mr K.B. Limaye, an old-time Hindu Mahasabha loyalist who had been the chief of Maharashtra RSS, wrote to Deoras,

> You have been given the position of the chief of the RSS of Dr Hedgewar. Kindly run that Sangh and try to foster its growth. Do not try to change it. If you think a change is necessary start a new RSS. Leave the RSS of Doctorji for the Hindu consolidation to us. If you change this RSS....I will not be able to have any relationship with that Sangh. (Chouthaiwale n.d.)

This letter reflected the confusion and the unhappy, bitter turmoil of most of the loyal RSS workers. Many senior level workers in Kendriya Karyakari Mandal, the highest body of the RSS, too expressed their displeasure. The organisation and its cadre could neither digest the idea, nor grasp the strategic significance of the move, the time at which it was made, the credibility and acceptance it would gain them in the society and rid of them of the problems they were faced with, the paradigms it would change in the national life. At that time—and even more so now, in hindsight—it became glaringly apparent that Deoras was light years ahead of his organisation.

The Media and the Opponents of the RSS over the Muslim Entrance

How did the media and the erstwhile political opponents of the RSS react to Deoras' initiatives? There was a huge blockade on the Mumbai civic reception. The *Times of India* accorded it a small place, that of a 4-inch column on the third page. The media boycotted the reporting of this event completely. All those who had hounded the RSS as a communal organisation, the quintessence of Muslim hatred, did not have one word of praise for this man. No one even welcomed it. No one extended any support for this idea. Were they suddenly of the opinion that 'it is wrong on the part of RSS to do this?' Did they think that here was this one organisation which would save Hindus, and by implication, all of them who were critical of it as well, from Muslims? Did they believe that the RSS should not turn Muslim-friendly? After all, whatever one may say about the RSS, do we not know better than to trust Muslims? We cannot say this openly, but we will certainly not praise this initiative.

Those who should have been most delighted pointedly remained non-committal and reticent to acknowledge the turn of events. Were they suddenly aware that if Deoras changed the scheme of things, their favourite whipping boy would lose its charm? Whither pleasure? Whither vendetta? All those who should have come in support of Deoras' initiatives in 1977 but failed to do so have to answer for their inaction. Today if they want to blame the 'hardliners within RSS', where were they when the more egalitarian, the softer, the better element was asking for their support? They also have to answer for the fact that the combined effect of this deliberate withholding of support from without and the cold reception of this idea from within the rank and file of the RSS led to an entirely different turn of events, later taking the shape of something the nation is still stuck with.[4] For two and a half years Deoras persisted with the idea; gradually he withdrew from it. Everybody seemed to have missed the point then.

Was Deoras naive enough to think that Muslims would make a beeline for the RSS *shakhas* as soon as he made his announcement? Was the RSS so naive that it was rattled or frightened by the prospect of success of such an initiative? Were the hitherto opponents of the RSS thinking that Deoras had taken the wind out of their sails and left them nowhere in the game of political expediency, despite his apparent innocence? After so many years, it has still not occurred to the polity that it was a strategic move on Deoras' part, a concrete practical move to begin a new era. Symbolically, I would rank it on the same level as the Dandi March. Deoras knew well enough that things were not going to change overnight. He also knew the necessity of such a move.

Imagine for a moment that Deoras' move had received extensive popular support. Within the perimeter of appeasement, what is the problem of Muslims in this country? The problem is that appeasement keeps them in ghettos under the orthodox, deprives them of modern education, uses them as a vote bank, but does not emancipate them. Those who want to appease them do so to remain in power, at the cost of the Muslim community at large. This is increasingly being realised within the Muslim community. Imagine Muslims breaking this ghetto and joining hands with the RSS and the other opposition parties, as they did when they overthrew the Indira Gandhi government. I need not wax eloquent any further, but merely point out that it could have been the beginning of bringing the Muslims to the mainstream, which the orthodox *mullah*s have not allowed to happen. If this alliance had remained, if the opposition, then in power, had the wise sense to continue in power instead of devising policies of subtraction, rooted in prejudice and hate, which way would we have gone as a nation? Would we still have gone in that direction we ended up going in reality, or perhaps were forced to go towards?

What Did the Nation Lose in the Janata Experiment?

The issue was wonderfully summarised by Nayantara Sehgal, who herself comes from the Nehru family. Ms Sehgal wrote an article titled 'For Whom the Bell Tolls' in *The Indian Express* on 15 May 1979, where she wrote, 'The RSS has grown stronger and obviously has a role to play that can either set Hinduism on a progressive path or turn it inward upon itself in a self satisfied growing exclusiveness.' Ms Sehgal thought very strongly and highly of the RSS, to the extent of appearing to plead the RSS people on their own behalf not to do what appeared to be in the offing at that time,

> Can RSS become a movement for revolutionary change? In this kind of confusion where no logic seems to prevail, it is certainly not beyond the possibility that the RSS which fought a dictatorship should rally itself along new lines and pit itself against evils that no legislation, no government and no party have so far been able to eradicate. (Sehgal 1979)

Deoras had to get his cadre to the new position of admitting Muslims. He had to keep the initiative alive without allowing his own men to accuse him of dilution of the original stand and standards. The later events do suggest that the RSS, in the late 1990s and early 2000s, decided to go back to its own shell, and as predicted by Ms Sehgal, in the 'self satisfied growing exclusiveness' (1979). Yet, with all that was happening, the pitch got queered and the initiative over the entry of Muslims in the RSS was lost and was, in the end, quietly closed.

Deoras was busy with something as significant as opening doors to the Muslims in 1977. He was busy keeping the Janata Party alliance intact and in power. People like Madhu Limaye, once the pleasures of the initial camaraderie and the honeymoon with the RSS died, started thinking of utilising the strength of the RSS for their own promotion. The first move occurred by inviting and then demanding the RSS to dissolve itself and merge with the Janata Party. None of us — and least of all Deoras — were naive young children, unable to recognise the true worth of Limaye as well as others like him who had not even done a day's hard work and dirtied their hands in the building of an organisation. That there was a double game was obvious — one to use the RSS' strength, numerical or otherwise, its disciplined nature for their own ends, as their handmaiden; the second to destroy it once it was dissolved within the Janata Party. The RSS rejected the demand.

Displeased, the Janata Party leaders found another ploy. In order to retain the Muslim vote, they also started the process of appeasement. In the campaign, they started saying that the RSS has changed, and in order to make others believe the same, a number of uninvited suggestions were made. These suggestions were: the RSS should allow Muslims to come in, should give up the staunch Hindu stand, should change their flag, should allow the appointment of the RSS officers only through elections, and so on. Some prominent leaders who had a sympathetic attitude towards and a good relationship with the RSS sent forth these suggestions. The newspapers wrote articles to that effect. Deoras reacted by keeping quiet, neither challenging nor supporting these suggestions, not even talking about them, and continued to work as before. The RSS cadre thought this quiet response to be very queer.

The other fear of the few constituents of the Janata government was the increasing influence of the erstwhile BJS cadre and ministers within the Janata Party organisation and in the government itself. The constituents could have started feeling that they would appear belittled in front of the former BJS cadre and lose their grip on the organisation. As the suggestions to 'reform' the RSS were ignored, they were restless. The insistence on making Hindutva an unholy icon did not succeed. It was only natural that the mischievous leadership found some other idea to insult the RSS and the loyalists who were sharing power with them. The ruling coalition parties did not like the stability.

The new ploy was 'dual loyalty'. An erstwhile RSS member who was a MP in the Janata coalition, it was said, would have to disown and severe his links with the RSS and should whole-heartedly lay his loyalty at the altar of the Janata Party. The erstwhile BJS members could not accept any post in the RSS organisation (which incidentally never was a practice), could not talk or propagate the RSS' principles and had to abandon the concept of Hindutva. They were also expected to give up their RSS affiliation, even the daily RSS branch activity. It is difficult to imagine the arrogance of those who made such demands. These were people sworn to be the ardent believers of the system of our democratic nation, and were abusing the RSS for its fascist tendencies even as they dictated terms to the RSS. Ironically, these people were free and in power in the centre and several state governments because of the RSS! I have never encountered anything more astounding in my life. Here was Deoras balancing his organisation cadre and the new move, which he knew would meet with dire opposition. In the Janata Party, people were neither ready nor able to understand his position. Or perhaps they were unwilling to do so in order to strengthen his attempt, which is why they busied themselves queering the pitch.

Day in and day out, the 99 BJS MPs were being insulted. In order to keep the alliance, they endured the insults, sometimes silently, sometimes vocally. The stridency for separating them from their mother organisation increased. The forward-looking intelligentsia and the leading, respected (whither respectable?) journalists accepted these demands as legitimate. It was calculated that the BJS members would not tolerate these insulting demands and leave the cabinet, leaving the government open for these people to do whatever they feel like. Other leaders in the Janata Party, however, were aware of the dirty game and decided to approach the Sarkaryavah Prof. Rajendra Singh, who was based at Delhi, as well as other office bearers of the RSS in Delhi. Chandrashekhar was given the responsibility to speak to Deoras, to request him to ask the former BJS members to bear with these insults for some more time. In order to preserve the alliance in power, Deoras went to the Nagpur airport to meet Chandrashekhar. It was a one-to-one meeting in the VIP lounge of the airport, which lasted about 90 minutes. The nature of the discussions and the decisions reached can be inferred by the events and the policy followed by the RSS in particular afterwards, and in informal discussions, of which Chouthaiwale has drawn a neat picture and brought out the innards of this dirty game.

Chandrashekhar was clearly told that the RSS would not change its ideological base, and would not allow any section, group or party to conduct anti-national activity. Except for the RSS office bearers, any other *swayamsevak* was free to participate in any party or organisation, according to his taste and inclinations. There would be no need to put any restriction on that. The Jan Sangh members should follow the party discipline and work accordingly. They would decide about the RSS on their own—the RSS would not take any part in the decision-making process. Yet, the constant and uninterruptible bond between them and the RSS was such that the RSS would never tell them not to participate in the RSS in any form whatsoever.

Given the arrogant, impractical and cantankerous nature of nearly half the Janata ministers as well as their lack of sound understanding of constructive work, their blind hatred of the RSS, their megalomania and its preservation without regard to the national interest, it was clear that they were not interested in the continuation of the Janata rule. The people of this country therefore concluded that parties other than the Congress are incapable of ruling—which is precisely what they brought home and forced upon the Janata Party in 1980. If the Janata Party was to break on the issue of dual loyalty, the BJS and the RSS would have been blamed roundly. This was not acceptable to the RSS–BJS combine.

Hindutva Plank Rolled Back

In order to preserve the Janata experiment, the RSS–BJS combine adopted some cautious changes.· Except for a few and inevitable functions as a *swayamsevak*, the RSS workers in politics would not keep any close contact with the organisation. Since the Hindutva icon was the bone of contention and maligning tool, even the senior office bearers of the RSS decided to sidestep the matter, minimise the mention of Hindutva in their public speeches and press releases, even in the lectures delivered before RSS-only gatherings like officers' training camps, winter camps, and so on, and other speeches for nearly 18 months. It is for the polity to understand how much the RSS had to give up in this effort. Prof. Rajendra Singh, Mr Bhaurao Deoras, who was the mentor of the professor of physics, and Deoras himself were among those who enforced this. Including Deoras, they all made it a point to see that they observed these restrictions.

For whose pleasure did Deoras do this? Prof. Rajendra Singh has described the then leadership of the Janata Party as follows, 'He [Deoras] came from a different mould from those who deliver themselves of the most astoundingly imbalanced statements as soon as they are installed in office, however small and insignificant and equally ephemeral, because with the least popular support their egos are inflated' (Chari unpublished). The sins committed by the constituents of the Janata Party in pulling the RSS down by hook or crook have not been sufficiently punished, even after 30 years. The successors of the same elements continue to see to that a strong alternative to the Congress does not emerge. The polity are equally to be blamed, or even more, for not forcing these pseudo-intellectuals to the small niche they deserve.

Simple men like Deoras, Rajjubhaiya and Bhaurao defeated the machinations of the politically astute Janata leadership. When all this did not seem to work, the next extension of the perversion was brought out. The Jan Sangh MPs were asked to get a declaration from the RSS that they need not be bound by any manner of expectations as *swayamsevak* on the part of the parent organisation. There was a furore in the RSS–BJS camp. Initially, the whole exercise was ridiculed. When the Janata leadership insisted on this demand, there was an open rebellion of all the BJS MPs, and the even larger number of MLAs in the seven or eight north Indian states that went to election after the Janata Party came to power. Insults were mounting. It was getting clearer by the day that the Socialists had restarted their old game and were going back to their old brand of hatred. That they no longer wanted to stay with the erstwhile RSS–BJS combine and were out to create mischief became evident. It was more than apparent that they had no concern over the price the nation had paid for this victory. They had no realisation how important it was to keep the Congress away from power. It was a pitiable show from those who claimed to be intellectuals and who had the nation's sanction to rule because of this claim.

As a last resort, a letter signed by Deoras was handed over, saying that all the MPs and MLAs who had an allegiance to the RSS were thereby freed from the expectation to attend the daily *shakha* functions of the RSS (Joshi 1996: 35). Deoras was questioned over this act within the organisation. His smiling reply evinced his faith on the followers of his creed,

> Whatever I may write to these people, will any one of our MP or an MLA ever give up his loyalty to RSS? But, on the other hand, if such a letter satisfies the partners in power and if they remain in power because of that it will be more desirable. (Chouthaiwale n.d.)

We wondered at his attitude. The message that went out was clear: Roll back Hindutva. It is important that this alliance should remain in place. It should keep Mrs Gandhi and her Congress away from power. Get accustomed to power. Get to know how to use it. If we cannot talk of Hindutva for a while lest the alliance breaks, let us not do it.

A few years later, Deoras spoke of Abraham Lincoln. The parallels are striking and no comments are necessary.

> The noble idea of removal of slavery was paramount and dear to Lincoln. He could clearly see that any assertion to that effect would lead to civil war. He put aside even his noble goal of ending slavery for a few years. Later when he could not take it any longer he abolished it at the cost of civil war. (Bondale unpublished)

The Hindu chauvinists who merely go around shouting the *'Garvase Kaho'* slogan, need to listen to these episodes more attentively. They were not even remotely aware of the gory spectacle that they were portraying by continuing to raise the slogans of Ram Janmabhoomi and embarrassing the coalition led by the BJP. They had forgotten that some of them were raised with the purity and probity of the intensely polite former RSS chief called Golwalkar. They were calling their own man, the premier of the country, impotent because he was not moving in a direction they wished him to. Was Ram Janmabhoomi the alpha and omega of all that remained to be done in the country and still is? Were there no other issues whatsoever of greater importance for their very own government to deal with? They were not able to recollect that Deoras considered rolling back Hindutva, much more of their life's creed and soul than even Sri Ram is, putting it aside for other important practical reasons, just about 30 years ago.

To what extent was Deoras ready to roll back Hindutva to keep the alliance in place? An example will make it clear. One of the compulsions for the Ramakrishna Math was to preserve the institutes of the Math from predators. The only way to save them was to declare themselves a minority sect and obtain the permission to be free of audit from any agency under Section 30 (i and ii) of the constitution. Every Hindu was angry and denounced the move. Deoras was the only one to say, 'Try to understand the circumstances under which the Math would have had to go and do this' (Chouthaiwale n.d.). Obviously during that time he was not prepared to allow or give rise to any strident Hindu sentiment, lest it hurt the continuation of the alliance.

Deoras had appealed to the Janata Party to do the 'works that would be of help to people, of developmental nature'. They did not have time for that. Morarji Desai, instead of concentrating on that, was making a fool of himself by pursuing the single-point agenda of vendetta against Mrs Gandhi at all costs, not heading Deoras' plea to 'forgive and forget'. By simply refusing to appear before the Shah Commission, not even to defend herself, Indira Gandhi had defeated the very purpose of the commission easily. The Indian public did not like men going after a defeated woman, once the premier of the country, in this manner. Thengadi, a colleague of Deoras, asked him, 'Forgive we will. But how can we forget what Mrs Gandhi has done to us?' Deoras is reported to have said, 'Are we going to hand over to the new generation a legacy of perpetual hatred and alienation to create such a distance with the Congress that will never be bridged?' (conversations with an insider who does not wish to be named, August 2007).

Imprinting the RSS on the Polity

We have come ahead in time. Knowing what these people were worth, Deoras was busy imprinting his RSS on the minds of people of this country at large, and did so effectively, without any ambiguity and apology. The story will have to date back to 19 November 1977, when one of the most horrible disasters hit coastal Andhra. Before anyone could hear of that, the defeated former prime minister of the country, Mrs Gandhi, was there. What she saw before her were people in *khaki* shorts, burning and disposing of the dead bodies of people, a work no one wanted to do then or thereafter, because of the stench and the fear of disease. She asked who they were. *The Times of India*, Mumbai did justice to their work by placing in a box in the centre of the first page, with Mrs Gandhi's question and its answer, 'They are RSS.'

That one news item changed the world for the RSS for the second time in six months in 1977. Characteristically, the RSS named itself there as the Shava Sena—the army for (disposition of) corpses. Deoras did not lose time. He, as is said in the business parlance, thought through the problem. After the rescue and disposal of the dead, and control of diseases was accomplished, he got the Deendayal Research

Institute, Gonda, Uttar Pradesh to reconstruct the village, building many more amenities and facilities in it than existed before. He named it himself as Deendayalpuram, and dedicated it to the nation. He proudly went around telling everyone of the heroism of his *swayamsevak*s. He virtually enacted a thesis that the RSS is not just synonymous with *shakha* activities, but with each and every idea and work, man and event, meant for the betterment of the society. This, in some way, was also the beginning of his thesis of *seva karya*, the work of service, as the work of the *shakha*. Later he made it formal by saying that one *shakha* is one *seva karya* attached to it.

Deoras had turned the earlier ideas of de-recognition on its head:

> RSS work alone does not necessarily mean good work. Any good work that sustains or makes society better or stronger is RSS work. Anybody who thinks this to be 'his' country and did good work does RSS work. Becoming or remaining a formal swayamsevak, doing a ritual of attending a shakha did not remain a precondition. (Conversations with an insider who does not wish to be named, August 2007)

With his very vocal and emphatic descriptions of the deeds of his *swayamsevak*s, an extremely large section of 'sympathisers' developed in society who had a good word for the RSS, helpful and influential. Deoras knew the potential of this combine — the RSS worker and the sympathiser; he was aware of the strength it could carry.

The year 1973 saw him going out to the old *swayamsevak*s and bringing them back to the fold. In 1974, he moved to bring the Dalit brethren in. In 1977, he went out of his way to get the Muslims in. And now, in the post-Emergency days, while he was trying to save the government, he decided to thrust the RSS upon the minds of people. In doing so, the one conceptual barrier which did not exist in his case was the centrality paradigm of the RSS. I have talked about this in detail. Each good work was his, but there were special ones. Gonda had emerged as the brainchild of Nana Deshmukh. His models of rural development had started gaining acknowledgement. In the Gangetic alluvial planes of Uttar Pradesh, where a low level of water was available in the subsoil, they made wooden tube wells and a dozen other experiments possible. Deoras decided to hold a much-publicised ceremony and called the then president of India, Mr Neelam Sanjeeva Reddy, to inaugurate the ceremony, dedicating the project to the nation.

There were interesting pictures of Deoras sitting with the president on the ground for having food among the poor and the downtrodden as well as the workers of DRI. Interesting stories were heard (hopefully not true but cannot be vouched for) of Mr Reddy being warned of the possibility of the RSS using mesmerism and even black magic. The rumours could be true or false, but since Mr Reddy came out of the event unscathed, it can safely be assumed that the mesmerism and the black magic was either not practised or remained ineffective. The symbolic significance of the event, bringing together disparate political denominations for social reconstruction, was great. Here was a political party in diehard opposition to the one which had ruled for so long. The president, appointed by the premier of the defeated opposition party, who had signed the declaration of Emergency, was attending the function of the RSS, the so-called evil incarnate of modern India. Looking ahead in years, it is noteworthy that when Atal Bihari Vajpayee was the premier, the president chosen and installed by him never came anywhere near the RSS' functions. The far-sightedness and largesse of the Deoras era was gone.

Deoras would not be satisfied with just this, however. He then decided to play another message out by organising a fantastic rally of young children, all trained by the chain of Saraswati Shishu Mandirs across the country. Sixteen thousand children took part in the rally in New Delhi, with Deoras presiding over it and proudly declaring the Shishu Mandirs' work as the work of the RSS. The *Organiser* published beautiful pictures of that rally of smartly dressed children performing wonderfully well-trained activities on the ground.

Deoras had a natural concern about the downtrodden, the underdeveloped and those in remote places, in jungles, in the remote areas of the North-East, and so on. Critics will do well to remember that the RSS has done yeoman's work in those remote jungle areas, inhabited only by tribals, the *vanvasi* brethren of us mainland Hindus, since 1952. The Bhavani Shankar Niyogi Commission's report of the same year listed approximately 17,000 foreign and nearly 177,000 native Christian missionaries in India then. Tribal work has been one of the toughest challenges of our country, and apart from these missionaries and stray works done by others, it is only the RSS which has consistently taken up, expanded and qualitatively developed the life of *vanvasis* in this belt, stretching from Mumbai, cutting the country in two halves as it traverses through the lower Gujarat, Khandesh of Maharashtra, through Chhattigarh, Orissa, south Bihar (now Jharkhand) and marching on to the north-eastern states. Five crores of people of 350 castes and as many dialects stay in the jungles, stay for and by the jungles. They have a rich culture of their own, but are for millennia a perpetually starved section of the Hindu society. The RSS genius, intelligence or the bright conception of how work should be done has reached its culmination in their tribal work. It will take volumes to describe it, but suffice it to say that Deoras made it into an all-India body and gave the reigns of the body to one of the most imaginative, clear-headed and capable man in the RSS—Bhaskar Kalambi.

Mrs Gandhi Returns to Power

Even Deoras failed against the colossal intellectual bankruptcy, the stupidity, the monumental vanity and megalomania, both within and outside the Janata Party. Has history, the press or the electronic media, ever blamed them? Have they come down forcefully on the conceited self-centred attitudes of Morarji Desai, Charan Singh, Jagjivan Ram and the Socialists that led to the fall? Choudhary Charan Singhji went to the funeral pyre with a fulfilled desire to be the prime minister of this country. Mrs Gandhi, who had retained her base in the southern states, was now rooted in the northern states as well, where the *matadar raja* or the voter king literally gave all the Janata Party members a hack. The ones who suffered somewhat unjustifiably were the erstwhile BJS members. The Emergency had shown the ordinary man the power of his ballot. In 1980, when he saw that these jokers were incapable of handling power, he handed it over to Mrs Gandhi again. With the additional support of the southern and north-eastern states, she returned with a thumping majority. This is the biggest tragedy of independent India, surpassing even the Partition. We will see in the next chapter the horrible consequences of this India went through, the remedy Deoras tried to implement and where it led us to.

Notes

1. I have drawn extensively on the accounts of Mr Baburao Chouthaiwale to describe the events in the troubled era of Janata Raj of 1977 through 1979. Mr Chouthaiwale was the office chief of Deoras for long years. Some more information has been taken from *A Fruitful Life* (Chari n.d.).
2. There were many key people who had gone underground during Emergency. These were the ones who were called the chiefs of RSS by Deoras, contrasting himself as a chief who was sitting in jail. They included D.B. Thengadi, M.N. Pingale, Madhav Muley, Bhaurao Deoras, Bapurao Moghe, Nanaji Deshmukh, Rajjubhaiya and others, and they were not in favour of Deoras undertaking a fast unto death.
3. Atal Bihari Vajpayee wrote an editorial article in *The Indian Express* on 2 August 1979. On the face of it, the article appeared to advise various

players, including the RSS, on a few matters, apparently trying to please those within the Janata Party who were hell-bent on accusing the RSS–BJS of a variety of things. It can, however, be clearly read as a ploy to mellow things down so that the regime could continue.

4. The failure of the Muslim inclusion for reasons described above led to a very different turn of events, not necessarily helpful, and far more tragic, which left a vitiated atmosphere of hatred in the 20 years to follow. This is the thesis I have defended in the subsequent chapters.

6

The BJP, the Parivar and Deoras: 1980–85

———— • ✦ • ————

The Formation of the Bharatiya Jan Sangh[1]

The Bharatiya Jan Sangh (BJS) was formed after Gandhi's murder, out of the reality that the Congress had closed its doors to all RSS men. Thus the birth of the BJS was in the womb of untouchability. Had that not happened, the Congress as a bigger political force and the RSS as a social force facilitated by the government, becoming bigger day by day, would have drawn a different picture of the country. The BJP also took birth because the Socialists and others in the Janata government found the RSS untouchable.

Shyama Prasad Mukherjee was a pariah in the Hindu Mahasabha because he demanded that Muslims should be allowed to be members as well. The RSS decided to go with Shyama Prasad. Deoras was not sheepish about saying that he considered political power necessary to forward his work and thesis. The hypocrisy or the double game that the RSS had played over years with respect to their relationship with the BJS was not Deoras' creed.

Deendayal built the BJS as a political cadre-based party till 1968. Walter Anderson (please refer to note 1 for further information) has given a lucid, vivid and factual account of how this cadre-based party grew, how Deendayal shaped the party as a common man's party and how he slowly put it in the agitational mould (Anderson and Damle 1987). Finally, in 1967, they had to be counted for power sharing. The first temporary removal of the BJS' tag of political untouchability was in the Sanyukta Vidhayak Dal (SVD) ministries formed in many north Indian states in 1967. The BJS cadre opposed the notion of sharing power with the Communists. Deendayal overcame the opposition by reminding them that rejecting the alliance would be tantamount to fostering political untouchability from the BJS' side, which they otherwise complained of (Advani 2008). They had also shared power with the Communists then in the Delhi Municipal Council, under Advani (Advani 2008).

The experiment did not last; it was a prediction and preview of what was to happen in 1977. Both the parties, the BJS and the Left-wingers, were uncomfortable with each other. They were happier being critical of the government, whichever in power (and that would mean the Congress), by being in the opposition. Deendayal, having made limited progress in terms of electoral success for power or sharing it, philosophised that coalition was the way to power. At that time, it may have been considered pragmatic, but it also offered a hint of how difficult political progress was, or how the BJS was lacking in confidence or vigour. They did not give the impression that they wanted power desperately, not so much for the usual reasons, but with an indomitable belief that they were the ones who could deliver the goods best and do good for the society. The BJS remained in essence an RSS institute, disciplined and cadre-based.

The BJS kept on reacting to issues Mrs Gandhi acted upon. They could never become a forceful spokesman of definite socio-economic policies of an alternate variety. They were opposed to the Nehruvian model of development, but the people never heard of what alternative they wanted. Most of their time was used up to react to the National Integration Committee, or to defend themselves and the RSS from accusations of being Muslim-haters, Gandhi-murderers and communalists by Subhadra Joshi and co. From 1967 to 1984, Indira Gandhi succeeded in her gamesmanship, and the BJS looked as if their single-point agenda was 'Indira Hatao' (Remove Indira), especially after 1980.

The Politico-social Philosophy of the BJS

It would not be unexpected to find one who is amused or surprised to learn that the BJS had plenty to say on politico-socio-economic issues, since not many of their ideas ever reached the popular media. In the early 1970s (probably), they published a detailed but small book named *Siddhant Ani Neeti* (The Founding Principle, the Policy and Strategy). It does not have the publication date, making it difficult to relate to time. No one, not even the cadre, came to see or possess the book. It does not matter whether one agrees or not, but the fact there was an avowed opinion presented in it. This booklet (*Siddhant Ani Neeti* n.d.), Deendayal's *Bharatiya Artha Neeti* (Upadhyay 1957) and elements of Gandhi and Lohia's thought (Parameshwaran 1978) form the basis of their philosophy, which has been analysed in Anderson and Damle's (1987) book.

For the BJS, democracy was the tool. A theocratic state was not acceptable to the BJS. It believed in the rule of law and the state's responsibility to provide the necessary facilitation for the individual to do his work and duty and protect his rights. The BJS also believed that the state must guarantee the rights of the individual as well as his choice of religious practices with full respect to any and all religions.

The BJS advocated not only political but social as well as economic democracy as an integrated system. Representation by election, freedom of enterprise and consumption, equal opportunity and respect in social milieu and equality before law are the main characteristics of democracy as advocated by the BJS. Within the right of accumulating private wealth, there was the idea of limits placed to the extent this ownership could be allowed.

The BJS advocated decentralised means of production geographically, integrated through the different classes of industry. They had identified, even then, modern science and technology as conducive to decentralisation. They wanted to restructure economic and social institutions. This was in stark contrast with the centralised model of Communist Russia and Nehru's infrastructural development model. Centralisation of economic as well as political power was not acceptable, since it led to restriction of the democratic processes and human freedom. The BJS considered a strong centre and a unitary state as necessary because of the need to check the centrifugal and divisive regional and linguistic forces. While Schumacher's small was beautiful, a minimum bigness was considered necessary by the BJS.

The individual, the BJS believed, should be the centre of all planning. Education, it believed, should enable development, employment and leisure. It opposed government control of education and demanded free education till middle-school level. The language policy of the BJS advocation was education through local and Hindi language from primary to higher levels.

The political agenda of the BJS spoke of a united extended India, and that the people who love this land and stay on it are one people, despite diversities. It believed that many perverted practices needed to be routed out to bring homogeneity to the Indian society. It offered an alternative administrative structure featuring Panchayats, development blocks and a Janpad on the basis of commonalities, which would be governed by elected representatives. These

Janpads were not states — they could make local subordinate legislation and suggest all-India legislations to be enacted at a central Parliament. Administrators would be required to coordinate several Janpads. The BJS was, however, fairly ambiguous about the relationship between these Janpads and the provincial states, which they did not negate completely.

The BJS' wage policy stated that the ratio between the highest to the lowest paid should be 1:20. There should be parity between the local and central wage structures as well. It upheld agitation for the rights of workers. Instead of being only reformist in orientation, the BJS decided to organise discontent of the weaker sections and take on as a party a more militant and dynamic stand. They made it a policy to approach all problems from the common man's viewpoint and welfare. A share in the decision and management for the workers was an important declaration. Attempts were made after the 1971–72 electoral debacles to shed its conservative image and to develop a base among the poor.

Some of its most vocal stands, which were never projected very well for the outside world but caused internal organisational damage, was the insistence on abolishing *zamindari* (ownership of a large landmass by an individual or a family, often tilled by landless labour), putting a ceiling on the maximum landholding, as well as their insistence on the land belonging to the tiller. The BJS clearly opposed large dams and were in favour of small dams, canals and other irrigational methods to reduce the dependence of the farmers on rain and its vagaries. They called for common pastures, acknowledged the need for manure but suggested a more supportive action for choosing the right ones; they were uncomfortable with chemical manure used without organic manure. They made a prominent argument on hybrids and other foreign varieties of crops, which might hold even today. They were against rash replacements of the disease resistant, environmental condition resistant, native crops, developed over millenniums, which did not fail completely under adverse conditions. Crop failures (even today) being common in India due to the vagaries of monsoon, the BJS' claim was that hybrids could not stand these irregularities as strongly as the native crops were able to (conversations with Golwalkar, late 1960s). Hybrids also required higher resources like water and were less disease-resistant, but had the power to produce more.

Despite the small size of Deendayal's *Bharatiya Artha Neeti*, it was replete with action-oriented plans. What was projected to the public instead was Deendayal's integral humanism (1967). This is not to say it does not deserve to be projected, though we have seen the kind of sense it conveys, then and even today. The Bharatiya Mazdoor Sangh also had considerable details for implementation and practice in the labour area in the late 1960s (Thengadi, Gokhale and Mehata 1968). The *Labour Policy*, published in 1967, had nothing much to do with Hindu Rashtra as such. But it certainly had many operational details which they saw fit to implement then. As late as in 1972 and later, Thengadi (1972b, 1984a) was arguing over industrial guilds and functional representations, though he was making the fundamental error of basing things on the *Chaturvarnya* model. Thengadi's otherwise reticent attitude and derisive comments on anyone asking for a 'blueprint' disappeared there, to be replaced with the effusive descriptions of how this model would work. Subramanyam Swamy, the Harvard scholar, dutifully paid homage to this model.

Gandhi, Lohia and Deendayal

Vasant Nargolkar, a Sarvoday leader, explicitly states that it was Lohia and Deendayal who spoke the language of Gandhi in abolishing poverty and rural unemployment. Political and economic decentralisation was the remedy for all three of them. In economic terms, it meant decentralisation of the means of production, simpler machines and appropriate technology. All three were opposed to the Western kind of industrial revolution. They were also opposed to both Capitalism and Communism, since both concentrated power, economic and political. All were, in principle, agreed on the idea of trusteeship of property.

None of them were opposed to the nationalisation of a few key industries like defence, but on the whole believed that production should come from smaller units and small factories, even from one's home. All of them were in favour of planning from the bottom and upwards. Minimalisation of state power and devolution of power to lower levels were their main themes. Non-violence and identifying with the poor was common to all three as well. Their conception of man was identical. Deendayal's Dharma and Gandhi's application of moral principles to politics were the same thing. In a joint statement in 1964, Lohia and Deendayal urged for a loose federation of Pakistan and India (Advani 2008). Both criticised the non-alignment policy of India, replacing it with enlightened self-interest of the nation. Differing ideologies did not figure in their statement. They were Indians to the core, not Westernised Anglophiles like Nehru. Their agreement is in the fundamentals, their differences peripheral.

The BJS in fact had plenty to say, much of it worth its while, which could make them look a far more inclusive party, representing more groups than just the urban middle class. The popular media never gave the BJS a chance to put up their thesis. Their political untouchability had assumed a new form — media blockade.

Deendayal was found dead in the yards of the Mughalsarai railway station during the reign of Mrs Gandhi in 1968. The most important event in the life of Mrs Gandhi had taken place. The one man who could have kept the scholarship within the BJS alive, its character vibrant and its ideology against political expediency intact, who could have solidly built the organisation, coupling it with its legislative wing and caused steady political advancement of it, was gone (conversations with Raghunath Ganesh Kelkar, a close friend of Moropant Pingale, and Balasaheb Deoras since 1948, also well acquainted with Golwalkar).

The BJS was then reduced to a party reacting to Mrs Gandhi. The abolition of privy purse was a symbolic act. The BJS' opposition to it was probably perceived as a party protecting the interests of the rich. The nationalisation of banks by Mrs Gandhi was a huge blunder economically, and therefore rightly opposed by the BJS, but it did not earn them any points with the common man. Then, in 1971, Bangaladesh was liberated by Mrs Gandhi. The BJS joined the bandwagon of praising her to the hilt. But they also had an electoral debacle in 1971–72. 'Garibi Hatao' (Remove Poverty) was again a cruel symbolism on the poor, but it carried the masses with Mrs Gandhi. The BJS had no effective slogans to counter. The drought years of 1971 and 1972 followed. In 1973, Golwalkar died and Deoras succeeded him. The whirlwind of the Jay Prakash movement, the Emergency and the fall of the Janata Government is now history.

Thus, in 1980, Deoras and his RSS found themselves in a situation where the country was in unrest, and divisive and secessionist tendencies were developing all over as a series of setbacks, ripping through the fabric of nation and its unity. Sans the political power, the RSS was now the lone and last man standing to fight it back, its political ally not being of much help. Every attempt to hold the nation together was getting pushed back, getting defeated badly. We in the RSS had a distinct sense that no matter how much we strived, there were just too many forces, too big for a single organisation to counter and set things right. I will review these years briefly to bring it to a different perspective, not hitherto presented, about what Deoras and the RSS did from 1980 onwards, till December 1992, when the Babri Masjid was demolished.

The Ineffective Decade-long Pathetic March of the BJP

The signal deviation of the Bharatiya Janata Party (BJP), formed in April 1980, was to adopt 'Gandhian Socialism'. This had several fakes associated with it. As the BJS, they were not identified in any manner with Gandhi or Socialism. Mrs Gandhi had not won on the plank of either. The two terms themselves are neither congruous nor synonymous, nor can they be juxtaposed together. It was, and rightfully so, viewed as abandoning their base, their forte, their very character. The BJP may not think so, but the thousand-eyed people of this nation saw and disliked it. Assuming so unconvincing a character shattered the unseen sympathy. People credited them of gimmickry, political or otherwise. There was no credibility, authenticity and the power of ringing truth associable with this new stance. In less than four years, the BJP abandoned it. Had the BJP become so smug that they thought the fact that it was coming from Vajpayee would make the cadre and the people accept their new, changed stance as the sure-shot mantra, or did they feel that there was no need to take cognizance of the feeling of their cadre?

The RSS reacted vociferously; Vijayaraje Scindia in the open session lambasted the slogan and had to be somehow placated to accept it. Deoras bore with it stoically, even defended the Vajpayee–Advani duo by mentioning their experiences. I asked one of the seniormost RSS functionaries, Yadavrao Joshi, for an explanation for it in 1981. He said, 'Don't worry. The bird will come home to roost.' 'But the time lost before it did?' 'In the life of a nation a few years is not much.' We knew that the BJP was doomed if they did not see sense, even if the party cadre did what they were told (it was predictable then, not so nowadays). A Hindu-minded party of cadre base was necessary. The people believed this was necessary. Even the other opposition parties thought it was necessary. Everyone laughed at the BJP. Vajpayee, in particular, went on in his ways oblivious to the reality under his feet, the reaction of his colleagues and others.

The other step the BJP took was to change its constitution by adopting the presidential kind of system, which is the Congress' system (conversations with M.G. Vaidya in November 2007). Nehru and all the subsequent Gandhis till date have used the system to make the party machinery subordinate to them. Most of the Sangh Parivar organisations are, including the RSS, tightly controlled by the General Secretary. Contrary to the belief that the Sarsanghachalak is the reigning deity, it is very much the General Secretary who is in command. Presidents have a different profile. They are accountable to none, although they may be questioned and opposed. Secretary functions more effectively, and is accountable. When the person-centric model comes in instead of issue- or party-centric ones, the voice of democratic freedom goes out by the backdoor.

The BJP returned with two seats in the parliament in 1984. It was a reactive party, aping others, without strategy, without credibility and without its roots and its old character. Having lost the ground contact, it was a caricature of the erstwhile BJS. Deoras took it to his heart. As early as 1984, Dharmadhikari (1989) reported that he was told that Vajpayee never responded, never met, the press in particular included, and is never found at home. Stories about Vajpayee circulated; it is more than that he lead a cavalier life and was involved with the organisation only to a meagre extent. He was the orator of the party, so what else he did for it or with himself no longer mattered. The BJP was the only Parivar organisation not growing.

The Assam Unrest[2,3]

In 1979, the All Assam Students Union (AASU) and the Assam Ganasangram Parishad (AGP) started a peaceful students' agitation (Dharmadhikari 1989). Through this agitation they wanted to end infiltration, a growing menace from Bangladesh, threatening the Assamese individuality and entity. Also important was the fact of Assam being drained of its resources while receiving nothing in return. This accusation was made by Girin Barua of the Assam Jatiyabadi (meaning nationalist) Dal. It became an agitation by the whole of the Assamese society. It was pointing out the neglect of Assam at the hands of the Centre. The Assamese were bitter about Bengalis for long years for various economic and social reasons, principally the superiority complex of Bengalis, their unwillingness to merge with the Assamese people and their attempts to force their language there. The Bangladeshi infiltrators had managed to secure the rights of citizenship, which caused a feeling of insecurity among Assamese people there.

Despite the peaceful and nationalistic nature of the agitation, Assam was declared as a 'disturbed area'. On 6 April 1980, Mrs Gandhi made a perfunctory show of discussions and went to Nagaon to address a Muslim rally. The rounds of talk for deciding the base year to evict refugees repeatedly collapsed around two dates, 1951 and 1971. There was no willingness on the part of the Congress to sort the matter out, one more way of appeasing Muslims.

Deoras in his path-breaking observation, identified a Bangladeshi Hindu coming to India as a refugee and a Bangladeshi Muslim as an infiltrator. He made the world understand what was going on in Bangladesh as far as the Hindus were concerned. Initially, the AASU and the AGP expressed their differences over the infiltrator/refugee differentiation, but later could see the wisdom in Deoras' statement and accepted it as their line as well. In effect, later, it was the AASU and the AGP leaders who went around in mainland India, with the help of the Sangh Parivar, extolling their theories on the infiltrators, even though they remained silent over the issue of Hindu Bengalis coming across (conversations with Shrikant Joshi, a long-time personal secretary to Deoras). Later years did show the nation, through the writings of Taslima Nasreen, the torture Hindus were undergoing in Bangladesh and why they were fleeing from it. Nasreen asked for and was given political asylum in India.

The Divisive and Disruptive Forces Rock the Country

Divisive tendencies in the North-East — Nagaland, Manipur, Meghalaya and Mizoram — were becoming powerful. The revolts had armed backing, with guerrilla warfare as their tactics. Their principal point was that mainland India had never paid much attention to the North-East. No one from mainland India had gone there and resurrected the cultural–emotional bonds. Nobody had or could convince them that it is the mainstream nationalistic flow to which they not only belonged, but also had a secure future in. None had made them understand that by playing into the hands of foreign powers, they would merely become a tool at the hands of a second world power. China, Burma and the CIA had played their part in the tragedy India faced. Missionaries had enormous funds coming from many different Western world agencies, including the CIA. They contributed their human labour by working there for over 100 years, backed by their large-scale conversions.

Virag Pachpore, a journalist who has spent 14 years in the North-East, part of the years as a full-time worker of the Vivekananda Kendra in Arunachal, in his extremely well-documented book, *Indian Church?* (2001), has drawn a detailed picture of how the activities and thinking of the missionaries evolved. The missionaries first fostered the seeds of secessionist tendencies using conversion as a basis. From that they invoked a feeling of alienation, then provoked the people to say that they were not Indians, they were Christians. They destroyed the local traditions by denouncing it as animalistic and gave them a Westernised style of living. The Church then went on to identify tribals and untouchables as the next front and sowed the seeds of the idea of a separate Dalitasthan breaking away from India. The last phase, overall, was the strangest when they married Christian theology to Marxist jargon and came out openly in support of inciting all forms of disobedience, including full-fledged violence. Their targets were two groups: the tribals and the Dalits.

The encirclement theory was current at that time. The American Navy was in Diego Garcia. Relationships with Sri Lanka over the Tamil problem had deteriorated as never before. Bangladesh and China were very much there. Nepal viewed India with suspicion. The American representative in the UN was always at loggerheads with Indian interest, and sided with Pakistan; the veto went either in favour of Pakistan or against India. Punjab and Kashmir were ready to secede; Tamil Nadu sometimes had spoken of autonomy as well, as had Kerala. And all these unrests were supported and fostered by external and big powers. They did not want the country to be stable and become a superpower.

31 May 1981

By May, the demand for a separate Sikh state, Khalistan or Des Punjab, had taken roots in various political factions within the Sikhs. The Sikhs denied having anything to do with Hinduism and insisted that these two were separate entities.[4] Premature dismissals of Akali governments in 1966 and 1977 had made them suspicious of the 'Hindu Government' in the centre. The feeling, as the twisted logic went, was that Sikhs should be a separate nation. Sikhs were made to feel that they were the only ones to have done tremendous sacrifice for the country, but they had not received their dues. Bhindranwale, speaking with the Dnyan Prabodhini group, invented the story that thousands of innocent Sikh youths were being slaughtered, 'We want to remain as equal in this country'.

175

Their fear (concocted or otherwise) was that Hindus will swallow them up and destroy their identity.

As a relief and solace in this atmosphere of fissiparous voices was the universal expression of the completely ignored ordinary men, both Hindu and Sikh: We are one and one with the Indian National Life Stream. The demand for Khalistan is completely impractical, improper and self-destructive; it is a political stunt as a part of the power game. It is the adventurism of a miniscule minority of the extremists.

Yet, the real efforts were to inflame the emotions of people for a separate Khalistan and to spread terror. The poison of hatred being spewed was going down the veins of each Hindu and Sikh, and the damage being wrought was getting bigger. Whatever happened anywhere in Punjab, the point of origin was the Shiromani Gurudwara Prabandhak Committee, the unofficial government of all Sikhs, rolling in money.

The nation has since seen the senseless killings of innocent people for years to come. Punjab killed, therefore Haryana killed, and it continued to rise in geometric proportions. To gain politically, Mrs Gandhi had played people against each other, Hindus and Sikhs had thrown any ideas of nationalism and national unity away. Secession was and remained in the air for four more years.

According to V.N. Gadgil, the former Congress spokesperson, Kashmir was a festering wound, a base for training Khalistani extremists and terrorists and giving them asylum. This was supported by Farooq Abdullah who had even gone and spoken in those camps. He also had headed the UNO delegation loyal to Pakistan. Dr Abdullah had close links with the undoubtedly communal Pak loyalist organisation of Jamiat Tulba and had an electoral pact with them. Moreshwar Tapaswi has reported there were slogans in Srinagar, 'Sikhs and Muslims are brothers. From where has this Hindu creed come?' (Dharmadhikari 1989). There were boards in Srinagar, 'Indian dogs go back!'.

According to Indresh Kumar, the full-timer in charge of the RSS in J&K (accused of having terrorist links in July 2010), anything happening anywhere in the world led to the Hindu in Kashmir coming under threat. This led to widespread fear in the hearts of the Hindus and made them flee the valley. There was also a systematic attempt to destabilise the Hindu-majority Jammu area through colonisation by Muslims, reorganising the Assembly seat areas and or by forcibly converting Hindus. Meanwhile, in as small an area as Jammu, the BJP was divided in three groups actively kicking against each other, giving up their Hindu plank and losing badly. The in-fighting was so bad that Indresh Kumar had to admit that it had been a rude shock to their ideas of discipline. The manoeuvrings of the ruling Congress was not conducive to the emergence of national unity. In Kashmir the terror was unabated, unrest reigned and killings continued. Only the efforts of the military ever since have managed to retain Kashmir in India.

1981

Gujarat had bled badly due to weeks of killings and riots over the issue of 'reservation for the backward classes at the post-graduate levels in medicine'. The society was getting split vertically. Mrs Gandhi met the anti-reservationists by flying them to Delhi, and cowed them down (*India Today* 1981). On 18 March 1985, the state was once again in flames over the matter of the reservations. Politics motivated the crime and the conflagration, divided the people, snatched or retained power at the cost of the nation and the people.

Dalit Conversions Rock the Nation

Meenakshipuram! An entire Dalit village converted itself to an alien faith. Everybody, including the Prime Minster of the country, Mrs Gandhi, sat up and took notice. There was anger and anguish piercing the heart. The secessionist tendencies were afoot, as were killings, riots and animosity. To that was added the sense of alienation from the land that sustained one, evident in this act of change of faith. Everything that common sense dictates people to do for the welfare of the nation was pushed back or destroyed or most callously tossed out of the window. India was aflame and the BJP was touting its 'Gandhian Socialism' as their new tool for political manoeuvring. It was no longer a credible political alternative. The enthusiasm of the common worker, the strength of the party had gone.

The nation needed a destination where one could lead people to meet and unite.

Energising the RSS from Within

This was the situation that the RSS and Deoras found themselves in after the glorious, and in a way, ignominious era of nearly three years after the Emergency. He turned his energy inwards, to rebuild the RSS on a massive scale, raising its spirit and enthusiasm. Finally, whose strength but that of the RSS, and through it the Hindu society, in the long run, mattered? In March 1981, the Karnataka RSS saw an unprecedented concept executed with consummate organisational skill—the Hindu Samajotsav, festival of the Hindu society itself, as a whole. Spearheaded by the RSS machinery, the festival cut across all barriers of caste, creed, language and politics. Tamil Nadu started an initiative called the Hindu Munnani. The RSS, through Hindu Munnani and other initiatives, entrenched themselves in Meenakshipuram and reconverted a large number of people. The Karnataka RSS and the VHP took the lead and strongly persuaded the *Dharmacharyas* and other orthodox monastery *swamis* and *mahants* to go out and visit, eat and sit with the Dalit brethren.

In January 1982, a magnificent Hindu Sangamam was held in Bangalore, a winter camp of some 21,000 volunteers in full uniform to declare the brotherhood of everyone who was born Hindu. This was followed over years with larger versions elsewhere. Deoras' rallies with millions of people in attendance in Kerala continued; the participation of the Ezhavas and the Pullaiahs, the downtrodden of Kerala continued, with women from the *swayamsevak* families attending as well (Bondale unpublished). The RSS was breathing fresh and confident.

To cap it all, the Samarasata Manch (the Forum for Homogeneous Society) was inaugurated in Maharashtra in 1983. The day 14 April was chosen as the date of inauguration, which was also the date of birth of Dr Ambedkar by the English calendar and that of Dr Hedgewar by the Hindu calendar, also its first day, that of Chaitra Shuddha Pratipada. The Samarasata Manch declared the creation of a Hindu society without social inequities and discriminations by synthesising the thinking of these two great men. The position taken by the RSS became decisive in two of the most contentious issues that lent credence to its claim of attempting a homogeneous society. One was the upheaval caused by Dr Ambedkar's book, *The Riddles of Rama and Krishna*, which was not a traditional interpretation. Feelings had run high. The RSS did not allow people to go berserk, exercising its control over the situation. The other one was the change of name of the Marathwada University to Dr Ambedkar University. In the name of social justice and other democratic considerations, the RSS stood by the name change. Had Deoras not been there, it would not have happened.

The RSS, under the banner of Samarasata Manch, took out the Phule Ambedkar Yatra (the two men who had critiqued Hinduism, and Brahmanism in particular, for long years), that traversed Maharashtra for 47 days, covering 7,000 kilometres, attempting social enlightenment and unity. It was followed by the Saint Gadgebaba Samata Award and the institution of the Samarasata Sahitya Parishad (the Literary Federation for Unity and Homogeneity). A developmental agency was started for the nomadic and roving tribes of Maharashtra, the Paradhis, Bhills, Gopals, Mariaiwale, Medhangi Joshi and Devdasis, who lived in extreme poverty without any steady means of sustenance. That was an instance of the visionary and exemplary work done by the RSS volunteers. The tremendous response the society gave to these initiatives wrote new chapters towards the betterment of the down-trodden (Idate 2003).

In a rare amendment in the constitution, the RSS made the service projects an integral part of the daily *shakha* work. The total number of social service projects that are run by the different Parivar organisations today is a few thousand more than 100,000 (conversations with S.D. Damle, RSS officer in Mumbai, official figure as of October 2007). A large number of them are in the tribal areas of Madhya Pradesh, Chattisgarh, Bihar, the North-East, Maharashtra and elsewhere. Since the first writing of this book, three years ago, the updated figure now has gone well over 150,000 (conversations with Virag Pachpore November 2009). Vidya Bharati alone runs 16,000 educational institutes with 7.5 million children in it and 75,000 teachers, with 5,500 Ekal Vidyalayas (that is, where there is only one teacher who teaches several classes together). This was an idea Deoras gave, in view of the paucity of both children and teachers (conversations with an insider who does not wish to be named, August 2007). All these works have gone into the social reconstruction of the country, besides aiming towards a homogeneous society based on equality. More importantly, these initiatives honourably seek cooperation from those who may not have an ideological allegiance with the RSS but have a lot to contribute by way of experience, experiments and ideas.

The all-India body of farmers came a little too late in the scheme of things. The first attempt to form it was done by Deoras in 1968. Deoras was a farmer himself at heart. Sharad Joshi is credited to have said that farmers should be given a price which covers all the expenses, including labour of the household – a single-point landmark solution. At least 15 years ago, Deoras had gone a step further and said out of five, two crops are good, two bad and one average. The losses of the other years need to be considered and prices fixed for the farmers' produce.

In 1982 itself, the VHP had taken a lead in organising a fund collection drive to start social service centres, students' hostels, vocational training classes, training non-Brahmin priests to guide and perform worships, aiming at a number of 500,000, and such other initiatives to pose a deterrent to proselytisation. All these projects came up in villages and remote places. The actual figures of what was achieved on ground, however, could not be obtained.

The way these works have gone forward is a tribute to the imagination of both Deoras and the other RSS workers from top to bottom. No one knows much about it, simply because the media do not like to talk about it and the self-righteous social workers of other, particularly the Left-leaning creeds, effectively suppress any inclusion of these works. Milind Bokil, in his scholarly book, *Katkari: Vikas ki Visthapan?* (2006), mentions dozens of projects done by the Left wing, dismissing the more numerous projects inspired by the RSS in that area in just one line.

Attempts to Forge National Unity

The RSS inspired the beginning of another RSS, the Rashtriya Sikh Sangat, to bridge the gap, to keep Hindus and Sikhs united, to exhort them to remember that Sikhism came to protect Hindu Dharma, that every Hindu household sent their eldest son to become Sikh. The VHP floated an international body for the unity of Hindus and Sikhs, in which six influential organisations were party (Advani 2008: 159).

The Vivekananda Kendra from Kanyakumari had started attracting youth to dedicate their life for social service and prepared them to work in the most adverse situations. The Vivekananda Kendra focused itself on Arunachal Pradesh and Assam, sending full-timers there. The missionaries resisted their entry at first. The people treated them indifferently, but slowly, through medical and school work, they entrenched themselves in the areas, served and brought people together. They stood as a deterrent, if not particularly strong numerically or monetarily, but a deterrent all the same, to the missionaries. One does not like to be strident about it, but the various Christian activities and means used by the missionaries in the North-East particularly and elsewhere generally is one of the causes of unrest in the North-East, just as China and Burma are (Pachpore 2001).

Later, the Arunachal government wanted the Vivekananda Kendra to run schools for their children. The condition was to teach them in English medium. The government was ready to give land, build buildings and provide furniture and equipment. It was a great offer, handed to the Kendra on a platter. Deoras did not find anything wrong in teaching in English, especially when such a huge opportunity to entrench themselves in so difficult a province was coming their way, and gave the green signal for the project. Mr Sudarshan, then looking after the North-East, flatly denied the offer, saying that 'these schools will not teach in English, take it or leave it.' The colossal myopia needs no comments (conversations with Virag Pachpore November 2009). In the North-East, the RSS has delegated each province to a state in mainland India, attempting to serve them through numerous projects and inculcate in them the feeling that they belong to nowhere else but this India.

The VHP then took another lead in bringing this strife-ridden society together, especially after the shock of Meenakshipuram. The Dnyan Ratham or the knowledge chariot traversed 900 villages of Tamil Nadu, covering the backward districts and places where the Dalits and other backward classes were particularly concentrated. The deity of Murugan was worshipped by 600,000 people. Kerala followed suit, covering 580 localities of Dalits and tribals, contacting 210,000 people.

The VHP was then busy organising Dharma Sansads (religious parliaments), declaring that all Hindus are brothers, targeting particularly the removal of the notion of untouchability. Their momentum was rising. The Ekatmata Yatra, the voyage for homogeneity, was the next nationwide initiative. Emboldened by the response to its earlier ventures, it then actualised organisational wizardry through the 3 main and 312 subordinate chariots to bring together all the castes, creeds and the sects of Hindu society for the worship of Ganga Mata and Bharat Mata, the Mother Ganga and the Mother Bharat. They were to exchange the local waters with the water of the River Ganga. The 312 chariots, traversing the length and breadth of the country were to (and did) finally meet in Nagpur. People mad with devotion ran after the trucks to throw money, obtain the water from the Ganges and pour the water from their local rivers in the huge earthen pots. People were intoxicated with happiness. The truck chariots were worshipped by millions. Every sect, creed and religious denomination related to Hinduism, even Muslims, Christians and Buddhists from all over, without a trace of the feelings of high and low, of untouchability or otherwise, participated. Every province, even Nepal, Burma and Mauritius, participated in the Yatra.[5] There is room to believe that Deoras and Pingale were aware of the beehive they had touched.

There was unprecedented awakening somewhere in the heart of Hindus: 'I am a Hindu, I am a Hindu.' It looked like the colour of India was changing. It was all aimed to bring about unity among people, with a sense that they were above all and first Hindus. It was a meeting of minds and fraternity, an awakening of the sense of upliftment and solemnity. It aimed at placing in front of everybody an ideal acceptable to all, under which and for which the whole society would come together. All the Yatras covered 531 districts, 4,432 of the 5,129 blocks and 184,592 out of 564,342 villages. Upwards of 72.39 million people participated, of which 51 per cent were males and 49 per cent women. Over 155,000 men and women worked for the success of this project (R.P. Sharma 2007). At many places, Christians and Muslims welcomed these chariots. There was not a single untoward instance in the 85,000 kilometres these chariots went through. A massive wave of unity and fraternity went through the country.

Sometime in the year 1983 or so, the serial *Ramayan* started on television. Soon it was the rage of Hindustan. The anti-Hindu elements in Kerala switched off the electricity officially at the transmission hours of 9:30 in the morning. Protests erupted and the government had to yield. It was rumoured that even Rajiv Gandhi's cabinet meetings on Sunday began only after *Ramayan* was over.

Mrs Gandhi was killed on 31 October 1984. Unprecedented killing of Sikhs took place in New Delhi after the assassination. Rajiv Gandhi became the Prime Minister, went in for a mid-term poll and won hands down.

The Bombshell Call Comes from Deoras

Vijaya Dashami, that is, Dashera is the day of birth for the RSS, since this was the day Dr Hedgewar founded the organisation in 1925. With the gigantic divisive problems abounding, the nation in unrest, the BJP in doldrums (mainly their own doing), the nation needed to be told what to look for. Here came the most landmark speech of Deoras from Nagpur on the day of Vijaya Dashami in 1984 (*Tarun Bharat* 1987).[6]

> The tendencies of secession, terrorism, the broken down economic situation, are serious matters. The cost of items needed for even daily living have touched the sky. Corruption has become the norm of life. The public and private character has deteriorated as have the ethical values. The law and order situation is beyond control. The relationship between the centre and the states has become bitter and both the centre and state governments have become aimless and directionless.

In times of Nehru, Patel and Rajendra Prasad the leadership had character; they had a dream about this nation. They had quality leaders even at the provincial level and since Congress was everywhere, the centre state relationship was healthy. But in a short while, this type of leadership disappeared. The new leadership [referring to Mrs Gandhi without apologies] was self centred and did not have any allegiance to the principles and ideology. The only objective was to be in power all the time. The leadership that was fostered in the centre as well as in the states was to dance to the tune of only one person. As a result opportunism grew and the opportunist selfish leaders became powerful. Corruption, infiltration increased as did the self interest and the party interests. It has now grown and has assumed horrifying proportions. The ruling Congress is disorganized with the internal conflicts. Groupism has pushed Congress on the brink of destruction. It may not be able to rectify itself. The bureaucracy is also disorganized. And we feel pain and fear that it will lead to anarchy... We do not wish this to happen especially to the central power... We do not think about any one party but what is beneficial to the nation as a whole...[And yet] we do not see any other party which can capably take the place of Congress.

This was where the BJP was put in discomfiture and everyone else was baffled. Deoras continues,

In some provinces there are some parties which are influential. In some there are governments by opposition parties. But the opposition parties are also fighting with each other. They cannot come together and work. Nor can they project a strong alternative to Congress. And such a possibility does not seem apparent in the near future.

Having bundled all the political parties together and having shown them what they were worth and what they should be doing, he then actually turned to the common man of the country and not to any political party, 'The common man is bearing the brunt of the situation, is experiencing insecurity, inflation. Yet it is necessary that without crying or shouting over this, it is the common man who will have to come forward and produce action.' Deoras mentioned of the dangers to the integrity and sovereignty of this nation, and the clear threats of Muslims and Christians to it, as well as the inability or the unwillingness of all the political parties to solve these problems.

Having said that, he again turned to the basic strength of this country – the Hindu society, which is the support system of this country:

> Hence, if the circumstances have to be changed it is the responsibility of the Hindu Society. The responsibility to enforce upon the rulers to go the right way also finally devolves around the alert and conscious, proud and disciplined, nationalistic Hindu patriots; creating this force is the work that should take precedence. We need people who will say – we will not allow corruption, we will not do it ourselves. The RSS is precisely trying to achieve this for the last 60 to 62 years but in the terrifying situation our success is not sufficient. Increasing the momentum of this work a hundred times is the answer for these problems.

The RSS had the strength to facilitate, but not to restrict and restrain. Deoras was invoking the higher power of the society here to make rulers go the right way. The trouble arose since he described all political parties as incapable of delivering the goods and said that there was no alternative to the Congress. Whether he meant it or not, the interpretation right or wrong, the message rang through quickly, and every political party had to take notice. The BJP more than anyone else had to understand the situation and put an end to the foolish way they were behaving. In the Deoras' tour following the Dashera speech, this theme recurred and took stronger shape to actually spell out that the country needs a government that will 'care for the interests of the majority'. Various independent versions started making rounds, and like a message that keeps changing, it probably assumed the form of: 'The RSS would like to see a government that will protect the interests of the majority community, Hindus.'

A further slew of speculations arose. Was it disillusionment with the BJP? Or a hand of friendship offered to the Congress?

Or was it an appeal to the Congress to turn to Hindu interest if they wanted to win? Or was it a promise that the RSS would help them win if it was done? Speculations that Deoras had actually helped Mrs Gandhi to win the 1980 elections added to the confusion about the exact pointer of this speech.

Why was this speech interpreted as a Hindu vote bank speech? People had so far heard of a Muslim vote bank, a Dalit vote bank, of the backward classes as a vote bank. No one had even heard that there was something like a Hindu vote bank. But what else could this mean? Deoras, however, saw the disintegration of this country all around, consumed by every force divisive to the society at work. He saw the Hindu society as unprotected, unable to protect itself, in need of preservation against its own doing.

Unless Hindu interest is protected, Hindu unity is a far cry, something that the RSS had been striving for and not succeeding. For that unity, the society had to be sensitised on the matter. Having set that stage, it was necessary to either create an apparatus or strengthen an existing one that would do the job and unite the Hindus. In other words, it also means that the means were relatively unimportant as compared to the paramount end, which is Hindu unity. Deoras was aiming to bring to centre stage the Hindu interest, and the RSS as its saviour, governments and political parties notwithstanding. For the integrity of this nation, there was no other answer.

All the re-energising of Hindus that happened through the RSS was due to the imagination of Deoras and Moropant Pingale. Pingale, much more robust in health, executed most of these projects with superlative organisational skills and imagination. Deoras had the imagination which few others had. Yet, barring the Ekatmata Yatra, none of the works had gone on to acquire a long-term character to continue to hold the imagination of people over protracted periods for them to continue to hold the sense of being Hindu. Deoras' mind was searching for such a project.

Notes

1. It must always be remembered that the RSS was quite well aligned with the Congress till the death of Sardar Patel. Till 1937, while he was the Sarsanghachalak of the RSS, Dr Hedgewar was actively associated with the Congress. He left it on the grounds that it no longer remained nationalistic and inclusive as before (Thengadi 1989: 86).

   Golwalkar, even during the period of the ban, had written several letters to Sardar Patel. The gist of one in this context is: The RSS and the Congress should be complementary to each other. I have tried wholeheartedly for a holy meeting of hearts between the efficient present Congress ruling the country and the RSS working to create an extraordinary camaraderie, strong feeling of nationalism and self sacrifice (Letter of Golwalkar to Sardar Patel, 5 November 1948 [translated by the author]; printed in full in Golwalkar 1979).

   Golwalkar went with Dr Mukherjee to form the Bharatiya Jan Sangh only with reluctance as the Congress cleansed itself of the Hindu-minded leaders after the death of Sardar Patel.

2. It is extremely difficult to understand why government after government has not been able to think of Assam more imaginatively to address the upliftment of social and economic conditions. A government sitting quietly over the infiltration of Bangladeshi refugees is fully understandable in terms of political considerations. Although a major issue, that is not the only issue of Assam before or after the carving out of seven states.

3. Two significant facts about the Christian missionary work in India: First, after all the effort they have put in the conversion rates in mainland India have been low, but in the north-eastern region, they are significantly high. This is primarily because the mainland has never effectively supplied the North-East with effective alternative models for social and economic emancipation.

   The second development is the increasingly fissiparous and secessionist tendencies and, at times, violence the Christian missionaries have been indulging in over the last several decades by aligning themselves with Dalit interests. Church of North India delegations had met Mrs Gandhi to demand reservations for Dalit Christians. Mrs Gandhi, in a counterpoint, agreed to it provided the Christians were ready to declare that they also have among them caste hierarchies. The delegation could not agree with it and the discussions fizzled out.

4. Simple historical facts illuminate the path to unity. Sikhs became a sect with the tradition of at least one son of the Hindu families being sent to become a Sikh. Guru Gobind Singhji who converted the pious Sikhs

into a fighting army did it with the idea — Jage Dharma Hindu — so that the Hindu religion lives on. Such efforts alone can resolve problematic issues.

5. The idea of a joint federation of India and Pakistan is old. Including Deoras, many have expressed this same idea. There is a need and possibility of a second loose federation of the South East Asian countries which are dominantly Buddhists. Its perimeter is larger than that of SAARC. Needless to say, these ideas have potential in terms of stability, trade, economic development and as a force to reckon with.

6. I owe these ideas to Prof. G.B. Kanitkar, during our discussions in 1989.

7

Catapulting the Hindu to the Centre Stage

———— • ✦ • ————

In 1985, Deoras was asked to speak to the Nagpur *swayamsevaks* on the occasion of the RSS completing 60 years. Blunt and to the point, he began by saying, 'We have done thousands of works of social significance. And still RSS has no effect on the society as a whole. We have to shake our complacency and find an answer' (conversations with D.B. Ghumare, senior journalist, June 2007).

Deoras was aware, more clearly than anybody else, that each project undertaken by the RSS tended to think only of itself, and failed to see itself as a part of a larger whole or a chain, or a joint effort towards national reconstruction. The evidence of growing institutional egoism was also apparent. There was an overall myopia regarding the effective and result-oriented consideration of all works. The sense that the final justification of all works was to lift the RSS ideologies, and through it the welfare of this country to the centre stage in as urgent a manner as can be was missing.

Deoras Marks Time

By 1983, 1985 and 1987, Deoras was marking his time while marching ahead forcefully and speedily to bring the Hindu interest of this country to the centre stage. For Deoras, 1989 was the year of his greatest achievement.

Two great men had been born a hundred years ago, Dr Hedgewar, and Dr Ambedkar in the following year. Dr Hedgewar's birth centenary was celebrated by the RSS with gusto and effulgence. The RSS also actively and wholeheartedly participated in the 100th birth anniversary of Dr Ambedkar in 1990. The surprise and paradox, however, was about the Dr Hedgewar centenary celebrations. Dr Hedgewar had explicitly said that the RSS was not interested in celebrating its jubilees. Dr Hedgewar wanted to create a situation where the RSS becomes redundant by achieving the goal of a consolidated and organised nation of men with character. Dr Hedgewar dreamed that the RSS ultimately would 'wither away' in the organised society. And yet, his own *parama shishya*, his best disciple, Deoras, imaginatively and meticulously planned his centenary celebrations, initiated and undertook a whirlwind tour of the country in his failing health so that the nation could 'celebrate' the 100th birth anniversary of his mentor, the great Dr Hedgewar.

Final Unity of the Purpose

But what was the picture of Hindu initiatives at the beginning of 1988, whose core cadre were the RSS men who were meant to carry forth these initiatives? The Vishwa Hindu Parishad (VHP) had begun to feel powerful and become militant. The BJP, typically, was vacillating on the frequency and consistency of their hardcore stand on Hindutva. Vajpayee had already distanced himself from it. The Mazdoor Sangh was busy becoming the number one trade union of this country. The Vanavasi Kalyan Ashram had become an all-India body and was probably enjoying its newly earned status. The members of the VHP and the BJP were distrustful of each other. Years of practice had created a picture where these Parivar organisations had an independent image of their own and were now enjoying their all-India status. At that time, it had become obvious that 'this collective consciousness' of their RSS origin was getting diluted and fragmented, that it was slipping out of their minds. The 'end goal' was being forgotten. To put it even more bluntly, the 'institutional egoism' had become hardened and was surfacing rapidly (Varhadpande, unpublished).

The twin task Deoras set himself to was to bring Hindu interest to the centre stage and to forge an apparatus out of all the scattered RSS might, which would achieve that end. The shortest route to this end was through political power. Equally difficult was eradicating the institutional egoism within, bad enough an obstacle for the unity of the Parivar. Removing it from the minds of literally millions of *swayamsevak*s, sympathisers, co-passengers and intelligentsia in so vast a country with thousands of levels of understanding, backgrounds and prejudices would be considered impossible. Deoras did both the jobs single-handedly. The compilation of the events will amply testify to that strategy (Varhadpande 1988).

How could this egoism be submerged to be forged into a single force? The only name and the only place where all travails, doubts, disturbances, rumours, despairs and frustrations disappeared, where the only sense that emerged was of profound tranquillity and indefatigability was the name of the founder of the RSS, Dr Keshav Baliram Hedgewar. Deoras was a contemporary. Golwalkar had not been visible for quite some time. The concept of Hindutva also had its pinches. The only lustrous place, without blemish, was Dr Hedgewar. To that place each one could do away with his self without any pain in the act of relinquishment.

By celebrating Dr Hedgewar's birth centenary, the single aim was to submerge the individual consciousness into the 'collective original consciousness', to develop the sense that 'from beginning to end we are *swayamsevaks* of that RSS' whose the founder was Dr Hedgewar. There could not have been any defeat in the aim. The only result was a united Hindu force aimed at political power. The effects were singular. Once the centenary celebrations were over in a year, the RSS Parivar rose as one. It lent all its strength from one massive movement to the next.

The common knowledge is that the RSS desired to start *seva karya* or service projects of varied nature, numbering 5,000 across the country, in the name of Dr Hedgewar Janmashatabdi Samiti (Committee for the Celebration of the Birth Centenary of Dr Hedgewar). The society at large had already become familiar with this *seva karya* attribute of the RSS, for which it was well known and admired. The *seva* thus was an added dimension of *shakha* work. The enormous drive for mass contact, mass propaganda, collection of money for the said work, transparent distribution and safety of all this money, the meticulous programming across the country, the enormous enthusiasm of the RSS cadre and its Parivar organisations are marvels of the achievements of this 'organisational wizard'. Coming at the heels of the Sanskriti Raksha Yojana, Ekatmata Yatra, and so on, it was a truly great year for the RSS. It showed the world the enormous acceptability that the RSS had gained over the years from all sections of the society, and its ability to move masses. The birth centenary of Pandit Jawaharlal Nehru, on the contrary, with all the money a government can spend, was a pale, unnoticed and an unmoving affair.

Elevating the RSS, the Parivar and Hindus to a Cause

The Ram Janmabhoomi Mukti Andolan (Movement for the Freedom of the Birthplace of Sri Ram, hereafter Mukti Andolan) was one such cause which could fulfil both the conditions, that of rousing the RSS and the Parivar as well as the Hindu society at large for its sake. Deoras and Pingale picked it up and decided to arouse the society around the cause, to make it submerge their differences and divisive tendencies, and to make the Hindu cause and its protection the most important concern.

Any movement begins with one principal reason. The more magnificent the original conception, more ideas, purposes and reasons get attached to it. Later, the prime mover cause of starting the movement becomes secondary or even forgotten. Every subsequent cause becomes important. A stage may often and later come when for some odd reason which did not feature in the original conception at all it may appear that the programme cannot be stopped, or its tone or the direction or any such dimension becomes unalterable. The Mukti Andolan has gone through all these stages. It is unfortunate that it has stuck upon that one odd and utterly impossible reason when it should have been de-escalated long back and left on a back burner.

Mandal versus Kamandal, Mukti Andolan Uniting the Society

In 1990, when the call for *karseva* was reverberating through the country, the Mandal Commission report was accepted by V.P. Singh for implementation. The day to declare it was chosen for the sake of purely political one-upmanship, in order to divert the attention from the huge farmers' rally planned by Devilal, the vice premier (Loksatta Research Bureau, 21 October 2007). It produced immediate and severe reactions in the North, starting with demonstrations and culminating in self-immolation of youths. The Somnath to Ayodhya Chariot travel of Advani was on the cards and it was feared that the Yatra would now incite caste violence. Somebody imaginatively proclaimed it to be a war between Mandal and the Kamandal, a traditional pot used by *sadhus* for penance and worship. The slogan 'Mandal vs. Kamandal' was intended as a jest of the orthodox Brahminical ways of the Hindu organisations. Mandal was dividing the society vertically and the Kamandal was representing the Mukti Andolan, trying to bring it together.

The Mukti Andolan was presented as one that would restore Hindu honour, obliterate the insult of centuries, and serve as a strong negation and demolition of the atrocities committed over the Hindu sacred places. These factors, however, slowly became a part of the movement, mainly because of the brilliant and staged manner in which it was escalated. But the prime purpose of starting this movement in 1986 was the unity of Hindus. I often said those days that 'if by painting Babari Masjid green we can bring about unity in Hindu Society we will do that. But it will not happen'.

The massive book compiled by Raghunandan Prasad Sharma (2007) on the 42 years of the VHP gives the following account.[1] Ironically, the idea of Mukti Andolan arose from Mr Dau Dayal Khanna, the health minister in the Congress cabinet of Chandra Bhanu Gupta of Uttar Pradesh. He presented it to the VHP. In 1983, the liberation of Ayodhya, Kashi and Mathura was mooted in the VHP congregation in Muzaffarnagar. In 1984, it was reiterated and the *sadhus* and *mahants* accepted it as a mission. A lawyer by the name of Umeshchandra Pande moved the Faizabad district court and on 1 February 1986, the lock was opened. All the appeals of Muslims were dismissed by the High Court. To arouse the sentiments of all Hindus and to bring them together under it, 200 Sri Ram Janaki Chariots went around the country, in each village for the next three years. Girilal Jain (1991) hailed it as the magnificent and benevolent renewal of the timeless Dharma of Hindusthan. Four hundred million people participated in the welcome and worship of the statues of Ram, Sita and Hanuman. There were no conflicts, nor was any law of the land broken. Tension was not allowed to escalate either. It was not publicised in newspapers, nor were any handbills printed. Even then this programme took place at 275,000 places in the country. Every locality of a town sent one brick for the cause, just as small villages sent one brick each to build the Ram temple.

One need not agree with the purpose and intentions of all these mass contact movements for so bourgeoisie a cause. But the idea! Each place of human habitation in this country will come together, people will worship local bricks and send them in trucks to Ayodhya for future utilisation. It is an unparalleled concept of mass mobilisation for a single cause. The world could borrow it from the VHP and make use of it for one's beliefs, creed, ideas and ideals by appropriately adapting it. It is a lot of back-breaking work; it needs a cadre which rises to the occasion and works hundreds of days for it.

The nation saw the Mukti Andolan and how the VHP literally churned the society. The systematic demolition of isolation was the prelude to something else Deoras was planning.

A Dalit Places the First Brick

Having achieved a great degree of social upheaval and unity, the next programme was to undertake symbolic placement of a brick for foundation at a designated place. Except for the BJP, each and every political party opposed it. The Centre and the Uttar Pradesh government agreed upon the place, and Mr Kameshwar Choupal, the organising secretary of the VHP's Bihar unit, who is a Dalit, was chosen to be the person to lay the foundation. There would be hundreds who would have given their life for the chance. Without much ado about it, the foundation laying happened first at Choupal's hands. Others placed some 141 bricks at that place, all the *sadhus* and *mahant*s and VHP officers coming next.

The 1990 *Karseva*

In 1990, it was decided that a symbolic *karseva* would be held on 23 and 24 June. The Hindu synthesising genius picked up a concept from the Sikhs, in vogue for hundreds of years, and applied it to the symbolic movement of building the temple. Uttar Pradesh was sealed. It turned into a jail. A total of 800,000 people from all over the country reached Uttar Pradesh. A few hundred thousands were arrested on their way. The capacity created to jail them was exhausted. Most of those not caught had to walk not less than 200 to 250 kilometres. They were supported, looked after and hidden from the police by the illiterate villagers who believed in their cause. They helped them to reach the subsequent destinations with safety. With 800,000 people entering the state, not one unwanted, undesirable or untoward incident took place on their way to Ayodhya. Nowhere in the world has there been so peaceful an agitation on so large a scale. The undemocratic government failed miserably in front of the will of the people. Cordons were broken as thousands reached the place and the saffron flag went up on the three *gumbaz*. The police killed the peacefully chanting devotees of Sri Ram. The rally on Boat Club in New Delhi was considered the biggest ever rally in the post-Independence era that resulted in all rallies being banned on Boat Club subsequently. Hindus had won hands down.

The Demolition Takes Place

To put it in a nutshell, the Supreme Court procrastinated over the appeal of the Uttar Pradesh government and postponed the decision till 11 December 1992, knowing very well that hundreds of thousands of people were going to be there for a second *karseva*. Provocation and frustration took the toll and the Masjid was demolished. Hindus won the second time over the issue. Within minutes, Deoras himself said, 'Whatever happened is not a good thing. But now at least the Muslims will know how it feels when a place of worship and faith gets demolished at the hands of others' (Chouthaiwale n.d.). This was not arrogance. That was verbalised by the Shiv Sena supremo. Having taken the credit of the demolition, Bal Thackeray did not speak the language of Hindu pain over this kind of act. In Deoras' voice spoke the Hindu mind that had tolerated and respected temples, churches and mosques alike for thousands of years. There was no apology. It was a plain statement of fact. All the same, history was created.

That said, the ordinary man has to get on with his life, to revert back to the everyday. He cannot sustain such an agitational state continuously. He cannot look after himself then. Now was the time to start de-escalating the Mukti Andolan, remove the stridency of the sloganisation. It was the time to show the magnanimity of the victor and say: Okay. Let us sit down and find a way of how we can build the Mandir but also restore a Masjid for you. Demolishing places of worship is not our way of life. Now everyone knows what Hindus are capable of and we do not wish to prove it again and again. Let bygones be bygones.

The VHP and the Parivar Immaturity

The VHP and the Parivar failed to show the maturity to de-escalate the Mukti Andolan. They had proven a point. They had shown the world the power of Hindu sentiment when aroused. They had done something which Hindus had never done in their long history, that is, destroy a place of worship. They had to understand that all said and done, the Hindu sentiment and mentality dictates that we need not boast about it all the time. The sentiment would not like that. Having demolished the Masjid, the issue was now over. As

Deodhar points out, Vajpayee and Advani went to ask Deoras in 1987 how to get out of the situation the BJP was stuck in at that time among other things. Deoras had suggested that they hijack the Congress' initiative of Ayodhya as a road to political power. Deoras had clearly instructed both of them to rise with the movement but not remain stuck with it, get entangled especially in religious turmoil, but to move on (D. Deodhar 2004b). This was ignored, forgotten or not understood, at least by the VHP. The guerrilla warfare of Shivaji, with which the Maharashtrian leader Deoras was familiar, could neither be understood nor could the Western and the northern leadership in the Parivar be trusted to carry it out nimbly and in right proportion. They remained stuck with the Rajput ideas of 'war till (often their own) end, without thought to Guerrilla Warfare or tactical retreat' (D. Deodhar 2004b). The elementary wisdom that constantly harping upon and continuing with this movement would soon lead to the loss of popular sentiment and, indeed, might even lead to the rise of popular sentiment against the movement did not dawn upon the VHP. The idea was to establish a Ram Rajya, not just a symbolic Mandir.

Somewhere in 1993, the old hatred of the Muslims resurfaced. People like Singhal, and later Togadia, started dreaming of a strident Hindu force, bringing about their Hindu Rashtra symbolised by the Ram Mandir. Emotions overtook reason. Suddenly, nothing else seemed to matter. They were blinded. Getting drunk over the deed was not very far. The intoxication demanded for more action and more destruction for its own pleasure and satiation. The new-found strength went to their heads. The VHP continued to escalate the issue in more and more inflammatory language.[2] Muslims, thus, reacted strongly. The Bombay riots occurred in March 1993. The society stood against each other as Hindus and Muslims.

It appeared to everyone outside the pale, and rightly so, that the issue of Ram Mandir was being unnecessarily kept alive. The BJP-led coalition government was not being

199

allowed to do its work. It looked as if there were no questions or problems remaining in front of the nation and their government except this. The VHP, in fact, was told by the RSS leadership to de-escalate the movement. The concrete programme given to them was to get into the management of every temple, raise the level of management there and utilise the funds for works that would locally foster nationalistic attitudes, reduce casteism and numerous other things as a fallout. They were also requested to bring about some harmony between the different religions of the country and take up constructive work that would change the face of India. The VHP did not listen, did not realise that any good work is RSS–VHP work. Apparently, as Dilip Deodhar insists on saying (and I agree with him),

> [The] RSS is no longer following the open system of Dr Hedgewar's time but has taken up the Hindutva mire created by Golwalkar and adding to it the Hindu Mahasabha type of religious/sectarian Hindutva, getting caught in to the maze and getting sucked in to the whirlpool of the latter. (Conversations with Dilip Deodhar)

The Bajrang Dal–Durga Vahini Creations

From the book of Raghunandan Prasad Sharma (2007), it is clear that the Bajrang Dal and Durga Vahini were developed as the fighting arms of the VHP. On probing this issue and on the balance of things, it looks as if the VHP had sensed the backlash which occurred in the form of March 1993 Mumbai blasts and the riots that erupted at other places (conversations with M.G. Vaidya September–November 2007). In that way they seem to be justified in developing a protective armour. It is possible, but cannot be proven and only guessed, that this development dissuaded the Muslims from erupting again and again. Yet, the VHP, the Bajrang Dal and the Durga Vahini were riding the wave of valour and achievement. Such forces are not easy to control. They can flair up with a desire to provoke and hit out.

End of the Deoras Saga

Deoras' saga essentially ends in its first phase here with the demolition of Babri Masjid. He had started becoming seriously handicapped under the ravages of 50 years of diabetes. His body was eaten up from within. His brain was alert but his expression had started suffering. He was no longer in the position to actively control the behemoth of the RSS and the Parivar. Deoras' strategy, however, continued to work. The Parivar worked in a united manner. That the leadership left behind was well trained but did not have Deoras' touch has become obvious over the years. My analysis of the situation in the remaining pages will indicate this missing touch more than amply. Deoras died a few days after seeing Vajpayee become the Prime Minister of this country.

The Mukti Andolan remained alive. The globalisation, liberalisation and privatisation of the economy began and continued in full force. By fostering it, Prime Minister Narsimha Rao who had earned notoriety for doing nothing except pouting his lips in the Lok Sabha reached the same distinction that Gorbachev reached for Russia, by active work. Each one started the process of transformation of his country and met with unprecedented and unexpected levels of success. Both of them also affected an effective change in the world map, the way it functioned thereafter and progressed, Gorbachev contributing much more than Rao. The Sangh Parivar made an effort and in 1996 Vajpayee came to power as the premier of the country.

We will meet Deoras again in the remaining pages but it might be a good idea to say something more about his thinking and actions. There was a pre-programmed quality and refinement that years of thinking and profound understanding alone could have given to his actions. His expression and actions had the unostentatious ease, a masterly character, a downright 'to earth' quality and immense relevance with which he went about the whole business. Although pre-programmed, it was free from prejudice, bias, narrowness, rigidity and therefore could take in its stride almost anything, however disadvantageous it might be, like the Emergency, or however advantageous it might be like the Ram Janmabhoomi issue. He did what he wanted the RSS to do in 1950 or thereabouts, when he distanced himself from the day-to-day work, in this period of 1973 to 1991. It forced every one to take note, ponder over everything that he said or did.

Forcefully he brought 'the original theses' of this nation being a Hindu Rashtra and Hindu interest being paramount to centre stage, a feat considered almost impossible in 1973. If people think that the BJP finally attained power by their doing and persistence, it would be an expression of naivety. Deoras and then Rajendra Singhji led them there. Deoras was bold. In worldly pragmatism he was far, far ahead of anybody then and now. His era is characterised by initiation, emphasis, maintenance and containment of many movements, changing at different times, having character not greatly common to each other. It needs an intrinsic inborn sense of balance, proportion, priority and propriety, which he had demonstrated in ample measure. The RSS centrality paradigm gave him this sense of balance. The need for this balance is far more today and tomorrow than any other time of our lives.

The greatest tribute paid to him, at least as I see, was the one that came from Mr Lal Krishna Advani. He said, 'He taught us how to keep our balance between "the principles and its practical application"' (Advani 1996). The massive multifaceted character of the RSS is awe-inspiring and difficult to gauge. And by no means is balancing it an easy task. Take for example the balance between the constructive and the agitational work. This was changed by Mr Deoras without losing balance, doing away with a need to be defensive, apologetic or overly argumentative over facades the organisation had built over years around itself. Many have expressed themselves in uncomplimentary terms on this politicised aspect of Deoras' regime. It is true that he was not at all averse to politics. In fact, he was concerned about it and extremely vocal. However undesirable, it is true that politics dominates our social life excessively, to the extent that even the non-political targets need political powers and support for executing them. The balance, proportion and priority accorded to it by Deoras were in the most optimal measure. Therefore, he remained unadulterated by and from politics, and resisted to an extent the defilement of the original ethos of the RSS, which happened after he was no longer there. Deoras was an open and reactive individual, who did not believe in assuming unnecessary stances. Hence his reactions were spontaneous and to the point. Somehow, he was put into the limelight by the print and the electronic media. He did not seek it, neither did he deny it. Probably it was his way of going about that brought the press to him, a mark of his authority. Authority cannot be demanded, nor can it be wrested — it has to come to one by itself, naturally.

Publicity today is an accepted norm in the RSS and the Parivar. But it has assumed a most detestable form. In yesteryears, the deeds were publicised. Today, the individuals are publicised. In yesteryears, birthdays, travelling programmes and availabilities were not the norms; the heroism of the RSS was the norm. Today, it is felicitations galore. In yesteryears, movements were at the centre stage. The RSS and the Parivar have lost the intrinsic balance of Deoras. In less than a dozen years, we are not even able recognise them in the original form.

No one can deny that all paradigms of national life today have changed since that time. The people have seen an RSS *swayamsevak* becoming the Prime Minister of this country, loved it, felt the pain when the government fell after 13 days, and again when it failed to come back to power in 2004. The Ram Janmabhoomi has come and unfortunately stayed on.

To me Deoras' thinking is the basic mode of thinking that the RSS leadership and cadre have lost over years. This is what has to be retrieved and handed down to the future generations. There is nothing great or uncanny or scheming about it. If this thinking does not perpetuate, if the central, principal aim is not recognised to be the strong national character and Hindu unity, then whatever else that may remain is of no consequence at all.[3]

In the next few chapters, I will analyse the ways in which important people in the RSS Parivar, including the BJP, thought and behaved, what was right and wrong in the expectations, the nature of the relationships and how they deteriorated or improved in the post-Deoras era. I will also try and highlight what is to be learned from the Deoras era, and how beneficial it may prove for the future.

Notes

1. In 1987, Vajpayee and Advani had gone to Cochin to ask Deoras how to get out of the rut they were in. They also discussed the Mukti Andolan. Deoras' clear instruction was to continue with the Andolan, but not to get stuck with it.
2. It is the Hedgewar–Deoras axis that represents the original characters of the RSS. The author sincerely believes the line that changed since 1940 till 1973 changed in an unacceptable manner and direction. After the Deoras era, the same line is getting restored and adding to it the regrettable violence and rabid jingoism, chauvinistic tendencies so characteristically absent in the Deoras era.
3. It is necessary to emphasise the contributions and thinking paradigms of the Deoras era, especially because there are strong grounds to suppose that people high up in the RSS are active in suppressing the impact of the era. It may be a worthwhile question to ask why so little of Dr Hedgewar has been published in the last 50 years, when adequate material is available for use to teach the ethos of the founder.

8

Road to Political Power and Its Aftermath

———•✦•———

Power Comes Too Late

The BJP came to power nearly 16 years after the Janata Raj. Atal Behari Vajpayee was in his 70s at that time. The RSS had already carried the burden of its work for 71 years—those at the helm of affairs had aged and tired, physically and mentally. This was not the only problem, however. Age brings out certain tendencies in people, that of dwelling in the past, of expressing oneself in a set manner and revelling in the same, of losing one's grip on logic. With age, one becomes slow to react to important issues—nor is one capable of having a reaction startling enough to make an impact. We will see an instance of this in Chapter 9, in connection to the poor or no response of the RSS leadership to the Communist debacle in Russia. Age makes it difficult to assimilate or even understand newer ideas, their likely effect and implications. As more aged people accumulate in an organisation, accommodating them within the organisational structure becomes necessary but difficult, and the result is a non-productive asset. These unproductive elements cannot do much work, but demand accountability from the cadre, which increases the pressure on the declining number of working hands.

To restate the thesis of this book briefly — the RSS lost and aged by 24 years between 1949 and 1973, when the processes making this loss pervasive, effective and dominant were subdued. Deoras took charge of the organisation 24 years too late. The biggest limitation that thus arose was in terms of delivering goods, which fell upon those who had aged significantly. That is why even after the BJP attained political power, it did not utilise the same to foster its work for reconstruction by itself and through the various Parivar organisations. This was one of the most important consequences of having an aged leadership. It must be noted that ironically, the leadership of the RSS was younger in age than the stalwarts of the BJP after the passing away of Deoras, his brother Bhaurao, and when Rajendra Singhji laid down his office in 2004. The leaders of the other Parivar organisations were now taller figures than the leaders of the RSS.

The BJP, the RSS and the Parivar Disconnect

With three successive and two successful attempts at gaining political power, the BJP's financial situation became easier. Over-'reliance' on reliable parties fetched money. The legislative wings not only in the centre but also in the states became fairly 'independent'.

However, they did not govern well. There were many we know in Maharashtra at least who would not even turn up in their offices till noon and then would vanish just as fast. They shamed their Congress predecessors in the show of their self, of their degeneracy and arrogance.

In the course of my research, I sought clear information on whether the Vajpayee government built bridges of collaboration between the Parivar, the RSS and the BJP party organisation. There are two schools of thought here. Some think that the initiation of ignoring the RSS and the Parivar started with Vajpayee. The other school of thought blames the RSS, the Parivar and their non-political leadership for the increasing lack of communication and collaboration. The bottom line, however, is that neither theory does any credit to any of the parties concerned. Even the elementary lessons that Golwalkar, Deendayal and Deoras had tried to drill in were forgotten by this time.

The clear answer from one of the seniormost RSS functionaries, who was connected with the BJP for many years, on the matter of approaching the Parivar was, 'The legislative wings did not even care to keep contact with the party cadre' (conversations with M.G. Vaidya, former editor of *Tarun Bharat* September–November 2007). Keeping a live contact with the Parivar was completely out of question. The fundamental principle of Deendayal stated repeatedly in 1960s and held in high esteem by many thinkers like Prof. G.B. Kanitkar within Jan Sangh was completely forgotten by those who were holding ministerial positions. The Deendayal mantra was:

> Whether in power or not, it is the party cadre which takes the programs of the party or the government to people, translates them into realities for the people. These programs by implication become the reasons and cause for the public contact. They become the vehicle to continue to build and take the organization from strength to strength.

The same functionary also said, 'Vajpayee believed that the government machinery will take all the programs his government formulated to people and divorced the party from an active role,' undermining the organisation (conversations with M.G. Vaidya, former editor of *Tarun Bharat* September–November 2007). It is difficult to understand how Vajpayee of all people could be so naïve as to not know that this is one job the government machinery has never done and will never do. The bureaucracy is apathetic. Such a position, therefore, is simply not pardonable.

The RSS has evolved with social service projects in at least 35 different fields, as Deodhar has stated. Organisationally, the first thing that was necessary was to establish a liaison with the thousands of workers in these fields, which is the least controversial aspect of RSS work. They had a huge need for funds to further their work, to fight proselytisation and to establish and entrench projects in tribal areas which were the most susceptible, in the North-East and elsewhere. The onus for the safeguarding and the welfare of the North-East, to a large extent, lay with the central government. There were over 150,000 projects, many of which, if fostered, would be beneficial even to the BJP at the grassroots level. The BJP alienated the people fighting in the field rather than strengthening them. In 1977, the people in power had a little more sense, were more awake to the situation around them and had passed on some help to these projects. But there was no sense of Parivar or RSS centrality during the BJP's reign — they denied help to their own people who were making sacrifices in the field.

I know from my personal knowledge that the Christians and the missionary activists have created a jargon with the help of which they lift huge funds from the governments in health care. The mushrooming of NGOs lately is an example of similar lifting of funds. It is an open secret that funds are allowed to come in for the proselytising organisations under various names and garbs. Despite knowing this fact, the BJP government failed to pay attention to the cadre of the Parivar organisations of the RSS to counteract them. What were their priorities, their perspectives?

Backing the grassroots projects of the Parivar would make tremendous sense even from the point of view of the BJP returning to power in the centre. The stretch of land extending from Mumbai to the tip of Arunachal Pradesh houses nearly 80 per cent of all the 50 million tribal population, talking in 350 languages and of as many castes. The Vanavasi Kalyan Ashram has literally thousands of projects for the upliftment of the tribals. Education and residential hostels, propagation of agriculturally productive methods and a dozen more effective ideas made these families self-reliant. These projects were involved in rehabilitating the tribal families economically and culturally and bringing them closer to the mainstream without dislocating them from their natural surroundings and their land. These hostels have thrown up artisans, well-trained farmers, doctors, lawyers, legislators and even chief ministers. This is the power of the people they had accumulated. The message is clear, and the cavalier attitude of the BJP in its treatment of the Parivar is equally a fact. The blame needs to be placed upon the senior leaders in the BJP.

On the practical front, the BJP leadership forgot that the Marxists have retained their power in West Bengal for over 30 years because the party cadre actively pursues the perpetuation of their party programme with its grassroots activities. They do many other savoury and unsavoury things for the sake of it. The party cadre has a stronghold in the state. The BJP need not go to that length, but making the party cadre totally ineffective, leaving them politicking for positions, is no way of running the party. The presidential structure made it apparent to the cadre that their salvation lies in getting to a position of power (constitution and rules as amended by the National Council at Lucknow on 24 December 2006). One had to find a place among the powerful, using means fair and foul (no one in the BJP cares about the nature of the means utilised nowadays). With this recognition, the cadre stopped doing all the other work that was required.

Disregard of Its Own Manpower

The RSS has, among political parties and NGOs, one of the largest pool of technocrats, scientists and science graduates who vouch for the organisation. Dilip Deodhar says, 'In the Communist Parties most of them have their orientation in humanities and very few with science background' (2004a). This perhaps goes a long way to explain the greater obsolescence one has amply witnessed in the Left parties, particularly in connection with the nuclear deal. That said, what did the BJP do with these experts? Did the government try to tap their talent? Why did the BJP continue with the same bureaucratic bandicoots? When will the BJP learn to induct people, like the ones mentioned above, who will do better work?

Incidentally, this is an old and deep-rooted aspect of the RSS–BJP psyche. They either have no confidence in their own men or do not wish to project this confidence to the world, or they do not feel comfortable unless someone from the outside endorses them, even after enjoying power for so long, as late as 2006. Edward Luce (2006) has commented upon this tendency, of seeking approval of foreigners in particular (Yerkuntawar 1960).[1]

To run the Prime Minister's Office (PMO), as I understand, the prime minister needs the assistance of about 400 highly knowledgeable people. Not a single trustworthy man from the various Parivar organisations went to the PMO during Vajpayee's reign. It would have benefitted everyone with the experience one needed. On the other hand, tragically, Bhaurao Deoras questioned the RSS cadre if they had qualified manpower necessary for the job. Even Advani had no say in the way the PMO was run in general by the confidants of Vajpayee. At one point, Advani was close to asking Vajpayee to choose between his confidants and Advani. He also mentioned to a senior once that he failed to convince Vajpayee that he was not a rival to him. Even then one wonders, if these achievers from the cadre had gone in as special executives, whether they would have come out more disgusted or fulfilled.

Vajpayee as the Premier

Unfortunately, Vajpayee has a lot to answer here, in his present as well as from his past. If we consider the way the issue of the Ram Mandir has been reported and developed in the media, the VHP looks like the prime culprit in keeping the communal fires blazing in the name of Hindu honour. A little more analysis may still not minimise the role of the VHP, but the way Vajpayee has played with these men leaves a lot wanting. Vajpayee lives in a world of his own. He has his own ideas about what he wants to look like. He wants to be seen as the moderate, the liberal; he prefers being called the right man in the wrong party, as opposed to the 'hardliners', a word coined by the media or rediscovered after the Tilak era of radicals. The discussions, numerous as they have been, leaves an impression that Vajpayee thought of himself in a manner akin to the way Nehru thought of himself. Both did not have their feet firmly on ground and both were more drawn to the notion of being famous in posterity than anything else, even political power. Vajpayee is even said to have attempted for the Nobel Peace Prize. This is said to be one of the reasons why the imminent war after the 2002 Parliament attack did not ultimately take place. Patel, Gandhi, Deoras and Rajjubhaiya, on the contrary, had their feet firmly on the ground.

Vajpayee has been accused by people like Sachhidanand Shevade (2006), who has stayed in the interiors of Kashmir for months together, for nearly costing the nation Kashmir by virtue of his various acts and failures to act, not to mention his desire to have Muslim backing in the elections at all costs. Accusations of Vajpayee's insistence on employing 20,000 Kashmiri Muslims in sensitive areas like the army may be difficult to prove if records are not made available. But the fact that there could be room for such talk in the grapevine is bad enough. It is consistent with what I have learnt from inside sources. Prior to the 2004 election, the Shahi Imam

Abdullah Bukhari of Delhi issued a *fatwa* telling the Muslims to vote for the BJP. The reasons for such an action are not known. Hindus within the RSS and the Parivar had lost all interest in voting for this party. A highly placed doctor from Delhi told me a few years ago that it was Mulayam who suggested Dr Kalam's name for the post of the President, under the logic of refurbishing the secular image of the BJP as well as his own party.

The BJP, on hindsight, appears as though it wanted to do away with the RSS and the Parivar. The Parivar, in its turn, has not behaved well either. The barren woman BJP has ignored its husband, 'the main constituency of Hindus' (Dharmadhikari 1989), which helped it come to power. Nonetheless, Vajpayee still does not realise that in the 13 days of his first regime, all those who called him the right man in the wrong party did nothing for him to survive in the office. He continues to do nothing for the main constituency, that is, the Hindus who have voted him to power.

Vajpayee has ambivalence in him. His continued variance with the party, and even with the RSS, has been 'tolerated' by both for the sheer force of his personality. He seems to take this tolerance for granted. Vajpayee was never a builder of organisation like Deendayal. Did he consider all those in the other organisations to be his juniors who could not possibly have anything to teach him and did not need to be taken seriously? No one can tell. However, these were the people who had worked for the success of the BJP. The BJP was in their debt, which should always be paid. Vajpayee did not pay his debt.

The Parivar on the other hand failed to understand the international pressures upon the government and the obligations that needed to be honoured. That you cannot keep defying international pressures without internal political support, which, at that time, was always precarious, must be understood. For a long time, Vajpayee ignored taking any action on Ram Mandir under the plea that the coalition partners would not tolerate that and he had a government to run. There are many who believe that he has made the issue more complicated (conversations with a long time Nagpur unit secretary, who does not want to be named [2008]). The land under dispute was just 2.77 acres. The remaining 67 odd acres had already been given to the rightful owner by the earlier regimes. Vajpayee need not have gone to any court and would have broken no law if he had simply handed that land back. He also did precious little to withdraw the Ayodhya court cases and made Advani susceptible to political blackmail. We have seen this come full circle with the Liberhan Commission report in December 2009.

The saints who had spearheaded the Ram Janmabhoomi Mukti Andolan once went to meet Vajpayee for a discussion. They were made to wait for an hour and not even a glass of water was offered to them. I am no admirer of these saints, but elementary civic sense tells me that they should be treated well, even without considering the fact that they, with their hard work, had propelled Vajpayee to power. The year 1999 onwards, the distance between the BJP and the VHP continued to increase. What was Vajpayee trying to prove? Perhaps that he was more secular than all his predecessors, so much as to not allow religious work to take place in his regime. Who was he trying to please? Could he not have talked to the Telugu Desam Party and other such powermongers in the NDA?

The Thin Veneer of Acculturation

From 1998 to 2002, Vajpayee had to face severe opposition from K.S. Sudarshan, Thengadi and Singhal. These three abused their position of power in a most unseemly fashion. Singhal and Togadia were also allowed to and did make flagrant statements that were not in good taste. The reaction of anyone who has seen the civility of Golwalkar and Deoras was: No, this is not the kind of language the RSS or any of its constituents speak. We have not spoken like this throughout our long history. We were not like this, never. Now this kind of utterances will give legitimacy to the argument that 'the devil has always been there within these fanatics, right from the beginning. It has now acted and continues to spit venom. They are in power and without fear. What we have always known, they have now proved to be the case'. It is unfortunate that no one seemed to realise this, or brushed it aside arrogantly.

This is another instance of how thin the veneer of their acculturation, the *samskar* the RSS is so fond of talking about, really is, and how easily it is lost.[2] The other manifestation of the loss of this veneer was in the people who were placed in governance and their behaviour and character. There are many stories and not all of them are baseless. The many episodes where fingers were directly pointed at the characters of many BJP men, some of whom were RSS full-timers, true or false, planted, fabricated or otherwise, was something unthinkable to the cadre. This had become the day-to-day reality. At the whiff of power, the BJP men at the central and the state governments run by the party deteriorated. The party touted as a party with a difference became a worse and a poorer imitation of the Congress. Even the *pracharak*s lent for the BJP work did not have the moral power to control the arrogant ones and so no one managed to reign them in. Singhal and Togadia have finally been restrained for the last two years or so. When I asked a few highly placed individuals as to why it took so long, there was no answer.

That there are factions within the BJP, that the old guard is not yielding its place to the new generation of leaders are obvious. There is no moral authority arising out of character within the party. It is a game of power and nothing else. Herein lies the tragedy — only one organisation in India talked of character-building as a precondition to the betterment of the country (refer Note 1). This organisation said that it did not distinguish between the private and the public character of an individual. Both should be above board, without a trace of doubt about them. They found a method for building that. In the initial years, they seemed to have succeeded with a few known and notable exceptions. And by the time they were exposed to political power and mass movements and their power, they lost their balance, as well as civility, which is an important aspect of human character, along with many other facets. People across the RSS find it convenient to blame Deoras for getting them in this imbroglio and its revelations of character. The point is, however, that Deoras at least got them to power. Even without it, the possibility of retaining character and moral authority would still have turned out to be a huge mirage.

The Misconceptions about the Rapid Changes

The rapid changes taking place all around led to reactions from the RSS and, of all people, from Sudarshan. Thengadi too reacted, as did Singhal. The VHP asked the BJP to give up secularism and embrace Hindutva—failing to do so, they were called the enemies of Hindus by the VHP. Golwalkar and Deoras had always maintained that India is a secular state, and the guarantee of secularism's safety is the Hindu society here, which is secular by nature. Political power was neither the root nor the instrument of creating a Hindu Rashtra in India. It was merely a strong facilitator. If the Hindu Rashtra had to be created, it had to be organised, made aware of itself, of what was there to be proud of, and to destroy what was not good. It was the job of the RSS and the Parivar, not the BJP. Demanding the same through political power, through the symbolism of the Mandir, was ridiculous. I cannot but go back to Deoras in 1977, who put the issue of Hindutva on backburner just so that the Janata Party continued in power and Mrs Gandhi continued to remain ineffective. This is in sharp contrast with the actions of these people, their blindness and their revelling in symbolisms of rewriting history such as building a temple and preserving the Ram Sethu. The RSS resolution of 2007 did not take into account the environmental hazards for Kerala in undertaking the project of tunnelling — faith was the issue. As late as the Dashera rally of the RSS in Nagpur, in 2007, Mr Sudarshan spoke on these matters. When are they going to learn? When are they going to come out of their narrow moulds and understand the world?

Even without considering the 27 coalition partners of the BJP-led government, such reactions can only be termed the height of stupidity. The state is merely an apparatus that the society has thrown up for certain functions, and it must carry them out.[3] The Parivar and its leaders forgot the elementary lesson of keeping requests and admonitions private, or even working towards making the political party aware so that it might facilitate the work of the Parivar in general. They undertook public lynching instead. What showed through was the intoxication of the success of demolition, and the newly erupted traits of rabid chauvinism, Muslim-hatred and such, which had never characterised the RSS in the past. Vajpayee was being lambasted publicly in indecent language.

The kind of position that the Bharatiya Mazdoor Sangh, the Bharatiya Kisan Sangh or the Swadeshi Jagaran Manch were taking were obsolete and anachronistic in nature. None of them had any idea, or had decided to ignore the way the world economy by then had started working. They failed to understand that the word *swadeshi* had acquired a different connotation in the new globalised world.[4] I read some debates on the definition of *swadeshi* in 1999 (Wagale 1999a, 1999b). The participants in the debate were not RSS sympathisers, though many of them were well-trained economists, along with a few orthodox, obsolete Marxists. Within a span of eight years, even that debate has become obsolete in form. Their brand of *swadeshi* obviously is neither able to grasp the changes fully nor can see the future clearly. Thengadi took a strong stand against the disinvestment of the PSUs. It was perceived as going against the interests of the labour unions of the Bharatiya Mazdoor Sangh. Thengagi conceded to Sudarshan that he took this step under compulsion, in order to please the labour unions. He also requested Mr Sudarshan to maintain a distance from the matter (D. Deodhar 2004b: 21). The Parivar did not realise that they needed more time to understand the rapid transience of change. They did not wait to see the change slowing down around a stable, a more global and equitable economy to redefine things. It was merely the uncomfortable feeling that what they preached for so long was being overthrown and something they thought was defective was being put in place that led them to react in such a way. What Dilip Deodhar (2004b) says is an apt summarisation of the tragedy:

> Golwalkar and Deoras were not alive during the time Vajpayee was the Prime Minister. The chiefs of the Parivar organizations did not have a comprehensive understanding of issues, which created widespread confusion.... Vajpayee and Advani managed the opposition parties and their co-passengers well, but the RSS leadership could not manage the Parivar Leadership and organizations.... Some workers and the leaders of RSS were trying to prove Vajpayee a big zero and were feeling great about it... Five big defects of the Hindu Society viz, indiscipline, ingratitude, distrust, complete lack of information and misalliances came to the fore strongly and it made the RSS Parivar completely ineffective...

The rapport and coordination between the Parivar had broken. Now it was not 1 behemoth with 10 heads, but 10 different figures. No one bothered about the overall design, about cooperation and a common strategy.

The Mephistopheles of Publicity

The RSS and the Parivar had fallen prey to the habit of being in the strong spotlight of publicity. The most glaring example of this was Mr Sudarshan. He had to speak about something, indeed anything and everything, every day. A day would not pass without one controversial statement having been made somewhere. We have witnessed the RSS' extreme reticence and avoidance of publicity in Golwalkar's time, bordering on a shocking excess. We have also seen the optimum handling of the media in Deoras' time. He dealt with the press well, and the media liked him. He was always of an uncompromising belief, well-thought arguments and firm, polite and convincing speech. We agree that Mr Sudarshan is an extremely well-read man and has knowledge of a thousand different subjects in tremendous details, but we also think that there is no need for it to be on display all the time.

Thengadi, as late as 1990, answered my question by saying, 'There was no need to break the stranglehold of Left on the media. People understand and know.' It was nothing but an act of voluntarily wearing a blindfold, or hiding one's head in the sand, like an ostrich. The media also entrapped the BJP and all the Parivar leaders in these years of power, cornering them over negatives to make them appear repulsive in their defensive postures. The Left-dominated media caught them on the defensive, after already having created a sense of illegitimacy surrounding these organisations by virtue of a false, insistent and vicious propaganda. The lure of being in the limelight threw aside wise choice. Singhal, Togadia and Sudarshan, and everyone else, allowed the media to carry on with the game, and made a fool of themselves in the process. The failure of the BJP to get the media to support them has cost and will continue to cost the RSS and its Parivar in the future. All their achievements, if any, will be nullified.

Deteriorating Relationships and the Impossibility of Working Together

Arun Shourie, among other things, started the process of disinvestment of the PSUs. This was a clear notice to the labour unions of the country that their hegemony and evil chokehold over the PSUs would no longer be tolerated. Labour unions have been one of the major reasons why the PSUs became the white elephants that they are now, by common consent. The Bharatiya Mazdoor Sangh did not like disinvestment. Typically, the PSUs had stuck to an archaic mould of thinking. Even then, Thengadi probably took disinvestment as a personal insult — or more honestly, he could not do otherwise but to oppose it. Even if the latter is true, it was clear that the mindset of the unionists was still that of the smokestack economies or Britain in the 1860s.

The Left also opposed the privatisation of the PSUs and all other things that went with it. During the 41 years of the Nehruvian model of mixed economy, India never achieved a foreign exchange reserve of USD 300 billion, which she has today. Is there any chance the Left-ruled states would have created a proportional foreign exchange reserve for India? When are the Left and the conservatives in the RSS Parivar going to realise that whatever their model, it has already been beaten or overtaken, and has no chance now in this rapidly globalising world? When are they going to realise that it is globalisation which has given India the strength to protest at the WTO, and not accept what they do not like? What do they have to say when Ratan Tata buys Corus and Indians are routinely venturing into buying sprees all over the world? When will they realise that their model of India existing in isolation from the world did not appeal to the valour and the creativity of our people, who have redeemed themselves when they were forced to compete?

The RSS, the Parivar and the Left were concerned only about their own goals and not what will cause the overall benefit of the nation. The BJP had cut off the possibility of dialogue between the Parivar and itself. Not so long ago, in 1989, Deoras had taught everyone that the RSS, along with the Parivar and the BJP, would have to take the nation forward. The biggest drawback was that the mechanism of coordination which Deoras had established was no longer operative. Ultimately, the RSS had to step out and establish what they call the *Samanway Samitis* or the Coordination Committees. All the Parivar organisations desired that the RSS should conduct this coordination, since they are the only ones who can think of things with the broadest overarching perspective (conversations with M.G. Vaidya September–November 2007).[5]

I found this stance strange, and I said the same thing to Mr M.G. Vaidya, the person who first explained it to me. My point was that whoever has gone from the RSS to a different field has the primary responsibility of developing that field, a point upon which everybody agrees. But because they are RSS men, their final responsibility is to be able see the wider, bigger picture, and which action is more correct and more beneficial in that overall context. Singhal and Thengadi are not ordinary men. They are RSS men. How can they think so narrowly and only of their own field, throwing the bigger picture out of the window? The RSS *swayamsevak*s have not shown that maturity; their mediocrity has carried the game in an undesired direction.

The Parivar's Disconnect, Failure of Prioritisation and Politicisation

Prioritisation has been one of the weaknesses of the BJP governance. Dr Murali Manohar Joshi was accused of saffronisation of the contents of the various academic courses in the nation. My issue with Dr Joshi, however, is different and simple. Less than three years after the BJP lost the election in 2004, the need for trained manpower increased tremendously and the standards of what was being taught deteriorated. That Infosys needs a school of their own to train people after they are employed, as a precondition to taking them on the actual job, says it all. Dr Joshi was supposed to be the Human Resources Development (HRD) minister. Did he sense the need for trained manpower? Did he anticipate the growth? If he did, why did he not devote his time to improving the standards, setting up mechanisms to increase the manpower production in the required areas? And, much worse, if he did not understand that the job market was going to explode and that human potential was going to be the biggest potential to earn money for India, what sort of an HRD minister was he? An insider who worked with Dr Joshi, however, said that technological and other secular educational upgradation was attempted, but Joshi could not overcome the bureaucratic attitudes and hurdles (conversations with an RSS member with a key position in New Delhi, who worked with the Government from 1999 to 2004, name withheld on request [2007]). The subsequent boom and activity could, however, be partly credited to Dr Joshi. By building manpower, you make India a big force and a proud nation — this is the stepping stone to the construction of your Hindu Rashtra. The world has come to you, may be with just the back office jobs, but it has given you power. In time, better jobs and research and development (R&D) laboratories have also ultimately come to India. The RSS should also understand that there is no need to tell people to be nationalists and proud of their country anymore, like in the 1920s. They already are. Patriotism is no longer the RSS' monopoly as they still seem to believe.

Indra Nooyi became the worldwide chief of Pepsi. The RSS had no business with it, nor was it particularly necessary to say anything on the matter. They denounced her for serving a foreign company when every other Indian was feeling proud that an Indian woman had risen to such a high level. Disconnect with popular sentiments as well as the failure to recognise the right thing is obvious here. Obviously, sensationalism is the perverse habit that has overcome the RSS now. Sonia Gandhi met the astronaut Sunita Williams, who has later gone on to say that her ability to withstand the tough training of the American Navy is on account of her father's connection with the RSS, who gave them a good drilling in fitness (Chivhane 2007). The RSS did not see it fit to extend the same gesture as Sonia Gandhi. By their own standards, they would probably have denounced her as 'not Indian', since her mother is of Slavic origins. The RSS also did not see it fit to congratulate M.S. Dhoni and his world champion cricket team.

Instead of sitting down and talking it over, each leader of the various organisations started telling the other what they wanted through the media. As the insider observed,

> ...we have five third year trained swayamsevaks of fifty years standing in the organization, Vajpayee, Advani, Singhal, Sudarshan and Thengadi. But they can't even talk to each other; they do not even tolerate the presence of the other. That was not the RSS culture. There was a vacuum of issues for RSS to defend, react to or argue. The itch of old fault finding habits was left unfulfilled. It appeared that the RSS and the non BJP leadership was instead allowing personal likes, dislikes, biases, envy and jealousy of those in power, resulting in loss of balance, poise, dignity, largesse, civility, probity and an egalitarian way of speaking or dealing with tricky issues, while breeding irrelevance. The way all the parties behaved it did not appear that they realized the preciousness of political power. (Conversations with a RSS member with a key position in New Delhi, who worked with the government from 1999 to 2004, name withheld on request [2007])[6]

Issues of Public Image

Many of the issues faced by the RSS and the Parivar are ultimately related to that of public image, both nationally and internationally. On this account, it would be interesting to see how a person like Edward Luce (2006), a British journalist, views what has become of these people and the organisation. He describes gory incidents of massacre by Hindus in great details, while deliberately making no mention of the trigger for Godhra.[7] The tone and tenor of his argument are as if no one in human history has ever done a thing called 'state-sponsored terrorism'. Luce labels the RSS and all its Parivar organisations on the basis of their reactions to the Godhra incident, terming them perpetual, rabid, irredeemable chauvinists and fanatics, the most condemnable creatures on earth. He would have at least been politically correct if he had in equal measure talked about the carnage against the Sikhs in 1984 in Delhi. I do not justify the Godhra incident in any way. My point is that of the injustice in singling it out as a never-before phenomenon as well as the non-historicity of such viewpoints. This is the image the world is being shown, about which these people do not seem to be bothered at all.

The Luce narrative completely ignores the fact that Muslims had conducted such killings in the past, raped, plundered and destroyed in the cruellest manner and a greater degree than what is believed to have happened in and after Godhra. Will Luce tell us what it was if not state-sponsored terrorism? Do I have to remind him of the way the white man, who went as an emissary of their kings and governments, has displayed his cruelty, and the manifold ways in which he has wreaked destruction in Africa, Australia, America, or in short, wherever he went? The impunity with which Luce denounces Godhra is unbelievable.

I do not blame Luce. The people in his close circle may not be able to provide a clear or in-depth picture of the RSS and the related issues (refer Note 6). Whatever might have happened at the hands of Modi or whoever in charge, has there been any effort on the part of the RSS and the Parivar to highlight any different image of themselves? Deoras once said in the 1980s, 'I want to change the image of RSS as a *lathi* wielding organization doing route march on Dashera. I want to change the image to an organization devoted to service of polity' (Bal 2008). The BJP does not have the courage to introspect how the Congress remained continuously in power for 27 years in their first spell, and for 16 more years in their second spell. The BJP also does not seem to be concerned that they failed to get themselves elected a second time because of their own internal contradictions.

The inevitable happened once the Parivar lost touch with reality. The Vajpayee government was defeated in the premature elections of 2004 in a most unexpected manner. After the numbness was over, the blame game started. The worst happened when Mr Sudarshan publicly advised Vajpayee and Advani to transfer authority and leadership to the younger generation. The man at the helm of the affairs of the entire Parivar was publicly denounced by the BJP. The RSS volunteers in earlier years would have gone berserk over such an insult to their leaders, but they did not do so in this instance. Mukund Sangoram, a journalist, had to tell Mr Sudarshan about the impropriety of language Sudarshan used in his coloumn (2006). Ram Madhav made a ridiculous defence of Sudarshan, and embarrassed every one by going a step further and saying, 'If he had not said it, it would have been better' (Sangoram 2006). It may also be recalled that throughout the time they were in power, even the lowest ranking BJP man never opened his mouth to criticise the RSS and the Parivar leadership (Khandekar 2006). Journalists went to the extent of telling Mr Sudarshan he did not realise the power of the media, and that he should be careful with them (Bal 2008).

The last setback to the whole outfit was the way Ms Mayavati has stolen the show right from under their nose in Uttar Pradesh. Many reasons have been cited behind her rise, and clever analysis has been extended by all. The victory is being underplayed and predicted to be ill-fated due to her uncontrollable vindictiveness. I believe there are at least 40 people in her fold who had belonged to the RSS at some point of time or the other. Why has this been hidden? The whole of the RSS Parivar needs to understand that the failure on their part is that of imagination, of initiatives, of political acumen, of strategy, of coordination and of poverty of vision compared to what Mayavati has shown. They have to take into consideration that despite the ill-feeling and hatred between Brahmins and Dalits, they could be brought together and made to work together on the basis of a simple idea, that of having a stake in power. Had anyone restrained the BJP from making this offer to the various groups, especially since this is something they do all the time in a clandestine manner to remain in power? Why could they not build bridges across castes or give a slogan of Sarva Seva Samaj themselves?

Leadership needs to have a brilliant scintillating imagination in order to attract people. Mahatma Gandhi had it in ample measure. The overall RSS perspective and profile of action has been far more like Gandhi than anyone else for a very long time, but they never possessed his imagination. Yet, at least six times in the course of the Deoras era, the man in charge took landmark steps that changed the scenario of the nation completely and permanently. The RSS and its Parivar have a far wider base among the non-Brahmin castes, even the lowest of the low castes across the country, than one may think, represented in every rung of the hierarchy. Still, that last imaginative leap to scale it up massively, to bring big chunks of different populations within the fold, to publicise it and remake the Parivar's image, has been absent. No one is conscious about this either. If you want to survive, there is a great need to develop imagination to attract people.

The RSS and the Parivar have become everything that they were never to become. They have become men without largesse, men who have lost an egalitarian vision of mankind, men with a disconnect with the reality.

The bigger question, however, is if they at all understand the world today. Do they understand the challenges today? Are they willing to re-examine their premises, not so much because they are false, but with a view to expand the same in congruence with the modern-day reality? The even bigger question is if they at all understand the future? There are dozens of questions for today and for tomorrow that they need to first find out and then answer in order to survive. Making a mark of their ideology upon the nation would be a long shot after that. In the last chapters of this monograph, I will turn to these issues.

In 1996, Vajpayee was aware of the likely defeat of his party on the floor of the Parliament. It was the first BJP-led government and all efforts to win the support of parties outside the allied partners had not yielded fruit. Vajpayee was reluctant to make a claim. Deoras sent a personal message to Vajpayee, saying that no matter what happened next, Vajpayee must make the claim and form a government (conversations with V.S. Tamhankar alias Anna September 2008). One had to cross the finishing line, let people see that the party had, on its leadership, formed a government with its coalition partners, allotted portfolios and was ready to rule the nation. If there was to be a debate, then let the whole nation see it. The government lasted for only 13 days, leading to a series of people making their appearances as Prime Minister, finally leading to a midterm poll in 1998. This time the BJP formed a stable government that lasted for nearly five years.

The nation did see the debate. All attempts at garnering support on the part of the BJP had failed. All the old Hindu hatred, Hindu derogation, Hindu baiting and insult, and blatant Muslim appeasement gathered together, venomously and vehemently opposed the new government to see that the BJP–RSS principle does not attain full power. They saw the vilification of this principle. They saw the lone Vajpayee fighting it out with the hordes of predators. The debate watched by the nation brought Vajpayee back even after this government failed. The people also saw the mockery of the constitutional democracy, with a series of Prime Ministers coming and going. By the time the Lok Sabha dissolved and the polity had made up its mind to give the BJP and its allies one more chance.

In undemocratically pulling down the Jharkhand and the Goa governments in 2007, the Congress and Sonia Gandhi have once again shown the same hatred for the BJP and its principles. In Karnataka, the government was not an unholy alliance till Kumarswamy became the Chief Minister, and Ananthmurthy and Girish Karnad made a point to proclaim it as such on a public platform.

Notes

1. This has been apparent to me personally when the VHP higher-ups simply failed to garner the strengths of some of us who offered them help in experimenting with the situation in health care when Kalyan Singh came to power with a resounding majority.
2. I have come to seriously negate the thesis of the RSS that acculturation can build character and create men who can and will remain unblemished. That these men will ever create systems that will run the various areas of our national life, or will continue to do well, is seriously in doubt — the temptations of power or an unnatural life has negated that in more than ample measure. I have come to believe that without bothering about the man and his character, there is a need to build a system so strong that any one flirting with it wilfully will be the recipient of severe damage. We do not need men with character to build good systems; we need good knowledge of those entrusted to build them and a clear vision that does not allow the deliberate creation of loopholes.

   The absence of an institutional mind in the rank and file of the RSS is either the offshoot of the failure of acculturation or stems from the Hindu psyche which lacks the same. On the contrary, the RSS men, more often than not, take the course of desecrating institutions rather than building them professionally and solidly. Consequently, they have little of quality to show.
3. That there is a limited role of the state in the affairs of the national life, that its nurture and development on desired lines lie with separate agencies which need to be active and well has been a fond thesis of Golwalkar. Thengadi, the most enthusiastic articulator of that thesis of Golwalkar, as well as others should have known better than demanding so many things from the already beleaguered government — a government that had come to power because of their hard work. They were transferring the failure of their responsibilities to the government to be corrected. These were the people who persistently said that they did not need the state apparatus, to the

extent that they were not interested in power. They must now look back and reflect — is the thesis defeated?

4. There is a chain of cooperative banks set up by the Parivar. In the 1980s, many of them, particularly in western Maharashtra, were doing very well. When computerisation was proposed to improve operations in these banks, the Bharatiya Mazdoor Sangh unions, at the insistence of Thengadi, did not allow that to happen for many years. Consequently, these banks, instead of becoming the frontrunners in this sector, lagged behind. Only a few have slowly recovered from that. Incidentally, the work culture of the Bharatiya Mazdoor Sangh, the professionalism of its management and its institution-building capacity has been poor.

5. M.G. Vaidya was a former editor of *Tarun Bharat* and a high-level BJP functionary, who was a member of the RSS Central Executive for long years, and was well known to Deoras.

6. My source, the insider who worked in the Central Government from 1999 to 2004, also pointed out the unseemly way the RSS, the BJP and the other Parivar organisations behaved. The way the BJP persistently sidelined the Hindu issues left no enthusiasm among the cadre to go out and vote for them in 2004. This may be one of the many strong reasons for the party's election debacle in 2004. My source also consented to my contention that none of the ministers of the BJP government had any on-paper agenda of what they wanted their ministries to do.

7. The strident election campaign over the Godhra incident by these intellectuals and secularists, as well as the Congressmen of Sonia Gandhi, shows an anachronistic habit they have developed. All of us need to understand why Modi won twice in Gujarat. In 2002, the popular sentiment was with him for what he allegedly did or did not do in Gujarat after the burning of the carriage of the Sabarmati Express. He won in 2007 on the developmental plank on one side, but also because everyone else tried to raise the issue of Godhra and still do, in order to blackmail him and scare the voters. For even the common illiterate man, Godhra was a dead issue for long, no longer something to talk about or fear. People were happy with what development they had received.

The television media maintained an unprecedented silence over the Karnataka state elections of 2007. The element of injustice to the BJP, the deceit and treachery, was glaringly evident. With the failure of the coalition, it was clear that speaking against the BJP would have boomeranged on them — they sensed early that the BJP was going to win. This was despite Girish Karnad and U.R. Ananthmurthy coming to the fore to defend the Janata Dal when they started the treachery of not transferring power as agreed, saying that that was an unholy alliance.

9

The Unipolar World and the RSS' Response

———•✦•———

The quick collapse of Communism is the one of the greatest wonders of the 20th century. Ironically, according to Milovan Djilas (1969), Martial Tito's vice premier, the new physics of Einstein, Plank and other physicists had already formed the weapon that destroyed the physical, theoretical and materialistic basis of Marxism. The idea of Communism rose rapidly, became the noble creed for progress, social justice and human emancipation. It was accepted with a passion by half the world in a very short time post Marx, Engels and Lenin. The spread of Islam required a much longer timeframe and more violent struggle than Marxism before it was finally established. The Muslim stranglehold on irrelevant social constructs and fundamentalism continues and has only been strengthened over hundreds of years, but Marxism lost its fervour in just about 70 years.

What looked indestructibly permanent in the world structure was exposed to a whiff of an idea that 'we will change, open and widen the form'. The pent up emotions, thoughts, desires, needs and ideas of the people burst forth. Gorbachev's lovely book, *Perestroika: New Thinking for Our Country and the World* (1987), draws an extremely vivid account of the massive change, its speed and emotional content, and the massive upsurge of popular sentiment. The spread of this idea like wildfire led to the collapse of the USSR. The fact that everything about the earlier regime was archaic and irrelevant to the times came to the forefront. The Communist Party sought to master the art of running so vast a country through the central control of the Communist Party apparatus. This led to a stifling, suffocating, claustrophobic atmosphere, affecting the minds of the people. The thought of such suffering makes one's heart go out to the people who had to endure it. Having been reared in free India, and in a democratic atmosphere, which the illiterate masses of this country have preserved over long and troubled years, the contrast is excruciatingly painful.

Communism had clearly fallen short of the life Capitalist economies gave to the rest of the world, in smaller or greater measures. It fell short of democratic systems, with all their imperfections. *Perestroika* also gives a moving, futuristic picture of the transformation that Russia would undergo, beginning with a loosening of state control, leading slowly to a mixed infrastructure-oriented, defence-dependent economic model, to greater and greater liberalisation — strikingly close to the process India has undergone between 1950 and 1992, the subsequent years being a different story altogether. It was not the Marxist ideal of social justice, economic basis of life or the power of dialectical materialism as a change agent that collapsed — it was the utter irrelevance of that model of governance to time that was singled out for destruction.

The RSS and the Parivar failed to put up an appropriate response to the unipolar world that took birth with the collapse of Communism. The RSS, as well as its political and labour affiliates, did not attack the Communists, showing a singular lack of energy, imagination and initiative. It was the best opportunity to destroy any legitimacy that the

Communists have ever had, to destroy any stand or position or arguments that they have ever held as sacrosanct truths, and to destroy them even politically. The act of charging them of being irrelevant to the times, to modernity, of projecting them as a colossal failure of a social upliftment theory did not happen. The theory that failed in spite of the violence the Communists perpetrated on their own subjects or on the rest of the world was neither exposed nor attacked. Despite the fact that the RSS and Golwalkar considered them the enemy of nation since their loyalties were rooted outside the country and that their ways of thinking did not match with the Hindu world and its ways, the RSS and the Parivar did not react.

A few years after the Communist collapse, Joseph Stiglitz, in his landmark book, *Globalization and Its Discontents* (2002), drew a detailed account of the massive corruption under the Communist rule. More surprising was the paucity and poverty of legal, economic, banking and contractual framework, of a level of banking norms, systems, and so on, that a mature economy, market-driven or otherwise, normally should attain. The whole structure erected around the Cold War psyche started crumbling. Russia broke into smaller nation state units, and there were suddenly a lot of them to deal with, to bring back to the mainstream (as they did not become mainstream immediately) and rewrite the attitudes and the rules. In and around that time, China started shedding its Communist methods, and did so wisely. The change most noticed rather late was that the world was now a unipolar world, not so much of single political clout, but of one ideology.

As long as Russian Communism existed, there was a model for people to adhere to, to work and live by and for, to compare and contrast with the Capitalists. It also allowed the Capitalists a convenient target to blame things on. Now the onus was on the only system to deliver goods: Capitalism. The mixed economy model India adopted through Nehru was more Socialist than Capitalist or Communist, a hybrid, following a middle path. In and through the 1960s and 1970s, there was Euro-Communism. Each country had its own brand. It had led Thengadi, the ideologue and the creator of the Bharatiya Mazdoor Sangh, to rechristen World Communism as World Deviationism (Thengadi 1982: 38). Socialism was a huge contradiction, the most ill-defined entity. There existed other models, such as Anarchism of Prince Kropotkin, Bakunin and Proudhon, which never gained much currency (Thengadi 1972a: 8). Then, of course, there was democracy. In India, we have also had to experiment with the Panchayat Raj model, which was in transition and seems to have evolved well.

The populist Rajiv Gandhi regime and his subsidies and concessions to all and sundry had emptied the treasury and landed the country in debt, and repayments were just not possible. Twenty tonnes of the country's gold had to be mortgaged. Political instability had set in. In 1991, Rajiv Gandhi was killed. The BJP's strength was steadily rising from 1986 onwards. Narasimha Rao became the Prime Minister and with Dr Manmohan Singh as the Finance Minister he was faced with a situation where other than getting dictated over how to run this country, there was no option. The much-famed globalisation and liberalisation of India began under these ignominious circumstances. They were forced to start opening the economy, slowly but inexorably.

In the heydays of Mrs Gandhi, a systematically fostered Licence–Quota–Permit Raj of attaining government favours at a certain cost was prevalent. It preserved the protectionist economy controlled by the big businesses in order to maximise their profits — both parties benefitted in the process. It also protected labour unions in the public sector units (PSUs). In the 1970s and 1980s, unionism was the single factor which would not allow any productive unit to prosper. It was the greatest deterrent to creativity, to modernisation, to the continuous elevation of the quality of goods and innovation. The Indian economy, therefore, had become stagnant. It was not growing, whereas everything else such as population, prices, inflation and scarcity was rising alarmingly.

Economic liberalisation, modernisation and globalisation of India met with stiff opposition. The RSS led by Thengadi did not want it under the mistaken but fond assumption that 'India was a self contained market which did not have any a priori necessity to deal with the world or had to depend upon the world either' (Thengadi 1984b: 35).[1] The RSS and the Communists did not see computers as efficiency builders and enablers, as means to control human errors, important data-storing devices and powerful tools for analysis. They saw it as a labour-killing device. Technology and information technology was considered anti-labour, leading to loss of jobs. How terribly mistaken they have turned out to be! Their insistence was on human-intensive methods, typical of their fossilised mode of thought. Obviously they did not understand the future trends and their power, the benefits of technology and the way it upgraded the quality of human life and facilitated human work and efficiency; neither did they understand the importance of 'human independent systems'.[2] The RSS shared the Left's attraction for archaic models.

The RSS continued with its age-old habit of perceiving any system of functioning other than the decentralised, interdependant, slow and scattered system it was familiar with, which had not moved beyond the use of intermediate technology, as dangerous. Thus, along with the Left, the RSS and its Parivar denounced the changes sweeping over India. Thengadi's big slogan was, 'Modernisation without Westernisation' (1984b). This was an oxymoron. When cultures mix, they do not come in different separable packages. They come as a whole, and must be dealt with as one prefers and has the strengths for. Slogans such as the above then become individual preferences and convictions as to what is modern but not Western. A dozen versions emerge, and people fight about whose version is right. This has happened very often to the Socialists. If the technology is superior and enabling, it no longer remains either Western or Oriental—it becomes universal.

The Left theorists and the RSS men also failed to understand that 42 years had passed since independence, which is when the liberalisation process started. The Gandhian model of the village-based economy had long been discarded. It was not a wealth-creating model. It was an attitude of contented life. The Nehruvian model had created a dysfunctional economy and had failed to create wealth. The concept and model of the welfare state resulted in a popular psyche that assumed that the government would do everything. The heavy industry and infrastructure development model had made India into an industrial society, but did not give economic growth. It merely led to the urbanisation of parts of the country. Overall, that model and the concept of the welfare state had not succeeded at all going by the indices. There was little one could do to stop the exodus of people with little or no means from the villages towards the towns and cities.

In the role of the critic and the watchdog, it is not only easy but also fashionable to reel off impossible theories and prescriptions with all the self-righteousness one can command and be glorified as a great thinker. Both the Leftists and RSS men like Thengadi are guilty of this. In the field of my expertise, health care, I have seen unworkable solutions being offered while workable solutions are systematically spurned. I have observed behaviour for long years before reaching the conclusion that many of these theorists do not want a problem to be solved, but instead wish to keep it alive. Their existence depends on that. The Left in particular is interested not in solutions, but conflagrations.

The Indian Communists were shocked by the collapse Russian Communism, the basis on which their system was built. China also betrayed them by opening their economy gradually and wisely, adapting the Capitalist ways of development. Indian Communists have still not acquired an iota of wisdom to change their approach to either governance or development. Thengadi and the Left could not accept that the only surviving economic model was Capitalism. It had turned out to be strong, technologically superior and continuously evolving.

It is understandable how difficult it could be to accept this. In the minds of these people, Capitalism was still associated with the free market, the unbridled, cruel and exploitative economic system of 1760. These people did not realise that none of these things were present at the time of discussion, and that most of the exploitative aspects of Capitalism had been humanised. The industry had a stake in employee loyalty and development, which could not come about when the employer–employee relationship is exploitative in nature. This free system, in fact, had led to a stable and mature market, with regulations well in place, be it banking, social security or safety nets. The most glaring achievement was that this system had created wealth as no other system had done. It had made life interesting, set man and his rationality, his imagination, capabilities, creativity free to do things for himself, as most volubly lauded by Ayn Rand (1986). Capitalism succeeded precisely on this strategy — the production of the desire in a human being to earn for himself and earn profits. The third way or the Hindu way, more akin to the Gandhian model with its Panchayats and Janpads, was a system of slow and static progression, which had no chance at this time.

The hard-headed ideologues of the Left and the Right typically went after Capitalism by isolating certain elements for criticism. One such element was consumerism and the 'now and more' phenomenon that came along with it: the general rise in materialistic tendencies, the surrender to mere physical gratification and airy pleasures, hedonism, loose morals, drugs, mafia and gun culture.[3] Not even the Capitalists deny these problems. While denying these ills, however, Indians also denied themselves an otherwise strong and alert system. The threat of exhausting renewable resources of energy had come much earlier, but Indians ignored the strong drive and ability of science to develop alternate fuels. Lastly, and only lately, have serious environmental hazards been highlighted, which can be overcome through effort. Just as the RSS' hand was seen everywhere in the 1960s and 1970s,

American imperialism became the choice for abuse against the acceptance of the Capitalist model of economy in the late 1990s and the new millennium.[4] Funnily, both the Leftists and the Rightists use this abuse time and again.

In the hindsight of the last 18 years, the claim of imperialism appears somewhat ridiculous. In these years, more Indians have trained themselves to use foreign systems and made their country one of the most sought after nations. Would this have happened by keeping the economy closed? All those who spoke all the time of awakening the valour of the soul of the nation, of its people, be it Golwalkar or Thengadi, were in fact unwilling to confront the world and put up a fight against the challenges. Meanwhile, the Indians who did not subscribe to this vocabulary put up a stellar effort and a fight when confronted with global challenge. Despite all the talk of economic sanctions after Pokharan II, what happened in the end? The market realities did not allow anyone to dictate terms. The sanctions just went away. The process of opening up the economy made India stronger. Could we have thought of defying the whole world in Cancun and elsewhere, and reject the WTO terms not favourable to us with a weak economy? It is rather strange that the moment China and India came together and the BASIC nations backed Africa and the G-77, their power in the 2009 Copenhagen summit became massive and intolerable for Obama. He forced the door to enter a meeting uninvited. The Copenhagen exit of the Africans and the G-77 was dramatic in nature. Not opening up the Indian economy was never the correct answer—it was necessary to open doors and make the system work, which is precisely what has happened.

The only bastion to defend that the Right wing was left with was the danger posed to Indian culture in the liberalised age. Such objections are merely attempts to build walls around oneself, not allowing any new thoughts or ideas to come in. Resisting new thoughts and ideas is a difficult proposition, but there is no need to do so either. After all, what does culture mean to these orthodox Hindu thinkers? The first is the limiting of bodily desires, which degenerates into denial as an ideal, and surfaces elsewhere in a morally offensive and morbid manner. The defenders of culture, meanwhile, deceitfully claim that societies driven by earthly desires are not capable of understanding the meaning of the wonderful concept of renunciation championed by them. Another idea they think the modern world will not understand is to look at all forms of life as manifestations of God and their oneness with Him. The third element that concerns them are rituals. Furthermore, their idea of sexual morality centres around *yoni shuchita*, that is, the prevention of deflowering. Much of their 'culture', therefore, lies in the presentation of the instinct for incest in some sublimated transformation. Consider Rakhi or Bhai Dooj in the north as an example of sublimation.[5] Typically, all they present are unattainable prescriptions. Attempts to follow and achieve these states give rise only to subjectivism and deceit. One need not go into the effects it has on polity. It may be far more embarrassing to ask the very people who have supposedly given their life for the service of society as to how far they have succeeded in emancipating themselves from their bodily desires.

Deoras once asked Thengadi what he meant by Hindu economics. To Deoras, any economics that helped Hindustan and its people was Hindu economics. All in all, these Right- and Left-wing philosophers remained powerless, even as they kept shouting against the process of liberalisation of the Indian economy. The world as such had then become a unipolar world, with its collapsing national boundaries, incredible mobility (particularly that of Indians lately) and its power, the fading distinction between *swadeshi* and *pardeshi* (the national and the foreign). The new contours of this unipolar world, the new face of power and shift in power structures, the new functional peculiarities and strengths also led to a change in the role played by the business world and the government. All the divides of this world now resided in one unipolar Capitalistic world, in the single system of Market Capitalism. Some of the divides were new while some were older divides which have taken somewhat altered or new forms. There is now an accentuated rural versus urban divide, underlining the divide between the poor and the rich in the rural context of the agrarian Indian community. The rich and poor divide in larger towns and cities now revolves around the employable and the non-employable since this world has now set up a demand for skills that cannot come without the modern, formal education. Mr Narasimha Rao recognised this very early, but his ruling party did precious little for the same.

Technology has changed. It is no longer based on the physical capacity and capital of human beings, but becoming more and more based on mental capacity and strength. The technological changes have also led to old technology becoming obsolete, and with it, those who operated the same. Peter Drucker has given excellent accounts of what happened to the blue-collar workers in the mid-1950s in North America, which continued for the next 30 years or so. There is also a new divide, that of growth versus stagnation and decay. The changes have been vast. The question is whether the RSS or the Communists have understood this change to rise to the new challenges or not.

The RSS Response, Earlier and Now

Perhaps the most significant thing that happened in the life of Mrs Indira Gandhi was that Deendayal Upadhyay died in the year 1968. Deendayal was the one person in independent India who could have given two very important things to the Indian polity. Firstly, he could have possibly slowed the development of the degenerate state of today's BJP, thereby creating the most difficult challenge to Mrs Gandhi, and later, to Rajiv and Sonia Gandhi; second, he could have offered a third way, of incorporating the new developments, new models of thinking in his integral humanism (Upadhyay

1967). This was the most awesome challenge of the time. In his integral humanism, he attempted and achieved broad outlines of his thesis (Upadhyay 1967). Deendayal thought a great deal about the economics of this country and wrote about it in surprisingly original detail and a humane manner in his *Bharatiya Artha Neeti, Vikaski Ek Disha* (The Indian Economic Policy, A Way of Development) in 1957. Deendayal did not get time to produce more scholarly writing. He had to spend his energy in building the BJS. If anyone had to be chosen for the post of Sarsanghachalak after Deoras, it was clearly Deendayal. It is unfortunate that in spite of Deendayal's desire that someone should fill in the details in the broad outlines that he had drawn, no one chose to do so and the outlines remained unfulfilled as a result. There are a few treatises I have glimpsed through, but I am fairly certain that they do not expand Deendayal's thesis materially.[6] The only thing the subsequent ideologues of the RSS did was to avoid giving details, deriding blueprints in all manners possible.

Time and again the RSS men had taken refuge in saying that the eternal guiding principles were all that needed to be enunciated by the *darshnik*s, a grade of people higher than the philosophers. They quoted Marx and Engels extensively to show that even they desisted from offering blueprints, and quoted Lenin to show that both wrote precious little on economics (Nene 1986: 50–55). The clever arguments they put up are, at the least, somewhat reprehensible. A quote that has been attributed to Lenin, speaking with Savarkar in London, says,

> Blueprints tie the hands of the future generations. They become irrelevant and are more likely to fail. Those who are in charge of affairs have to decide. Till such time one does not acquire the ability to implement, the blueprints cannot be developed. (Nene 1986)

Quoting Golwalkar, the ideologue D.B. Thengadi says, 'Hindus are free to make any societal formations depending upon the circumstances as long as it is in light of the eternal principles of the Sanatan Dharma' (Nene 1986). The worst of the dishonesty over this issue was the argument that even Marx's predictions failed on the future of Communism. This was bad logic, even in those days.

Vague generalisations in place of adequate details do not tell the worker in the field how to go about solving the current problems, but, in fact, bind him to nonsense, as the Golwalkar quote above does. Unmistakably, these principles of the Sanatan Dharma are also, one may grant, the principles of the 'original' *Chaturvarnya*. Is it possible to implement such principles today?

It is the responsibility of the leaders to develop plans, to plan as carefully and in as much detail as possible, and to make predictions, however tentative, so that one has some idea about the probable success and failure of the plans. You cannot avoid this responsibility. After Deendayal, Jay Dubhashi tried to do this job. P. Parameshwaran attempted to do the same later, as did Nanaji Deshmukh, who made a serious attempt at experimenting with the Deendayal Research Institute. But to the best of my belief and knowledge, they have not been able to produce an imprint of their thinking on the BJS, nor create treatises that the political apparatus of the BJP could use later. Apart from being the doomsayer for decades, the RSS has shown a fundamental limitation in its intellectual apparatus in its incapability to make any fundamental contribution that could make this world a better place, before or after it became unipolar.

This duplicity of the RSS to criticise and comment but not contribute or involve itself in any of the processes and come forward to clearly express itself have cost both the RSS and the nation dear. One notable contribution was the remarkable treatise called *Labour Policy* (Thengadi, Gokhale and Mehata 1968), which put forth certain ideas on economics. The treatise consisted of well thought out and fundamental objections to the Nehruvian model of infrastructural establishment of not just large, but huge projects. The objections were based on the costs that would continue to go up as the years rolled by. The country could not afford these costs in the face of the reality of having to sustain and feed a large and poor population, especially since the fruits of these projects would be reaped too many years later. The treatise had further objections to the destruction of the soil of the sites of the dam once the construction was over, and to the rising salinity levels. It also termed the large PSUs as white elephants maintained by the government. Indeed, decentralisation and appropriate technology were the two mainstays of Deendayal's thinking. In today's world, we frequently speak of sustainable development, organic food products, the paucity of non-renewable sources of energy and developing alternate sources, such as windmills, to generate electricity. Soil erosion has become an issue to reckon with. These RSS men thought of these matters 50 years ago, but they failed, for whatever reason, to forcibly imprint their ideas on the minds of Indian politicians, thinkers, the industry itself as well as the agriculturists.

The situation is even more dramatically against the old RSS mode of thinking today. Market Capitalism is taking great strides, creating wealth, benefitting India in particular; it is talking of inclusive models of economic growth, and has become more kind, as epitomised by individuals like Narayana Murthy of Infosys. And, suddenly, the RSS is now left with few issues and even less alternatives. The third Indian way has been swept aside. The so-called world mission seems suddenly overtaken by powers the RSS is clueless about. It is equally clueless of its own role in this world and the strategy it should follow.

There is no point in continuing to curse Capitalism without even acknowledging what it has given this world. The kind of life and quality that Capitalism has offered people is unmatched. It has provided people with tools to build a new world and provided them with strength to fight those who seek to use Capitalism to oppress them. There is a need to shed archaic ways of behaviour and thinking in the name of ancient wisdom—I cannot say this as forcefully as I want to without repeating it a hundred times. It is high time that both the RSS and the Communists realise that there has been no fresh contribution from them about their basic or the world mission in terms that will make sense to the modern world, in a language that appeals to modern individuals and on issues that are truly relevant today. There are many more demands, but in the context of today's unipolar world, the responsibility to contribute and to expand with understanding is great.

Does the RSS Understand the Future?

Does RSS literature and experience reflect an understanding of global cultural fluxes beginning around 1975? Does it understand the role of the government to foster wealth, the new economic institutions and the new give-and-take? I do not see much to look for in whatever I have seen recently. In fact, one of the manifestations of the return of lost years is their perpetual preoccupation with the old symbols, exemplified by their obsessions with the Ram Mandir and the Ram Sethu. The RSS has recently spent about ₹1 crore to remodel their headquarters, Hedgewar Bhavan, on the lines of *Vastu Shastra*. Today the RSS gives the impression of an organisation perpetually mired in the past, having turned its back on the future and the present. What do the strident cries from the highest level suggest in opposing the ringing in of the new world?

Does it have a good understanding of the changing circumstances, of the changing psyche of the people, changing priorities of the people and the governments, the foci of power as well as vulnerabilities of the people and the governments? Is this knowledge and understanding clear, unbiased, deep and far-seeing? Or does it just have a vague idea of the Hindu way of living, where the details revolve around rituals and no modern details has been added to have a clearer idea of how it is done? In *Among the Believers* (1981),

V.S. Naipaul tried to painfully find out what the Islamic way of living meant. Other than *Zakat, Namaz* five times a day after washing one's hands and feet, some obscure reference about washing the private parts, fasting in Ramadan, going to Haj and that of Islamic banking not allowing usury, he could not find any sixth element of daily ritual which would have to be observed by a Mussalman. Travelling through Indonesia, Naipaul visited a few Islamic village schools called *pesantren.* The preoccupation of these schools is to teach how to pray, Arabic grammar, stories of Islam and Islamic law, apart from practising to live in poverty according to the Islamic tenets. The last was too strenuous an exercise. When it came to the daily rituals as the way of living, it left major issues completely out of context.

The Hindu way of life seems to go the same way identifying itself with the daily observances to be considered and identified as Hindus', like Tulsi Pooja (worshipping the Basil plant every morning), and such other rituals. People of both the religions need to understand that these are but the most superficial and inessential parts of being religious.

The RSS' Resolutions about the New World (2007)

A consideration of the RSS' resolutions over the course of 11 years, from 1996 to 2007, I believe, is an extremely useful approach that will show the changes that have occurred in the RSS' worldview over the years. In 1996, the RSS levelled criticism on many issues. Foreign direct investments (FDI) in the power sector and the negligence shown by the governments, resulting in losses upwards of ₹50,000 crores, were among major issues. Allowing fishing contracts to foreign companies ignoring the Murari Commission, thereby putting 100,000 fishermen in dire straits, was another issue. That allowing cigarette companies to manufacture small cigarettes is likely to make 10 million *tendu patta beedi*-makers jobless was the third issue the RSS brought up. The RSS felt that the import of Australian pulses, while banning indigenous production, created dependency. They had also objected to FDI in fast moving consumer goods (FCMG) — they may have been right in their thinking.

I am not a trained economist, but I do see one obverse aspect from the example of China, and the American and European investments that have gone to China.[7] These investments have become a strong restraining factor for the US and Europe as they grow increasingly dependent on the invested capital and seek to preserve it and help it grow, instead of being destroyed somehow or nationalised by the Chinese authorities. In fact, it appears more significant to them than it does to China. This is because America and Europe have become more vulnerable today. Similar developments could take place in India, which is why there is no point in opposing FDI to please the labouring classes, perhaps the RSS' sole constituency.

In 1997, RSS reiterated its demand of banning FDI in telecommunication, mines, insurance, agriculture and nuclear power, in addition to the areas already discussed earlier. It demanded an upper limit on foreign loans under Article 262 of the Constitution of India, and made a case for monitoring the same. The 1997 resolutions also cited several examples in surprising details to claim that liberalisation and globalisation will result in economic slavery, which is why they advocated *swadeshi* in its place. GATT and the WTO were naturally criticised. They further demanded a nine-year postponement in allowing FDI in FMCG. They also drew attention to the various local plant and biological species being patented by Americans.

In March 1998, the old objections were retained and a new emphasis was placed on resisting the imperialistic designs of the WTO, the G-7 and the multinational corporations (MNCs). The RSS further cautioned against a currency crisis that could be precipitated by foreign nations. In 1999, the RSS objected to the airing of sexually titillating content by some television channels. It also castigated America for insisting on the supremacy of American laws over those of other world-level market instruments, but not allowing the same to the developing nations. In 2000, the RSS came down heavily on 'cultural aggression' by the West, leading to materialistic, hedonistic attitudes, uprooting Indian culture and bringing about mental illnesses and physical deterioration. After 2000, the highest body of the RSS shifted its critique from economics and concentrated on all matters that threatened the territorial and cultural integrity of India, its sweep far-reaching and wide. Are we to assume that the RSS finally started to see the good globalisation had done to India? (Refer to note 7.)

From this, we go on to the next chapter of this monograph, wherein we discuss the survival of the RSS in such a situation, and all elements connected to the matter.

Notes

1. Thengadi started expressing these views in 1990–91, in a congregation held at Nagpur under the name of Swadeshi Vidnyan Sanstha, devoted to elaborate on Indian solutions for various issues. I heard some of them in informal discussions. Earlier, in 1984, he had published his thesis on Modernisation without Westernisation (Thengadi 1984b), emphasising intermediate technology and characterising the Western culture and development.

   As the leader of the Bharatiya Mazdoor Sangh (BMS), he started opposing computers, especially in banks run by RSS men, some of them among the best in the country. All of these banks have now fallen behind their competitors. Thengadi later admitted to Sudarshan that many of those activities were done under the compulsion of being the head of the BMS.

2. It is not just the human-independent systems of computer technology that the RSS failed to grasp. As I have argued earlier, the importance of building strong systems is a new idea that the RSS needs to understand. Emphasis only on man-making is only doing half the job. The second enormous problem with the RSS is their failure to comprehend the huge potential of computer-based information technology, even at

the highest level. Part of the problem is the accumulation of old age in the organisation. We will return to this again in the next chapter.

3. It was as late as 1958 that John Kenneth Galbraith called America 'The Affluent Society' (Galbraith 1958). Even Galbraith had warned Americans over the hazards – to health in particular – of consumerism but also knew the road to wealth it creates (Galbraith 1968).

4. I have no desire to give a clean chit to the Americans or condone what the British have done in the realm of economy. The arm-twisting, pressurising, sanctions, blockades are too well known to be detailed here. The issue was to meet the superpowers head on, use their own systems effectively and efficiently and get the best we could for the nation's development.

5. Mr K.P.S. Sudarshan raised a lot of hue and cry over the young generation's enthusiastic participation in Valentine's Day as a non-Hindu practice. I have dealt with this matter in the next chapter.

6. I have already alluded to the discussions on what fundamentals integral humanism should pay attention to, that which would result in a complete abandonment of the traditional approach. This illustrates the approach of some of the new writings on it as mere repetition.

7. The strength India has gathered today has come to be praised by the world in the course of the terrible recession that hit world economics in mid-2008 and lasted nearly till the end of 2009. It was the Indian and the Chinese economies that held on, bringing in sight the end of the recession in a relatively short period.

10

The Future, If Any

————•✦•————

The only sociopolitical body in India capable of reinventing itself today, albeit on a low scale of probability, is the RSS and its Parivar. Despite the mediocrity enshrined within the Parivar, they 'may' achieve the feat because of their enduring concern about this land, its people and its future. The Congress is unlikely, for at least another 50 years, to come out of its impotent dependence on dynastic rule. One fears that their hardened tendencies of Muslim appeasement and that of other non-Brahmin Hindu sections, at the cost of bringing about divisive effects within the society, will become stronger.

The RSS was ridiculed for wearing 'perpetual blinkers'. That distinction should now pass on to the Leftists as well. Their obsolete and irrational ways still hold the polity at ransom. We saw that during the issue of the nuclear deal with America, when they virtually brought down the government they were supporting. Over the last few months of 2010, the CPI (M) seems to be losing their ground rather quickly in their own bastion. The so-called pro-poor people of both Communist parties seem to have benefitted hugely in their personal life, economically, from their engagement with the Western system. We cannot expect them to provide solutions for the future for India since the old guards are still deceitfully engaged in their irrelevant old-world imagery.

The Socialists, in the form of the various alliances they keep forming and breaking, have tremendous nuisance value in Indian politics. They are so smug, shameless and megalomaniacal about the third and the fourth fronts they form every six months that the egos that break these fronts, or even abort them in the womb, does not seem to affect them in any way. These ridiculous fronts are a travesty of Indian democracy. Their diehard habits of high individualism, conceit and megalomania will not allow them to either learn or to reinvent themselves to offer concrete solutions for the nation's problems.

The task of reinventing, redefining, reinvigorating, re-looking at inconvenient truths, modifying or expanding or abandoning what was sacrosanct till yesterday, demands an extreme degree of boldness, strong political will and even greater intellectual honesty. Still greater strength is needed to overcome and overthrow the emotional likes and loves of the past. Such strength is not easy to garner. A couple of assets may take the RSS there. For one, they are not born anti-Americans. They are capable of responding to completely new situations, fully outside their area of training, especially when their backs are pressed against the wall. For example, they had the resilience to continue what Manmohan Singh and Narasimha Rao began. It is, however, unlikely for the RSS to develop a transcending, overarching, far-seeing intellectual capability, or the emergence of a visionary among them. The advent of Dr Bhagwat in the last quarter of 2009 raised hopes. The media liked him enough to talk to him. With Gadkari as the President of the BJP, talking of 'indiscipline is a matter of execution and not discussion'. 'Discipline and building the party'—he has at least struck the right notes. We wish him good luck. Let us hope Gadkari and Bhagwat manage to bring about this change in a wholesome manner and fast enough to become a sound, strong and meaningful opposition soon.

When it comes to the structuring of the RSS and the Parivar like a postmodern corporation that is able to respond to contemporary challenges, vision within the Parivar is rather limited. It threatens to become, or perhaps has become, a dinosaur. The survival of the Parivar itself is in question. Yet, they may be able to find a way, based on a couple of characteristics. To illustrate my point, I will discuss the New Wave Companies in the light of what is commonly accepted about the surviving and growing organisations of today's corporate world, and see if we find any parallels between them and the RSS–Parivar organisations. I will identify areas where the Parivar is lagging behind and use them as a guide for the future. It may be wise for organisations based on other ideologies and their supporters to also think in this manner, comparing various models and descriptions of thriving organisations with their own and drawing lessons from the same.

Does the RSS Have a Future?

The RSS has a long future ahead as the cult that it has reverted to being after the Deoras era — it is, however, a long but unproductive and sterile future. The lost years have returned post-1992, with the addition of some vile elements. Its dominant mentality still is cultish, although it has mercifully receded from that prospect to some extent.[1] Does it have a future as a highly influential body in the welfare of this nation? Stated otherwise, does it have the capacity left within to bring itself in that position? What would be the preconditions for it to be able to transform itself to that? Without answering these questions right now, we will look at some more questions.

What will happen to the RSS in the next 25 years? Will it disintegrate? Or will it be able to hold itself together? It is old, tired and too bulky today to remain agile. Its speed for change in the inner structure is grossly limited. It is manned by the bachelor full-timers, who have held sway over the organisation for long years. This is coupled with the householders who form a large part of the cadre that financially supports the RSS, assists in the management of the day-to-day affairs of the *shakhas*, including the various rituals and programmes. The RSS needs to manage a proper balance of involvement of these two groups. They have to think hard about the system of having celibate/bachelor full-timers. Their moral authority seems to have eroded beyond all expectation — they have to now decide how much of that is their own doing and how much the result of short-sightedness of others. Deoras had called the celibate full-timer system a social evil and also confessed that they had continued with it for the want of an alternate, equally good or better. Golwalkar was aware of these matters, but putting up impractical ideals was either a part of his way of dealing with his people or a way of keeping them under control by withholding crucial information.

Preserving the Ethos, Acquiring Credibility

With the passing of Mr Deoras, the rope that continued to tie the true ethos in Sangh has been severed. A large part has been played by the Hedgewar legacy in shaping the ethos of the Sangh. They will have to go back to that, rediscover it, reimplant it in their lives and then step out in public life. Unless that is retrieved, almost anything can happen to the RSS. The RSS ethos is the same as the centrality paradigm I have discussed earlier. The organisation's ethos lays down the only distinction that *swayamsevak*s can and should ever desire to achieve: credibility. This has taken a severe blow. It is foolish to expect credibility by virtue of being (or declaring oneself) a *swayamsevak* (voluntary worker) or an officer alone—it will have to be acquired first and then maintained and kept without blemish for a painfully long period if they want people to believe in them. Credibility comes out of character and its demands are ever more stringent.

Man-making Mission

As we have already discussed, the man-making mission is the primary cause for which the RSS needs to exist. The RSS and the Parivar have failed to write a coherent philosophy or an action plan for each of the areas of national life where these men were supposed to contribute and leave their imprint upon by virtue of their character. This task is not as difficult as it looks. If the man-making has to continue, then the deployment strategies for those workers in the areas of need should be planned where they could practice what they imbibe.

It is surprising how little appreciation has been accorded to this goal of man-making of the RSS by all and sundry. Whatever the system of governance, of political structure or philosophy, it cannot succeed unless honest men run it. With all the glorious achievements of India Inc. painted daily in the pages of *The Economic Times*, the ground reality is still that of *Khosla ka Ghosla*. Whatever the level of our national pride, the operational reality is still as glaring as depicted in *Chak De! India*.[2] There is no substitution to the development of the notion that the nation comes first, and one has to serve it with honesty, even if it makes one's own life much harder. A mechanism has got to be in place for this. But the RSS also needs to change its approach to the same.

System-building with Character-building

The RSS needs to revamp its system to intensify this man-making process and achieve it. The RSS has not lived up to the claim that by creating men with a capital M, they will create the required form and action in various fields of national life. They must persist with it since only they can do it effectively on the level of the common man. So now they have a twin task: that of creating men as well as creating systems where they work properly, character or no character. Men with impeccable character and incisive intelligence, or either, are hard to come by. In the general absence of them, creating a detailed system or operational patterns becomes even more difficult. Any attempts to do the same will only be non-professional caricatures of ineffective work. The kind of economic methods you apply, the business techniques you use, the kind of export–import policy you adopt or the brand you chose to implement, be it *swadeshi* or liberalisation — all these are important considerations. To make the right decisions, they need men with not just character, but vision as well. This is not an abstract discussion. There are many ways in which it can be done.

What More Does the RSS Need to Rethink About?

On an ideological plain, the RSS will have to redefine Hindutva and Hindu Rashtra, taking into consideration at first the constitutionally established state. Is it a purely emotional, amorphous and a mordent concept that binds people together? Or is it a formed social entity that is not co-extensive with the polity but is a subset thereof? Or is it some kind of an extra- or supra-constitutional force, like the Quran Sharif or the Vatican? Which of its contents — religious, social, and so on — are likely to undermine the supremacy of the rule of law or that of the Constitution, if at all?

After this, the RSS has to consider if their concept of
Hindutva comes into conflict with the rights of citizenship
granted by the Constitution or if it reinforces these rights in
some way. Does the RSS think that Hindutva is a precondition
to citizenship, or do these two concepts run parallel to each
other and are not a threat to each other? The RSS also has
to clearly define its attitude towards the constitutionally
established state vis-à-vis Hindutva. I would be very happy
if the RSS truly believes that these are hypothetical questions
and that they have clear answers for all of them. I would also
then insist that they publicly offer these answers so that the
polity may understand where they are coming from.

The social behaviour of a man or a woman, as dictated
by their religion, vis-à-vis behaviour as required under the
Constitution, in and under a civilised social system, is another
civic/civil issue. It has created enough conflict in the polity for
last 80 years. The RSS should take the lead in redefining this
for its own members and, by implication, for the traditionally
recognised Hindu society. This will lend justification to their
demand to similarly redefine these aspects of all the major
religions and cults in India. Diversity, plurality vis-à-vis
Hindu ethos needs a more liberal interpretation in the RSS.

Sovereignty and democracy have come to stay. How
does the RSS view these values? The edifice of modern
India is built with the recognition of the individual as the
fundamental unit of the nation. How does the RSS view
this? Furthermore, they will also have to do away with the
hypocrisy that has prevailed since the inception of the Jan
Sangh, either by declaring their allegiance to political goals
or complete separation from politics.

Surviving in the New Postmodern World Corporations

Alex and David Bennet, in their 2004 monograph, have
discussed organisational survival in the new world, as many

others have before them and since. The Bennetts consider the Intelligent Complex Adaptive System (ICAS hereafter) to be a way of describing the characteristics of the New Wave or the Postmodern Organisation of the late 1990s. Such corporations have been defined in many ways. The ICAS, however, pithily represents both the concepts of the New Wave and the Postmodern Organisation, and best sums up the other descriptions.

It may come as a big surprise, but the RSS is, even now, at the cities, district towns and in the sub-district levels a striking example of the ICAS. The volunteers behave like an ICAS instinctively. How could the singular massive organisation of the Ekatmata Yatra and the Ram Shila movement and other such massive campaigns succeed otherwise? What exposure did they have during the 1947 genocide, or in the Andhra or Morvi or Killari and Bhuj disasters?[3] The character of the RSS in general is well in place and the belief in the aims, work and the leadership quite adequate for the organisation to be called an instance of an ICAS (conversations with an RSS man who worked with the government from 1999 to 2004 and does not wish to be named).

The volunteers come together for different Parivar organisation works, group and regroup themselves, adapt to different roles, to responsibilities outside their general expertise, training or the formal responsibilities within the organisation, and share and work with camaraderie. However outdated in form, the *shakha* work holds them together. Barring the narrow-minded hierarchy, which dwells on the ifs and buts of their kingdoms and domains, the perceptions of rules and regulations, the ordinary volunteer ignores all ifs and buts and throws himself into the fray. Bhaskar Rao Kalambi had spoken to me of this paradox, 'Whatever may happen at the top, the RSS work does not suffer at the ground level. That way, it is an ingenious system Dr Hedgewar developed' (conversations with Bhaskar Rao Kalambi in 1980, 1987, 1988, 1990).

Some Negatives—the Downside of the RSS

While the volunteers understand, the CEOs of the Parivar have long forgotten that they are directly responsible for creating the collaborative working ethos, the seamless informal formations and reformations of the cadre across the organisations (conversations with an RSS man who worked with the government from 1999 to 2004 and does not wish to be named). One of the major expectations from all Parivar organisations has been to bring capable people from the society in contact with the RSS. This is where they will achieve their final transition to being different men. No one even remembers this today.

In the New Wave Organisations, the CEO and the senior management need to create and foster such a positive working culture within the rank and file of the organisation and make a habit of doing the same. Today it is a cliché to say that companies with the industrial wave smokestack structure, with rigid hierarchies and standardised static work practices, and replaceable blue-collar work forces will collapse under their own weight. Today when products are standardised in quality, have parity in prices as well as being of large variety, what sells is the relationship and value-added services. Typically, the RSS used to offer that to an individual, but this function has declined significantly with such a vast organisation. The BJP in particular has forgotten to maintain this contact with the ground for a long time, and has paid dearly for that.

The new world needs organisations that are knowledge-driven, which use information technology to collate and analyse all possible relevant information through automated processes to the greatest extent possible. New Wave Organisations are knowledge-based organisations, and have knowledge workers who are difficult to replace. The RSS was never a knowledge-based organisation, or even driven by the same. Little did they understand that knowledge is not a need-based acquisition. It stands for itself, and not acquiring it will make mediocrity the norm, will make scholarship go out of the organisation or never come in at all. The RSS must, therefore, learn to use these tools to develop effective strategies for their work.

The New Wave Organisations are flexible and adaptive; the RSS in its day-to-day working is not. In fact, it is the very opposite: rigid. This rigidity extends all over. It has become an instrument in the hands of the hierarchy to keep people at a distance and to control their behaviour. It also results in killing their energy, creativity and enthusiasm. It stops contact and interaction between the lowest and the highest levels. Rigidity has become sacrosanct, nay, it is an age-old malady in the RSS. It is stifling. It creates small terrors about the highly placed officials in the hearts of the volunteers and makes working for the RSS mechanical, without much joy or fun. It merely enhances the prestige of those in the hierarchy, often unearned.

Democracy within Organisations

The new organisations in the postmodern era are much more democratic. In Dr Hedgewar's time, there was unlimited democracy within the RSS—it was a boisterous, energetic organisation, untiringly argumentative and founded on the bedrock of mutual trust. Hedgewar was democracy personified. Talking to him and listening to him was the living experience of it. In fact, despite the ridiculous charge of fascism, one characteristic of democracy has always been present in the RSS till date. In formal forums, difference of opinion has always been expressed strongly. Informal discussions among the workers, without fear of recrimination, have always been a feature. There is, however, a flip side to this story. While the charge of fascism levelled against the RSS is nothing short of ridiculous, it is true that dissenters had been shown the door in 1950. Egos rather than fascist and dictatorial tendencies in the hierarchy were behind this. Deoras, the major dissenter, had distanced himself from the organisation without any prompting and had remained away without voicing further dissent or leading rebellions. The RSS, like any other organisation that has lost touch with democracy, had the techniques to isolate dissenters and then defame or degrade them. Golwalkar was not fond of dissent—most of us are not—but if you consider his speeches till 1960 at least, Golwalkar pleaded with his people to accept his point of view, pleaded with them to allow him to do what he liked best, which was RSS work. The charge that he was a dictator does not hold (Golwalkar 1974b, 1978, 1979).[4]

Democracy got its due in the Deoras era once again in far more ample measure. He started the question–answer sessions, the process of two-way communication in all the gatherings of the *swayamsevak*s and at all levels, small children included. It was a free for all. In case of small children and young ones, the questions ranged from hilarious to ridiculous to queer; they were also often blunt, audacious and sensible. Deoras never spurned, snubbed or ridiculed a person, however small, but patiently explained the answer, most often in surprising details in the most humble manner, even to young children. The long-time General Secretary of the RSS, Mr H.V. Seshadri was so enamoured with the process and found it so important a step that time and again he mentioned it when he spoke about Deoras in later years. It merely indicates to me that the dialogue with the grass-roots workers was not so free-flowing in the Golwalkar era. After the Emergency, Deoras replaced the term that allowed the RSS to be labelled as fascist, *Ekachalakanuvartitva*, or the unquestioned obedience to one supremo, to *Sahachalakanuvartitva*, or decision by consensus. Today, however, the sad story is that all the men who gather to make decisions in the RSS seem to think alike, in the same old manner, finding refuge in the received, conventional wisdom. Otherwise, they are just yes-men with no opinions of their own. We do not want this kind of unanimity. There are no landmark initiatives, no startling imagination to be found within the organisation anymore, despite the existence of a form of democracy.

However, an antithesis to democracy has also been long built within the RSS in the form of prevailing internal and external terrors. Despite the long-standing culture of expressing differences of opinion, one is not easily given to expressing dissent. There is, however, a difference between dissent and outright indiscipline. The RSS will have to uproot this tendency of conflating the two, which now holds sway within the organisation. Dissent often leads to withdrawal of support by the RSS, especially of its manpower and financial support; both members of the RSS as well as Parivar organisations fall prey to this tendency. An instance of this is the 2004 general elections. Even L.K. Advani did not dare voice dissent against the RSS.

The surviving and rapidly growing organisations of the modern age are team-based, generally requiring its employees to undertake extra and special tasks outside their hierarchical job descriptions. The functioning of the RSS is hierarchical. There may be committees, even cells for special purposes, but not teams as described here. Teams are embedded within organisations; they have special functional characteristics, urgent and deliverable timelines, as well as the capacity to create knowledge, leading to strategies. Teams have multiple talents. In the RSS, it is the organisational structure itself that is embedded. Unlike postmodern corporations, changing functions all the time as per the needs of the situation is not a routine characteristic in the RSS, and has not been for a long time. The groups stick to one kind of work. They are not allowed to network freely. There is a huge network built within the RSS, but it has not attained at the intellectual, perceptual, understanding and working levels that are characteristic of a networking organisation which has habitually free-flowing information. In their routine day-to-day work, the volunteers are not conscious of all the other work undertaken by the Parivar, of the issues, priorities and emergencies elsewhere in the Parivar. The RSS still needs a deliberate effort for the first meeting to get it all in, after which things get going.

The New Wave Organisations are keenly aware of the need for systematic thinking, speedy connectivity, digitisation and access to knowledge, and smooth flow of information throughout the organisation in dealing with an environment that is complex, uncertain and changing all the time. The systematic and holistic thinking of the Hindu thought is well explained in theory in the RSS, but it ultimately waters down to the 'old model' in practice. Connectivity with speed is a notion which is far away from taking birth in the RSS — matters take a few weeks at its minimum to percolate down. The information that passes down is smooth, but there are filters at each level.

Intentionally building the 'organisational intelligence' is a necessity for survival. This is meagre in the RSS cadre and supporters today — as a result, the spoken word in meetings does not get translated into organised knowledge on paper, in knowledge banks with its accredited source or the expert behind it. What comes to hand is the concise or paraphrased list of general conclusions and somewhat vague directives. Using organisational intelligence through innovation is also a far cry in the RSS.

The New Wave Organisations are complex, non-linear and hence diverse. They have a shared purpose and multi-dimensionality, all qualities that are also possessed by the RSS. But their internal linkages across the departments (read Parivar) is neither well formed, nor well informed. It is neither constant nor do they care about it enough to put an end to inconsistency. This is a problem which has made the RSS much less live to reality now than in the past. Through creativity and the use of organisational intelligence, they should learn to solve problems and take right decisions. The RSS far too often resorts to conventional wisdom and suggests or receives insubstantial remedies, which have no effect on the situation, be it their own or a national situation.

Porous boundaries are an important concept. It is the guarantee of the direct contact of the senior/higher management with the frontline managers and customers, based on a free exchange of communication and ideas. This culture has not survived in the RSS after Deoras. For instance, I had made it a habit to go and meet Deoras to sort out the various issues I faced. A couple of discussions that I have had with him were a face-to-face, free affair. On one occasion, the discussion turned out to be a path-breaking one for the general thinking of the RSS, welcomed by people like Bhaskar Rao Kalambi. This mode of open interaction did not extend beyond Deoras.

New World organisations can neither survive in the power culture of entrepreneurial organisations, nor in the bureaucratic rote culture. The culture of personalities that results in little organisational cohesion is also antithetical to them. For the RSS, a culture of action would be the best option. Today the RSS genius is unable to produce a culture of action that can operate in timely and effective manner, capable of turning the tide of the event. It has within itself the trappings of power, role and the culture of personalities; this is also true for many Parivar organisations that have grown big.

The New Wave Organisation typically relies on creativity through brainstorming, problem solving and a dozen other methods. Both creativity and brainstorming, characterised by out-of-the-box thinking, lead to decision making. Decision should be taken at the highest level only after considering the inputs from various team decisions taken at different levels. In the RSS, the quality of data and the reliability of lower-level decisions and perceptions suffer, which is reflected in the high-level decisions in the organisation.

One of the important signs of the New Wave industry is collaborative leadership. It nurtures and allows the various employees of the organisation to co-evolve within a culture of collaboration. The collaborative leaders, through their integrity and vision, earn the right to influence others. They serve as role models and help others to get the work done. Today, this long-standing culture within the RSS has been corrupted. Neither the organisation nor the culture is evolving. Unfortunately, the RSS leadership is on a somewhat brittle foundation for being considered worthy of emulation, or as role models of integrity and vision. Hence, it does not have the moral standing to advise the Parivar on issues; they cannot bring the entire Parivar together for a common purpose, since the leadership at the highest level cannot sort out matters by dialogue.

Furthermore, collaborative leadership is driven by values and moral principles. Today, the RSS and its Parivar seem to be driven by the irrepressible desire to politicise issues, to indulge in high-pitched rhetoric and cantankerous fits over matters of utter irrelevance to the national situation or to the RSS itself. They revel in being in the limelight, irrespective of the consequences. It may go unnoticed, but Dr Bhagwat has, at least initially, succeeded in reigning in many stalwarts.

The collaborative leadership is a guide with moral authority. One major function they perform is to reign in the knowledge workers who, by nature, training and job requirement, are freethinkers. But at a point they need to understand the common ground to which the whole process is heading. The leader needs to bring the knowledge workers and other workers to some common ground, where they can complement their competencies for a given task. These processes do take place in the RSS and the Parivar, but the authorities are rigid and do not allow a full role to the knowledge worker so crucial to the modern and changing contexts. I have doubts about the effectiveness of this process and whether it is working any longer in the RSS and the Parivar. The level of understanding the context at its widest is low since the ability and willingness as basic tenets of being a *swayamsevak* are no longer mandatory or routinely available traits.

Trust in other organisations, including that of schooling others, especially in an organisation like the BJP, is a far cry.

Ability to trust others also defines a collaborative leader. Many seniors feel the need for establishing a healthy feedback system in the RSS. Others think that the existing feedback system functions well enough for the organisation. Taking a middle view, I suggest that it is necessary to make the feedback as well as the feed-forward mechanisms stronger. This will be naturally empowering. Trust and empowerment leads to easier alignment, which is the process of continually assuring that the activities of all the workers are directly or indirectly supporting the organisation's common vision and purpose. For very long years, these processes in the RSS could be cited by any management expert as the best of examples, especially in the Deoras era. The unfortunate part is that no one has looked at it from the point of view of management of men of diverse characters, wedded to a common goal and functioning smoothly as a machine. Deoras used to call the RSS 'the wizards of organisation'. Organisation, for Deoras, was their main attribute who claimed no other expertise. This machine had the capability of utilising the combined pool of talent of its men through this managerial process. But no one inside the RSS listens to anybody today—alignment of purposes is no longer visible.

The activity of evaluating, or the post-mortem of an event or project or an initiative, is considered extremely important today. But such evaluations may occur in the RSS and the Parivar today only when failures happen, so that the blame game can begin and the buck may be passed around. Even more frequently, when things go wrong or dissent occurs, the RSS does not show the courage to face the unpleasant truths, to bring differing people together to sort out the issues in the open. Instead, they would attempt to do the same by indirect and circuitous routes of dialogue in order to not hurt their own people. Even more frequently, they deal with such matters by following the old adage, of pushing such issues under the carpet. If and when the analysis of failures do occur, it has often taken the route of rationalising or of building elaborate facades of involved and clever facetious reasoning so as to not admit the failure has indeed occurred. When situations worsen, they often take to the final refuge of telling each other that it is not their job to sort the matter out, or that external situations were *force majeure.*

Discovering tools that will enable the teams as well as the hierarchy to do their job well is one of the foremost concerns in growing companies. The RSS and the Parivar has virtually forced their cadre to use outdated tools that will not do the work. Albert Einstein famously said, 'You cannot solve a problem by working at the same level of thinking at which you created it.' Daring, audacious thinking and thinking outside the box have not been among the virtues of these bodies.

Promoting learning and development of the people, leading them to envision an even greater future, a great concern of the New World companies, seems to have been pushed back by eons in the RSS. They do not probably even have the elementary centralised databases on almost any parametre one could lay down where information is invaluable. In the absence of hard data that has been collected in a 360-degree manner, presented in written or non-verbal state for discussion, viewed in different perspectives, using newer methods of analysis, how will the organisation learn of how the situation on ground fully is, and envision action at micro levels? The reason probably lies in the fact that the RSS and its Parivar organisations are unfamiliar with the computer culture, the enormous capabilities of these tools and are suspicious of it. At best, they have a qualitative impression about their work in various pieces, the difficulties, mainly of finance, and worry over keeping the work going. Thinking of the effectiveness or otherwise of the work has never been there. As a result, having a handle on the full picture is a far cry. Any possibility of systematically understanding the need for an effective counter strategy, systematically developed by analysing what data they have at hand, is too remote.

There is another longstanding tendency in the internal structure of the RSS, which requires massive — albeit very difficult—corrective measures. Over the Golwalkar years, it has accumulated a subset of cultural purists whose stances are archaic and near impossible to maintain in today's context. It has accumulated a number of aged office-bearers everywhere, and no one is ready to give up their honourable (but often empty) positions. People have gone on record saying that even the post of the Sarsanghachalak should be abolished in the manner the tenth Guru of the Sikhs, Govindsinghji, had done during his tenure. The point is they will have to think boldly.

In large, complex organisations, balancing the long- and short-term organisational priorities, allocation of resources to its functioning parts, central control over these parts versus the freedom they get, are matters of dynamic action. Post-1992, and even more so post-1999, this balance is in a state of perpetual and perilous disequilibrium in the RSS and the Parivar, which it needs to urgently regain. It is heartening to learn that there have been efforts within the organisation to regain this balance and that the process is now in place—we only wish that it becomes strong, steady and yields positive results. Structuring an overall strategy will also hopefully follow and strengthen these achievements. Furthermore, for a longer-lasting future, there is also a great need for the RSS and its Parivar organisations to become learning organisations that draw relevant inferences for winning actions.

A Little More About the Existing Strengths and Weaknesses of the RSS

The RSS has a sprawling network of literally thousands of organisations, of service projects. Its strength arises from the grassroots level, where its contacts are close to a million people. Nonetheless, these network organisations and contacts are scattered, and therefore ineffective.[5] Why have there been sub-optimal achievements? Declining quality of forward-looking scholarship is one of the foremost reasons behind this. The process was not consciously continued. Nana Deshmukh made different rural models of socio-economic upliftment, but they could not be used by the Parivar by lifting them to a popular level, with concrete programming across all Parivar organisations. These models, in fact, suited the grassroots needs of these grassroots projects. Mediocrity arose within the organisation, and with that was gone the backroom data acquisition and processing, analysing for problem issues and their likely answers.

The RSS through the 1950s and the 1970s, and the RSS now are financially different institutions. Today it can afford to think of different ways of ensuring a reasonable future for those who have family responsibilities, who need to be freed from their other vocations since they are useful to the organisational development and growth. People who have been exposed to the different ground realities of life while having to work for their livelihood bring in different perspectives to the organisation. Their lifetime expertise could be utilised to actually build on paper strategies and schemes, or priorities which they could implement among the Parivar, and offer to their political affiliate, if or when it comes to power again. This also has another huge internal advantage, that of lending the same expertise to the over 100,000 social service projects run by the RSS-supported organisations. To get the idea approved and ensure a respectable relationship within the RSS and the Parivar will be a huge task involving coordination and drilling the benefits attained from the same into the minds of the people.

The Ineffective Network

The RSS and the Parivar have an unqualified enthusiasm to start organisations, small or big, without much forethought. That results in multiple organisations, at times doing the same thing. Today, the majority of these organisations will claim that they are trying to push forth the RSS ideology and influence their respective fields. They may even forward some sketchy ideas of how they will achieve this, but the concrete, detailed programming and the process arising out of these ideas will undoubtedly be vague. Their performance on the ground level is poor in terms of the business they are supposed to transact. The Cooperative Banking Sector can be cited as an instance of this (Godbole 2007). Their personal conduct and financial and business acumen leaves much to be desired. Even their integrity is not beyond question. Their vision is limited, the future planning, at best, is inadequately thought of. The expertise available to the entity at the board level is not spectacular, nor is their achievement significant (Godbole 2007). There are sterling exceptions to this general rule, but we are talking of more prevalent types. The situation of other organisations is similar. The bottom line is they are not counted, they are not effective, they can neither lead nor influence.

The greatest contribution the RSS can make today is to work with the various models it has created and replicated in thousands of different projects in the various fields of national life. Only the RSS can do it. They need to first assess the basis on which these models work, to determine the relevant and practicable against the obsolete and irrelevant. Then comes adjusting and aligning their goals as well as methods to the modern era and the reality of today's India. They must make an assessment of what their needs are, and how and from where could they be fulfilled. The next important consideration would be how to consolidate them far more effectively as the torch-bearer of its own new thesis to reconstruct India while riding the new currents. The last consideration should be over how many of them should be dismantled, or merged within larger units.

Some of us in the headquarters have already made a little campaign for bringing all the Parivar work onto an excel sheet on a computer and consolidate the statistical information, the output so far and its possible effect on the local situation in which these works are in progress. The idea has not been rejected. It will take time and energy, and help of software experts to bring all information to the level of statistics. We are aware of the tremendous potential benefits of this exercise. It will need a little bit of convincing and judicious allocation of work. The strong feedback mechanism and the contribution of experts in the various fields, abundant in supply, will crystallise the knowledge of the lessons learnt. This is something that needs to be achieved. More importantly, the lessons must be implemented. The RSS needs to write everything down. What has it done? How was it achieved? What was the vision behind it? How far have they been successful? This can teach them the required lessons. Equally importantly, the world will draw quite a few lessons from what the RSS has achieved. This is the form in which the RSS should contribute to the reconstruction and rebuilding of this nation in all fields. This is a far better way than sloganised, obscure and obsolete activities like the Swadeshi Jagaran Manch (Forum for Awareness of Nationalistic Ideas).

Also significant is how well it is able to coordinate, nay, integrate the functioning of its Parivar and give it an agenda to sharply focus on and work. The RSS has an enormous strength that lies dormant. It has not been effectively utilised throughout its history. If they cannot organise themselves and utilise their strength, they will disintegrate as a Parivar, and then the RSS mainframe will be left with little power.

Wanted: An Institutional Mindset

The failure of the numerous social work projects undertaken by the RSS and its Parivar to make an impact lies in the inability, or unawareness, of those connected with these projects to develop an institutional mindset. This appears as a paradox to me, because I am more than convinced that the RSS training and workings of the Parivar should directly lead to the development of an institutional mindset. Instead, they have merely focussed upon and glorified the individuals who sacrificed. The RSS and its Parivar has never made a conscious effort to help their members to develop this institutional mindset and take their work to an institutional level with all its characteristics. This is why they have failed to raise quality institutions and to continue with those that built quality for long. The longer their institutions lasted, the poorer they became in terms of their functional characteristics and declined. Deoras was conscious of the need of an institutional mindset and used to talk about it. Deoras was appreciative of English institutions like Eton. He often said that the battles of the World War II were won on the grounds of Eton. Harrow still displays the stick with which Churchill was beaten and shaped into the man he became. It never dawned upon the *swayamsevak*s who started these institutions that institutions should create a norm of behaviour and a benchmark for performance, should control and make it difficult for corrupt practices to flourish, and should produce quality output and work. This is an approach that Deoras helped me evolve. The RSS and its Parivar did not take the same lessons to heart and, as a result, they could not sustain institutions for long. Institutional egoism rose, and factionalism became ubiquitous within the Parivar people running them.

Hindus seldom have the likes of Ida Scudder, who established the Christian Medical College, Vellore, or Mother Teresa or Albert Schweitzer. And while being incapable of building quality institutions that last, the people in the RSS and the Parivar, time and again, have shown great ability to destroy their own institutions, particularly those that did well, where ability, originality and creativity showed. Only those among the able who gave the officials unearned credit, bent over backwards to please them and projected them as providers of assistance they did not give were spared. More particularly, such able institutions were destroyed if the RSS bosses thought that the leaders of such institutions might be seen as taller figures than they were themselves.

Professionalism

Professionalism was never a characteristic of the majority of the *swayamsevaks*. They are not even aware of it. They failed to realise that behaving in the manner the RSS taught them in the *shakhas* in any work they undertook was not warranted. The job at hand in other areas demands different skills and competencies, erudition, precision, and so on. With an RSS background, one may perform the tasks within the organisation more effectively. The sequential nature of these two skills, RSS training and professionalism in their field of expertise (making use of the RSS training) never dawned on them. Non-professional individuals were more acceptable than a professional due to the loyalty of such individuals to the organisation and their longevity in it, regardless of whether their core competencies suited the job or not. Generally speaking, the most significant disease with which all their social projects are plagued is non-professionalism, arising out of often inadequate training, of being unaware of issues of quality, of an absence of a restless enthusiasm, agility and alacrity to build the man of tomorrow. One glaring aspect of this non-professionalism is the inability of these wonderful and high sacrificing individuals to write a coherent, adequately detailed project report, or using them by adding relevant details to an application of grants or donations. That professionalism is a precondition to the thinking of new, bold and effective ideas which would change their effectiveness in their areas of operation never occurred to them.

Becoming Aware of Their Power

The on-ground psyche of the grassroots workers of the RSS and the Parivar, their vision, their understanding, cannot be said to be a part of the massive power structure they are a part of. In fact, it has not dawned on them that this powerful structure needs to be leveraged while dealing with people outside from a position of power (D. Deodhar 2004a: 23–30). The principal reason behind this plight is the long-standing tendency of the RSS to not recognise and disseminate such information in the general cadre. Many working in these projects are dissatisfied with the working conditions and are looking outside for a better and more economically assured position for their future. This is because neither they nor their leaders ever had any ideas about how to professionally develop their projects. Expectations of path-breaking work or even a powerful workplace is unrealistic. These factors are making them ineffective, unable to dictate any aspect of the national life, unable to make an imprint or to come out with a new vision of programmes and coordination.

Need to Change the Externalities vis-à-vis Its Man-making Mission

The RSS is still sticking to the age-old archaic model of its programme of contents, its old-world psyche, in the ever non-appealing form and content of their day-to-day work of their *shakha*, the great man-making machine Dr Hedgewar invented. It had transformed itself in 1975 after the ban in a hundred forms. In 1977, it received a great boost after the Emergency, which lasted for some years. All attempts to give it a more acceptable and appealing form have failed, although none of these attempts were in any way very forceful.[6] That the existing model was appealing in 1925, but would not be so now, has been completely overlooked. The sacrosanct status was not allowed to change. Talking about changing externalities became a taboo. What was once a rigorous and vigorous playground of manly games like *kabaddi*, or many other imaginative, low-cost, low-input games of immense pleasure and fun have watered down to dull drills performed with or without *lathis*, chanting songs and reciting Sanskrit *mantras* and edifying passages, mostly from Golwalkar. It has become even more unattractive, Brahminical and boring. It is sans modernism, sans imagination, sans any thoughts about how the world of today's youth has taken shape, sans any consideration of job timings and constricted timeframes available for people to come to the *shakha*, and the various fads of aerobics and *yoga* and other such things where the youth still manage to spend time, difficulties notwithstanding.

There should be a change in the RSS' outer structure to be conducive to its man-making mission. Will the RSS evolve methods of binding individuals strongly by a few fundamentals and using their capabilities in a hundred different ways inside and outside the organisation? This will help them attain true success in their man-making mission. However, for this purpose, they need to appear liberal and convincing to the intelligentsia, the creative and capable stalwarts as well as people with a generally liberal outlook, not to mention the new generation, or anyone who has the capability to contribute to the task of nation-building. For that they will have to internalise the new cultural mixes, exchanges and acceptances across different strata of people, evolve a much grander, more inclusive and plural culture than they have. Their behaviour itself will have to change.

RSS for Hindu Interests First or Hindu Rashtra?

Is the idea of Hindu Rashtra as unhistorical and as irrelevant as the rubble after the Communist collapse? Like the Communists, has the RSS also stuck themselves in some kind of a rut from which they are not able to extricate themselves? Is the Hindu Rashtra or the Ram Mandir that rut? Is it holding on to the old models of social construction and working to bring them about, an enterprise completely useless against the strong winds of change? Will the speed of this hurricane of change be the RSS' undoing? What does the RSS stand for, Hindu interests and Hindu unity, or the notion of the Hindu Rashtra? If Hindu interests are primary, then the country's need for the RSS is truly the greatest because no one else is concerned about the same. However, if the interest of the RSS lies only in Hindu unity, without also looking after Hindu interests, then it is probably doomed to fail. Of course, then the question arises: is Hindu interest synonymous or co-extensive with Hindu Rashtra? I do not think so. The former, Hindu interest, is a more immediate concern for survival in a manner one would like to. I believe that the RSS and its Parivar needs to be the guardian of Hindu interests, since no one else can be or will have sufficient acceptance or mass appeal. They will have to make a distinction. The latter, Hindu unity and the Hindu Rashtra arising out of that, is impossible unless the Hindu interests are looked after. It does not appear to be an absolute necessity to talk about Hindu Rashtra all the time, because it will become manifest when this ground condition is met.

Today's icons are different. Today's concepts are different. The RSS needs new words, contemporary words to express them. Talking in the same scriptural language of the remote past will not gain acceptance. Newer generations need new appeals. This is a big drawback in the RSS system. We appeal to its genius to make new icons for the new world. They can do it more effectively if they decide to do away with some of the ancient notions.

The RSS itself is such a big mass that if it comes together for newer or more appealing causes, it need not look for more mass. What is important is that the RSS arouses its mass over such causes. The difficulty is to find new images and icons for new purposes of direct national benefits instead of holding on to old ones. Ram Sethu, first and foremost, is an ecological issue.[7] Politically exploiting it smacks only of the chauvinistic (and therefore disgusting) rabidity that has now come to be associated with the RSS. Even more disgustingly, it demonstrates the inability of the RSS to identify newer and more relevant issues. The preservation of the Ram Sethu does not equal preservation of Hindu culture. The RSS will have to refrain from such moves and concentrate on the more sedate and groundbreaking work of thinking anew.

Does the RSS Understand the Future?

Knowing the shape of the future world, which is not a mono-chromatic world of American imperialism or the supposed cultural disintegration it causes, is essential. No one really disputes the economic imperialism of the USA or other developed nations. Educated people are vaguely aware of that as a diffuse background of their world. However, the spectre of economic imperialism recedes while dealing with the multicultural milieu of today on a daily basis. What stands out is the enormous facilitation and strengthening of communication, of the development of new techniques and capabilities by the new media. These developments, arising, supposedly, out of this economic imperialism, have given to the developing, or shall we say the rapidly lunging forward world, great strength to stand up to the imperialism itself. These developments, furthermore, are assisting the developing countries to move away from the prehistoric agrarian and industrial worlds, and moving into more contemporary systems. With the placement of these tools in the hands of others, there must be limits to the imperialistic design of the developed economies. This is an absolute necessity for the process to take place. Instead of harping on imperialism, therefore, one needs to focus on the increasing interdependence the world has got accustomed to and is getting comfortable with.

The RSS, and many other conservatives, often and unnecessarily talk of Western and American influence on our culture. If it is indeed affecting us, there is no way of getting rid of that effect. It is not necessary either. Is our culture so flimsy that sibling relationship finds itself endangered due to one Valentine's Day celebration? If the occasion in some way brings out the instinct for incest, or allows the expression of sexual interest towards another person in the open, then it is better to face it and then remove it from the psyche. Why does the RSS want to build walls and disrupt the flux of culture? As Deoras would say, it is the sign of insipid people. Is that what the RSS is?

They also need to understand the vision the Western world is capable of today. A cursory look at a magnificent book written by Alvin and Heidi Toffler on the business of war, *War and Anti-war*, as early as 1993, will show the eons the West is ahead of us. Instead of harping on the negatives of the Western culture, one needs to find out where the benefits for the nation lie. Even prior to that, the RSS as well as the conservatives and the society at large must change its mindset to accept the reality that they are better off integrated in the world economy and the globalised society, in competing with the world than remaining in isolation. The laptop computer on which I wrote this monograph was manufactured in China for IBM, purchased by a Danish multinational and given to their ex-Director in India to facilitate this work. This is the world today.

Once this attitude of acceptance is in place, matters will become simpler. It is high time India realises that the old Hindu model of social construction and the model of the Welfare State dampened the appeal as well as the need to rouse the initiative, imagination, intelligence, creativity and strength of the people of India. The new economy forced us to do precisely that, and L.N. Mittal, Mukesh Ambani and Ratan Tata compete for the top posts in the world today. Call it, as some have done, reverse Indian imperialism and rejoice when these corporate bosses buy companies in the Western world instead of blaming them. Today a Hindu congregation in London has the courage to call Gordon Brown 'Govardhan Brown', and he accepts it jovially.

The fast-shrinking world with collapsing national boundaries is a reality. Being born in Mumbai, brought up in London, trained in the US and holding a high office in Singapore is the reality of the global Indian, the global Dane or the global Chinese manager. Collapse of national boundaries does not mean collapse of nationalism. It is there, it is intact, and the RSS need not remind the Indians about it again and again. These Indians have fantastic mobility across the globe. They have influence; their power is recognised as much as that of a Dane or a Chinese. It is for India to make use of them for the country, to give them an additional mission.

In the preceding chapter we have seen the way the RSS reacted to these issues. The last comprehensive review was perhaps the *Chintan Baithak* of 1998, which sought to review the journey of the RSS over the years, the Ayodhya issue, the Partition, the crisis of character in the nation and the daily work of the organisation. There was an analytical review of the major Parivar organisations (The RSS 1999). Hindutva, with its spiritual lineage, formed a dominant trait of thought in the *Chintan Baithak*. It identified as challenges the internal security of the nation, terrorism, secessionist movements and infiltration, all of which are undoubtedly correct (S.H. Deshpande 2006: 126–27). It took note of globalisation, the multinational corporations, economic imperialism of the developed countries, caste-based politics and conflicts, cultural aggression, corruption and status quo-ism. On another front, it spoke about the participation of non-Hindus in national life and a proper place for women.

On the political front, the *Chintan Baithak* tried to review its thinking on political parties, the ground realities and expectations from the party and from political power, the limitations of power, the RSS' attitude towards power and social transformation vis-à-vis power. It showed concern about their workers' quality, contribution and character and touched upon today's perspective in the world. These deliberations reflect the sedate and polite ways of getting a point across in the RSS, even on contentious issues.

Yet, the basic framework of their reference frame or thinking, as evident from a review of the *Chintan Baithak*, still does not reflect how they are going to adapt or fight the new challenges. The overall approach is there, but the details are lacking, and therefore the force behind it. Whatever their approach, the fact remains that the RSS could not manage the burdensome and huge task of adapting with changing equations. It has sadly come to narrow behaviour and patterns of thinking. The open and unbiased comprehensive understanding such intellectual exercise should have is absent. We have seen instances of this throughout this monograph.

Failure of the Tenets of the Deoras Era

Perhaps the most serious matter on which the RSS needs to reflect is the failure of the tenets of the Deoras era. The Deoras era of the RSS was free, welcoming and exceptional. What are the reasons of the tremendous influence Golwalkar had—and still has—on the RSS before Deoras, and even after him? The reasons are clear. In the Golwalkar era, there was no demand for hard work on ground; the platitudinal lectures demanded sacrifice for the mother nation. Taking responsibility for immediate, result-oriented behaviour was not required because there was no time-bound programme, there was no urgency for achievement, there was no official responsibility of the Parivar. There was an atmosphere of virility and valour, but an opportunity to utilise the same was not allowed to surface or was backtracked upon, like in 1946–47, so that there was no need to display this valour and embrace suffering. This gave everyone a sense of doing something great towards the national cause, feeling happy and fulfilled while achieving little in actual terms.

Deoras demanded that responsibility for everything that happened or would happen was 'ours' — hence, complacency should be left behind. No one wanted this accountability towards achievement. No one wanted the hard work. Deoras was a competent manager, and managers always demand achievement. Merely trying is not sufficient. That is why the Deoras legacy ended. This is also the reason why the Deoras era failed to influence the future course of the RSS.[8] When I speak of Deoras to the RSS cadre, I hit a wall, without exception. The distinct feeling is that everyone is uncomfortable with or disinterested in him. Instinctively they are afraid of reference to an earlier era of Deoras' exit, which they do not wish to discuss. However, speak of Golwalkar, and the same individuals are vocal, happy and enthusiastic. There are people who have told me that the hierarchy does not want any comparison which might show Deoras in better light. Karandikar (1999) wrote a voluminous 600-page book where a meagre and sketchy 100 pages have been allotted to Deoras. Bhishikar, a lifelong friend of Deoras, wrote a small book on Dr Hedgewar (1988). In the few pages devoted to the Deoras era, he has not been mentioned by name. Since Bhishikar is a balanced and experienced journalist, I do not think this is an oversight on his part. There is enough evidence that Deoras is being systematically blocked by the RSS machinery in order to continue with the Golwalkar stamp. That is the sole reason why I continue to say that the lost years have now returned: the RSS has gone back to the era of the lost years.

If I have managed to bring out the need for embracing an egalitarian, modern, inclusive, unprejudiced way to work together, to develop an image which is powerful but tolerant, that of a welcoming majority party actively trying to rope people together for a modern India, I have fulfilled my mission. Scholarship, along with a desire to critically look at everything they have accumulated over the years, is all that is required for the RSS to redeem itself.

What holds true for the RSS also holds true for Leftists of all hues and creeds, and the Socialists as well. A lot exists in common between the three, and therefore the maladies for betterment are also common. If this book stimulates a debate among these parties as well, the higher purpose this monograph acquired as it unfolded in my thoughts will also be fulfilled.

After all, it takes all kinds to make the world.

Notes

1. The morbid attraction to the old symbols has not died down. The VHP was inclined to start agitating on the Ram Mandir issue again in September 2010. The way it was planned it would have certainly led to the exacerbation of communal tension and hatred, and would have vitiated the atmosphere in society.
2. *Khosla ka Ghosla* is a feature film that brings out the deceit, dishonesty and hooliganism at the ground level in cases of land acquisition and building houses. The picture it draws is disconcertingly out of tune with what counts as humanity. The consciousness it depicts is barbaric. *Chak De! India* is a portrayal of politics, absence of a nationalistic vision over personal gain and furtherance, false egos and complete callousness towards the end goal of victory for India in an international hockey tournament. Both these portrayals are true and bring out the fundamental difficulties in making India a superpower.
3. The 1977 Andhra disaster was like the tsunami of 2006, causing huge destruction and mortality. The Morvi deluge and disaster occurred because of the rupture of the Morvi dam. Killari and Bhuj were two of the biggest earthquakes in India. The RSS response to all these calamities was gallant.
4. In 1949, Golwalkar was pained that different ideas other than that of the Sangh *shakha* were being considered. He called such thinking strange. In 1954, he was surer of his grounds and altogether eliminated the mention, but pleaded with all to rejoin the work. The language of appeal to sacrifice and that of request are so obvious in Golwalkar's statements that only perverted, bigoted or highly prejudiced critics could call it a dictator's order.

5. Two things stand out for the future of RSS. One is the multiple appealing form their exterior should take in order to draw the youth of this country to them. The second is the knowledge that they have accumulated in around 35 fields where they have worked should be systematised, conclusions should be drawn from them and successful forms given a boost in hundred different ways. The final task of course is to break the cordon of publicity and media vilification to project the enormous good work they have done over the last 82 years for this country.

6. In 1960, in the Indore *Chintan Baithak*, his appeal to take up the work is also a pained acceptance that the main machine of *shakha*s is moribund and that they need to revive it.

7. The RSS also learns! The submission to the President of India to ban cow race slaughter that it has submitted in 2010 is based on only economic reasons. It does talk of the medicinal value of the cow excreta, but the claim is made in terms of research, even US patents obtained for products developed out of that, and so on. It says that the medicinal value benefits all humans, hinting even other alien faiths. There is not a single word about cow being the holy animal and a point of honour for Hindus and all the usual rubbish.

8. During this period, from 1952 to 1961, of pain and sacrifice, Deoras was not involved with the day-to-day work of the RSS. The details of how he held the organisation together during this trying period have already been mentioned. But this non-involvement may be a reason for a possible antagonism towards his policies and way of thinking when he became the chief in 1973. That may also be the reason why the RSS did not continue to follow his line after his demise. However, this is a speculation based on the understanding of psychology of the people of the RSS at various organisationally important levels and with respect to the Parivar.

11

The New Hindutva (Violent)
Forces

————•✦•————

The rise of the new and violent forces of Hindutva should
not be a matter of great surprise to anyone, since violence
is not alien to the RSS. Any organization as controversial
as the RSS could not have survived and grown without the
use of it. The question I would like to address, especially in
connection to the Malegaon incident, is whether violence
is constitutionally embedded in the minds of the RSS men,
resulting in automatic, uncalled for outbursts.

Malegaon, like Godhra, as we have already discussed, is an
old story now. Yet, a complex web appears to be spun around
the RSS ever since the incident. The most recent instance of
this web becoming more intricate is the CBI's charges against
Amit Shah, the Home Minister of Gujarat, of being party to
the fake encounter that killed Soharabuddin and Kausar Bi,
and the CBI's subsequent complaints that Amit Shah has been
uncooperative. Does it mean that the CBI allegations are not
only being challenged by Amit Shah, but also that the CBI is
not able to force Amit Shah to capitulate? The CBI is further

claiming that 15 IPS officers behind the bars for many months have turned friendly witnesses for the prosecution, ready to depose against Amit Shah. Geeta Johari is being depicted as someone who first assisted the Modi government and then cooperated with the judiciary, worked against Modi's interest and was then shuffled around as a result.

I have a small question to ask here. The arrest of Amit Shah, the Home Minister of Gujarat, was alive in news for as long as he was in jail. On the other hand, Dr Ketan Desai, a surgical specialist (urologist), was reportedly found in possession of a sum of ₹1,800 crores and 2 tonnes of gold. Yet, the media is silent on this issue. Does it mean that only the political connection of a person decides the treatment he receives from the media when prima facie there appears to be a case against him?

By common knowledge, Soharabuddin was a criminal. Yet, this fact is not being highlighted in media reports. He was killed in a fake encounter ordered or planned by Amit Shah and the 15 IPS officers who are presently in jail. The term 'fake encounter' amuses me a great deal. The fact is that no encounter is legal, none genuine and none fake. It is a lawfully unlawful, or unlawfully lawful, way of getting rid of dangerous criminals. Which crime is greater — Amit Shah's plan to rid the world of an extortionist, or that of Ketan Desai, who amassed unimaginable wealth by certifying sub-standard medical institutes as first class? If these institutes produce sub-standard doctors who may misdiagnose and eventually mistreat patients, who may die, is not the schemer an accomplice after all? Why is he not behind the bars?

In 2008 and 2009, there were allegations against the Bajrang Dal workers for having raped some Christian nuns. Later it turned out that it was the local Christians who had done that heinous act. There were angry reactions to the murder of the Australian missionary, Graham Stein, and his family, as well as the burning of churches in Orissa after the killing of Sadhu Laxmanananda, holding the RSS and the Parivar to blame. However, none of the allegations against the

Parivar organisations held water. While the immediately useful device of labelling these organisations as culprits satisfied the media, due judicial processes did not confirm the allegations.

A bona fide full-time worker of the RSS, along with two other prominent members and officials, were shown on videotapes being interrogated by the CBI in connection with the Ajmer blasts. These three individuals, according to sources close to the people in the RSS who were shown these tapes, unambiguously stated that the persons on the tapes were not the ones being referred to. These three people have also been reported to have gone to not one but two places when the CBI called. The possibility is that the footages of these people talking to the CBI can later be produced as a pointer to their involvement in the blasts.

The terrible blast in the Samjhauta Express is another case in point. This is one case where the CBI and other investigative agencies seem to have played a dubious role. The evidence indubitably pointed to non-Hindu forces at work behind the blasts (I do not know which word would be the least controversial with respect to these terrorists—Islamic terrorists or Muslim or pro-Pakistan terrorists). The version that was produced for the world, however, was that Right-wing Hindu extremists were responsible for the blast.

On the other hand, the RSS chief, Dr Mohan Bhagwat, has issued public statements that the RSS does not believe in violence and will cooperate with the CBI. In July–August 2010, a senior member of the RSS' Central Working Committee, Indresh Kumar has been linked with terrorist outfits of the Right-wing extremists. Indresh Kumar is an individual who has been in touch with a large number of Muslim communities across the country to build bridges between them and the RSS. The basis of his appeal is that Muslims are also the sons of this land of Bharat. He proclaims that Islam states that heaven lies at the feet of the mother. Is this new initiative something that has started scaring some people, who therefore wish to spoil Indresh Kumar's image among the Muslims? We must ask if some agency, internal or foreign, is interested in creating and maintaining the hype that the RSS is a terrorist organisation. Is it likely that in the near future, the same agency will declare it to be so and ban its activities? Going further, has there been a deliberate series of such accusations and media propaganda being undertaken to provoke the extreme Right Hindu groups to act rashly? Once these groups fall prey to such temptations, it is child's play to declare that groups connected to the RSS are dangerous to society, and therefore carry out the nefarious designs to ban the RSS as a terrorist organisation.

The RSS should have the alacrity and the agility to make its stand clear and set up a counter-mechanism to expose these nefarious designs. Or is it that the RSS is actually a terrorist organisation and these episodes are genuine depictions of reality? These are the questions that have not been taken note of, or are being systematically spurned from being asked.

Whatever be the veracity of the charges, Malegaon and the incidents described above have given me an opportunity to reiterate a few issues I believe I have not been able to emphasise upon so far.

Let me state my position in clear terms: any violent attacks, especially if they come from the Hindu camp, are against the interests of the nation. Hereafter I will be reporting facts, and offering analysis of events, even suggesting conclusions and actions. I would also like to point out that henceforth any mention of the RSS will include the Parivar, and no separate mention of it will be made unless the context is different.

Violence by the RSS in Yesteryears

The first episode of the so-called violence happened in 1927 in Nagpur, within two years of the birth of the RSS. In east Nagpur, the Mahalaxmi festival is closest to the heart of the local people. Muslims from the outlying areas of Nagpur and other nearby areas which have a high Muslim population had planned to march with *lathis* in order to disrupt the festivities. The RSS had an inkling of these plans. Unnoticed by anyone, Dr Hedgewar organised their defences. Remaining hidden and armed with *lathis*, the RSS men allowed the *lathi*-wielding mob to enter the narrow lanes of Mahal, beat them up, and sent them running back the way they had come. Nagpur saw the next instance of communal violence around 1967, between the Dalits and Muslims. With the RSS' intervention, it was not allowed to escalate.

The Quit India Movement of 1942 saw hundreds and thousands of RSS men participating on their own. Accounts of the many deeds of the RSS volunteers in the movement are available, but none of these accounts include deliberate killings of Muslims, Christians or Dalits. Most of the accounts tell of the shelter the RSS gave to those who were involved with anti-British activities, The Saint of Love, Shri Sane Guruji, who hated the RSS, and Aruna Asaf Ali were among those sheltered for months by RSS activists.

The years 1947–48 was a terrible time for the nation and for the RSS. The only Hindu forces available to protect the Hindus, the Congress leadership and the people of Delhi were the RSS men. Hindus as a whole reacted to the Muslim carnage of Hindus from across the border. The organised forces of the RSS were at the vanguard of the defence of Hindus. A 600-page book as well as other writings detailing the various defences, attacks and fights that the RSS men put up for Hindus and against Muslims at that time is available.[1] The carnage from across the border stopped only when counter-carnage was effectively undertaken.

Did the RSS men have any specialised training to deal with such situations? Were they men possessing firearms and trained in using them? If they were, they did not use these firearms till the carnage started. To put the record straight, most were not trained in combat. Army generals asked Golwalkar about the source of the courage of these ordinary men which surpassed even that of the soldiers.

Golwalkar's reply was that they had acquired this courage from playing *kabaddi*, and from the love of the motherland that was inculcated in them. The generals saw Golwalkar's point, but may not have understood the mechanism behind it. To Gandhi, Golwalkar was polite but blunt, saying that the RSS volunteers would act according to the situation, and he therefore could not give any guarantee for their acts (obviously including violence).

I have already dealt with the communal violence in 1960s and the 1970s. None belonging to the RSS and the Parivar were ever convicted, probably because none participated in it. The well-known pattern, at least in Maharashtra, was that a provocation started clashes, which then turned into fights between gangsters and criminals, which eventually hogged the limelight and took centre stage. Another phenomenon of the 1970s, within the folds of the RSS, was the presence of groups of musclemen who did not like the generally peace-abiding approach of the RSS towards what they conceived as anti-Hindu elements bent upon destroying the signs of honour of the Hindus in Maharashtra. There was the Patit Pawan Sanghatana (the emancipators of the morally degenerate), there were various groups in Nagpur allied to the Vidyarthi Parishad, or independent ones like the Chhatrapati Sena, prone more to fights than arguments. But none ever went as far as killings. These forces were almost always under control. The primary targets then were the Socialists and their creed, not Muslims.

The author has witnessed many fights in this era. One notable example of hatred towards Socialists, which sparked clashes, was the Marathi Literary Congregation, an important yearly event. The Socialists and Leftists found it intolerable that Mr P.B. Bhave, a great Marathi litterateur with a strong Hindu ideology, could be the constitutionally elected President. The hatred spilled over. During Bhave's presidential address, a strong and fairly successful attempt was made to disrupt the speech. Another was the perversions of the writings, bordering on pornography, of a great Marathi novelist, N.S. Phadke. Attacks on the RSS branches have been numerous as well, and they were fought back brick for brick. We knew about the RSS disruptions of Communist meetings in Uttar Pradesh, effected with the use of *lathis*. None ever went as far as killings. Here, only for decency's sake will I refrain from mentioning the names of the Congressmen who got RSS men killed, except that of Dattaji Bhale, connected with one of the most honoured names in Maharashtra Congress.

The years of real violence were seen in Kerala again in the 1970s. Kerala, like Bengal, was a difficult province for the RSS to develop due to the Marxist stronghold and many Muslim- or Christian-dominated areas. Here, the fights typically took place between the Marxists and the RSS, not with Muslims and Christians. The RSS ranks had started swelling in Kerala in the late 1960s and early 1970s when Marxism no longer appealed to the sensitivity of the ordinary men. Their emotional and cultural needs attracted them to the RSS. For a time they remained Marxists politically, after which they gradually gave up Marxism altogether. This was intolerable to the Marxists. They started killing RSS volunteers, initially singly, then in groups, attacking the branches. The RSS bore with it for years under Golwalkar as well as Deoras who succeeded him in 1973. When such organised violence went beyond tolerance, the RSS decided to retaliate—two teeth for one. These killings lasted for about two or three years and abated once the Marxists stopped attacking the RSS. The rallies of Deoras touring Kerala swelled, totalling a million. During 2008, the Marxists again tried to invoke violence in New Delhi, at BJP offices, and in Kerala, but this was short-lived.

Violence against the RSS

The most terrible form of violence against the RSS was seen during the infamous Emergency period, one of the worst examples being in Kerala, where heavy printer rolls were used to crush the muscles of the thighs and legs of volunteers who offered peaceful Satyagraha against the Emergency. Many IPS officers were summoned by Mrs Gandhi, who unanimously told her not to play with fire. They clearly warned her that about the fact that so far the RSS men had neither raised their voice even once, nor a finger in protest, but if the torture continued, the situation would go out of hand. There would be retaliation. Shortly after this, the torture stopped.

In the Gandhi-murder ban alone, a great deal of violence had been used against RSS followers, destroying property, means of livelihood, and so on. After the ban was lifted, the violence took the apparently civilised form of threats, exclusion from the services, general ostracism and the use of government machinery in an attempt to demoralise the cadre. This, to a considerable extent, succeeded. The response of the RSS, on both the occasions of ban, was to forgive and forget. In 1948, it was Golwalkar and in 1977, it was Deoras who appealed to the cadre with this message. The message was complied with.

Violence Prevented by the RSS

One of the two most notable instances of violence prevented by the RSS would be the Shia and Sunni skirmishes, something that routinely takes place in Lucknow. Time and again, it fell on Nanaji Deshmukh, the then RSS full-timer in Uttar Pradesh, to stand between the warring factions and broker peace. The second instance would be the part the RSS played during the name change of the Marathwada University to Dr Babasaheb Ambedkar 'Marathwada' (interposed as a compromise) University. Here the entire Socialist, Communist, Maratha and even the Brahminical lobby was hell-bent upon not allowing the change of name. Narahar Kurundkar, an arch-enemy of the RSS and a critic of Muslim issues, was against the name-change. Anant Bhalerao, a Brahmin editor of the widely read daily *Marathwada*, was against it. The issue of adding the name of Dr Ambedkar was less important than the deletion of the word 'Marathwada' from the title. But it all got too mixed up and came to be seen as a vertical split between the Savarna Hindus of all varieties against the Dalits. The violent tension was in air for months. The RSS again brokered peace, this time standing by the Dalits and pacifying the upper castes to effect the change of name.

There are instances strewn throughout this book which testify to the non-violent character of the RSS. Nothing more needs to be written about it.

The New Forms of Hindutva Intolerance and the Malegaon Blast

The thesis of this monograph is that the RSS has become everything it never was and was never meant to become, especially after December 1992. In the Golwalkar era, it avoided even democratically initiated conflict, confrontation or agitation over time-relevant issues, making it irrelevant to the day and age. Violence then was a far cry. Yet Golwalkar is held to be the breeder of Muslim- and Christian-hatred among the RSS, and of translating this into violence. The temperance of Golwalkar had at least one great message, that of not reacting violently, or in an ugly manner, to each and every thing that happened. He had true sophistication. The new forms of intolerant Hindutva are too far away from that sophistication. The RSS is not able to eliminate the Savarkar-leaning tendencies itself and strongly follow the Dr Hedgewar path. If it fails to do so in the near future, one might say they are digging their own graves. Some of the recent examples will make it clear.

Today violence breaks out if M.F. Hussain paints the Hindu goddess Saraswati naked. The Baroda School of Arts is attacked for similar reasons. The Shiv Sena and at times the RSS, with its Parivar, rises, allegedly using force, to ban movies or books, such as Mr Lain's book about Shivaji, which is not in good taste to say the least. The Library of the century-old Bhandarkar Institute is burnt. A professor is allegedly attacked in Ujjain by the Vidyarthi Parishad activists and dies. The RSS reacts to Sachar Committee's report, to the demand of reservations for Christians who were earlier Dalits, to the Ram Sethu, to almost everything.

Is There Another Side to This Violence?

Prima facie, the army would not have surrendered their ex-Lt. Colonel Purohit to the ignominy of being arrested for being responsible for the Malegaon blasts by a state Anti-Terrorist Squad (ATS) unless strong evidence was put before them. Then, within days, a *sadhvi* was arrested, a *sadhu* followed suit, and all the threads seem to have come together in a rapid-fire sequence. It can therefore be assumed that there is indeed a case. The question that needs to be asked is whether one such as yet unproven act is worthy of the title 'Hindu terrorism'. This will also lead to the question whether the Hindu mindset is that of a terrorist?[2] And if there is a strong strand of such intrinsic cruelty in the Hindu psyche, where and how has it been expressed?

The second unproven conclusion to which the Hindu-baiters have jumped is that there are large numbers of fringe groups within the RSS behemoth who will time and again cause violent disruptions. I have raised this issue merely to allow a proof of this to come from those who have alleged it.

It may, in the name of truth and justice, be valid to ask a few questions about the various incidents which have provoked Hindu violence. Will Mr Hussain be bold enough to draw even a clothed picture of Mohammad? Will the Muslim community worldwide allow such a drawing to be made? Ramakrishna Paramhans, according to the testimony of Swami Ranganathanand in the Introduction to *The Gospel of Sri Ramakrishna*, had a spiritual vision of Mohammed, Jesus and Buddha (Swami Ranganathanand n.d.). There is a Muslim artist in the city I live in, who has confessed to a Hindu leader that he has actually had a *darshan* (a vision) of the *Paigambar*. He is mortally afraid of discussing this vision with his religious brethren. If this extreme intolerance is considered justifiable, then why should a protest against a naked Saraswati not be acceptable?

What happened when a Denmark resident drew a cartoon of the Prophet has been internationally reported about. Shri Shri Ravishankar is not a Hindu hardliner by common understanding, yet he wrote about Mr Hussain's painting of Saraswati. How are the Hindus supposed to react when what they revere is defiled as a nude?

With all the hue and cry over the violence in Orissa, there is no actual proof against the Hindu activists. The Malegaon blasts, if they are indeed proven to be the RSS' handiwork, will be the first such instance. Professor Sabharwal who died in Ujjain allegedly had leanings towards the Left and was actively blocking the election processes in the University so that the already strong Vidyarthi Parishad did not get elected. The Baroda incident is equivalent to the Hussain drawing.

Five Sets of Reaction to Malegaon

How are the Malegaon (and possibly the events of 2010 cited above) being projected and viewed? There are five sets of reactions we have to consider, to know where it will all be heading. First, and the most visible, is of course the press and the electronic media. They have had a field day, as they thought that they had caught their favourite whipping boy red-handed. The press and the electronic media, within 24 hours, popularised and entrenched the words Hindu terrorism within the Indian psyche. One act was equated with all the other serial blasts successfully undertaken by the Muslim terrorists. It is somewhat childish to glorify Malegaon this way. The more cogent expression would have been The New Hindutva Violent Forces.

But the media did one more job well. The ATS put its foot in the mouth by making too many claims (or they were pushed into that position by the media or their political bosses), first about Nanded, then about the Samjhauta Express, and so on. But the press also revelled while it revealed the rapidly shifting stand and statements of the ATS, to create doubts about the veracity of everything they seem to say so confidently. The story about a Pune-based Chitpawan Brahmin funding the operation providing close to ₹1 million, which was either withdrawn later or not emphasised upon, gave ammunition to other reactions and logic by equating the Malegaon incident with the murder of Gandhi, and holding Golwalkar's tendency of perpetuating communal hatred responsible for such acts.

The second set of reactions was equally predictable and came from the Hindu-baiters, the Socialists, the Communists and the Congressmen. They erupted in full-throated cries of this being another RSS act resembling the murder of Gandhi, including its link to Pune and the key accused being a Maharashtrian Brahmin. The charge they make, most clearly brought out by Prakash Bal in his letter dated 16 November 2008 to the editor of the *Pune Sakal*, is that the RSS creates an atmosphere of hatred and distrust. They have individuals, groups or organisations within them or their fringes which plan such violent activities, of which the high-ups are fully aware. If it succeeds, the RSS leadership will not own up to it. If it does not, the RSS will make noisy protests about Hindu discrimination and cry foul. The chances to prove the charges, however, are slim because the police force, the army and the judiciary have been widely infiltrated by the people who belong to the creed of political Hindutva of the RSS, and will see to it that such a verdict does not come out. Bal indicates by several examples how deep the 'infiltration' is.[3]

Most importantly, Bal states at the end of his letter that there is no difference between the fundamentalist (read rabid) mindset of the *jihadis* and the political Hindutva mindset. They are feeding on each other and will soon lead India to become what Pakistan has become. His last contention is that this is what the RSS and the other Hindu fundamentalists are aiming at.[4] The *sadhvi* and the Colonel, as well as those from the Parivar who are duplicating the *jihadis* are the worst enemies of the idea of (multicultural, multi-religious and multilingual) India, just as the *jihadis* are.

The third set of reactions was also equally predictable. The BJP did not react immediately in denouncing the act. They kept mum till the *sadhvi* filed an affidavit of torture, and then put it on their website. The VHP gathered their irrepressible, volatile and vitriolic *sadhus* and *mahants* in protest against the dishonour being meted out against a *sadhvi* and sought to stir the nation against it. Mr Sudarshan reacted after a long time, only to say that terrorism has no religion, and that the law must be let to take its own course. It was, however, also declared that the *sadhvi* will be defended against the charges. The sad thing is the RSS and its Parivar has lost the sense of time and timing, of what the correct political reflexes are, what the right things to say are, and so on. The *sadhvi*, or a couple of other *sadhus* like Aseemanand, who became fugitives or went incommunicado, become a strong indication of their being the accomplices, and the RSS should take note of this.

The first words that escaped the mouth of Golwalkar when he heard about the assassination of the Mahatma were, 'The great ill fate of the nation' (Golwalkar 1979). Today, we do not see any semblance of these sensitivities and sensibilities in the RSS. They have become militant, rabid and do not really care. In December 2009, when the Liberhan Report 'leaked', by design or chance, controversy followed and lasted for several days in the press and the media through July and August of 2010. The nation was gearing up for the Ayodhya verdict as well as the Bihar election. On 30 September 2010, the Ayodhya verdict was delivered. Dr Bhagawat set the tone well and the nation received decent reactions from all quarters. When confronted, however, Dr Bhagawat expressed that there was no question of 'regret over the demolition' (*Tarun Bharat* 2010). Such a statement stands in contrast to the one made by Deoras on Babari demolition, that what happened was not a good thing.

The fourth set of reactions comes from Hindu sympathisers outside the RSS fold. Francois Gautier made his case strongly by saying, 'When the Mahatma's cowards erupt in fury, it hurts. It isn't terror' (2008). Pointing at the history, he says,

> Hindus had also given refuge to persecuted minorities from across the world — Syrian Christians, Parsis, Jews, Armenians, and today (since 1955) Tibetans. In 3,500 years of existence, Hindus have never militarily invaded another country, never tried to impose their religion on others by force or induced conversions. It saddens me when I see the Indian and western press equating terrorist groups like SIMI, which blow up innocent civilians, with ordinary, angry Hindus who burn churches without killing anybody. (Gautier 2008)

Gautier also points out that

> most of these communal incidents often involve persons from the same groups — often Dalits and tribals — some of who have converted to Christianity and others not, implying thereby that the new Hindutva forces are maligned by dragging them in the slander of wrongful accusations.
>
> However reprehensible the destruction of Babri Masjid, no Muslim was killed in the process; compare this to the 'vengeance' bombings of 1993 in Bombay, which wiped out hundreds of innocents, mostly Hindus. Yet the Babri Masjid destruction is often described by journalists as the more horrible act of the two. Hindus, since the first Arab invasions, have been at the receiving end of terrorism. Blasts after blasts have killed hundreds of innocent Hindus all over India in the last four years. (2008)

Gautier has well tracked this reaction after the Malegaon blast,

> At some point, after...centuries of submitting like sheep to slaughter, Hindus—whom the Mahatma once gently called cowards—erupt in uncontrolled fury. And it hurts badly. It happened in Gujarat,...in Jammu, then in Kandhamal, Mangalore, and Malegaon. It may happen again elsewhere... this is a spontaneous revolution on the ground, by ordinary Hindus, without any planning from the political leadership. (2008)

To quote from what might be the most popular and beautiful poem by Vajpayee, titled 'Parichay' (Introduction),

> Tell [us] how many Masjids have we destroyed in Kabul
> How many we killed in the name of Gopal and Ram?
> Not the land but winning the hearts of hundreds of people
> Is my determination
> [and as a Hindu this is my character and identification]
> (Vajpayee n.d.)

There is also a fifth response, which is the most silent and insidious response to the Malegaon blasts—it is the silent logic working within one's mind. I take no position regarding this being good or bad, but simply emphasise that it exists. The relentless targeting of the Hindu community as the harbingers of communal violence sets this silent logic to work. The real danger lies in the possibility of such a continued vilification, aligning Hindus more towards the Hindu hardliners. The possibility is strong that this may already be happening, and it is not the doing of the RSS at all.

Look at the Amarnath controversy, fuelled by the language of Dr Mehbooba Mufti! Why has the Amarnath movement lasted for a month or two, going beyond the political agenda, with hundreds of thousands of people joining the struggle? And finally the PDP lost power and could not gamble it back, with the BJP winning 11 seats. It is edifying for all to see the BJP-led movement becoming a people's movement, and lasting over a month. Somewhere, the sense of non-facilitation of Hindus and a feeling that Hindus were being short-changed by the powers-that-be worked, as the government continued to sponsor Haj pilgrimages instead.

Most Hindus believe that missionaries do excellent work in health and education, but they also take note of the conversions through inducements and financial traps. People do not fail to notice a cross-like mark appearing on the two rupee coin, Ajit Jogi and Y.S. Reddy being preferred for chief ministerial positions and their antecedent Christianity. They understand the slant the Orissa incidents are given, that the Christian missionaries are peace-loving, who do not undertake violence and divisive, subversive acts, and who are not engaged in forced conversions. It is the intolerant RSS brand of Hindutva, with their brutal mentality, that leads to attacks on these harmless people. When an 84-year-old Swami gets brutally murdered, the only relentless projection is that of the Church burnt and its attribution to Hindu intolerance, without going into the antecedents of all this.

When Hindu gods are blasphemed in the form of a naked Saraswati, Hindus are supposed to tolerate it. Crores of Muslims pouring in the streets over a Danish cartoon of Mohammad is flashed across as a rightful protest. The Madison Avenue of New York City is blocked for about two hours by the overpowering number of Muslims who come for midday prayers there. It is arrogance that is being played out as America seems reluctant to act. The attacks in Baroda Art College arise from similar anger, which is condemned by the media by subtle emphasis, nuances and innuendoes. That there could be a reason behind the attack against the Ujjain professor is effectively suppressed.

Underestimating the ability of people to think and act accordingly has been a chronic error of judgement. Mrs Gandhi made the same mistake in imposing Emergency. When all the MPs attacked the nascent 13-day-old government of Vajpayee, people saw the injustice of it on television and voted him to power again. It will be useful to look at the examples of the Karnataka elections granting the BJP a victory and what I have discussed earlier regarding Narendra Modi's vilification. These, I believe, are a few recent and high profile examples that highlight the issue. Hoping to cash in on Muslim sentiments and get them to vote against Modi, everyone persisted with this mode of vilification in 2007. Muslims either could not save the Congress or they did not vote for it, simply because Godhra no longer featured in their scheme of things. Now it was, for Hindus and Muslims alike, the development agenda alone that mattered.

The more the press and the politicians denigrate Hindus attacking back, and the RSS and the Parivar being behind it, violence being their credo, and so on, the more the silent logic will work to escalate estrangement. This is the biggest threat. The RSS is not a holy cow; not many like the organisation. But by constantly targeting the RSS and alleging its hand behind the Malegaon, Kandhamal and Mangalore incidents, the press is in fact legitimising their actions, refurbishing their image as heroes in the minds of the common man who think that the RSS at least have the guts to counter-attack when Hindus are vilified by one and all.

By a similar logic, people question, how is it that about two to three weeks prior to the five large state legislative assembly elections, a Lt. Colonel is caught, a *sadhvi* is arrested at lightening speed, followed by a Pandey in a short time? Why is it that even months after the serial blasts in the Mumbai locals, no trace of the perpetrators is available? Why is it that the Muslims are being given the prop of the Sachar Committee report?[5] The situation here will ultimately be like that of reservation quotas for the backward castes, where the seats are remaining unfulfilled.

The Congress, in the course of these long years, has not prepared the Muslims to make them able to pass the minimum qualifications for entering such jobs. It is ironic, therefore, that a Congress-appointed committee is crying hoarse that there are no Muslims in the civil services! And now in December

2009, the report from a desultorily functioning committee, whose official members have neither seen nor signed the report, has been submitted to the government, advising a referendum on the Article 370 in Kashmir to provide more 'autonomy' to the state.

The point I am making is: the way the situation is being handled is counterproductive to everything that we, as ordinary citizens, want. Do we want terrorism of any kind, Muslim, Hindu or Christian? No. Yet it is being glorified and constantly publicised. We want inclusivity to be shown by the larger Hindu society towards accepting others. Hindus are getting alienated due to a perception that Muslims are getting preferential treatment. Perception may not be truth, but it strongly dictates emotions and action. Despite the assumption that no one wanted Narendra Modi or Yediyurappa to win because of what they are, they still won.

A look at how the 2007 elections in five states were handled by the media may give an insight into the undesirable way the news was presented. In reality, the BJP lost only Rajasthan, by losing 40 of their earlier strength, rebellion being the clear cause. There was no question of losing Delhi, since it was never under the BJP for the last 10 years. Yet that lone partial defeat in Rajasthan was drummed up incessantly. No one seemed to have the time to find out what made Shivraj Chauhan win, or for that matter Raman Singh! This is not helping the Congress to go to the root causes of their defeat in both places. This is neither a credible nor an enlightening media, akin to the media of the 1950s, or that of Tilak's time. It is a media of sensationalism and nothing else, which can be highly damaging. If Malegaon was a political ploy to increase Muslim votes, it does not seem to have worked, because otherwise the Congress would have won in Madhya Pradesh and Chhattisgarh convincingly. This only means that the Muslim reaction to the Malegaon episode is different and, I would say, rational. Was the Hindu mind so sharp that it sided with the BJP because it sensed that Malegaon was a political ploy? The media has no answer.

Failure of Right Actions and Responses

The answer to the Muslim terrorist attacks is not the counter-offensive of Hindu terrorist attacks. The answer is political and strategic, that of mobilising the world against such attacks. The answer is for the political leaders to use the available information to nip it in bud. Everyone seems to believe that enough information is available to effectively smash all terrorist training camps. On the contrary, in the last two months of 2009, doubts had been raised about the quality of the bullet-proof jacket worn by Hemant Karkare, the fallen hero of 26/11. The jacket was first lost, then was found in a dustbin; important papers in connection with Kasab, the captured terrorist, disappeared. A strong suspicion that the government is trying to befuddle the issue is unmistakably taking root. Highly placed sources in Mumbai say that there was a possibility 26/11 itself was known to the people concerned. This source also confirms that the death of Karkare was a plot. I have eyewitness account of three terrorists being sent to a prestigious hospital in Mumbai for treatment by a central Home Minister many years ago. Where will all this lead?

The Christian missionary conversions in various parts of the country cannot be tackled by violence against them. What is needed is a larger network of nationalist, social and political network of Hindus for protecting the polity if they believe they are under threat. The solution is in imparting modern secular education to all so that minorities become equal to the mainstream. It is important to build a strong India that can withstand all the pressures that prevent a politically effective response to Pakistan-sponsored terror.

Mumbai has already cried hoarse over the political, police and terrorist nexus, the lack of political will and the failure of the ATS and the intelligence agencies to act on information received regarding the latest terror attack. Deshmukh was virtually sacked. If the USA does not allow a single terrorist attack to occur on its soil after 9/11, there is no reason why India cannot do the same. The right action is not only about preventing terrorist attacks by Muslims, but also about not provoking Hindu retaliation in a similar direction. What leads me to despair is the recurrent experience that men take the rational course of things only as a last recourse.

In the last 20 years, the Indian Muslim is increasingly identifying himself/herself with India. They are themselves tired of being targeted as traitors, tired of the violence and terror, being pointed out as people who shelter refugees and terrorists. The all-India gathering of *ulema*s in Hyderabad came out strongly against a Mumbai attack within days of its happening. There were other voices as well. Has any one fostered these forces the way they should be? Are we going to learn from the groundswell of affection shown by the ordinary Pakistani to our cricket team a few years back? Are we not going to stop considering the Indian Muslim as a traitor, a refugee or anti-Indian? If I may go a step further, it is a need of the hour that some one stands by the Indian Muslim with faith and trust, asking them to join us to root terror out. The Congress has long lost the credibility. The BJP never really acquired it. The Hindu-baiters are a suspect in the minds of Muslims.

Unfortunately, the RSS also does not seem to see this as the right path. They are the only ones to whom the Muslim community will give some credence if an appeal is made.[6] M.J. Akbar, in a beautifully written piece during one of the worse blasts in the recent past, pleaded with Hindus not to react in violence but to keep peace, to keep the fabric of harmony intact. Hindus are not just a majority in this land, they are the elder brothers. They have to hold the Muslims close to their heart. In a household, it is always the elder who takes the least.

Is this not another form of appeasement? Vehemently I will say it is not. Today the strength of Hindu forces lies in asking Muslims to come along with them. When the Hindu forces were not strong and appeasement was afoot, we have seen what happened, the worst being the vivisection of the nation. Today the strong Hindu forces have even managed to rule the country for six years.

Such a vicious atmosphere of hate and suspicion exists in the Indian society today that unless a clean break from the past is made by someone, the situation will deteriorate much more. We have to not only save this country, but also its long-standing cultural groups. No one seems to be interested in saving the culture of the country. Waging a civil war is in the interest of no one, including the RSS. We need seers who can look across generations and centuries, and not politicians who look from elections to elections – to quote Lord Charnwood on Abraham Lincoln.

Deoras made this attempt of broadening the concept of Hindutva, its base and relevance. I have extensively written on what happened to it in 1977. The thesis I have propagated herein is of the failure of that attempt, the subsequent strong secessionist movements across the country, violence against factions of Hindu backward class communities in Gujarat and injustice in Assam, leading to various actions taken by the RSS and its Parivar to keep the Hindu society united. These movements led to unfortunate consequences at the hands of mediocre individuals, bigots and rabid chauvinists within the RSS. Something similar to 1977 will have to be undertaken. And it is my belief that only the RSS can do it. It will take the wind out of every other divisive sail and work wonders for the nation. This is the true Hindu psyche. For that they do not have to give up their Hindutva, only make it broader and more inclusive.

Does the concept of Hindu Rashtra and undivided India come in the way of such unity? I think not. I will end this monograph by quoting a poem popular in the RSS after the Partition, that tellingly summarises the sentiment of vivisection:

In the epochs and millennia of history
Even the present will become the past

But these shattered and divided hearts will continue to burn till
They reunite, and till then they will continue to burn
And while burning will they reunite.[7]

It is there that we all have to go.

Notes

1. Titled *Jyoti Jala Nij Pranaki*, meaning, 'by sacrificing their life and spirit' (in the cause saving Hindus from Pakistani carnage in 1947), this book tells all that the RSS volunteers did during that period (Vajpeyee and Paradkar 1999). For a less emotional but equally factual account, one may refer to H.V. Seshadri's *The Tragic Story of Partition* (1998).

2. To keep the record straight, it must be stated that the claim of the news channel that their office was ransacked is completely false. The channel offices were on the 4th, 11th and 13th floors. The demonstrators could not even access the first floor, as it was blocked by the security forces. Eyewitness accounts, which the media will never circulate, deny all the vengeful projections done by this channel.

   On 6th August 2010, the right hand of an auto-rikshaw driver was cut off. The driver had accosted the eve-teasers of his sister. NDTV was the only channel which reported this instance as being the handiwork of RSS–BJP hooligans, without making any clear attempt to offer evidence behind the same. All channels which received the same brief for editing did not choose to report it as the handiwork of RSS–BJP hooligans.

3. Much has been talked of Hindu RSS infiltration in the army, the judiciary, the police and the government by those who are eager to offer quotas to Muslims and every other non-Hindu in precisely these institutions. The numerous RSS volunteers are also citizens of this country, seeking work through all possible avenues to be able to live here. Infiltration happens in a foreign country, not in one's own. By that token, in the era of globalisation, every native community can start calling all the legal immigrants infiltrators. Furthermore, by the same coin, what have the Left and the Socialists to say about the way they have 'infiltrated' the media, to the exclusion of all others?

4. As late as 19 November 2009, about 1,000 Muslims from different North Indian states assembled in the Haj house in Mumbai. In a walkathon to the Gateway of India their slogans were, 'Terrorism is

not *jihad*, it is treachery to religion (*fasaad hai*)'; 'There is no religion to terrorism'; 'Our slogan is brotherhood'; 'Our children we will educate, education is for life, life is for the nation Hindusthan'. They held a symbolic protest to denounce 26/11. There were many impassioned speeches by many *fez* cap donning Muslims, declaring their allegiance to India as their country. A long poem pleaded Mother Bharat to treat her beloved sons not as traitors, but her own. It ended by all these Muslims singing *Vande Mataram*. It was as beautiful a rendition as any coming from Hindus. The author has all this as evidence filmed in his personal camera. The next day one, and only one, channel, STAR MAZA, telecast the *Vande Mataram* he had sent to them.

5. If one goes through the critique of the Sachar Committee Report by the India First Foundation, even the few excerpts are terrifying, because it was the same language that led to the vivisection of the country. I do not believe that even Muslims want another partition or riots over such an issue.

6. It is a welcome development that the RSS is now involved in bridging the Hindu–Muslim divide by joining hands with the Rashtriya Muslim Manch at various places in north India. The RSS leaders, particularly Indresh Kumar, whom we have seen as a full-timer in Jammu and Kashmir, and whose effort Mr K.P.S. Sudarshan is backing, are supporting it. It is unfortunate that they are (as usual) late by about 30 years. Deoras was defeated in his effort to do the same. Even today, the strong possibility that the cadre still will not like such an initiative looms large. In 1977, the circumstances were conducive for such an effort. Today the motto, if suspected, will have no justification. Fortunately, it is the magnanimity of the Muslims of the Rashtriya Muslim Manch that they do not have any such suspicions.

7. This poem was written by R.G. Kelkar after the partition. This poet had another memorable poem, famous in the RSS in the 1940s, written on Dr Hedgewar when he was on his deathbed, requesting Death not to take him at that time since there was so much to do still. Collected in *Paris Sparsh* (the Midas touch of the RSS), it was released in Nagpur by Balasaheb Deoras.

Epilogue

The Problem of Ideologies

———— • ✦ • ————

Why do people need an ideology? Above everything else, this is the question that intrigued me. The ideologies themselves as well as the reasons why people choose particular ones was the second issue I was intrigued by. Why do they not, or why — even more importantly — *can* they not choose any other? Despite possessing intelligence and the best of reasoning power, why do they fail to see something worthwhile in ideologies other than their own? After all, making these choices results in behaviour that leads to division and acrimony, bitterly opposed sentiments, strife and violence, which is evident in the history of the last ten thousand years of civilised life. Vinoba Bhave once said, 'To understand is to forgive.' This attribute seems to be singularly lacking today in anybody who swears by a particular ideology.

Allegiance to an ideology runs counter to the basic instincts of human beings — the perpetual quest for pleasure, leisure, avoidance of hardships and the need to maximise fulfilment. It is the principle of unlimited, non-restricted pleasure and freedom that human beings want, without bothering about consequences or its effects on others. Contrarily, swearing by an ideology only brings severe hardships on oneself, demands hard work, sacrifice and monetary losses. Why make this choice, then?

Perhaps the answer is that an ideology gives us something larger than life to stay with. An individual gets a powerful sense of fulfilment when he follows an ideology — a sense that he is answering a higher call or fulfilling an obligation to society. At other times, it could even be a mechanism for atonement of sins one has perpetrated. Sometimes it is a cultural imposition. Most frequently, it gives the sense of belonging by making an individual a part of something larger. It is thus a more primal need (Kandel 1991, Brodal 2004, Kruk 1991).

An ideology also provides the best opportunity for self-actualisation. This is the 'most selfish act', giving immense pleasure, and is a great need — the pinnacle of the positivism of Maslow's psychology. Deoras, the RSS chief, was a living example of this intense self-actualisation among the thousands of RSS followers I know. Deoras himself found its best resonance in the founder of the Sangh, and his ways and thinking.

What happens to the ideologies in the long run? People adhere over long years to the name and the core of the ideology, even when the external situation changes so much that it makes the core irrelevant. Adherence is also an aspect of the pleasure principle. The other question that remains is: why do people refuse to change? An ideology attracts people of a similar make-up, who react similarly, emphasising the validity of the idea. Hence they stay for long years and often rise in the organisational hierarchy.

An intellectual endogamy, giving rise to inbreeding of ideas therefore inevitably begins. The thinking is no longer productive, nor vigorous or outward-looking, but more and more inward-looking. This is the beginning of the loss of contact of the organisation heads with their cadre and their frontline grassroots workers. The larger implication of inward-looking, unproductive thinking is the organisation's inevitable loss of contact with society and reality. Any one who is familiar with FedEx couriers will know how important they consider keeping in touch with their frontline managers. It is a common malady in industries, where the loss of this contact starts spelling doom for a company. The vitality with which the race began starts fading. This loss is best reflected in the ever-increasing unwillingness of those at the core of the organisation to stir themselves up, mix and be one with people. With the loss of contact with society, they lose the strength and the energy required for that.

These ivory towers are the breeding ground of politicking that typically leads to the failure to expand and broaden the ideological moorings. Instead, it spells ruin. With increased cerebration, not just the decisions but also the pattern of thinking or the quality of arguments, if any, tends more and more to arise from obsolete concepts, viewpoints and situations. The cerebration is either based on the data the organisation collects or ignores. Most organisations or companies talk of using it as a feedback, even feed-forward, but few actually work in a timely fashion on the data. The time lag that occurs between the generation, analysis and a ruling on the data makes the conclusions inappropriate as well as irrelevant to the changed situation. Working with figures or basing decisions on evidence is talked of, but many key decisions still continue to arise from the biases and from the 'gut feeling'.

The core of the organisation is conscious of this change, but does not face it fully or rectify it. They simply project the old routine thinking, more generally without any basis. There is neither emotional nor intellectual appeal, nor pleasure. It is reflexive and recursive. Having thus enshrined obsolescence as the eternal unalterable truth, the defence of obsolescence becomes the biggest pastime of the organisation, leading to the rise of rationalisation as one of the major mechanisms — a crime in psychology — used to the point of ridiculousness.

A colossal fraud like this can be sustained only by those who have stayed in the organisation for long and have vested interests—the need to somehow perpetuate themselves is dominant—and hence no other path is open. In social and political organisations, the members do not have to earn their own keep. It either comes from the followers outside the hierarchy or through corruption in politics. Thus, defence of a repetitious status quo becomes a need in itself. It serves the purpose of all. Add to that the lures of leisure and habits of luxury which the followers of the organisation or acts of corruption have provided. Who then would ever be ready to displease people by breaking new grounds or subject oneself to hard work?

The story is as true of the RSS as it is for the Communists, the Socialists and the Congress. Some movements like Sarvodaya have lived through the cycle and are dead, dying or moribund. Rigid religious organisations or sects are no exceptions. Imagine the terrible state of affairs in a group where now even the pleasure principle has died. To an extent, this progression will lead us to understand the basis of irreconcilability between ideologies and the men who follow them. The original tends to become more sacrosanct (read rigid) or gets corrupted; the defence of it becomes more foul smelling and farther from moderation and reasonable appeal. The effects these processes have had on all ideologies in general, on their travel, progress, unfolding and deterioration, and the factors responsible for this over years have been the same.

It is the behaviour of the followers which becomes the final determinant of the way ideology is received by society. Ideology demands a lot in terms of the quality of behaviour and utterances by the followers of the same. Such a psychological conglomerate also shapes and governs its expression. The individual finds it difficult to consistently live on an egalitarian, exalted plain all the time. An individual almost always falls short of living up to one's ideology. This discrepancy is a major factor in the discordance people feel towards an ideology they do not subscribe to. The preached and the professed do not match with the practised. The viewer believes that if this is the practice, then the thesis itself has got to be at fault. The world has neither the time nor the wish to think of the proposed as the pure thesis to consider, even if it is not practised; it also is generous or forgiving enough to do the same. Ideologies thus come to be blamed.

The distorted behavioural versions get entrenched in minds of the warring factions, further reinforced in debates in the electronic and the print media. The pleasure principle dictates the actions of the defenders and the critics of the ideology, whether there is a rational call for it or not. Accretions of false beliefs occur, making it impossible to reach the truth. Any attempts at different or differing interpretations then are scorned, blamed and considered fake; they become unacceptable to the majority, and are not believed even if they are true. Truth thus becomes the casualty, and with that any hope for doing justice is gone forever.

Truth and Otherwise of These Warring Perceptions

Despite the vehemence of differences over an ideology, the truth is that there is more common ground for acceptance that can, if considered, submerge the differences that are there. This fact has been the driving force behind writing this book. A number of examples that illustrate the necessity of each warring faction to look at others objectively, without biases clouding their vision, are listed below.

Mr Balasaheb Deoras, the former chief of the RSS, had said openly that Marx indelibly imprinted in the minds of people that economic inequality and exploitation of masses are unacceptable.[1] Deoras, in the early days of the RSS, was called 'the Communist in RSS', and he never really gave up many of his ways of thinking. Again, years ago, P.L. Deshpande, a great Marathi litterateur and no sympathiser of the RSS, wrote a long foreword to one of the anthologies of Dr Ram Manohar Lohia's writings (P.L. Deshpande 1968). A dominant part of this foreword was spent on elaborating the mechanisms put in place by Lohia to impart nationalism, character and strong cultural influences, including religious and social, in the Hindu culture prevailing then in suburban Bombay in the 1930s and 1940s. His account seems so close to the ideas of the RSS that it is as if he was interpreting the mechanisms of the RSS *shakhas* and its acculturation methods.

There are people within the RSS who can understand the Naxalites and are not prepared to call them anti-national or traitors. They recognise the emotion, but disagree with the methods. Meanwhile, Hiren Mukherjee, the Communist Trade Unionist, read the *Mahamrityunjay Japa* in the bitter cold of Moscow early in the morning, confessing, 'We cannot but have to do this.' Many of the Communists of Bengal are, surprisingly, enthusiastic supporters of Durga Puja. And there are a fair number of atheists within the RSS, who, though in minority, do not like the religiosity of the RSS cadre. Then there is the fact that the speeches of Mr Jay Prakash Narayan in 1975 and later, on the RSS, sound more like the speeches of Golwalkar, in contrast to his earlier speeches. The Socialists might call these speeches wayward, but the fact remains that he delivered them.

People believe that there could not be anyone who hates Muslims more than the RSS. Let me present a little-known fact: the most sacred monument for the RSS is the one erected in honour of Dr Hedgewar, the founder, in Nagpur; the chief stone dresser of that monument and his 20 subordinates were all Muslims. Hakim Bhai, the chief stone dresser, was honoured by Golwalkar in a public ceremony by wrapping a shawl around him. No purification ceremony was performed, then or ever.

Did the Socialists and the Congressmen not decide to submerge the differences among themselves and with the RSS, and come together in order to restore democracy in

1977? Was there not then mutual respect and admiration, even when they agreed to differ? Did the Muslims not vote against the Congress, at least in the north? Meanwhile, in the south—as Mr Shrikant Joshi, who had been Deoras' personal assistant for long years, pointed out—Muslims as well as the remaining polity stayed with Mrs Gandhi by and large. Did the Jamat–e-Islami shy away from meeting Deoras wherever he went, including visiting the RSS offices and offering *Namaz* there at the appointed time so that the dialogue could continue?

My appeal therefore is to accept (without necessarily agreeing) that ideologies, behaviour and human needs are not watertight, not specific to particular groups and are neither inexplicable nor unintelligible. There is a common ground that we should be aware of, and we need to make an effort in order to see the commonalities. As Ayn Rand famously said, 'Contradictions do not exist. Check your premises' (1956).

Note

1. The occasion was a general body meeting of the daily *Tarun Bharat* in Nagpur, when the editor came under bitter criticism for writing an article hailing Marx on his 100th death anniversary. Defending him, Deoras praised Marx, also saying that *Tarun Bharat* should not sit out when the whole world would be writing about their debt to Marx. Deoras repeated this opinion of his later as well.

Postscript: Ayodhya Judgement and Bihar Assembly Elections

———— • ✦ • ————

This is the best of times to write a postscript to this book. The outcomes of the Ayodhya judgement and the Bihar assembly elections strongly underline the thesis of this book.

The nation had watched with baited breath the Ayodhya verdict, which, rather unsettlingly, could have gone either way. Nitish Kumar's victory in Bihar, on the other hand, was more predictable, though there are always uncertainties. On one side, there was the huge divide and emotional estrangement of the two major communities in India, for which no solution was in sight. On the other side, a new way of demonstrated governance in Bihar was pitted against many undesirable elements of history. In case of the Ayodhya decision, the apex court manifested the age-old Indian wisdom. In Bihar, the lowliest and the commonest demonstrated the same wisdom in returning to power the Nitish Kumar–BJP alliance a second time.

The Ayodhya verdict can be looked at in many ways. It stands taller than the other two major ones—the disqualification of Mrs Indira Gandhi's election and the Shah Bano verdict. Like the other two, prima facie it was an independent judgement, not interfered with by any forces, though we will never know if it was actually so. It has brought glory to the Indian judicial system, its competence, integrity and its ability to stand against pressure and deliver correctly. It was politically astute and wise. Socially, it diffused a likely explosive outbreak of unrest to an almost extinguished level. It respected the majority community's traditional strong feelings without cowing down to that. At the same time, it emphatically underlined the view that Muslims also have a place in this country side by side with Hindus. It opened many avenues for rapprochement between the two communities even as it disqualified the *locus standi* of some of the Muslim litigants. If one of the basic and major functions of law is to foster progress in a society, this judgement has achieved it effectively. It made religious extremism on any side incapable of conflagration while pushing it aside to create a sane atmosphere.

The days preceding and following the verdict also threw up healthy indicators. There were appeals for peace and respect for the judgement from all quarters: political, social, religious. The VHP and the Sangh Parivar, who had maintained for years that this was a matter of faith that law could not decide, spoke for peace and respect just as many Muslim bodies did. When all the litigant bodies were called to make an out-of-court settlement one day prior to the judgement, each one left it to the court to decide. This was wisdom.

The tone was set no doubt by Dr Mohan Bhagawat, the RSS *Sarsanghachalak*, which others followed. Bhagawat said, 'It is not an issue of victory for one party and the defeat of another. A Ram temple can now and will be built but with the cooperation of the Muslim community in an amicable way. This is an opportunity for both to come closer and work together. The way forward can be discussed' (*Tarun Bharat* 2010). A long-standing suggestion to build a mosque nearby had been talked about. There were a few who waxed eloquent over going to the Supreme Court but those, evidently, were patently hollow, being devoid of any conviction, and being merely habitual utterances that no one paid any attention to.

The nation had to wait a few more months to feel the full impact of the atmosphere created. It was the thumping, unprecedented majority vote the JD(U)–BJP alliance in the Bihar elections received. The alliance had focused totally on developmental issues, *vikas*, which came to be identified as BIPAS—Bijli, Pani, Sadak (Electricity, Water, Roads). In the preceding five years it had decriminalised society as well as politics with 54,000 convictions of criminals, over 10,000 of them imprisoned for life and 1,600 sentenced to death (Dani and Patna 2010). Measures for the upliftment of young girls and women were symbolised in the bicycles the girls received. Good governance brought investments and money to Bihar with a double-digit growth rate five times that of what earlier regimens had recorded. Corruption declined.

All the downtrodden, oppressed and suffering classes were brought into a grand alliance, of which Muslims became a major part. All of them voted for the alliance, leading it to win 84 per cent of the seats. Another outcome that came as a complete surprise was the BJP winning 30 more seats than the previous election. It sent an emphatic message that development, decriminalisation and good governance will make people united while religion and caste questions will unalterably divide, which they do not want.

The Bihar elections completed the process which the Ayodhya verdict had began. It de-religionised politics and democracy at one go. The rendezvous with Ram for both Hindus and Muslims was over, something which should have happened 19 years ago. The aspirations of the people are clear to all political parties. It has, after a long time, ushered a new, strong and stabilising paradigm to the Indian nation and its politics. In all political processes hereafter, it will (hopefully) change the tenor and the timbre of the discourse.

The disastrous, divisive, fissiparous and secessionist movements that threatened the integrity of this nation from 1980 onwards, as we have seen, led Deoras to found a movement that would unite at least the majority community of Hindus of all denominations. It led the BJP to power. Liberalisation, privatisation and globalisation were wisely continued by the BJP, but the convincing economic fruits were not manifest till the middle of the first decade of the 21st century. The religious card worked for some time. Now, with people aspiring for development, economic upliftment, containment of corruption, better governance and decriminalisation of social political life as a logical fallout of the new era, it will not work anymore. Even a Narendra Modi can win hands down if he is committed to development. These are the new values. Those who uphold them will flourish and do well to the nation. Those who do not will perish.

Now it is the farsightedness of leaders, their wisdom, their ability to see beyond elections, at least from decade to decade as statesmen, beyond dynastic continuation, that is on the anvil. Let us hope they will succeed. If they do not, let us hope that the nation has the potential to throw up such leaders and displace the old guard.

Amen.

Appendix 1

The 'Dashera' of Dalits and the Dashera of RSS*

By Sanjeev Kelkar and Virag Pachpore

———— • ◆ • ————

1992

It is a milling crowd, of half a million people. It is in the large ground of a few acres in the heart of Nagpur, a city at the heart of this country. The ground is bound by roads on three sides, no great compound wall to talk of, therefore innumerable sites of influx and efflux of people. The people are simply moving forward, in groups and in families, coming in all the possible directions. They are talking little among them. There are no slogans, no shouts and no hurray. They are just moving, moving and moving.

The center to which the crowd is moving is a large monument of six stories in the center of the ground, commandeering a 360-degree view of the ground from the top. The monument is illuminated, the ground is illuminated, the roads on all the three sides have jam packed juxtaposed shops — temporary stalls that sell from beads and rings and bunions to books and calendars and explosive, thought provoking literature. There are stalls titled of organisations, banks, credit societies and political parties of all colors and hues and creeds. There is dust everywhere, fine dust, dust that does not necessarily irritate, nor make you sneeze.

---

* Published in the English daily, *The Hitavada*, Nagpur, on 13 April 1997.

The people seem to have a uniform pattern. The children are in somewhat ragged clothes. Not torn, not pitiable, just a wee bit ragged. Older women have a big blob of a weight, wrapped in some kind of a *chuddar* that once had a good white or bright color. One of their hands is put to the weight on their heads. The other holds a child or a young man or a woman or her own old man. He also has some baggage. He is usually seen to wear a white *dhoti* and an old fashioned white shirt, somewhat altered in color, again poorish but not pitiable, torn but not ragged.

The young women have brighter saris, a round vermillion decoration on her forehead. A few rings, a black beaded string to show that they are married. Their clothes are much better than the old women. The younger men and the middle aged men are also somewhat better dressed. All of them are uniformly thin, not malnourished but not very well fed either. They are unmistakably not the city folks, but the villagers. The remaining 5 per cent are city dwellers. You can make them out even in the illumination of dust and lighted darkness that is present in the area.

The time is eight o'clock in the night. The day is Dashera. These are the Dalits, the untouchables, now converted to the Neo Buddhism by Dr Ambedkar, who assemble at Deeksha Bhoomi, the place where Dr Ambedkar was ordained in the Buddhist religion, in Nagpur, in great devotion, every year, in millions, move around, bow at the statue of Bodhisattva, listen to some lecture going on at the all-party podium erected for this day and go back.

After Relinquishment

I am moving around in this crowd, among these millions of people. They are pushing me from the sides to get past me. They are pushing me from behind as they are themselves pushed forward. These are the untouchables the Hindu society has denigrated, caste out, ostracised into further, downward abyss of unkempt ugliness and poverty. They, according to the scriptures, are not worth pouring water on the hands of or by the *Savarnas*, even from a distance; even their shadows cannot touch and cross the Hindus of upper castes. I am in them. A so-called high class, high caste Brahmin. They are touching me. I am touching them. There is certainly no revulsion. This is a touch that is like any other if I were to attend a rally on Shivaji Park in Mumbai addressed by Vajpayee or Thackeray. I am moving around hour after hour.

I relinquished my allegiance to the organisation of RSS in 1991. Ideologically I gave it up in its substantiality in the next year that followed. These years also made me an avowed, declared atheist. It was then that I went to see the Dashera celebrations of the Dalits, about half a kilometer from where I stay in Nagpur.

The two doctors — Dr Ambedkar and Dr Hedgewar — lived for a mission: a mission to emancipate the society, to take the nation to the highest pinnacle of glory, by organising it. The movements launched by them — *Dhammachakrapravartan* — and the RSS have been going on parallel lines ever since their inception. Now the time has come for these two powerful streams of national life to come together and work for the betterment of the nation. The confluence of these two will alone rid the nation of many of its present day ills and attain the desired goal cherished by both the 'Doctors of the Nation'.

The Backdrop—1

In 1956, I was over 3 years old on the day of Dashera. Dr Ambedkar relinquished the Hindu fourfold system and a mass conversion to Buddhism took place. Streams and streams of people were heading for this Deeksha Bhoomi in thousands. As my father described it to me years later, tears were falling down all faces, because they were going to leave their ancient religion. Any man with even minuscule sensitivity would understand the poignancy of the situation and disturbing potential of the image that he created. The image has stayed with me till date. Why should they be crying? For a religion that gave them humiliation and torture?

In all my years in RSS dating back to 1967, the problem of untouchability and the solutions that the RSS ideology could offer remained a matter of constant concern, debate, doubt, assertion and need.

The Backdrop—2

It was in 1964 that I first attended the two-day Dashera celebrations of the RSS in Nagpur, the citadel of the RSS. The clean sparkling disciplined atmosphere, the RSS dresses, the shining band, the tall flag mast, the well decorated dais, the military precision of route march, the months of preparations that had gone by. By 1969, we learnt that Dashera would set the theme of emphasis of the RSS for that year, depending upon the national situation. It would be repeated every year. The Nagpur Dashera became a central, focal point of our thinking.

The Backdrop—3

Between 1992 and 1995, in the circles and strata in which I was moving always had very vocal comments that used to begin a few days before Dashera and the first week of December centering around 6th December, the *Mahaparinirvan Din*, the day of salvation of Dr Ambedkar. Everybody was irritated, train travels were impossible. Nagpur swelled. People said it became dirty and horrific because of those millions of people who came. There was overt contempt, disgust, but dead were the 'sensibilities and sensitivities' of people; about that I was very sure.

The Backdrop—4

The history of the 'Dashera of Dalits', naturally dates back to 1956. It completed forty years in 1996. On 14 October, 1956 around half a million people abandoned their ancient religion and adopted Buddhism. The eyewitness accounts say there was enthusiasm and jubilation of a degree as had never in the past been witnessed by the city of Nagpur, in the people who were going to convert themselves. Such was the joy!

The event in its importance of multiple levels, dimensions and paradigms is great. Its consequences and long term effects may live up to the greatness, which will be a tribute to this land and its people. But by itself the event ranks equal to the Mahabharata war, Shankaracharya's victorious march, Shivaji Maharaj and his deeds, the Indian renaissance from 1820 to 1947, Tilak and Gandhi's freedom fight, the vivisection of India and the Ramajanmabhoomi movement, besides the birth of the RSS. It does not matter if people do not agree to this. But then it would be equally debatable if they understood what the event really meant! By and large the *traivarnik*s, the upper castes, do not; if they do, they will neither recognise it, nor do will they want to react and if they do, they will put out the wrong foot first.

To say the least it was one of the major religious revolutions the kind of which the world has rarely seen. The revolution was akin to Adishankara's travails to win people over to *Advaita* philosophy by debate and persuasion. The world knows Jihads and Crusades, Jew-hatred and pogroms. Silent religious revolutions are not in its character.

The revolution had been preceded by the inevitable persuasion, debate, demand for justice, the desperate cry for humanity and compassion, an appeal to the adaptation of the modern values of equality and freedom, made by Dr Ambedkar. It fell on deaf ears. It could not persuade the hardened hearts, the frozen attitudes and dead sensitivity, born out of the terrible, diabolically effective 'Chaturvarnya Vyavastha', the fourfold Hindu system of organisation of the society.

All that the frozen attitude did was to persuade the Dalit leader not to get converted, without offering him a convincing alternative and proposal of equality, honour, miscibility or oneness. There was nothing for Dr Ambedkar to reconsider his decision in the efforts. In the heart of his hearts, he knew that the *Savarna* (or the touchable) Hindu will not want Dalits to be reckoned equal at any cost. Then, there was a question of choice of religion. I wonder if the Hindu society ever realised the debt that Dr Ambedkar has put them in, by adopting Buddhism, a religion and sect from this land.

Dr Ambedkar chose Dashera, a festival traditionally celebrated 'to cross the frontiers'. He crossed the frontiers of a religion which keeps men unequal, views them as such, and has degenerated to such animalistic depths and abyss as to become loathful in its practice. Ambedkar used an old symbolism with far-telling effects. And yet, he choked in his throat, his eyes filled with tears when he said, 'I relinquish this Hindu religion.' Despite the millennia and generations of humiliations of extreme degrees on a moment to moment basis, Dr Ambedkar retained his sensitivity to his religion. He repeatedly referred to religion and its need for his poor people on that day when he spoke. He did not talk of equality, reservation, economics, but of Harijans and Dalits becoming educated, cultured and emancipated. What was his plea against Hinduism? It was the inability of the Hindu religious and social system to produce any enthusiasm in any individual for development, emancipation, rise and betterment. All he said was that the enshrined nature of inequality in Hinduism was unacceptable to him.

And yet, it did not move the people of the Hindu religion.

The account that *Tarun Bharat* from Nagpur gave of that day does itself some credit by calling it an 'unprecedented event', anticipating that 'this will make Nagpur the new center of pilgrimage of the untouchables and that the world is watching its occurrence'. Singularly, it spared the Hindu society from pointing out that it was their doing.

The Years of *Dhammaparavartan Din*

Over years this celebration has grown in its number and strength. The people around Deeksha Bhoomi and Nagpur have accommodated these millions of people. There has been no violence, no disruptions, none have been afraid of these people. Everything, houses, businesses, remain open, working. For years, the poor classes from all over have come. They use some facilities for an hour and a half of the localities, and go away. In one day everything is over. It is only in the last 2–3 years that more and better facilities are noticeable. It is only in the last few years that 'the class' of people attending has changed. It is emancipation at work! The number of places where it is held has also gone up as well!

1996

In the evening despite the fact that it had rained and the roads would be muddy, I put on my shoes and walked out in to the milling Dashera crowds, of swelling millions in the night. In the intervening four years the facelift and constructions in and around Deeksha Bhoomi had made remarkable progress. The mud notwithstanding, the illumination was better, there were many more people, many more stalls and much less dust. Lo and behold! The people I had seen in 1992 looked changed.

The Backdrop—5

I am at the airport, to pick my father, the day prior to Dashera. A pair of short, stocky, educated men are sitting by my side, waiting. Their talk makes it obvious that they have come to receive some Buddhist monk, whose name I forget, a *Bhadant*, along with other high ranking Dalits, not all of them political leaders, coming by flight from Bombay. The recipients are eager and proud. A group of tall young boys with sweaters and scarves around them have also come in. They are attempting not to slip into the crude Marathi that they have been brought up with. They are conversing in somewhat artificial looking Brahminical Poona Marathi. They are educated, confident and have tried to develop a style around them of behavior.

The Backdrop—6

I am in the streets of Nagpur next day morning, the Dashera morning. I am loafing around the Deeksha Bhoomi area. There are numerous vehicles, fiats, traxes and jeeps. Many of these jeeps and traxes bear the names of the families that have rented them. Godbole, Phatak, Phadake and so on. They are specifically Chitpavan Brahmin surnames. There are also many buses around. Even the villagers are quick to point of which ones they want to pick. Many vehicles hold within them from young children to old people, a large united family or groups. Their clothes are not rich but they are new and of a good quality. The air of poorish quality is gone. The ornaments give an indication of education, culture and awareness. There is more confidence and less diffidence. There is more joy on their faces, a more secure one, in the surety of their station. The dresses of ladies and young girls show much remarkable aesthetic escalations. The villager crowd that I had seen four years ago is also moving around. Many of them appear better off, better dressed.

I look at the roadside, trying to pick out mounds of dirt, to be exact. I go round and round these areas and roads. I don't find anything disturbing.

The Backdrop—7

In the night I am in the crowds again. I confirm my impression of a whole new generation, more affluent, better fed, better brought up and better oriented to aesthetics and manners. In the villagers again I confirm my impression—better than before.

A plethora of books and ideological literature bear a lot many more names. The change is neither drastic, fantastic, disproportionate nor of unlikely magnitude; it is substantial, noticeable, emphatic, stable, likeable, enchanting and desirable.

I move out; there is a dais on the left of the monument, large, long. Many leaders are perched on top. PWD Minister Nitin Gadkari, an arch Bharatiya Janata Party leader, is speaking in a Dalit Sammelan. I try to recollect. I have a feeling that in the '*Yuti* Raj' more attention has been paid to the beautification of Deeksha Bhoomi premises—to enable people to participate in a smoother manner.

A Tale of Two Cities

It was the best of times and it was the worst of times. It was a reign of light and there was a reign of darkness. There was a king on the throne of England and there was a king on the throne of France...

For last forty years, in one city there are two celebrations going on, the Dashera of the RSS and the 'Dashera' of Dalits. Their profiles, culture types, ethos and organisation are totally different. I decide to explore further.

The Reactions

I am talking to an Andhrite Marketing Executive of a Danish Company.
'Why did you go to see that celebration? It is too crowded. It is dirty, it smells.'
'No, it does not smell. It is crowded, but it is not dirty. Have you ever seen it yourself, having been reared in Nagpur?' I persist.
'No, I have never been there.'
I am talking to two brilliant young computer engineers staying less than half a kilometer from Deeksha Bhoomi.
'We see it every year from as far a distance as possible. For 2 to 3 days we cannot open our office on Jail Road. We have to take long detours.'
'Have you ever been "in it"?'
'No. We have not bothered to really feel the atmosphere by mixing in the crowd and going into the monument.'
I am talking to two young ladies; one of them is a dark, tall and elegant Marvari doctor.
'*Aap "wahanse" aa rahe ho?* Are you coming from there? Why did you get into so much crowd, rain, dirt, smell and mud.'
'It does not smell. It is not dirty. Have you ever seen it? Experienced it?'
'No I have not.'
I ask the other young lady, also a doctor from the Tiral Kunbi community with an English-convent accent.
'No. I have never been there.'
I ask a number of people. I ask a number of RSS workers.
'No. I have never been there in last 30 years. I have rarely failed to attend the Reshimbagh Grounds for the RSS Dashera in last 30 years.' This was the stock reply.

The Recollections

All my recollections are of the Dashera of the Nagpur RSS, the highly organised celebrations. The RSS at least has a section of Hindu society which salutes Dr Ambedkar for being so magnanimous about the decision of conversion to Buddhism. The salute is in recognition of the fact that he retained the loyalty of millions of untouchables to this land, to this society by not embracing an alien religion and an alien philosophy like Marxism to which he had diehard opposition.

There are elements in the RSS that are disturbed over this obstruction of untouchability that prevents the society from being one and homogeneous. The founder of the RSS from the early years of the organisation had banished all notions of it in the working of RSS and its mind. He adopted a method of derecognition of untouchability. It took sometime before it was realised that the method falls short of its intended achievements and time moves more rapidly. It took time for the RSS to become vocal as regards untouchability. It was Late Mr Deoras who forcefully declared that 'untouchability should go and go lock, stock, and barrel and that if untouchability is not wrong then nothing in the world is wrong'.

There is no point in hammering the RSS as the torch-bearer of orthodox lithic Hindus. It is not. It is ahead of Hindu society. But the condition and psyche of the society is so horrible that anyone trying to pull it out of abyss is bound to look inextricably entangled with it. Yet many an initiative has been developed within the RSS, over the issue.

The role of the RSS in the troubled period of Namantar of Maratthwada University (the change of name of the university to Dr Ambedkar University) is not insignificant. The emphatic thoughts expressed by Mr Deoras as regards reservations, in the highest body of Sangh, that is, the Pratinidhi Sabha, the establishment of Samajik Samarasata Manch, the inauguration of Dr Babasaheb Ambedkar Pratishthan Sanchalit Dr Hedgewar Hospital in Aurangabad and the need for a Human Rights Commission were the significant milestones. Had it not been for an inborn culture that the RSS has, Mr Kalyan Singh, a backward class worker, would not have been the natural choice for the chief-ministership of the largest state that the BJP won after 1977. It was an act of penance to have honorably placed 'the first stone' of Ram Mandir at Ayodhya by the hands of a Harijan. There is no point in ridiculing these events as misleading, deliberate or symbolic. In that case, it will become a moral imperative to all the Dalit leadership to denounce lethally the BSP–BJP coalition which has come to power in Uttar Pradesh. None of them have done it. Why?

The Most Earnest Appeal

The times are changing. The unity of these two societies is essential. It is possible because right-thinking people are there on both the sides. The bridges can easily be built. I met people during the filming of Dhamma Pravartan Din on 30 March 1997 who think not very differently. The tale of two Dasheras in one city must become different.

Is it impossible that in one year the RSS celebrates its Dashera function on the grounds of Deeksha Bhoomi with the countless Buddhist brethren of theirs? Let the RSS pay its tributes to the debts that Dr Ambedkar has put on Hindu society by celebrating their most sacred function of their rebirth on Deeksha Bhoomi.

Is it impossible that the next year the same function is held on the Reshimbagh Grounds with all the Dalits, Buddhists, participating in the function with the RSS. Let them also recognize the founder of an organisation with so lofty a vision as to want to embrace the Hindu society on an 'as is where is basis', untouchables included. Let them recognise the organisation that was described by no less a person than Dr Ambedkar as follows — 'stands as a barrier between communism and the upper castes just as I stand as a barrier between the untouchables and the communism'.

Buddhists or Dalits or Harijans or anybody needs friends whom they can trust. Political vitriol is from election to election. But just as Lincoln said, we need statesmen (on both sides) who can see from generation to generation and maybe seers who see from century to century.

Dashera can be the beginning!

Mr Deoras did once say — 'Let us not spoil the future by continuing to fight the wars of past, in the present.'

Can this make sense?

Appendix 2

The RSS Constitution

——— • ✦ • ———

During the Gandhi murder ban, the RSS continued to remain dispersed and the structure started loosening and becoming disorganised. The RSS withdrew the protests. Golwalkar stationed himself in New Delhi to get the ban lifted. There was no response from the government. Patel pressed for the RSS to merge with the Congress. When the deadlock continued, Dani and Deoras sent a veiled message to Patel that if the ban was lifted the RSS would enter politics. No one would want this parallel force to come into existence.

The absence of a written constitution has long been claimed as the most devastating evidence of the fascist nature of the RSS. At that rate, Britain should be considered the fountainhead of all fascism. The RSS had no written constitution. The government agreed to remove the ban if the RSS wrote a constitution, which they did. It could make interesting reading.

Shri
The Constitution of the Rashtriya Swayamsevak Sangh

(Translated from the original in Hindi)

(As adopted on 1 August 1949 and amended up to 1 July 1972)

Preamble

WHEREAS in the disintegrated condition of the country it was considered necessary to have an Organisation.

a) to eradicate the fissiparous tendencies arising from diversities of sect, faith, caste and creed and from political, economic, linguistic and provincial differences, amongst Hindus;
b) to make them realise the greatness of their past;
c) to inculcate in them a spirit of service, sacrifice and selfless devotion to the Society.
d) to build up an organised and well-disciplined corporate life; and
e) to bring about an all-round regeneration of the Hindu Samaj on the basis of its Dharma and its Sanskriti;

AND WHEREAS the Organisation known as 'RASHTRIYA SWAYAMSEVAK SANGH' was started on the Vijaya Dashami day in the year 1982 Vikram Samvat (1925 A.D.) by the late Dr. Keshav Baliram Hedgewar;

AND WHEREAS Shri Madhav Sadashiv Golwalkar was nominated by the said Dr. Hedgewar to succeed him in the year 1997 Vikram Samvat (1940 A.D.):

AND WHEREAS the Sangh had till now no written Constitution; AND WHEREAS in the present changed conditions, it is deemed desirable to reduce to writing the Constitution as also the Aims and Objects of the Sangh and its Method of Work,

THE RASHTRIYA SWAYAMSEVAK SANGH hereby adopts The following Constitution:

Article 1 Name

The name of the Organisation is "RASHTRIYA SWAYAMSEVAK SANGH".

Article 2 Headquarters

The Headquarters of the Akhil Bharatiya Karyakari Mandal is at NAGPUR.

Article 3 Aims and Objects

The Aims and Objects of the Sangh are to weld together the various diverse groups within the Hindu Samaj and to revitalise and rejuvenate the same on the basis of its Dharma and Sanskriti, that it may achieve an all-sided development of Bharatvarsha.

Article 4 Policy

a) The Sangh believes in the orderly evolution of society and adheres to peaceful and legitimate means for the realisation of its ideals.
b) In consonance with the cultural heritage of the Hindu Samaj, the

Sangh has abiding faith in the fundamental principle of respect towards all faiths.

c) The Sangh is aloof from politics and is devoted to social and cultural fields only. However, the Swayamsevaks are free, as individuals, to join any party, institution or front, political or otherwise, except such parties, institutions or fronts which subscribe to or believe in extra-national loyalties, or resort to violent and/or secret activities to achieve their ends, or which promote or attempt to promote, or have the object of promoting any feeling of enmity or hatred towards any other community or creed or religious denomination. Persons owing allegiance to the above-mentioned undesirable elements and methods of working shall have no place in the Sangh.

Article 5 Dhwaj

While recognising the duty of every citizen to be loyal to and to respect The State Flag, the Sangh has as its flag, The 'BHAGWADHWAJ' the age-old symbol of Hindu Sanskriti which the Sangh regards as its 'GURU'.

Article 6 Swayamsevak

I.
a) Any male Hindu of 18 years or above, who subscribes to the Aims and Objects of the Sangh and conforms generally to its discipline and associates himself with the activities of the Shakha will be considered as a Swayamsevak.
b) A swayamsevak shall be deemed to be an Active Swayamsevak if he pledges to devote himself for the furtherance of the Aims and Objects of the Sangh, and attends a Shakha regularly or performs any work duly assigned to him.
c) A Swayamsevak shall cease to be a Swayamsevak if he resigns or is removed for any act prejudicial to the interests of the Shakha or the Sangh.

II. Bal Swayamsevak—Any male Hindu below the age of 18 may be admitted and allowed to participate in The Shakha programmes as a Bal Swayamsevak.

Article 7 Shakha

a) Swayamsevaks desirous of propagating the Aims and Objects of the Sangh coming together in the form of a regular assemblage will form a Centre. Each Centre shall be a self-contained unit receiving its finances and making its own financial disbursements and is herein referred to as a "SHAKHA".

b) Each such Shakha shall constitute the primary unit of the Sangh, which shall be an autonomous body in respect of its administration and finances.

c) The Shakha shall function under the directions of its Karyakari Mandal.

Article 8 Programmes

For The fulfilment of the Aims and Objects as set out herein earlier, the Shakhas may undertake any or all of the following programmes:

"Arranging frequent discussions and lectures for imparting intellectual and moral education to Swayamsevaks and others and inculcating in them love for the Nation and the ideals of Hindu Dharma and Sanskriti.

"Establishing and running of Libraries and Reading Rooms for the benefit of the general public.

"Carrying on of activities or undertaking programmes for the welfare and benefit of the general public, such as extending medical care, propagation of literacy and improvement of living conditions of the poorer sections of the society; and flood and famine relief, study circles and free exhibition of educative films and advancement of oTher objects of general public utility, but not involving carrying on of activity for profit.

"Imparting physical education by means of exercise and games with a view of improving the physical and mental faculties of Swayamsevaks and others for the co-ordinated and disciplined development of The Society.

"Arranging periodical classes for Swayamsevaks to be trained as Instructors and Workers.

"Celebrating festivals of cultural importance with a view to providing opportunity for Swayamsevaks and others to imbibe the sublime cultural values of character, service and sacrifice to rededicate themselves to the cause of society.

"Adopting suitable means and establishing institutions to propagate the ideals and activities of the Sangh and to educate the people.

"Generally the Shakhas may do all such things as are considered necessary and are conducive directly or indirectly, to promoting and achieving any of the objects of the Sangh."

Article 9 Finances

Any voluntary offering made with devotion before The Bhagwa Dhwaj shall exclusively constitute the finances of the Shakha and shall belong to and be solely managed and disbursed by the Shakha for the promotion of the Aims and Objects of the Sangh and general advancement of Sangh work to be done by the Shakha according to the rules framed by it for that purpose.

Article 10 Elections

a) Elections shall be held after every three years.
b) The date, method and venue of election shall be determined by the concerned K.M. in consultation with the A.B.K.M.

Article 11 Qualification for Voters and Candidates for Elections and Appointees

a) **Voters**

Every Active Swayamsevak of at least one-year standing immediately prior to the date of preparation of the Electoral lists for the election, shall be entitled to vote in the election.

b) **Candidates for Elections and Appointees**

1) A Swayamsevak, who is an office-bearer of a political party, shall not be eligible as a candidate for election or as an appointee to any post so long as he is such an office bearer.
2) A candidate for election, or an appointee to any Akhil Bharatiya post, shall be an Active Swayamsevak of at least six years' continuous standing.
3) A candidate of appointee for Sanghachalakship shall be an Active Swayamsevak of at least one-year standing.

Article 12 Sarsanghachalak

The late Dr Keshav Baliram Hedgewar, the founder of The Sangh, was the Adya (First) Sarsanghachalak. He, in consultation with the then K.K.M., nominated Shri Madhav Sadashiv Golwalkar, who is the Sarsanghachalak since then. The Sarsanghachalak will nominate his successor as and when the necessity arises, with the consent of the then A.B.K.M.

The Sarsanghachalak is the Guide and Philosopher of the Rashtriya Swayamsevak Sangh. He may attend, summon or address any assembly of the Swayamsevaks, A.B.P.S. and Karyakari Mandals severally or jointly.

Article 13 Sarkaryavaha

a) The elected members of the Akhil Bharatiya Pratinidhi Sabha (vide Article 15a) shall elect the Sarkaryavaha.
b) The Sarkaryavaha shall act in consultation with the Sarsanghachalak.
c) In case of death, incapacity or resignation of the Sarkaryavaha. The A.B.K.M. may appoint a person to discharge his duties until such time as his successor is elected.

Article 14 Akhil Bharatiya Karyakari Mandal

a) The Sarkaryavaha shall form the Akhil Bharatiya Karyakari MandaI of which he shall be the Chairman with the following office bearers duly appointed by him.

   i) One or more Sah-Sarkaryavahas.

   ii) Akhil Bharatiya Sharirik Shikshan Pramukh (Incharge of guidance in physical education).

   iii) Akhil Bharatiya Bouddhik Shikshan Pramukh (Incharge of guidance in intellectual and moral instruction).

   iv) Akhil Bharatiya Pracharak Pramukh (Incharge of propagation of Sangh work and guidance to Pracharaks).

   v) Akhil Bharatiya Vyavastha Pramukh (Incharge of general management). and not less than five members chosen from among the Prantiya Karyakari Mandals.

b) The following will be The functions of The A.B.K.M.:

   i) The A.B.K.M. is the co-ordinating body of all the Shakhas in the country to carry out the policy and programmes laid down by the A.B.P.S.

   ii) The A.B.K.M. will frame rules and bye-laws in consonance with the constitution for the purpose of regulating its own affairs and for the general functioning of the Sangh.

Article 15 Akhil Bharatiya Pratinidhi Sabha

a) The delegates elected in accordance with Article 16(a) (i) and (ii) in a Prant shall elect from amongst themselves one tenth of their number as representatives of the Shakhas on the Akhil Bharatiya Pratinidhi Sabha.

b) The A.B.P.S. shall consist of —

   i) Representatives of the Shakhas as elected in 15(a) above.

   ii) Sanghachalak and Pracharaks of Vibhags and Prants.

   iii) Members of the A.B.K.M.

c) The Sarkaryavaha shall be the Chairman of The A.B.P.S.

d) The A.B.P.S. shall meet at least once a year.

e) The A.B.P.S. shall review the work and lay down policy and programmes of the Sangh:

Article 16 Delegates and Sanghchalaks

a)

   i) Fifty or more Swayamsevaks entitled to vote in Shakha will elect from among themselves one for every fifty such Swayamsevaks as delegates of the Shakha.

ii) Such of the Shakhas as are having less than fifty Swayamsevaks entitled to vote will come together to elect delegates. The delegates, as elected above, in a Jilla, in a Vibhag and in a Prant will elect the Jilla Sanghachalak, the Vibhag Sanghahalak and the Prant Sanghachalak, respectively.

b) The Jilla Sanghachalak, in consultation with The Prant Sanghachalak and Prant Pracharak will nominate Sanghachalaks for the various Shakhas and groups of Shakhas within the Jilla.

c) In case a suitable person is not available for the office of Sanghachalak, The Jilla Sanghachalak will appoint a Karyavaha.

e) In case of death, incapacity or resignation of Prant, Vibhag or Jilla Sanghachalak the K.M. of the larger area may appoint a person to discharge the duties of the respective Sanghachalak until such time as his successor is elected.

Article 17 Pracharaks

a)
  i) Pracharaks shall be full time workers selected from amongst those devoted workers of high integrity, whose mission is to serve The society through The Sangh and who, of Their own free will, dedicate Themselves to the Cause.

  ii) They will receive no remuneration. However their expenses will be met by the Shakhas.

b) Appointment of Pracharaks —
  i) The Sarkaryavaha will appoint Prant Pracharaks on the advice of the Akhil Bharatiya Pracharak Pramukh and in consultation with the Prant Sanghachalak concerned.

  ii) The Prant Sanghachalak on the advice of Prant Pracharak will appoint Pracharaks for different areas in the Prant for the assistance and co-ordination of the Shakhas in their respective areas.

Article 18 Karyakari Mandals

a) Sanghachalak of a Prant, Vibhag or Jilla elected in accordance with 16(b), or any groups of Shakhas within The Jilla appointed in accordance with 16(c), will form a Karyakari Mandal of the respective area, of which he shall be the Chairman, consisting of the following office bearers duly appointed by him —
  i) Karyavaha
  ii) Pracharak (appointed under Article 17(b) (ii))
  iii) Sharirik Shikshan Pramukh
  iv) Bouddhik Shikshan Pramukh
  v) Vyavastha Pramukh

b) The Sanghachalak of a Shakha appointed in accordance with 16(c), will form a Karyakari Mandal, of which he shall be the Chairman, consisting of the following office-bearers duly appointed by him.

   i) Karyavaha

   ii) Sharirik Shikshan Pramukh

   iii) Bouddhik Shikshan Pramukh

   iv) Prachar Pramukh

   v) Vyavastha Pramukh

   vi) Nidhi Pramukh

NOTE: In case suitable person/s is/are not available for appointment to any one or more of the above posts the same may remain vacant until suitable person/s is/are available.

c) Each Karyakari Mandal shall also have in addition not less than three members chosen from amongst the other Karyakari Mandals within its area, if any.

d) K.M.S will be executive bodies in their respective areas, guided by the K.M. of the immediate larger area for implementing the policy and carrying out the programme laid down by the A.B.P.S.

e) The K.M. of a Shakha will have the power to take disciplinary action against any individual Swayamsevak for breach of discipline or behaviour prejudicial to the interests of the Shakha or the Sangh. Such an action will be subject to confirmation by the Karyakari Mandal of the immediate larger area.

Article 19 Quorum

One half of the total strength shall form the Quorum for the meetings of the various Karyakari Mandals, and one fifth for the A.B.P.S.

Article 20 Undeveloped Prants

In case of prants in which the work has not yet developed to an appreciable level, The A.B.K.M. may provide representation to them on the AB.P.S. in a manner it deems fit.

Article 21 Interpretation and Amendments to Constitution

a) The interpretation of the Constitution and its Articles by the A.B.K.M. shall be final.

b) An amendment to the Constitution not inconsistent with the Aims and Objects of the Sangh can be proposed at a convention specially convened for that purpose by the A.B.K.M. on its own, or to, the A.B.K.M. by any P.K.M., or by any other Karyakari Mandal with the recommendation of the respective P.K.M. or by any twenty-five members of the A.B.P.S. The A.B.K.M. after due consideration will put the proposal of such an amendment before the P.K.Ms and the amendment will be deemed carried if two-thirds of the P.K.Ms agree by a simple majority.

c) The decisions of The P.K.Ms regarding such amendments may be brought for reconsideration before the A.B.P.S. on a requisition by any twenty-five members of that Sabha. The decision of the A.B.P.S. in this behalf, taken by a two thirds majority shall be final.

Glossary

———— • ✦ • ————

For the top key positions in the RSS hierarchy listed below see
Appendix 2— RSS Constitution.

1. *Sarsanghachalak*
2. *Sarkaryavah*
3. *Sahsarkarvah*
4. *Sanghchalak*
5. *Karyavah*
6. *Sahkaryavah*
7. *Boudhik Pramukh*
8. *Sharirik Shikshan Pramukh*
9. *Prachar Pramukh*
10. *Vyavastha Pramukh*
11. *Mukhya Shikshak*
12. *Pracharak*
13. *Swayamsevak*

Some Technical Terms

Dharma is not an individual's way of worship or that of a sect or religion. It
is a way of life, a system that 'sustains' societies with peace, calm, wealth,

etc., where all such relations are in essential harmony, and causes both the earthly and spiritual development. Hindu Dharma is a federation of religions.

Chakravartitwa of the *Chakravartin* may be regarded as a centre for coordination, helper, but even the large states who have allegiance to the *Chakravartin* (the Sovereign) would still be sovereign states. This concept is not the same as monarchy.

Samrats were similar to emperors.

Ashwamedha Yagnya is a ceremony wherein a powerful kingdom, desirous of establishing its hegemony by getting obedience from all other states, sets out a horse to go around the earth. The horse carries a charter on whether the kingdom whose boundaries it has entered wants to submit or challenge by war. If the kingdoms submit, there is a peaceful settlement. Otherwise, the challenger kingdom has to defeat the proclaimer. Once all the states are won or have submitted, the proclaimer performs a sacrificial fire ceremony in which the horse which has gone around is sacrificed.

Ekachalakanuvartitva means that there will be only one authority whose advice which will be followed unquestioned, one of the tenets of the RSS for long, also a ground for critics to accuse the RSS of being an undoubtedly fascist organisation.

Sahachalakanuvartitva, decision by consensus, is the idea Deoras mooted and implemented in the post-Emergency period. While in jail, he declared that he as one *Sarsanghachalak* might be inside, but six others were moving outside free, and had a better idea of what was going on. He further said that whatever they decided would have his full support and sanction.

Chintan Baithak is a conclave of all important functionaries of the RSS to freely deliberate on the issues facing them. For the understanding of those who label the RSS as fascist, it is well to know that every 10 odd years, RSS conducts a review of the decade gone by where the representatives express themselves fearlessly. So far there have been eight major such conclaves, in 1939, 1954, 1960, 1972, 1981, 1987, 1989 and 1998.

Peethadheeshas or *Mathadheeshas* are the sectarian chiefs of the monasteries each sect builds for itself, usually in one or more places, around which the followers of that sect revolve as a great place for religious congregations.

Ekadashi, the 11th day of the first half of the lunar month, is an auspicious day for fasting.

References

———— • ✦ • ————

Advani, L.K. 1996. 'Shradhheya: Homage to Deoras', *Tarun Bharat*, Special Edition, 16 July, p. 16.

————. 2008. *My Country, My Life*. New Delhi: Rupa & Co.

Anderson, Walter K. and S.D. Damle. 1987. *The Brotherhood in Saffron*. New Delhi: Vistaar Publications.

Bal, Prakash. 2008. 'Ata Jihad Hinduncha', *Saptahik Sakal*, 16 November, Pune.

Bennet, Alex and David Bennet. 2004. *Organizational Survival in the New World: A New Theory of the Firm*. Burlington: Butterworth-Heinemann. (First printed in India 2007.)

Bhishikar, C.P. 1982. *Sri Guruji Charitra*. Pune: Vichar Sadhana.

————. 1988. *Virat Sanghaswaroopachi Prerana, Dr Hedgewar*. Pune: Bharatiya Vichar Sadhana.

Bokil, Milind. 2006. *Katkari: Vikas ki Visthapan?* Mumbai: Mouj Prakashan.

Bondale, Rambhau. Unpublished. *Collection of Speeches of Balasaheb Deoras*. Collected over a period from 1977 to 1990. Dr Hedgewar Bhavan, Nagpur.

Brodal, P. 2004. *The Central Nervous System, Structure and Function*, 3rd ed. New York: Oxford University Press.

Chari, Seshadri. n.d. *A Fruitful Life*. New Delhi: Bharat Prakashan.

Chivhane, Dattatray, ed. 2007. *Keshav Prakash*, back page. Nagpur: Dattatray Laxman Chivhane.

Chouthaiwale, M.K. n.d. *Maine Dekhe Huwe Param Poojaniya Shri Balasahab Deoras*. Nagpur: Bharatiya Vichar Sadhana.

Covey, Stephen. n.d. *7 Habits of Highly Effective People*. Country Atlantis: Free Press.

Dani Ravindra and Badallele Patna. 2010. *Tarun Bharat*. Nagpur, 20 June.

Darwin, Charles. 1998. *The Origin of Species*. Hertfordshire: Wordsworth Editions.

Das, Durga. 1969. *India from Curzon to Nehru and After*. London: Collins.

Datye, Hari Vinayak. 1981. *Aarti Aalokki, Shri Guruji Ek Darshan*. Pune: Hindusthan Sahitya.

Deoras, Balasaheb. 1965. *Rashtriya Swayamsevak Sangh, Lakshya Va Karya*. Dombivali: Moraya Prakashan.

Deoras, V.D. 1974. *Samajik Samata Ani Hindu Sanghtan*. Pune: Bharatiya Vichar Sadhana.

———. 2000. 'Ajanma Bramhcharya Jaganara Grihasthashrami' (Lifelong Celibate Caretaker of the Family), *Tejonidhi*. Balasaheb Deoras Prabodhini, Nagpur, year 1, Vol. 3.

Deodhar, Dilip. 2004a. *Bhajapa, Genesis and Swot*. Nagpur: Vikram Sathe.

———. 2004b. *Chakravyuhamein BJP*. Nagpur: Vikram Sathe.

———. 2004c. *Hindusthan, 1920 to 2020. Dr Hedgewar Yanbcha Ekweesarya Shatakacha Vedh*. Nagpur: Vikram Sathe.

———. 2006. *Riddles of WE*. Nagpur: Vikram Sathe.

Deodhar, V.N. 1997. 'Hindutvala Rajkiya Vyaspeeth Denara Drashta' (The Visionary Who Gave a Political Platform to Hindutva). *Tarun Bharat*. 5 July, Nagpur.

Dharmadhikari, Avinash. 1989. *Eka Aswasth Dashakachi Diary*. Pune: Mehta Publishing House.

Deshpande, P.L. 1968. Foreword to *Lalit Leni* by Dr R.M. Lohia. Pune: Prestige Prakashan.

Deshpande, S.H. 1969. *Sanghane Tarunanche Lonache Ghalayache Tharavale Ahe Kay?* Mumbai: Mouj Deepavali Visheshank.

———. 1996. *Maharashtra Times*, 23 June 1996, Mumbai.

———. 1983. 'Israeli Kibutz'. In *Sanghatale Diwas*. Pune: Suparna Prakashan.

———. 2006. *Dharmanirpekshatechya Drishtitun Hindutvavadachi Fermandani*. Pune: Rajhans Prakashan.

Djilas, Milovan. 1957/1983. *The New Class: An Analysis of the Communist System*, paperback ed. San Diego: Harcourt Brace Jovanovich.

———. 1969. *The Unperfect Society: Beyond the New Class*. trans. Dorian Cooke. New York: Frederick A. Praeger Inc, 5th reprint.

Duncan, Isadora. 1927. *My Life*. New York: Boni and Liveright.

Galbraith, John Kenneth. 1958. *The Affluent Society*. New York: Signet Special Broadside and Mentor, New American Library.

References

Galbraith, John Kenneth. 1968. *The New Industrial State*. New York: Signet Special Broadside and Mentor, New American Library.

Gautier, Francois. 2008. 'The Hindu Rate of Wrath', *Outlook*, 10 November, p. 34.

Godbole, Arun. 2007. *United Western Bank, Uday, Utkarsh Ani Asta*. Pune: Dilip Majgaokar for Rajhans Prakashan.

Golwalkar, M.S. 1939. *We or Our Nationhood Defined*. Nagpur: Bharat Prakashan.

———. 1966. *Bunch of Thoughts*. Bangalore: Jagaran Prakashan.

———. 1974a. *Shri Guruji Samagra Darshan*, Vol. 6. Nagpur: Bharatiya Vichar Sadhana.

———. 1974b. *Shri Guruji Samagra Darshan*, Vol. 4. Nagpur: Bharatiya Vichar Sadhana.

———. 1975. *Shri Guruji Samagra Darshan*, Vol. 5. Nagpur: Bharatiya Vichar Sadhana.

———. 1978. *Shri Guruji Samagra Darshan*, Vol. 3. Nagpur: Bharatiya Vichar Sadhana.

———. 1979. *Shri Guruji Samagra Darshan*, Vol 2. Nagpur: Bharatiya Vichar Sadhana.

———. 1981. *Shri Guruji Samagra Darshan*, Vol. 1. Nagpur: Bharatiya Vichar Sadhana.

Gorbachev, Mikhail. 1987. *Perestroika: New Thinking for Our Country and the World*. HarperCollins.

Hassan, Mushirul. 1997. *The Legacy of a Divided Nation: India's Muslims since Independence*. New Delhi: Oxford University Press.

Idate, B.R. 2003. 'Amrutpath'. *Saptahik Vivek*, February, Mumbai, 49–51.

India Today. 1981. March–April 1981.

Jain, Girilal. 1991. 'Hindus Moving Towards Their Timeless Dharma', *Panchajanya: Parivartan Ank*, January 44 (32): 8–11.

Joshi, L.T. (ed). 1996. 'Shraddheya,' *Tarun Bharat*, special edition, July, Nagpur.

Kandel, Eric R., James H. Schwartz and Thomas M. Jessell et al (ed). 1991. *Principles of Neural Science*. USA: Prentice Hall International Inc.

Kane, V.S., ed. 1996. *Veervrati Balasaheb*. Pune: Ekata Prakashan Nyas.

Karandikar, V.R. 1999. *Teen Sarsanghachalak*. Pune: Snehal Prakashan.

Ketkar, Dr Shantarm Hari. 1985. *RSS Vividh Kshetratil Vyaktinchya Drishtikonatun*. Ratnagiri.

Khandekar, Rajeev. 2006. 'Sanghgach Shist Visarala', *Loksatta, Ravivar Vishesh*, 17 April, Nagpur.

Kruk, Z.L. 1991. *Neurotransmitters and Drugs*, 3rd ed. St. Edmunds, Suffolk: St. Edmundsbury Press.

Lokhiteishi. 1994. *Shradhheya Balasahab Deoras. Lokhiteishi*, editorial. Lucknow: Lokhit Prakashan.

Loksatta Reasearch Bureau. 2007. 'Satheecha Sakshidar,' *Loksatta*, 21 October, Mumbai.

Luce, Edward. 2006. *In Spite of the Gods: The Strange Rise of India*. London: Little Brown.

Malkani, K.R. 1980. *The RSS Story*. New Delhi: Impex India.

Mehta, Usha. 2007. *Anibani Ani Amhi*. Mumbai: Granthali.

Naipaul, V.S. 1981. *Among the Believers*. London: Andre Deusth Ltd.

Nene, V.V., ed. 1986. *Pandit Deendayal Upadhyay Vichar Darshan*, Vol. 1. Pune: Bharatiya Vichar Sadhan.

Onward March. 1974. Editorial, March, 22–45.

Pachpore, Virag. 2001. *The Indian Church?* Nagpur: Bhaurao Deoras Human Resources Research and Development Institute/Trust.

Pachpore, Virag, Afzal Mohammad Sushama and Shahnaz. 2007. *Rashtriya Pariprekhsyamen Bharatiya Muslim*. Delhi: Mai Hindusthan and Jaipur: Rashtravadi Muslim Manch.

Palkar, Narayan Hari. 1967/2008. *Dr Hedgewar*, 7th ed. Pune: Bharatiya Vichar Sadhana.

Parameshwaran, P. 1978. *Gandhi, Lohia and Deendayal*. New Delhi: Deendayal Shodh Sansthan.

Pimpalkar, Pandit, ed. 2002a. 'Divyatwachi Jeth Prachiti, Tethe Kar Maze Julti' (Where I See Transcendental Greatness, My Hands Offer Obeisance), *Tejonidhi*, Balasaheb Deoras Prabodhini, Nagpur, year 2, Vol. 3, p. 8.

———, ed. 2002b, 'Poorvottar Kshetra Kahi Doosara Kashmir Na Ban Jay' (Let us Hope the North East of India Does Not Become Another Kashmir), *Tejonidhi*. Balasaheb Deoras Prabodhini, Nagpur, year 2, Vol. 3, p. 8.

———. 2005. *Memoirs*. Nagpur: Pandit Pimpalkar.

Ramabhau Mhalgi Prabodhini. 1996. 'Drashta Sanghatak', Editorial, *Maharashtra Times*, 19 June, Mumbai.

Rand, Ayn. 1956. *Atlas Shrugged*. New York: Signet, New American Library, Division of Penguin Group.

———. 1986. *Capitalism: The Unknown Ideal*. New York: Signet, New American Library, Division of Penguin Group.

Rashtriya Swayamsevak Sangh (RSS). 1973. *Shraddhanjali to Shri Guruji*. Nagpur: Dr Hedgewar Bhawan.

———. 1999. *Chintan Baithak*. Nagpur: RSS.

———. 2007. *RSS Resolves, 1950–2007*. New Delhi: Suruchi Prakashan.

Sangoram, Mukund. 2006. 'Bedkala Jewhan Hatti Zalyacha Bhas Hoto', *Loksatta, Ravivar Vishesh*, Nagpur, 17 April.

Saptahik Vivek. 1974. 'Answering Questions of Invited Guests in Nagpur', 14 April, Mumbai, 2.

Savarkar, V.D. 1979. *Hindutva*, 5th ed. Hindi trans. Ramteertha Bhatia. New Delhi: Rajdhani Granthagar.

Sehgal, Nayantara. 1979. 'For Whom the Bell Tolls', *The Indian Express*, 15 May, Mumbai.

Seshadri, H.V. 1996a. *Lo Shraddhanjali Rashtrapurush He*. New Delhi: Suruchi Prakashan.

———. 1996b. 'Amrtya Veerka Mahaprayan', *Panchajanya*, June 1996, New Delhi.

———. 1998. *The Tragic Story of Partition*. Bangalore: Sahitya Sindhu Prakashan.

Sharma, Jyotirmay. 2007. *The Terrifying Vision*. New Delhi: Penguin.

Sharma, Raghunandan Prasad. 2007. *VHP kee 42 Varsheeya Vikas Yatra, 1964–2006*. New Delhi.

Shevade, Sachhidanand. 2006. *Kashmirnama*. PhD thesis, UNESCO.

Shourie, Arun. 1998. *Worshipping False Gods, Ambedkar and the Facts Which Have Been Erased*. New Delhi: HarperCollins.

Siddhant Ani Neeti. n.d. Mumbai: Bharatiya Jan Sangh.

Sinha, Rakesh. 2003. *Dr Kesheo Baliram Hedgewar*, 1st ed. New Delhi: Publicity Division, Information and Broadcasting Ministry, Government of India.

Subrahmanyam, K. 1997. 'Emergency Remembered, Stemming the Rot Within', *Times of India*, Bangalore.

Subramanyam, Vidya. 1997. 'Diluted Federalism Led to Emergency', *Times of India*, Bangalore.

Stiglitz, Joseph. 2002. *Globalization and Its Discontents*. USA: W.W. Norton & Company.

Sudarshan, K.P.S. 2006. 'Mumbai Lecture 11th December 2005', Editorial. *Saptahik Vivek*, 26 February, Mumbai, p. 7.

Swami Ranganathanand, n.d. 'Introduction', *The Gospel of Sri Ramakrishna*, in 2 volumes. Madras: Sri Ramakrishna Math.

Swaroop, Devendra. 2007. 'Rashtriya Ekataka Shubharambh'. In *Sangh, Rajneeti aur Media*. New Delhi: Prabhat Prakashan (originally published in *Panchajanya*, 9 April 1978).

Talwalkar Govind. 1980. *Sattantar*, Vol. 1. Mumbai: Mouj Prakashan.

———. 1982. *Sattantar*, Vol. 2. Mumbai: Mouj Prakashan.

———. 1984. *Sattantar*. Vol. 3. Mumbai: Mouj Prakashan.

Tarun Bharat. 1987. Full Speech of Shri Balasaheb Deoras titled as 'Sanghache Kam Hindu Sanghatit Va Jagrut Karanyache' (To Awaken and Unite the Hindus is the Work of the Sangh).

———. 2010. Nagpur, 19 September.

Telang, Shivrai. 1996. 'Yugapravartak Balasaheb Deoras,' *Saptahik Vivek*, 30 June, Mumbai, pp. 6–8, 31.

Thengadi, D.B. 1972a. *Chintan Samagri*. Pune: Bharatiya Vichar Sadhana.

———. 1972b. *Focus on the Socio Economic Problems*. New Delhi: Bharat Prakashan.

———. 1982. *Communism Apnehi Kasautipar*. Lucknow: Lokhit Prakashan.

———. 1984a. *Saptakram*. New Delhi: Suruchi Prakashan.

Thengadi, D.B. 1984b. *Modernisation without Westernisation.* New Delhi: Suruchi Prakashan.

———. 1986. *Pandit Deendayal Upadhyay Vichar Darshan,* Vol. 1. Pune: Bharatiya Vichar Sadhana.

———. 1989. *Sanket Rekha,* 1st ed. New Delhi: Bharatiya Mazdoor Sangh.

Thengadi, D.B., G.S. Gokhale and M.P. Mehata. 1968. *Labour Policy.* Nagpur: Bharatiya Mazdoor Sangh.

Toffler, Alvin. 1985. *The Third Wave.* London: William Collins & Co.

Toffler, Alvin and Heidi Toffler. 1993. *War and Anti-war: Survival at the Dawn of the Twenty-first Century,* 1st ed. Boston: Little Brown and Company.

Tupkary, R.H. 2008. *Sanghatana Ani Sanghatitata: Vikas, Rhas Ani Lay* (Organisation and the Organised State). Nagpur: Shri Mangesh Prakashan.

Upadhyay, Deendayal. 1957. *Bharatiya Artha Neeti, Vikaski Ek Disha,* 1st ed. Lucknow: Rashtradharma Pustak Prakashan.

———. 1967. *Integral Humanism.* Trans. Ramesh Seth. Mumbai: Bharatiya Jan Sangh.

Vajpayee, Atal Bihari. n.d. 'Parichay', poem number 26. In *Meri Ekkyavan Kavitayen,* edited by Dr Chandrika Prasad Sharma, pp. 55–57. New Delhi: Kitabghar.

Vajpeyee, Manikchandra and Shridhar, Paradkar. 1999. *Jyoti Jala Nij Pranaki.* New Delhi: Suruchi Prakashan.

Varhadpande, Bapurao. 1988. *Ham Kare Sankalp,* Bharatiya Vichar Sadhana, Nagpur.

———. Unpublished. *Notes on Balasaheb Deoras.*

Wagale Subodh. 1999a. 'Swadeshiteel Chakve ani Khare Swarajya'. In *Swadeshi Va Jagatikikaran Visheshank, Artha Bodh Patrika,* Vol. 3 & 4, 1–14 April. Pune: Bharatiya Arthavidnyan Vardhini.

———1999b. 'Note by Dilip Kulkarni: Swadeshi: Dhoran? Navhe Jeevanshaili', (Swadeshi: A Policy? No, A life Style), *Artha Bodh Patrika,* Vol 6, November, Pune, p. 28.

Yerkuntawar, B.S., ed. 1960. *Pradnya Lok.* Nagpur: Dr G.B. Vaze.

Index

•✦•

Abdulla, Sheikh, 146
Abdullah, Farooq, 176
Advani, Lal Krishna, 4, 40, 138–39, 164, 171, 194, 199, 202, 210, 213, 224, 258
Ajmer blasts, 282
Akbar, M.J., 299
Akhil Bharatiya Pratinidhi Sabha, 146
Akhil Bharatiya Vidyarthi Parishad (ABVP), 50, 117
Ali, Aruna Asaf, 284
All Assam Students Union (AASU), 172–73
All India Khilafat Parishad, 5
Ambani, Mukesh, 274
Ambedkar, B.R., xxxii, 74, 82, 90, 93, 179, 191, 315–18, 322
American imperialism, 19, 273, 275
Among the Believers, 242
Anandamargis, 16
Ananthmurthy, U.R., 227

Anderson, Walter K., 41, 73, 105, 164–65
Aney, Lokanayak, 36–37
anti-cow slaughter movement, 80
Anusheelan Samiti, 1
Aparigraha, principle of, 23
Aseemanand, 292
Ashoka, 28
Ashwamedha Yagnya concept, 28
Assam Ganasangram Parishad (AGP), 172–73
Assam Jatiyabadi Dal, 173
Assam unrest, 172–74
Aurangzeb, 28
Ayodhya judgement, 293, 310–13

Babri Masjid, demolition of, 197–98
Baitule, Narayan, 100
Bajrang Dal, 200–01, 281
Bakunin, 232
Bal, Prakash, 68, 291–92
Bang, Thakurdas, 118

Barua, Girin, 173
Bennet, Alex, 253
Bennet, David, 253
Besant, Annie, 4
Bhagalpur riots, 15
Bhagwat, Mohan, 248–49, 261, 282, 293, 311
Bhale, Dattaji, 286
Bhalerao, Anant, 288
Bharatiya Artha Neeti, Vikaski Ek Disha, 89, 165, 168, 239
Bharatiya Janata Party (BJP), 24, 67, 146, 156, 178, 184, 186, 191–92, 199, 202, 204, 238, 240, 248, 255, 261, 286, 292, 294–97, 299, 312–13, 322
  ineffective decade, 171–72
  political power, 205–06
  relationship with RSS and Parivar, 206–10, 212–15, 218–22, 224–26
Bharatiya Jan Sangh (BJS), 67, 93, 100, 103, 108, 138, 151–55, 161, 171–72, 239–40
  formation, 163–65
  Gandhi and, 168–70
  Lohia, Deendayal and, 168–70
  politico-social philosophy, 165–68
Bharatiya Kisan Sangh, 81, 216
Bharatiya Kranti Dal, 137
Bharatiya Mazdoor Sangh, 50, 168, 191, 216–17, 219
Bhatia, V.P., 145
Bhavani Shankar Niyogi Commission, 160
Bhave, P.B., 285
Bhave, Vinoba, 303
Bhide, Baba, 146
Bhindranwale, 175
Bhishikar, 277
Bhishikar, C. P., 42
Bihar assembly elections, 310–13
Bokil, Milind, 181

Bolshevik revolution, 89
Bombay riots of 1993, 199–200
Bose, Subhash, 5
Brahmadeo, 134
Buddhism, 28, 74, 82, 315–18, 322
Bukhari, Abdullah, 144, 212
Bunch of Thoughts, 35, 53

capitalism, 168–69, 231, 234–35, 237, 241
Capra, Fritjof, 91
Chak De! India, 251
Chale Jao (Quit India) movement, xxxiii, 71–72
Chandrashekhar, 138, 152–53
Charnwood, 300
chaturvarnya system, 85, 89–90, 120–21, 123, 125, 168, 318
Chauhan, Shivraj, 297
Chhagala, M.C., 17
Chhagala, Mohammad Karim, 143
Chhatrapati Sena, 285
Chhatra Yuva Sangharsh Vahini, 132
Chintan Baithak, 275–76
Choupal, Kameshwar, 196
Chouthaiwale, Baburao, 152
communism, xxxv, 3, 116, 169, 229–32, 234, 241
communist
  debacle in Russia, 205, 229–32
  ideology and RSS, 16, 60, 74, 87–88, 116, 164, 230–31, 233–34, 238, 242, 271, 291, 306, 308, xxxii
Communist Party, 230, 247
Congress, *See* Indian National Congress
Congress for Democracy (CFD), 137–38
Congress (O), 137
Covey, Stephen, 87
cultural nationalism, and territorial nationalism, 30–31

Dalits, 284, 288–89
  conversions issue, 175, 177–78, 182–83
  Dashera of, 314–23
  identity, 124–26, 158
  laying foundation of temple, 196
Damle, S.D., 41, 106, 165
Dandavate, Madhu, 140
Dandi March, 73, 149
Dani, Bhayyaji, 47, 108, 324
Dashera of Dalits and RSS, 314–23
Datey, Damodar Madhav, 50, 137–38
Deodhar, Dilip, 11, 42–44, 100, 119, 199–200, 210, 217
Deoras, Balasaheb
  activism and agitation issue, 116–19
  on Assam unrest, 173–74
  ban on RSS, 133–34
  changes in
    direction under, 113–14
    exterior of RSS *shakhas*, 119
  as chief of RSS, 111–12
  civic receptions, 143
  deal by free RSS, 139–40
  differences with Golwalkar, 98–103, 106–07, 109, 127
  divide in psyche of Sangh, 126–28
  efforts to bring Hindus to centre-stage, 190–91
  Hidutva plan roll back, 153–57
  imprinting RSS policy, 157–60
  inclusivity issue, 114–15
  interaction with press, 115–16
  Janata experiment and, 149–53
  misunderstanding about, 108–11
  open door policy
    media and RSS opponents on, 147–49
    for Muslims, 140–46
    Muslims reaction to, 144–46
    reaction within RSS on, 146–47

paradigm of centrality of RSS, 106–07
  peace and protest offers, 134–39
  return and ascent of, 98–128
  and RSS, xxxi, xxxiii–xxxiv, 11, 15, 39, 41, 47, 58, 60–61, 63–65, 69–73, 87, 92, 98–128, 163, 170–77, 179–83, 206–08, 211, 213, 215, 218, 220, 223, 225–26, 237–38, 257, 260, 262, 268, 274, 276–77, 286–87, 293, 300, 304, 308
  sense of time and timing, 104–05
  setting and achieving goals, 103–04
  speech from Nagpur, 184–87, 190
  stronghold on RSS, 105–06
  tenets of, 276–78
  thinking paradigms and master strokes, 119–26
  withdraws from day-to-day RSS work, 99–103
Deoras, Bhaurao, 154, 206, 210
Desai, Ketan, 281
Desai, Morarji, 138, 156, 161
Deshmukh, Nanaji, 90, 118, 159, 240, 265, 287, 298
Deshpande, P.L., 307
Deshpande, S.H., 94
Deval, Madhukar, 49, 114–15
Devilal, 194
Dhammaparavartan Din, 318–19, 323
Dharmadhikari, 172
Djilas, Milovan, 88–89, 229
Dnyan Prabodhini, Pune, 49, 114, 175
Dr Hedgewar Janmashatabdi Samiti, 193
Drucker, Peter, 238
Dubhashi, Jay, 240
Duncan, Ballerina Isadora, 43
Durga Vahini, 200–01

economic imperialism, 273, 275
Einstein, Albert, 263

Ekatmata Yatra, 183, 187, 193, 254
emergency and post-emergency
    period
  oppression during, 132–34
  RSS during, 131–60, 286–87
  civic receptions, 143
  deal by free RSS, 139–40
  Hindutva plan roll back, 153–57
  Janata experiment, 149–53
  media and RSS opponents on
    open door policy, 147–49
  Muslims reaction to open door
    policy, 144–46
  opens doors for Muslims, 140–
    49
  peace and protest offers, 134–
    39
  on polity, 157–60
  reactions within RSS to open
    door policy, 146–47
Engels, 229, 239
Euro-communism, 232

fascism, 11, 31, 54–55, 114, 256, 324
Fernandez, George, 137

Gadgil, V.N., 176
Gadkari, Nitin, 248, 320
Gandhi, Indira, 140, 143, 155–57,
    173, 176–77, 184, 187, 216, 232,
    238, 287, 295, 309, 311
  emergency period, 132–40
  return to power, 160–61
  RSS and, 139–40, 164–65, 169–71
Gandhi, M.K., 43, 78, 80, 83, 90, 165,
    168, 211, 215, 285
  Congress under, 4–8
  on Dharma, 25
  Hindu–Muslim unity and, 76–77
  murder, 46–47, 104, 140, 163, 287,
    291
  Muslim appeasement by, 7–8,
    14–15, 30

trusteeship concept, 23
Gandhi, Rajiv, 184, 232, 238
Gandhi, Sanjay, 133
Gandhi, Sonia, 43, 222, 226, 238
Gandhian socialism, 171, 178
Garvase Kaho slogan, 155
Gautier, Francois, 293–94
Ghosh, Aurobindo, 4
Ghumare, D.B., 42, 44, 52, 73, 103
Globalization and Its Discontents,
    231
Godhra incident, 223, 228, 280, 296
Golwalkar, Madhav Sadashiv
  aversion to
    political power, 42–45
    publicity, 64–66
  ban on RSS and, 45–46
  contribution for RSS, 93–95
  and democracy, 92–93
  on Dharma, 25
  differences with Deoras, 98–104,
    106–07, 109, 127
  Hindu Rashtra concept, 26, 29
  Hindutva notion, 22, 40
  letter from Sardar Patel to, 45
  nationhood concept, 34–39
  political
    ethnography, 34–61
    situation and, 59–61
    socio-economic philosophy,
      87–92
    thrust and sensitivity, 58
  politics to establish leadership in
    RSS, 41–42
  and RSS, xxxi, xxxiii, 34–61, 63–95,
    146, 170, 192, 207, 213, 215, 218,
    231, 236, 239, 250, 257, 264,
    271, 276–77, 284–88, 291–92,
    308, 324
  achiever's psyche, 55–58
  aversion to political power,
    42–45
  aversion to publicity, 64–66
  belief system in, 40

clamour and controversies, 35–39
Congress politics during first ban, 45–46
consolidation politics, 52
demoralisation, 47–49
dissidence handling, 49–50
dominant tendencies, 63–95
early years, 41–42
General Elections of 1952, 47–49
nationhood thesis, 34–36
need of political power need, 46–47
non-inclusive culture, 51–52
political situation and, 59–61
political thrust and political sensitivity, 58
sect, 53–55
trusteeship issue, 23
unity of universe thesis, 22
Gorbachev, 201, 230
Gore, N.G., 143
Govindsinghji, Guru, 29
Growth
Gupta, Chandra Bhanu, 195
Gupta, Lala Hansraj, 134

Harshavardhana, 28
Hassan, Mushirul, 75
Hedgewar, K.B.
centenary celebrations, 191–93
and congress, 9, 37
on Hindus, 2–3, 7, 16–18
on Muslims, 6–7
political philosophy, 8–31
long term goal, 12–31
short term goal, 8–12
and RSS, xxxiii–xxxiv, 1–2, 9–31, 34, 41, 55–56, 58, 63–65, 67, 70–71, 73, 102, 107–08, 111, 146, 179, 184, 250, 254, 256, 270, 277, 284, 288, 308, 316
anti-Muslim psyche, 15–16

behaviour and strength, 10–12
declaration, 10
Hindu and, 16–18
Hindu Dharma and, 16–18, 24–25
Hindu Rashtra concept, 25–30
Hindutva and, 16–18, 20–24
Muslim atrocities and arrogance impact, 14–15
nationalistic mind and civic discipline, 12
organisation for post-British Independent India, 12–14
territorial *versus* cultural nationalism and, 30–31
Hegde, Ramakrishna, 138
Hindu Code Bill, 16
Hindu Dharma, and RSS, 9, 16–18, 24–25
Hindu fundamentalism, 15
Hinduism, 20, 24, 30, 38
Hindu Mahasabha, 3, 46–47, 147, 163
Hindu–Muslim unity issue, 6–7
Hindu Nation, 39
Hindu Rashtra, concept of, 25–30, 34, 63, 69, 142, 168, 199, 202, 215, 221, 252, 271–72
Hindus
Hedgewar on, 2–3, 7, 16–18
Muslim League and, 75
organised behaviour and strength, 10–12
Hindu Sabha, 7
Hindu Samajotsav festival, 178
Hindu Samrajya Dinotsav, 11
Hindu Sangamam, Bangalore, 179
Hindu Sanghatan, 42
Hindu Society, 2, 9, 11, 17, 45, 83, 94, 123, 125, 178, 183, 186–87, 195, 217
Hindutva, 9, 40, 151–52, 252–53, 275

intolerance and Malegaon blast, 288–97
political and economic content, 24
rolled back, 153–57
and RSS, 16–18, 20–24, 146, 192, 215
violent forces and, 280–89
violent forces and RSS, 280–89
Huddar, Balaji, 11
Hussain, M.F., 288–90

imperialism, 19, 60, 236, 273, 275
Indian Church? 174
Indian National Congress, 3–4, 37
under Gandhi, 4–8
Muslim appeasement, 7–8, 14–15, 30, 247
RSS and, 45–46, 58, 79, 163, 172, 186–87, 214, 224
Indian National Life Stream, 176
Indreshkumar, 282
Intelligent Complex Adaptive System (ICAS), 254
Israeli Kibbutz, 89

Jain, Girilal, 195
Jamat-e-Islami, 133, 140–41, 144, 309
Jamiat Tulba, 176
Jan Sangh, 15–16, 24, 44, 47, 50, 100, 115, 142, 153, 207, 253
Janata Party, 138–39, 144, 150–54, 156, 160–61, 215
Jaysingh, 28
Jinnah, 4–5, 74
Jogi, Ajit, 295
Johari, Geeta, 281
Joshi, Appaji, 41
Joshi, Jagannathrao, 142
Joshi, Murali Manohar, 220–21
Joshi, S. M., 143
Joshi, Sharad, 180
Joshi, Shrikant, 11, 15, 309

Joshi, Subhadra, 165
Joshi, Yadavrao, 171
Jung, Carl, 20

Kalam, 212
Kalambi, Bhaskar Rao, 160, 254, 260
Kanishka, 28
Kanitkar, G.B., 207
Karandikar, V.R., 63, 277
Karkare, Hemant, 298
Karnad, Girish, 227
karseva, for temple construction, 196
Katkari: Vikas ki Visthapan, 181
Kerala, communal violence in, 281, 286–87
Khalistan movement, 175–77
Khan, Shamsul Haq, 145
*khap panchayat*s, 84
Khare, N.B., 42
Khilafat Committees, 5
Khilafat movement, 4, 15
Khosla ka Ghosla, 251
Kousarbi, 280
Koya, C. Mohammad, 146
Krinvanto Vishwam Aryam, 23
Kropotkin, 232
Kumar, Indresh, 176
Kumar, Nitish, 310
Kumarswamy, 227
Kurundkar, Narahar, 287

Labour Policy, 168, 240
Lal, Chaman, 102
Laski, Harold, 12
Laxmanananda, Sadhu, 281
Lenin, 229, 239
Liberhan Commission report, 213, 292
Licence Quota Permit Raj, 232
Life of Ramakrishna, 290
Limaye, Madhu, 137, 140, 147, 150
Lincoln, Abraham, 77, 155, 300

Lohia, Ram Manohar, 23, 165,
168–70, 308
Lok Sangharsh Samiti, 132
Luce, Edward, 210, 223

Madhav, Ram, 224
Malegaon blast
failure of right actionand respon-
ses, 298–301
Hindutva intolerance and, 288–
90
reaction to, 290–97
Mandal Commission, 194
Manipur, divisive and disruptive
forces active in, 174–75
Marathi Literary Congregation,
285
market capitalism, 237, 241
Marx, 229, 239–40, 307
Marxism, 229, 286, 322
Maurya, Chandragupta, 28
Mayavati, 82, 224–25
Meghalaya, divisive and disruptive
forces active in, 174–75
Mehta, Usha, 133
Minority Treaty of League of
Nations, 36
Mittal, L.N., 274
Mizoram, divisive and disruptive
forces active in, 174–75
Modi, Narendra, 296–97, 313
Modi, Sushil, 117
Moghe, Bapurao, 134
Moghe, Madhukar, 138
Mopla revolt, in Kerala, 6
Mufti, Mehbooba, 294
Mukherjee, Hiren, 308
Mukherjee, Shyama Prasad, 46,
100, 163
Muley, Madhavrao, 102
Murari Commission, 243
Murthy, Narayana, 241
Muslim League, 3–4
Direct Action, 75, 77

and Hindus, 75
Muslims
communalism, 6
Gandhi's appeasement of, 7–8,
14–15
Hedgewar on, 6–7
reaction to RSS open door policy,
144–46
RSS
anti-Muslim psyche, 15–16
open door policy, 140–46
reaction to arrogance of, 14–15

Nagaland, divisive and disruptive
forces active in, 174–75
Nagpur, communal violence in,
283–85
Naipaul, V.S., 243
Narasimha Rao, 201, 232, 248
Narayan, Jay Prakash, 73, 117–18,
132, 308
RSS alliance, 132–34
Nargolkar, Vasant, 168
Narkesari Prakashan, 102
Nasreen, Taslima, 173–74
National Conference, 146
nationalism, territorial and cultural,
30–31
national unity attempts, 181–84
Nava Nirman agitation, 116
Nehru, Jawaharlal, 30–31, 37, 47, 59,
71–72, 75, 77, 79, 91, 94, 166, 169,
185, 193, 211, 231
New Class, The, 88
New Wave organisations, 249,
254–56, 259–60, 263
Niyogi, Bhavani Shankar, 160
non-violence, concept of, 5
Nooyi, Indra, 221
North-east India, divisive and
disruptive forces active in, 174–
75

Pachpore, Virag, 174
Pal, Bipin Chandra, 4

Palkhiwala, Nani, 143, 145
Panchayat Raj model, 232
Pande, Umeshchandra, 195
Parameshwaran, P., 90, 240
Paramhans, Ramakrishna, 290
Paranjape, L.B., 71
Partition of India, 75–80, 98, 140
Pasha, Kemal, 6
Patel, Chimanbhai, 116
Patel, Sardar, 45–47, 71, 79, 211, 324
Patit Pawan Sanghatana, 285
Patwardhan, Achyutrao, 135–36
Pendsey, V.V., 49, 114
Perestroika: New Thinking for Our Country and the World, 230
Phadke, N.S., 286
Phadke, Sudhir, 146
Phule Ambedkar Yatra, 179
Pingale, Moropant, 137, 183, 187, 194
political ethnography
of RSS, 34–61
achiever's psyche, 55–58
belief system in, 40
clamour and controversies, 35–39
Congress politics during first ban, 45–46
consolidation politics, 52
demoralisation, 47–49
dissidence handling, 49–50
early years, 41–42
General Elections of 1952, 47–49
Golwalkar's leadership, 41–45
nationhood thesis, 34–36
need of political power, 46–47
non-inclusive culture, 51–52
political situation and, 59–61
political thrust and political sensitivity, 58
sect, 53–55

Pope, Alexander, 102
Proudhon, 232
Pulakesin, 28
Punjab, divisive and disruptive forces active in, 175–77

Quit India Movement in 1942, 71–74, 98

Rafi, Mohammad, 146
Rai, Lala Lajpat, 4
Rajjubhaiya, 154, 211
Ram, Jagjeevan, 137–38, 161
Ramaswamy, Cho, 17
Ram Janmabhoomi issue, 156, 193–200, 212
Ram Janma Bhoomi Mukti Andolan, 193–200, 213, 317
Bajrang Dal and Durga Vahini creation, 200–01
Dalit laying foundation of temple, 196
demolition of Babri Masjid, 197–98
end of Deoras era in RSS and, 201–04
Karseva for temple, 196
uniting society for, 194–96
VHP-Parivar immature decision, 198–200
Ram Mandir issue, 193–200, 211–13, 242, 272, 322
Ram Sethu issue, 216, 242, 273, 289
Ram Shila movement, 254
Ranade, Eknath, 52, 81
Ranade, Raghu, 76–77
Rand, Ayn, 235, 309
Ranganathan, Swami, 290
Rashtra Meemamsa, 34
Rashtriya Sikh Sangat, 181
Rashtriya Swayamsevak Sangh (RSS)
achiever's psyche, 55–58
aculturation, 213–15

anti-intellectual psyche, 66–67
ban on, 45–47, 133–34, 139, 287
belief system in, 40
changes in thinking of, 238–42
character-building, 252
collaborative leadership, 260–61
Communists and, xxxii, 16, 60, 74,
  87–88, 116, 164, 230–31, 233–34,
  238, 242, 271, 291, 306, 308
conception and creation of, xxxii,
  2
Congress politics and, 45–46, 58,
  79, 163, 172, 186–87, 214, 224
Constitution of, 324–32
Dashera of, 314–23
democracy within, 256–64
demolition of the Babri Masjid,
  197–98
demoralisation politics, 47–49
Deoras era, xxxi, xxxiii–xxxiv,
  11, 15, 39, 41, 47, 58, 60–61,
  63–65, 69–73, 87, 92, 98–128,
  163, 170–77, 179–83, 190–204,
  206–08, 211, 213, 215, 218, 220,
  223, 225–26, 237–38, 257, 260,
  262, 268, 274, 276–77, 286–87,
  293, 300, 304, 308 249–50, 313,
  322, 324
  activism and agitation issue,
    116–19
  ban on RSS and, 45–47, 133, 139
  call from Deoras, 184–87
  change in exterior of RSS *shakhas*,
    119
  changes in direction under,
    113–14
  as chief of RSS, 111–12
  deal by free RSS, 139–40
  differences with Golwalkar,
    98–103, 106–07
  divide in psyche of Sangh, 126–
    28
  efforts to bring Hindus to centre-
    stage, 190–91

emergency period, 131–60
end of, 201–04
Hidutva plan roll back, 153–57
imprinting RSS policy, 157–60
inclusivity issue, 114–15
interaction with press, 115–16
Janata experiment and, 149–53
media and RSS opponents on
  open door policy, 147–49
misunderstanding about, 108–
  11
Muslims reaction to open door
  policy, 144–46
open door for Muslims, 140–46
peace and protest offers, 134–
  39
Ram Janma Bhoomi Mukti
  Andolan, 193–200
reaction within RSS on open
  door policy, 146–47
return and ascent of, 98–128
RSS centrality paradigm of,
  106–07
sense of time and timing, 104–
  05
setting and achieving goals,
  103–04
stronghold on RSS, 105–06
tenets of, 276–78
thinking paradigms and mas-
  terstrokes, 119–26
unity for purpose, 191–93
withdraws from day-to-day RSS
  work, 99–103
early years, 41–42
on economic liberalisation and
  modernisation, 233–37, 244–
  45
emergency and post-emergency
  period, 131–60
energising from within, 178–81,
  187
enshrined mediocrity, 67–68
ethos and redibility, 250–51

failure of prioritation and politicisation, 220–22
on FDI, 243–44
founder, xxxiii–xxxiv
future of, 247–50
Gandhi's murder and, 46–47, 104,
140, 163, 287, 291, 324
Golwalkar era, xxxi, xxxiii, 34–61,
63–95, 111–14, 139, 146, 170,
192, 207, 213, 215, 218, 231, 236,
239, 250, 257, 264, 271, 276–77,
284–88, 291–92, 308, 324
achiever's psyche, 55–58
anti-intellectual RSS psyche,
66–67
clamour and controversies,
35–39
conflict-avoiding tendency,
69–74
consolidation politics, 52
constructive and agitational
work incompatibility, 68–69
contribution of, 93–95
and democracy, 92–93
differences with Deoras, 98–103
dissidence handling, 49–50
enshrined mediocrity, 67–68
fascination for past, 83–86
General Elections of 1952, 47–
49
model, 98
nationhood thesis, 34–36
non-inclusive culture politics,
51–52
obsession with symbolism, 80–
83
partition of India, 75–80, 98,
140
resolutions, 59–61
as sect, 53–55
stronghold on RSS, 105–06
Hedgewar era, xxxiii–xxxiv, 1–2,
9–31, 34, 41, 55–56, 58, 63–65,
67, 70–71, 73, 102, 107–08, 111–

12, 146, 179, 184, 250, 254, 256,
270, 277, 284, 288, 308, 316
anti-Muslim psyche, 15–16
behaviour and strength, 10–12
declaration, 10
Hindu and, 16–18
Hindu Dharma and, 16–18,
24–25
Hindu Rashtra concept, 25–30
Hindutva and, 16–18, 20–24
Muslim atrocities and arrogance
impact, 14–15
nationalistic mind and civic
discipline, 12
organisation for post-British
Independent India, 12–14
territorial *versus* cultural nationalism and, 30–31
Hindutva intolerance and
Malegaon blast, 288–97
ideological conception, xxxiii–
xxxiv, 252–53, 303–09
man-making mission, 251,
270–71
manpower disregard, 209–10
misconceptions about changes,
215–17
need of political power, 46–47
negatives and downside of, 255–
56
organisational intelligence, 259–
60
partition of India and, 75–80, 98,
140
political power and aftermath,
205–27
public image issues, 222–27
publicity issues, 218
reaction to Malegaon blast, 290–
97
relationship with BJP and Parivar,
206–10, 212–15, 218–22, 224–
226
resolutions about new world,
243–45

response to unipolar world, 229–31, 238–42
social service projects, 208–09
strengths and weaknesses, 264–78
 awareness about power, 270
 change in externalities of man-making mission, 270–71
 Hindu interests and Hindu *Rashtra*, 271–73
 ineffective network, 265–67
 institutional mindset, 267–69
 professionalism, 269
 tenets of Deoras era, 276–78
 understanding future, 273–76
surviving in New Post-modern World corporations, 253–54
system-building, 252
technology development and, 233–38
trust and empowerment, 261–62
trusteeship issue, 23
truth and perception about ideologies, 307–09
understanding future, 242–43
violence
 failure of right action and responses, 298–301
 Malegaon blast, 288–97
 prevented by RSS, 286–87
 against RSS, 286–87
Ravishankar, Shri Shri, 290
Ray, Satyajit, 17
Reddy, Neelam Sanjeeva, 159
Reddy, Y.S., 295
Riddles of Rama and Krishna, The, 179
Roop Kanwar episode, 84
Roy, M.N., xxxii, 74
Russian communism, 231, 234

Sachar Committee report, 289, 296
Samarasata Manch (the Forum for Homogeneous Society), 179

Samarasata Sahitya Parishad, (the Literary Federation for Unity and Homogeneity), 179–80
Samjhauta Express blast, 282, 291
Sanatan Dharma, principles of, 240
Sane Guruji, Shri, 284
Sanghatana Ani Sanghatitata, 53
Sangoram, Mukund, 224
Sanskriti Raksha Yojana, 193
Sanyukta Vidhayak Dal (SVD), 164
Saraswati Shishoo Mandirs, Bangalore, 115, 159
Sarva Seva Samaj, 225
Sastri, T. V. R., 54
Satyagraha concept, 4–5
Savarkar, Babarao, 34–35
Savarkar, V.D., 7, 16, 20–22, 34, 39–40, 239
Sayyad Bhai, 145
Scheduled Castes Federation, xxxii
Scindia, Vijayaraje, 171
Sehgal, Nayantara, 149–50
semitic religions, 24
Seshadri, H.V., 75, 127, 257
Sethu Samudram controversy, 80
Shah, Amit, 280–81
Shah Bano verdict, 311
Shah Commission, 156
Shalivahana, 28, 30
Shankara, 29
Sharma, Dau Dayal, 195
Sharma, Jyotirmay, 93
Sharma, Moulichandra, 100
Sharma, Raghunandan Prasad, 195, 200
Shevade, Sachhidanand, 211
Shewalkar, Ram, 109
Shiromani Gurudwara Prabandhak Committee, 176
Shivaji, 28–29, 76, 289
Shiv Sena, 198, 289

Shourie, Arun, 74, 219
Shraddhananda, Swami, 6
Siddhant Ani Neeti, 165
Singh, Charan, 137–38, 161
Singh, Hari, 46
Singh, Kalyan, 322
Singh, Manmohan, 232, 248
Singh, Rajendra, 152, 154, 202, 206
Singh, V.P., 194
Singhal, 213–15, 218
slavery, abolition of, 77
Socialism, 116, 171, 178, 232, xxxiii
Soharabuddin, 280–81
Sri Vitthal Sahakari Seva Sanstha, 49
Stein, Graham, 281
Stiglitz, Joseph, 231
Sudarshan, K.P.S., 69–70, 78–79, 93, 182, 213, 215–18, 224, 292
Swadeshi Jagaran Manch (Forum for Awareness of Nationalistic Ideas), 216, 267
Swamy, Subramanyam, 168
Swaroop, Devendra, 144

Talwlakar, Govind, 85
Tapaswi, Moreshwar, 176
Tata, Ratan, 274
Teen Sarsanghachalak, 63
Telugu Desam Party, 213
territorial nationalism
  cultural nationalism and, 30–31
  principle, 6–7
Thackarey, Bal, 43, 198
Thatte, Abaji, 138, 143
Thengadi, D.B., 44, 67, 93, 137, 157, 168, 213, 215, 217–19, 232–34, 236–37, 239–40
Tilak, Bal Gangadhar, 3–4, 78, 211, 297, 317
Tito, Martial, 229
Toffler, Alvin, 274
Toffler, Heidi, 274
Togadia, 213–14, 218
Toynbee, Arnold, 13
Tragic Story of Partition, The, 75

Tupkari, R.H., 53
Tyagi, Om Prakash, 60

Upadhyay, Deendayal, 67, 80, 85, 88–91, 93, 164, 168–70, 207, 212, 238–41

Vaidya, M.G., 220
Vajpayee, Atal Behari, 138, 142, 145, 159, 171–72, 191, 199, 201, 294–95
  as premier, 205, 207, 210–13, 224, 226
Vanavasi Kalyan Ashram, 191–92, 209
Varhadpande, Bapurao, 65
Vasant Vyakhyanmala, Pune, 119–21
Vidyarthi Parishad, 285, 289–90
Vikramaditya, 28, 30
violence
  failure of right action and respon-ses, 298–301
  Malegaon blast, 288–97
  prevented by RSS, 286–87
  against RSS, 286–87
Vishwa Hindu Parishad (VHP), 81–82, 178, 181–83, 191–92, 195–96, 211, 213, 215, 292, 311
  immature decision of Ram Janma Bhoomi Mukti Andolan, 198–200
Vivekananda, Swami, 42
Vivekananda Kendra, 115, 174, 181–82
Vivekananda Rock Memorial, 81

War and Anti War, 274
Watergate, 132
We or Our Nationhood Defined, 34–39
Williams, Sunita, 222

Yadav, Mulayam, 212
Yediyurappa, 297

About the Author

———•✦•———

Sanjeev Kelkar has seen the RSS at close quarters, and at all levels, for the last 43 years. He was brought up in a diehard RSS family in Nagpur. It had close connections with the founder of the RSS, Golwalkar, Deoras and many others.

As a part of his social commitment, he left Mumbai for a rural tribal area medical service project and worked there for 11 years.

He is best described as an institution builder, an excellent trainer, an educational technologist, a wizard at project management and a gambler with his life. The excellent second-level referral hospital that he created was for him a laboratory to develop models to address the numerous needs of rural health care.

He then made the unlikely leap from the rural to the highly complex tertiary care super-specialty practice in CIIMS Hospital, Nagpur. He won an award of ₹200,000 for his short essay, 'Program Proposal for Tuberculosis Control in India in 1995'.

Giving up his medical practice overnight, he joined a multinational pharma giant for the next six years. As their education director, he has trained numerous medical postgraduates in diabetes with extraordinary results.

Giving up medicine, for the last several years, he has engaged himself in political and literary writing. This book on the comparative study of the leftist–socialist, centrist and particularly the right-wing politics in India is an altogether different interpretation compared to the conventional wisdom.

He is presently working on his novel based on his experiences as a medical practitioner.